Routledge Revivals

International F ~~mics

This book, first published in 1983, and written ⌐y,
authority, presents the essentials of international economics in a ⌐   ⌐e
and straightforward way. The book contains the minimum of algebra
and avoids detailed proofs. It incorporates the most recent contemporary theoretical advances and discusses contemporary issues in
commercial policy. Moreover, it puts less emphasis than other textbooks on trade theory and more on balance of payments theory and on
questions of international finance and international monetarism.

International Economics

David Gowland

Routledge
Taylor & Francis Group

First published in 1983
by Croom Helm Ltd.

This edition first published in 2011 by Routledge
2 Park Square, Milton Park, Abingdon, Oxon, OX14 4RN

Simultaneously published in the USA and Canada
by Routledge
270 Madison Avenue, New York, NY 10016

Routledge is an imprint of the Taylor & Francis Group, an informa business

Publisher's Note
The publisher has gone to great lengths to ensure the quality of this reprint but
points out that some imperfections in the original copies may be apparent.

Disclaimer
The publisher has made every effort to trace copyright holders and welcomes
correspondence from those they have been unable to contact.

A Library of Congress record exists under LC Control Number: 83021386

ISBN 13: 978-0-415-61563-1 (hbk)
ISBN 13: 978-0-415-61564-8 (pbk)
ISBN 13: 978-0-203-83018-5 (ebk)

INTERNATIONAL ECONOMICS

INTERNATIONAL ECONOMICS
DAVID GOWLAND

CROOM HELM
London & Canberra

BARNES & NOBLE BOOKS
Totowa, New Jersey

© 1983 David H. Gowland
Croom Helm Ltd, Provident House, Burrell Row
Beckenham, Kent BR3 1AT

Croom Helm Australia Pty Ltd,
28 Kembla Street, Fyshwick,
ACT 2609, Australia

British Library Cataloguing in Publication Data

Gowland, David
    International economics.
    1. Industrial economic relations
    I. Title
    337   HF1411

    ISBN 0-7099-1135-1
    ISBN 0-7099-1138-6 Pbk

First published in the USA 1984 by
Barnes & Noble Books
81 Adams Drive
Totowa, New Jersey, 07512

ISBN 0-389-20438-2

Printed and bound in Great Britain

CONTENTS

1 THE CHANGING WORLD

1.1 International Economics

In international economic text books it is conventional to start by justifying the need for a separate branch of the subject. The reason for doing so is self-evident. The whole of economics should be 'international', for example all macroeconomic analysis must take account of overseas factors. In many ways international economics is the natural extension and complement to the other branches of economics. For example, the pure theory of international trade, Chapter 2, is an extension of the elementary analysis of the gains from exchange. Commercial policy, Chapters 3 and 4, is a complement to other analyses of government intervention. Balance of payments theory, Chapters 6 to 10, extends Keynesian and monetarist analysis to an open economy and analyses the exchange rate as another macroeconomic weapon. Chapters 11 to 13, international finance, similarly complement domestic financial economics.

However, to show the value of international economics does not explain why it should be studied as a separate branch of the subject. Hence some economists have tried to find a theoretical rationale for the existence of the subject. For example, it has been suggested that within an economy all the factors of production are (perfectly) mobile but that they are not mobile between economies. From this it is natural to derive a theory of international economics as the study of the relationship between these distinct economies. Unfortunately for this approach, however, factors are not very mobile within an economy and are not immobile between them. Even labour is quite mobile between countries in many cases, e.g. the 'guest workers' from Turkey, Portugal and Italy in Germany and Switzerland and between Canada and the USA. Indeed labour is far more mobile between Michigan (in the USA) and Ontario (in Canada) than between Ontario and Vancouver or Michigan and New York.

The justification for a separate and distinct international economics is, therefore, essentially a political one. Nation states, and groupings of them, are of fundamental importance in modern life irrespective of whether different countries do or do not represent distinct economies in any theoretical sense. Thus it is necessary to study the relationships between nations and to analyse them economically because of this underlying political reality. It is equally essential to be aware of the changing nature of the world which is being studied.

1.2 Some Developments

The major change in the world economy since 1950 has been the growing interdependence of economies, especially within the developed world. Underdeveloped countries have tried to reduce their dependence and perhaps thereby contributed to their continued lack of development. This interdependence has both caused and been caused by the very rapid growth of world trade which has risen six-fold since 1950, almost twice as fast as world output (see Table 1.1). The growing interdependence of economies is dramatically revealed in the US's import ratio which was a mere 3 per cent in 1960 but nearly 11 per cent in 1980 (Table 1.1). In 1980 one new car in every four purchased in the US was an import.

This growing interdependence is in part the result of market forces. These always work to intergrate economies but their effects have been especially prominent since 1950. The most important and dramatic manifestation of market forces is the Eurocurrency market (see Chapter 13). This has produced a massive degree of integration of world financial markets and consequent integration of real markets. Real transport costs have fallen substantially, mainly because of Japanese developments in shipbuilding and the 'container revolution' they faciliated. Communications have improved dramatically because of the impact of jet planes and electronics. Innovations of all sorts, whether dramatic, like television, or humdrum, like cheaper ships, have made the world in the popular, but accurate, cliché much smaller.

This growth in world trade and increasing interdependence has been encouraged by the movement towards the liberalisation of trade, i.e. the removal of restrictions on imports. This trend in particular has meant that most countries have reduced the discriminatory taxes on imports called tariffs (see p. 28 below). In the US, for example, the average tariff was reduced from over 60 per cent in 1932 to less than 10 per cent in 1970; although this is a very crude measure of the protective effect of tariffs, it reveals the very clear trend. The high tide of protectionism was in the mid-1930s, especially after the UK abandoned free trade in 1932. The sustained trend towards liberalisation began as part of post-war reconstruction programme which also remodelled the international financial system (see p. 163 below). The moves towards trade liberalisation were originally beset with difficulty, for example no nation ratified the Havana Charter (1947) which would have set up an International Trade Organisation, ITO. Such attempts were heavily criticised, e.g. Worswick and Ady (1952), p.31, but within a decade liberalisation had become unchallenged orthodoxy: in the US after Eisenhower's Reciprocal Trade Act of 1954, in the UK after the Conservative victory in 1951. The formal framework for these developments was provided by the General Agreement on Trade and Tariffs, GATT, established in 1944 with a permanent secretariat (see Dam (1973)). In practice, barriers to trade were reduced by hard bargaining amongst national governments, e.g. in the much-vaunted Kennedy round, which was discussed from 1962-7 before implementation. The trend towards freer trade ended in the later 1970s when quasi-protectionist views became widespread in most countries.

Political developments greatly changed the environment in which world trade took place. In 1946 the British Empire and Commonwealth was still a tightly knit economic bloc comprising a quarter of the world's population. By 1970 virtually all of this former empire was independent and, while the Commonwealth survived in name, it was of economic significance only in a few areas, notably the link between New Zealand and the UK. Successor states in Africa and Asia were usually protectionist. Less dramatic and slower, but almost equal in impact, was the demise of the French Empire. China became communist in 1949 with a consequent enormous reduction in its external trade. Trade between communist Eastern Europe and the rest of the world was much less important than had been trade with its predecessors.

All of these developments had a major effect upon the pattern of world trade. An ever-increasing proportion of world trade was between members of the developed world rather than between developed and underdeveloped countries. For example, as shown in Table 1.1, only one-third of UK exports in 1951 went to Western Europe and North America, whereas by 1980 two-thirds did. Trade in manufactured goods was also of ever-increasing importance, its growth rate being over twice that of food, raw materials and fuel and amounting to around two-thirds of world trade by 1970. Hence, whereas in 1950 the typical pattern of trade was that of an underdeveloped country exchanging raw materials for the manufactured products of a developed country, by 1970 it was of two developed countries exchanging their manufactured products. These trends were reinforced by the re-emergence of

Germany as a major trading power in the 1950s. Its share of exports rose from 10 to 20 per cent of world trade in manufactured goods between 1950 and 1960. Japan also benefited. Its share of world trade rose by 50 per cent in the 1950s (from 4.1 to 6.9 per cent), nearly doubled in the 1960s and rose by over a quarter in the 1970s (see Table 1.1). The UK and USA both lost substantial shares of world trade, between them falling from nearly half of all manufactured trade in 1951 to only a quarter in 1980. This reflected many factors, some external, such as the end of the sterling area (Commonwealth) trading bloc, and some internal, especially an inability to produce cheaper reliable goods as quickly and as well as Japan.

The tendency for world trade to become ever more concentrated as trade in manufactured goods between developed countries was encouraged by the development of the EEC (European Economic Community). The origins of this were in the aftermath of World War II. On the one hand, there was a desire to ensure that France and Germany fought no more wars. On the other, there was a desire to create a strong anti-communist bloc, especially amongst the Christian Democrat politicians who were prominent in Germany, France (MRP), Italy and the Benelux countries. They were inspired by Pope Pius XII's fervent anti-communism and by Catholic social philosophy to pursue (Western) European unity. Their schemes mixed political unity, military co-operation and economic policy, e.g. in the Western European Union, and sometimes were designed to facilitate co-operation with and sometimes to exclude the USA and UK. After the defeat of the European Defence Community in 1954 and the partial eclipse of the MRP in France after 1951, the schemes became entirely economic. The first major development was the European Coal and Steel Community, ratified in 1952. However, the main changes came after the Treaty of Rome (1957) which established the EEC, or Common Market. This was a customs union (see Chapter 5) linking the six countries of France, Germany, Italy, Belgium, Luxemburg and the Netherlands. Its major achievement was the growth in trade amongst its members which the EEC stimulated both directly, by reducing tariffs, and indirectly, by promoting a favourable climate. However, its major policy was the infamous Common Agricultural Policy, CAP. This was designed to increase farmers' incomes and to reduce food imports. It utilised very high guaranteed prices and a variety of devices designed to exclude imports (see p. 66 below). The sky-high prices meant that supply of agricultural products exceeded the demand but the EEC bought up the difference and stored it, the famous butter, beef and apple mountains. The policy was enor-

Table 1.1: World Trade Patterns 1950-80

The growth of world trade

	World trade[a]	World industrial[a] production
1951	100	100
1960	161	148
1970	330	254
1980	571	343

Share of world exports of manufactured goods (%)

	1951	1960	1970	1980
UK	21.9	15.9	10.8	10.3
USA	26.6	21.7	18.5	16.9
Japan	4.3	6.9	11.7	14.8
Germany	10.0	19.4	19.9	19.8

Import ratios[b]

	1950	1960	1970	1980
USA		3.0	4.1	10.7
UK	18.0	17.8	18.0	20.6
Germany		14.7	14.9	22.2

Goods traded

1. Volume

	1948	1960	1970	1978
Food and raw materials	100	180	277	397
Fuel	100	227	302	378
Manufactured goods	100	244	560	958

2. Share (%)

	1970	1978 1970 prices	1978 prices
Food and raw materials	23.9	20.9	18.6
Fuel	9.2	7.1	16.9
Manufactured goods	65.2	69.0	63.2

1978 world prices (1970=100)

Food and raw materials	231
Fuel	620
Manufactured goods	237

UK export markets (%)

	W. Europe (of which EEC)		N. America	Overseas sterling area[c]
1951	24.5		10.7	49.5
1960	25.7		15.3	40.2
1970	37.8[d]	(21.8)	18.7[e]	36.3
1980	55.7[d]	(42.1)	11.0	

Notes: (a) Volume (b) Imports (FOB) ÷ GDP (market prices); in current prices; (c) Commonwealth less Canada plus Jordan; (d) EEC plus EFTA; (e) USA only for 1970.

Sources: IMF, *Financial Statistics;* NIESR, *National Institute Economic Review;* UN, *Statistical Year Book;* UK, US, *National Accounts;* OECD, *National Accounts Principal Economic Statistics.*

mously expensive and seemed bizarre to observers, especially as it harmed relations with the USA, Third World producers of food and other efficient farmers who disliked being excluded from European markets. However, the policy was in line with both continental tradition and Catholic social philosophy. In addition, inefficient farmers were large marginal blocs of votes in France and Germany. The UK, Denmark and Ireland joined the EEC in 1973. The decision to join the EEC was bitterly contested in the UK. Moreover, few UK politicians shared the ideals of the CAP, so there was a long series of quarrels within the enlarged EEC. The EEC was further enlarged when Greece joined in 1982.

The final important change relevant to world trade concerned the oil market. In 1965 oil prices were controlled by a group of Western oil companies, often called the Seven Sisters (Shell, BP and five US companies). They ensured that oil prices were both low and falling. This economic control was reinforced by political muscle, e.g. the Gulf sheikhdoms were still largely ruled by UK political or resident agents supported by the Royal Navy. However, in 1968, the Wilson government withdrew from the Gulf. In 1969, the pro-Western regime was overthrown in Libya and King Feisal replaced his weak brother as King of Saudi Arabia. The oil-producing countries, who had formed an organisation called OPEC (Organisation of Petroleum Exporting Countries) in 1960, were now both willing and able to stand up to the Western governments and oil companies, which they did by blocking a price cut in 1970. In 1972 they forced a small increase in oil prices. The crucial change occurred in 1973 when the price of oil was quadrupled. A further rise followed in 1978. All in all, the price of a barrel of Saudi Arabian crude oil rose from $1.80 in 1970 to $34 in 1980. Energy prices rose 520 per cent in the decade, whereas other prices rose by about 150 per cent (see Table 1.1). In value terms fuel rose from 10 to 16 per cent of world trade, although it fell in volume terms. OPEC countries acquired enormous wealth with major effects on the world financial system. Oil production was stimulated elsewhere, e.g. in the North Sea.

Note

I would like to thank Brian Hillier who read the typescript of this book and made a number of helpful comments. I should also like to thank Janet Russell who helped in various ways, especially with the bibliography.

2 THE PURE THEORY OF INTERNATIONAL TRADE

2.1 Introduction

The purpose of the pure theory of international trade is to show why international trade exists and that it is beneficial. This might seem a redundant exercise, since there is no reason why the normal arguments used in elementary economics to demonstrate the existence of trade (internal or external) should not be applied at the international level. The argument in elementary theory is that trade will occur whenever it is profitable for two or more people to trade. If the price of a good is different in two places then it will pay someone to buy in the cheaper and sell in the dearer market. In addition to such *arbitrage* transactions, sellers will gravitate to the higher-priced market and buyers to the lower-priced until prices have been equalised. It is, in general, a sufficient condition for the existence of international trade of a good (in the absence of legal prohibitions or barriers) is that its price should be different in different countries. The gain to the participants may be regarded as self-evident or be proved using the familiar tools of welfare economics.

International trade theory, however, has set itself two slightly different and more precise goals:

1. to show that trade is beneficial to the nation as a whole, not just to exporters and importers.

This might be analysed using the 'market failure' framework to see whether international trade generates (negative) externalities but has usually been treated as a separate subject (for market failure, see Gowland (1982b), Chapter 8).

2. to show *minimum* conditions for the existence of trade.

It is easy to think of reasons for the existence of trade, such as different prices, but the theorists seek to show why prices differ and to find as many reasons as possible why they might differ. There are two principal approaches to these problems: the Ricardian and the Hecksher-

Ohlin (p. 16), besides the alternative theories reviewed in section 2.9.

2.2 The Ricardian Theory

The Ricardian, or classical, theory of international trade argued that trade would occur and would be beneficial because of *comparative advantage*. This was simply a way of saying that beneficient trade would occur if *marginal opportunity costs* differed between countries. Given competitive assumptions, different marginal (opportunity) costs will be reflected in different prices, as it is, of course, a basic prediction of competitive analysis that price equals marginal cost; so the existence of trade is guaranteed. It is desirable because it will produce a potential pareto improvement compared to autarky (no trade), i.e. that more of all goods will be available for consumption so there must be a conceivable distribution of income that will make everyone better off, the definition of a potential pareto gain. This argument is best demonstrated by an example, which abstracts and simplifies by using only two countries and two goods. The two countries will be labelled the USA and the UK; anyone not sharing this Anglo-Saxon chauvinism should relabel as 'the rest of the World'. The two commodities will be wheat and cotton, a gesture to textbook tradition. The example is shown in Table 2.1.

Without trade, the US produces and consumes 50 million bushels of wheat and 30 million bales of cotton. Its marginal opportunity cost of production of 1 million bushels of wheat is 1 million bales of cotton. In other words, for each 1 million bales of cotton by which production is reduced, 1 million extra bushels of wheat can be produced and vice versa. The UK produces and consumes 10 million bushels of wheat and 8 million bales of cotton. Its marginal opportunity cost of 1 million bales of cotton is 3 million of wheat. Hence, if it reduces production of cotton by 1 million bales, wheat output can rise by 3 million, and if wheat output is reduced by 3 million bushels, cotton output can rise by 1 million bales.

With the aid of a *deus ex machina*, perhaps the Walrasian auctioneer on his day off, the two nations decide to:

1. trade at a price of two bushels of cotton for one of wheat;
2. the US will sell 6 million bushels of cotton to the UK in exchange for 12 million of wheat;
3. the US will reduce its output of wheat by 10 million bushels and

Table 2.1: Gains from Trade

	No trade Production (= consumption)	Production	*Trade* Exports (−) Imports (+)	Consumption	Gain from trade
US Wheat	50	40	+ 12	52	+ 2
Cotton	30	40	− 6	34	+ 4
Marginal opportunity cost 1W:1C					
UK Wheat	10	25	− 12	13	+ 3
Cotton	8	3	+ 6	9	+ 1
Marginal opportunity cost 1W:3C					

Note: US trades 6 million bales of cotton for 12 million bushels of wheat; US reduces production of wheat by 10 and so can increase output of cotton by 10; UK reduces production of cotton by 5 and so can increase output of wheat by 15.

increase its output of cotton by 10 million bales so it will produce 40 of each;

4. the UK will reduce its output of cotton by five million bales and increase its output of wheat by 15 million bushels – it will now produce 25 million bushels of wheat and 3 million bales of cotton.

The outcome is shown in Table 2.1. The US now consumes 52 million bushels of wheat (40 it produces and 12 it imports) and 34 million bales of cotton (40 it produces less 6 it exports). This represents a gain of 2 million bushels of wheat and 4 of cotton compared to autarkic consumption. The UK consumes 13 million bushels of wheat (25 produced less 12 exported) and 9 million bales of cotton (3 produced and 6 imported); a gain of 3 and 1 respectively. Hence trade has made both nations better off.

A number of crucial aspects of the analysis must now be emphasised.

2.2.1 Independence of Productivity

The example assumed nothing about productivity. There might be 200 million people in the US or just one person. Nothing in the example would change. This reveals why a nation can be more efficient in producing both goods and still gain from trade. If the US population were 5 per cent of the UK's, it would be more efficient at producing both goods (since it produces more of both with less resources and by examination of the marginal opportunity costs). If the US population were five hundred times that of the UK's, the reverse would be true. In either case the gains from trade would be the same.

2.2.2 Distribution of Income

Nothing is said in the example about who consumes the goods. It may be that international trade produces so adverse a distribution of income that autarky is (socially) preferable. The pro-trade argument needs to be either indifferent to distribution or assume that income distribution can be costlessly altered by other means, see p. 34 and p. 49 below.

2.2.3 Full Employment

The argument above implicitly assumes full employment, when wheat production was reduced, cotton production was assumed to rise. There was no consideration of whether this would, rather than could, happen, or whether instead resources might be unemployed. Those arguing for the adverse effects of trade have always concentrated on this.

2.2.4 Price

The price was plucked out of mid-air; the theory says nothing about price, except that for beneficient trade price must lie between the two marginal opportunity costs. Relative prices of exports and imports are called the terms of trade, see p. 13 below. Many Third World countries have grumbled about unfair terms of trade — and so have some European nations since oil prices rose.

2.2.5 Incomplete Specialisation

The Ricardian theory does not imply complete specialisation. In the example, both the UK and the US continue to produce both goods. For complete specialisation it would be necessary both for marginal opportunity costs to be constant and for trade to take place at the level at which it maximises welfare.

2.3 The Gains from Trade

The gains from trade can conveniently be illustrated by Figure 2.1. XY is the production possibility frontier of an economy which can produce two goods x and y; the slope of XY is therefore the marginal opportunity cost of x in terms of y. Without trade XY is also the consumption possibility frontier. Some point such as A represents the highest possible level of welfare under autarky, i.e. without trade. If this nation starts to trade, its consumption possibilities are expanded. VW is a line drawn tangential to XY (at P) whose slope is equal to the world price of x in terms of y. The nation can produce at P and then exchange along VW. Between P and V the nation would be giving up some (exporting) y and receiving (importing) x; between P and W it would export x and import y. If the nation were to export x it would receive x times the (world price x/ world price y) units of y for each unit of x it exported. As the relative price of x in terms of y is, by definition, the slope of VW, it can be checked that VW does represent the trading opportunities open to this economy.

VW also represents the new consumption possibility frontier. The nation can produce at P and trade along VW, so it can consume anywhere along VW. The gains from trade are the expanded consumption possibilities, the shaded area between XY and VW. Any point in the area SAR represents a potential pareto gain compared to A, as more of both x and y could be consumed. Some new consumption point along SR, e.g. C, would clearly leave the economy better off than at A

Figure 2.1: The Gains from Trade

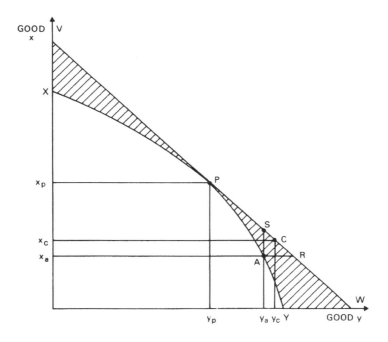

(subject to the reservations discussed in 2.2 above). Some poing along VS or RW might be superior to C but it would then be preferred to A as well. At C, this nation produces x_p and y_p and consumes x_c and y_c so it is exporting (x_p-x_c) and importing (y_c-y_p) in exchange. The gains from trade have enabled the consumption of both x and y to rise, by (x_c-x_a) and (y_c-y_a) respectively.

In this presentation it was assumed that the nation was a price taker in world trade, i.e. unable to influence the world price of x in terms of y. If this were not so, e.g. if the size of this nation's imports influenced the price, two minor changes would have to be made to Figure 2.1 since VW would be convex and there would no longer be a single optimal output P but many different Ps each associated with a point along or segment of VW. Neither of these would change the main thrust of the gains from trade argument.

2.4 The Terms of Trade

There have been various references to the *terms of trade* above, so it is useful to deal more formally with them at this point. The terms of trade are normally defined as the relative price of exports in terms of imports. When the price of imports falls, the terms of trade are said to improve. This happened to the UK in the 1930s and 1950s when the price of its imports fell very rapidly and on both occasions UK consumption per capita rose because of this. In 1973 OPEC's raising of oil prices (p. 6 above) dramatically worsened the terms of trade of oil importers such as Germany and Japan. (The UK's Terms of Trade, 1963-82 are shown in Table 2.2.)

Table 2.2: The UK's Terms of Trade (1975=100)

1963	114.9
1964	113.5
1965	116.4
1966	118.7
1967	120.3
1968	115.7
1969	115.9
1970	118.8
1971	119.8
1972	121.1
1973	106.8
1974	93.1
1975	100.0
1976	97.9
1977	100.2
1978	105.9
1979	106.3
1980	103.7
1981	101.9
1982	101.2

This measure of the terms of trade, i.e. export prices ÷ import prices, can be measured in various ways depending upon which price indices are used — e.g. wholesale prices, retail prices or GDP deflator. The usual index number problem arises when the price of some imports rises and that of other falls. If the UK used to import 10αs at 10 cents and 1β at 1\$ and now imports 1α at \$1 and 10βs at 10 cents, import prices could be said to have risen, fallen or remained unchanged.[1] However, great the practical and theoretical problems of measurement, the conceptual idea of the opportunity cost of exports in terms of imports is clear.

The above definition of the terms of trade is sometimes called the net barter terms of trade (as opposed to the gross barter terms when the *quantity* of imports is divided by the *quantity* of exports; the two measures are identical so long as exports equal imports). An alternative definition called the single factoral terms of trade seeks to measure the cost of imports in terms of home factor inputs such as labour time. For example, if an imported bottle of champagne cost an (exported) bottle of whisky in 1950 and two bottles in 1980, this definition asks how much time was needed to produce a bottle of whisky in 1950 and compares it with the amount of time needed to produce two bottles in 1980. A final definition (double factoral) compares the amount of labour used to produce both exports and imports in the two years. Despite the labour lavished by Viner, Taussig, Spraos and others on different definitions of the terms of trade, attention is almost invariably focused on the simplest – the price of imports ÷ price of exports, i.e. the net barter terms of trade.

2.5 Testing the Ricardian Theory

There are a number of major problems which render the theories of international trade exceptionally difficult to test. The first is that the predictions derived from the theories are of such a long-run nature that most conventional econometrics is irrelevant. Moreover it is very difficiult to imagine, let alone quantify, the pattern of production and costs in the UK if there were no trade so as to compare it with the post-trade pattern. A simple examination of *ex post* exports and imports cannot reveal all the *ex ante* information necessary to test the theories. Finally, there are horrendous conceptual and data problems faced by any investigator in this area. The Ricardian theory in particular is very difficult to set up in a refutable fashion so that it can be tested. It is possible to describe almost any pattern of trade in a fashion consistent with the theory. Nevertheless, a number of studies have attempted to test a modified and refutable version of the theory. The pioneer was MacDougall (1951-2), followed by Stern (1962) and Balassa (1963).

MacDougall sought to find a measurable version of the 'marginal opportunity cost' concept used on p. 8 above, and to apply it to the US and UK, using data for 1937. He decided that productivity differ entials were the most appropriate available measure of this, even though these were available only as *ex post* average rather than *ex ante* marginal relationships. Because of data availability he could only use labour productivity. The theory is concerned with comparative not absolute productivity, so MacDougall had to determine the average productivity differential because the US had higher productivity in all industries. Where the differential was above average, the US had a comparative advantage; where it was below average, the UK had one. MacDougall observed that US wages were about twice the UK level. This ratio would reflect the average productivity differential so long as the neoclassical (marginal productivity) theory of wages was valid. MacDougall made this assumption so that he could divide the 25 industries he was using into those in which the US had a comparative advantage and those in which the UK had one. Given the prevalence of trade restrictions he chose to examine US and UK exports to Third World countries rather than their trade with each other. In the purest case, if the US and UK competed on level terms in, say, Argentina, then the pattern of their exports should reflect the desired trade that the theory sought to explain, not the pattern that governments permitted. The pattern of trade was consistent with MacDougall's version of the Ricardian model, but the UK dominated markets where the US productivity advantage was less than 2.4 to 1 rather than 2 to 1 as he had hypothesised. This could be because of demand factors, i.e. reasons of taste or that British goods were more acceptable for political reasons. In addition British goods benefited from 'imperial preference' in some markets. Alternatively, MacDougall might have misclassified the boundary between US and UK comparative advantage.

Stern and Balassa (1963) obtained similar results using 1950 data but found that the UK had lost significant market shares to the US which suggested that the division between US and UK comparative advantage was closer to the theoretical value. This cross-section correlation between export success and productivity gives strong support to the Ricardian theory. In may seem obvious that industries with higher productivity are better able to compete internationally and so export more, but this is the Ricardian theory. The Hecksher-Ohlin model, for example, denies any role to productivity in explaining international trade.

2.6 The Hecksher-Ohlin Theory

The major rival to the Ricardian theory of international trade is the Hecksher-Ohlin theorem, which *inter alia* helped to win the Nobel Prize for Ohlin. (Both Ohlin's (1933) and Hecksher's (1919) contributions are reprinted in Ellis and Meltzer (1949).) Their work was based on the assumption, discussed on p. 1 above, that goods were mobile between countries while factors were immobile.

The argument used by Hecksher and Ohlin was that countries would like to trade factor services but were unable to do so, so they traded goods instead. Goods were traded as a method of indirectly trading the factor services embodied in them. A nation with a lot of capital and very little labour would like to import labour services and export capital ones. This was deemed to be impossible (except for special cases like Switzerland, which has always imported labour, traditionally Italian; now copied by other Western European economies). Hence the nation would export capital-intensive goods and import labour-intensive ones. In general it was argued that a nation will export goods which are intensive in the factor with which it is relatively well endowed and import the reverse case. Hence the Hecksher-Ohlin theory is often called the *factor-endowment theory* of international trade. This theory seeks to establish a minimum condition for international trade so its exponents usually rule out alternative reasons for trade by assumption – e.g. different tastes or different production functions; of course the latter is the *raison d'être* of the Ricardian theory.

The Hecksher-Ohlin theory has been subject to a lot of empirical testing which has not left it unscathed, e.g. the Leontief paradox, below. Hence it is worth emphasising that the theory is very useful in explaining trade within a firm. A large fraction of world trade is carried out within multi-national firms such as Ford or ITT and, undoubtedly, the location of factories by Ford could be explained by factor endowment, as modified by government intervention. ITT, for example, produces capital-intensive television components in California and ships them to Taiwan for the labour-intensive assembly stage.

2.7 Testing the Hecksher-Ohlin Model

The factor endowment theory has been much more extensively tested that the Ricardian theory (see Grubel (1977) pp. 62-5). The most famous and important of these studies was by Leontief (1969, originally published in 1953). Leontief was the pioneer of input-output analysis for which he was ultimately awarded the Nobel Prize. He used the US input-output matrix for 1947 to test the Hecksher-Ohlin model. Leontief calculated the factor inputs into $1 million of American exports; strictly he estimated what resources would be released if US exports were reduced by $1 million. He then calculated the inputs of factors that would be required to produce within the US $1 million of goods actually imported in 1949. Leontief regarded this as the appropriate measure of the factore-intensiveness of US imports. Thus he could compare the factor-intensiveness of US exports and imports. Moreover his methodology had created composite goods for exports and imports which represented all the goods actually traded in the correct proportions and so came as close a test of the two-good Hecksher-Ohlin model as was possible.

Leontief expected that US exports would be more capital-intensive than her imports since the US was obviously a capital-rich nation. Hence, according to the factor endowment theory, it should export capital-intensive goods and import labour-intensive ones. Instead US exports were more labour-intensive than her imports. This apparent contradiction of the predictions of the Hecksher-Ohlin model was called the Leontief paradox. There have been many attempts to explain it, either by showing that Leontief's results were wrong or by showing which of the Hecksher-Ohlin assumptions was inappropriate.

2.7.1 1947 Was an Atypical Year

This obvious comment on the results was first made by Swerling (1954). 1947 was not a typical year as economies were still recovering from World War II. However Leontief (1956) and Baldwin (1971) replicated the calculations for 1951 and 1962 respectively and still found the paradox.

2.7.2 Leontief's Results Were Not Significant

This proposition was advanced by Loeb (1954) who showed that the difference between the capital-intensiveness of US exports and imports was not statistically significant. However, the later work did find significant differences.

2.7.3 Capital Was Measured Inappropriately

This criticism was made by Buchanan (1955) who argued that Leontief had failed to take account of the different lengths of life of different capital goods. Leontief had used the capital stock to measure capital-intensiveness, not the capital services used (e.g. if good 1 were produced using £10 million of capital which lasted ten years and good 2 using £10 million of capital which lasted five years, Leontief said they were equally capital-intensive, whereas in reality good 2 is more capital-intensive). Buchanan is right but it is not clear if this mismeasurement would produce a systematic bias.

2.7.4 The Trade Pattern Reflects Protection Not Market Forces

This is another problem that arises in the real world. In 1947, the US was a highly protectionist economy. Hence *ex post* trade reflected what was permitted and possible rather than what was desired, whereas both Ricardian and Hecksher-Ohlin seek to explain desired trade. The US economy was much more open to trade by 1962 so this problem is less applicable to Baldwin's results.

2.7.5 Demand Effects

This proposition is that the US has such a differential demand for capital-intensive goods that it imports them in addition to its own production (see p. 22 below). It is plausible that the US (in 1947) was both the richest country as well as the best endowed with capital and that capital-intensive goods are highly income elastic (e.g. electricity). In this case, tastes would explain the pattern of trade, rather than factor endowments, in a pattern consistent with the Hecksher-Ohlin model. The evidence, however, does not seem to support the demand theory — Grubel (1977) says that 'it should be rejected' (p.67) and Sodersten (1979) that 'it is more of a theoretical curiosum than a very likely empirical possibility' (p.69).

2.7.6 Factor Reversals

One of the assumptions of the Hecksher-Ohlin model is that there are no reversals of factor intensity, that is that the ranking of goods by capital-intensiveness of their method of production is the same in all countries. If this assumption is not valid, the factor endowment theory collapses. There is a lot of support for this explanation of the paradox but little evidence, although it is clear that such reversals may occur (see appendix, p.25) but not that if they did it would explain the paradox.

2.7.7 US Labour Is Better

This explanation was advanced by Leontief himself in 1956. His argument is that the US is really labour rich, contrary to appearances, since each US worker is worth three workers elsewhere. Hence corrected for effectiveness the US is labour rich; rather in the vein of Sir Roger de Coverley's 'one Englishman could beat three Frenchmen . . . that London Bridge was a greater piece of work than any of the Seven Wonders of the World', and the rest of his 'honest prejudices' so gently guyed by Addison. As Leontief recognised, such a proposition is inconsistent with the simple Hecksher-Ohlin model. It is therefore useful to expand the model to bring in extra factors which may explain the superiority of American labour. The most obvious is human capital, discussed in section 2.7.8.

2.7.8 An n Factor World

This is the simplest and best way to redeem the factor endowment theory. If one extends the analysis to n factors, the US would still export goods intensive in the factor(s) with which it is well endowed but this need no longer be either labour or capital. The US is well endowed with land and natural resources and relatively well endowed compared to all but a few countries (Australia, Argentina). It exports products, like wheat, which are land-intensive but also labour-intensive. If one follows Becker's analysis of 'human capital', the US is certainly better endowed with human capital than other countries because of its expenditure on education and health. This factor is, however, embodied in US labour, so exports which are human-capital-intensive seem to be labour-intensive in a two-factor analysis.

2.7.9 Technology

The most radical departure from the factor endowment theory is to drop the common production function assumption and to argue that US technology was superior and explained its trade pattern. Such analyses are considered below, p. 22.

To summarise, the Leontief paradox may reveal the irrelevance of Hecksher-Ohlin to explaining trade patterns or it may be extended to 'n factors' and still be applicable.

2.8 The Factor Price Equalisation Theorem

Samuelson (1948) was the first to demonstrate the factor price equalisation theorem. However, it is a natural and obvious extension of the Hecksher-Ohlin theory. It is a fundamental result in elementary microeconomic theory that trade within a market leads to the equalisation of price within it, indeed it is a condition of equilibrium. As the factor endowment theorem argues that international trade is trade in factor services, albeit indirectly, the natural result would be an equalisation of their price. The stringency of the assumptions necessary to demonstrate the proposition is, therefore, more surprising than the theorem itself. Despite the apparent unrealism of the theorem, it has nevertheless been the basis of applied analysis especially within the context of the EEC, e.g. by Dosser in Shoup (1967). Before examining the factor price equalisation theorem it is important to stress that it could be proved using alternative assumptions within the framework of other models, e.g. free movement of labour in the Ricardian model.

The assumptions that are necessary to prove the FPET are:

1. perfect competition in all factor and goods markets in all countries;
2. perfect certainty;
3. the number of commodities must be at least equal to the number of factors (this can always be achieved by a redefinition of factors or commodities);
4. production functions should exhibit constant returns (empirically not unreasonable);
5. production functions should be identical in all countries.

This does not mean that the *method* of production must be the same in each country but that the same technique must be *available* to each country.

6. no reversal of factor intensities; this assumption ensures that in all countries the ranking of industries by capital intensiveness is the same, see appendix;
7. zero transport and transaction costs;
8. no externalities;
9. no total specialisation, i.e. each country must produce each good.

It is clear that these assumptions can be relaxed but not in exactly what manner. The major research into this area was pioneered by Batra (1975) and Kemp (1976). They showed that if either assumption (2) or (7) is relaxed, the FPET is valid only in the modified form, that trade reduces inequalities in factor returns rather than eliminates them.

The theorem is usually proved for two countries, one of which is relatively well endowed with capital, the other with labour; and two goods, one capital-intensive and one labour-intensive. Here the countries are C which is relatively capital-rich and L, the goods shoes (labour-intensive) and cars. The assumptions listed above ensure that for both goods in both countries price equals marginal cost and that factors are paid their marginal revenue products which are also equal to price times marginal physical product.

Wages are the same in both industries within each economy and so are profits per unit of capital, so marginal revenue products are the same in each industry. Two intuitively obvious results follow: under autarky, wages are lower and labour-intensive goods cheaper in an economy with more labour relative to capital. The labour:capital ratio is higher in L, so MRP of labour must be lower under autarky. Hence wages are lower in L than C (and capital rentals higher), given assumption (2). Marginal cost, and so price, for each industry in each country can be calculated as the sum of the marginal physical products of each factor times their price. Consequently the price of cars will be higher in L and that of shoes in C.

As shoes are more expensive and wages higher in C, trade leads to less production of shoes and more of cars in C. This reduces the demand for labour and increases that for capital in C. Therefore wages fall in C (and profits rise in L by the same argument). This continues until the prices of the goods are equalised between countries. When prices are equalised, as prices reflect marginal costs and marginal costs marginal products, the sum of the marginal revenue products must be the same in each industry across countries. This is only possible if marginal revenue products, and consequently factor prices, are equal.

2.9 Other Theories

There are a wide range of other theories of international trade besides the Ricardian and factor endowment theories. Some are implicit, or even explicit, within the two major theories. Others are extensions of them or involve manipulation of neoclassical economics. Others are overtly political or are distinctly hostile to orthodox economics or both. Some of the theories are intellectually coherent, some useful, but some are neither.

One theory which is implicitly accepted by proponents of the orthodox theories is the proposition that trade takes place because of *differences in tastes* between countries. No one denies that this could cause trade; it is for this reason that identical tastes are usually assumed so as to show that it is differential factor endowments which create the incentive to trade, not differential tastes. To take an extreme, simple example of this theory, imagine two countries with identical populations and equal GDP and factor endowments. A has a comparative advantage in producing good x so it produces 60,000,000 tons of it and B only 40,000,000. Nevertheless such is the desire of A's citizens for x that they consume 80,000,000 and B's only 20,000,000. Thus, A actually imports a good in which it has a comparative advantage because of the difference in tastes. Real world examples are hard to find. Tastes clearly help to shape the pattern of trade, e.g. UK imports of lamb and tea, but rarely determine them without the interaction of other factors. If differences in tastes are extended to include any difference in the proportion of income spent on goods, examples are easier to find, e.g. the US imports oil although it is a large producer as well. (Strictly this may not be a difference of tastes; the high US energy consumption:income ratio may reflect the level of income as much or more than taste.)

The theories that argue that international trade occurs because of *differences in technology* are really variants of the comparative advantage theory; the technological differences no doubt often explain why there are different marginal opportunity costs in the different countries. In their simplest forms, technological theories of trade are merely special cases of comparative advantage. However, more sophisticated variants claim to present a dynamic theory of trade and development. This is the *product cycle* or *imitation gap* theory associated with Kravis, Posner and Kindelberger. In the simplest case, there are three countries A, B and C, of which A is the most technologically advanced and C the least. A invents a product, x, and exports it to B and C. After a while B acquires the technology to produce x but by now A has a new discovery, y, so A exports y to B and C while B exports x to A and C. Finally, C acquires the means to produce x (and can undercut B) but B's engineers have discovered how to make y and A's inventors have a new high-technology product z. Hence each country exports one good to the other two, A exporting z, B y and C x. With the USA, Japan and Taiwan as the countries and computers, cars and textiles as the products, the story is plausible but it is not clear how generally applicable the theory is. The theory is, arguably, most useful as a reminder that comparative advantage may not persist and that a nation should not try to sustain old export industries after they have lost their cost advantage.

Kravis also pioneered another theory, the *availability* doctrine which is wrong in so far as it is not vacuous. This is that trade takes place principally in goods which are only available in one country and cannot be made or produced elsewhere. This could be interpreted as infinite comparative advantage. However, there are no such goods, barring those where the district defines the product: sherry, champagne, scotch whisky. In these instances, competition is provided by very close substitutes (Australian sherry, Asti, other grain-distilled spirits) and purchases are determined by comparative cost (and quality), not simple availability. In other cases, the theory is misleading. In one sense Kuwait and Saudi Arabia do export oil because it is available there. However it is also available virtually everywhere else in the world, the difference being one of cost. Even if oil were not available, coal (or peat) would be, or wood could be grown. Undoubtedly it would be much more costly for Japan to use alternative fuels or to obtain oil from the Tsuggru Strait. However, it is not that oil is available in Kuwait and not in Japan but that it is available in Kuwait at a minute fraction of the cost which explains why Japan imports oil.

The *monopoly* theory of international trade is logical and explains some trade, but a small, decreasing fraction. This is that every producer wants to be a price-discriminating monopolist and that the easiest way to become one is to export. Geographical segregation of markets is relatively simple in this case and different prices can be set at home and abroad, or even in each export market, so as to equate marginal revenue and marginal cost in each market. Price discrimination is rife, whisky is priced at about 30 per cent of its European level in Britain, cars at almost twice the level (in both cases net of tax and retail margins). However, whilst exporting provides opportunities for price discrimination, the latter may not be the motive for it.

The *economies of scale* theory is logical but empirically irrelevant. This argues that if there were economies of scale, identical countries could gain by specialisation. This is true. (Take two countries; either could produce 30x, 30y or 10 of each. Assume x and y are perfect complements, without trade each produces 10 of x and 10 of y. If either of them specialises in x and the other in y each will consume 15x and 15y.) However, there is no evidence that economies of scale exist such that national economies are too small to exploit them and much evidence that trade patterns are inconsistent with such a theory.

The *'vent for surplus'* theory is associated with Williams and Myint. In essence, their proposition is that many underdeveloped economies are inside their production possibility frontiers and that the stimulus of trade is necessary to ensure the full utilisation of resources. The argument would certainly have met with the approval of colonial governors in British Africa who deliberately sought to promote both internal and external trade for this reason. However, it is probably more relevant to a theory of development than of trade. Trade more often occurs because it is profitable than because of a belief that it is essential for development. Even in the colonial case, the actual trade was carried out by British (and Asian) entrepreneurs. In post-colonial Africa, governments have usually sought to restrict trade, not promote it.

The simplest of the *political* theories is that trade is an arm of diplomacy. Nations trade so as to encourage better relations. Often trade ties are imposed by the stronger as a means of making the weaker into a dependency. This theory reverses the economic theory of imperialism, whereby power was sought to promote trade ('trade follows the flag'). Instead, trade, even unprofitable trade, is sought as a means to power. Examples are legion: perhaps the most blatant being Franco-German competition in Eastern Europe between the wars.

Marxism argues that trade occurs as an essential stage in the self-destructive progress of capitalism towards its inevitable doom. Firms seek profits abroad as they decline at home but, of course, this merely intensifies the competition, as the same is happening in every country. Such ideas are hard to present in a way that is neither a caricature nor misleading but are nevertheless capable of penetrating insights, e.g. Glyn and Sutcliffe (1972).

2.10 The Pure Theory in the Real World

The acid test of the pure theory is to see if it can explain the patterns of trade that actually exist. Problems arise because many countries' exports and imports are remarkably similar, e.g. Britain both exports and imports cars on a large scale. France and Germany each exports large numbers of cars to the other. Britain both exports and imports high-technology capital-intensive goods like computers and has a similar two-way trade in low-technology labour-intensive shirts.

The factor endowment theory, while very successful at explaining the internal organisation of Ford or ITT, cannot explain such behaviour. There is no way in which it can be argued that French cars are more or less labour-intensive than German ones.

The Ricardian theory does somewhat better. It sometimes uses the rather formalistic device of saying that each make of car is a separate good and comparative advantage exists in them. Italy has a comparative advantage in making Italian cars, indeed no one else can make an Italian car. This is reasonable for a few goods — Paris fashions, British shotguns

— but is not generally very acceptable. More convincing use is made of Lancaster's 'characteristics' theory. This argues that all goods are bundles of 'primary characteristics'. Thus, a car is a bundle of, *inter alia*, performance, comfort, economy and style. It is then argued that different countries have comparative advantage in these characteristics but no one can buy a characteristic without a car. Hence Italian style or German reliability or Japanese gadgets have to be embodied in superficially similar cars. The problem with comparative advantage may be that it is so flexible that it could explain anything.

Appendix: Factor Reversals

The concept of factor reversals is best understood by reference to a diagram such as Figure 2.2 which has the capital:labour ratio on the horizontal axis and the relative cost of capital in terms of labour on the vertical axis. The optimal capital: labour ratio for each level of (relative) costs is then plotted as in Figure 2.2(a). If there are fixed proportions of factors in production this curve would be vertical, but normally it would slope downwards from left to right as in Figure 2.2(a). As the cost of capital falls relative to wages, it becomes profitable to substitute capital for labour so the capital:labour ratio rises. If one plots these curves for two industries on the same diagram it is possible to see whether a reversal of factor intensity occurs. If the curves intersect, as in Figure 2.2(b), a reversal occurs. x represents the optimal capital output ratio for industry X and y for industry Y. At relative cost level c_1 industry Y has a higher capital:labour ratio; r_1 compared to r_2. As the relative cost of capital falls there is a reversal of factor intensity such that at relative cost level c_2 industry X is more capital intensive since its capital:labour ratio (r_3) is higher than Y's (r_4). Where the curves do not intersect there is no reversal. For the FPET it is necessary only that there be no reversal over the relevant range, i.e. between the initial relative cost (factor payments) in the two countries. Hence the case illustrated in Figure 2.2(c) satisfies this requirement, even though a reversal would occur at an irrelevant ratio. The problem of factor reversals was extensively analysed by Minhas (reprinted in Bhagwati, 1969, pp. 140-68). Minhas argued that such reversals were important empirically as well as theoretically.

Figure 2.2: Factor Reversals

a) The relationship between relative cost and the optimal ratio

b) Factor reversal occurs

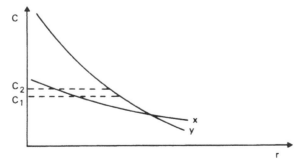

c) Irrelevant factor reversal

c_1 is initial cost ratio in Country 1 and c_2 in Country 2. Trade would equalise factor prices.

Note

1. The FPET can be demonstrated geometrically, e.g. Grubel (1977), pp. 48-52 and 54-8, and Johnson (1958), Chapter 1, which also discussed the case where factor intensities are reversed. An algebraic proof can be found in Batra (1973), p. 117.

3 COMMERCIAL POLICY I: TARIFFS AND THE THEORY OF PROTECTION

3.1 Some Concepts

Free trade exists if imports are allowed to compete on equal terms with domestic suppliers without any device introduced by governments to try to distort the choice of purchasers. Domestic producers may very well enjoy some *natural protection*, because of transport costs (or, in the extreme, geography). For example, a restaurant in Singapore cannot compete on equal terms for my custom with one in York. A painter in Germany could tender to paint York University, but his travelling costs handicap him such that he cannot be said to compete on level terms with York painters. Economists recognise this but normally simplify their analysis to consideration of only two types of goods:

1. *traded goods* in which free trade could exist if governments permitted it, i.e. there are no transport costs, and
2. *non-traded goods* in which there could never be any foreign competition, let alone free trade, i.e. transport costs are prohibitive.

This distinction is used in various places in the subsequent analysis, e.g. Chapter 10. Before leaving natural protection, it is worth noting that it may protect the importer against the domestic producer. A Californian firm, for example, has much lower transaction costs in reaching Vancouver than a firm in Quebec.

Protection exists when imports are handicapped in their ability to compete with domestic goods. By convention, 'protection' is restricted to those cases where governments have imposed the handicap, i.e. natural protection is excluded. There are many protective devices.

3.1.1 Tariffs

A tariff is a tax which is imposed on imports but not on domestically produced goods. The tax may be a flat rate or *specific* one – e.g. £500 per car. Alternatively, tariffs may be calculated as a percentage of the importers' price, an *ad valorem* tariff, e.g. 20 per cent. Tariffs can be calculated in other ways – e.g. the US government used to calculate them as a percentage of the domestic producers' price, the American selling price system. Often it is debatable whether a tariff has been imposed or not, since it is not clear whether the same tax is paid on imported goods as on domestically produced ones. This may seem strange, but stems from ambiguity about the definition of a good. Wine is imported into the UK and pays a high rate of tax (for the purposes of this argument the miniscule UK production is ignored). Bitter beer is produced domestically and pays a much lower rate of tax. This arrangement might be argued to be protective since imported alcohol pays a higher rate of tax than domestically produced alcohol; an argument advanced by the European Commission in 1981 and Gladstone in 1860 amongst others. Alternatively if wine and beer are separate products there is no tariff.

A tariff which is sufficiently high to exclude all imports is called a *prohibitive tariff.*

3.1.2 Quotas

A quota restricts the amount, either by value or volume, of a product which can be imported. Quotas, for example, are imposed by most OECD countries on textile imports, either through multilateral arrangements like the MFA (Multilateral Fibre Arrangement) or unilaterally. Quotas take various forms depending upon the arrangements made to determine who is allowed to supply the restricted quantity.

3.1.3. Subsidies

A subsidy may be used to induce domestic residents not to buy imports — e.g. at the time of writing the UK government is to give £10 million to Cunard to persuade it to have a replacement for the *Atlantic Conveyor* built in Newcastle rather than South Korea. Subsidies may be general, that is extended to all purchasers, or specific to the individual case, like the Cunard case. They may be paid to consumers or producers but the effect is the same.

3.1.4 Import Deposits

This device is overtly permitted by GATT (p. 29 above). An import deposit requires the importer to lodge, usually with the central bank, a large proportion of the cost of the import interest free for a period of time, usually six months or one year. Import deposits were used by the UK in 1968 and Italy in 1976. In both cases it seems to have been very effective but more because of the macroeconomic effects of the forced loan to the government than because of any protective effect.

3.1.5 State Trading Monopolies

These are probably the oldest and most widespread of protective devices, being used in Ancient Egypt and in virtually every country in the communist bloc, Africa, Asia and Latin America. The government permits no one but itself to import a named good. It then resells the good to domestic consumers, usually at a profit. Alternatively, the right may be delegated to a specific person or company — usually for a cash payment. Elizabeth I made extensive use of such trading monopolies but renounced them in 1601 after the 'Golden Speech'. They were just as controversial in the UK after World War II when used by the Labour government, although reducing substantially the cost of imports (Ady's analysis: pp. 553-9 of Worswick and Ady, 1952) but being selected by the Conservatives as one of the major oppressive devices from which they would 'set the people free' — the Conservative slogan in the 1950 election.

3.1.6 Non-tariff Barriers to Trade

Logically, a non-tariff barrier would include (1) to (5) but is usually, although not always, restricted to a barrage of administrative and regulatory devices which restrict trade. These range from preferential buying to sophisticated restrictions masquerading as health and safety regulations. Preferential buying occurs when public sector bodies buy more expensive domestic goods in preference to cheaper imports. This is enshrined in the 'Buy American' Acts (which lay down a percentage by which an import must undercut the domestic price before it is purchased) and was practised in the 1960s and 1970s by the UK government in its computer policy to help ICL against IBM. Even here the line is blurred, as protection may take .the form of specifying a feature that only the domestic product could have, even though not intrinsically desirable; this is especially common in defence purchases (Hartley (1983).

The regulatory and administrative devices used to restrict trade are legion but are impossible to distinguish from genuine safety and health regulations. For example, German brewers have always used a method of production which does not use the additives used by British, Belgian and Dutch producers. Is a regulation banning the sale of beer with additives in Germany discriminatory? The Germans argue that the additives are dangerous to health; the EEC Commission that it is a protective ploy. European producers of cars have argued that US safety and pollution regulations impose, and were intended to impose, a cost penalty on them compared to US producers. American producers deny this, with justice, but the Japanese government recently amended its regulations because it agreed that they had an (unintentional?) protective effect.

3.2 The Effective Rate of Protection

It is important, given the array of protective devices, that a measure of protection be available. The standard measure is the effective rate of protection. This is calculated so that as far as possible protection can be analysed as if there were a tariff on a good with no inputs, i.e. the simplest possible microeconomic problem. The calculations assume that incidence is always on the consumer; this follows from the 'small country' assumption below but would also follow from an assumption of perfectly inelastic demand, a common assumption in tax analysis. In this case any tariff will be added to the world price of the good and any subsidy will be retained by the producer.

The first problems which arise in calculating protection arise from the existence of inputs. Tariffs on these affect the competitive position of domestic firms, e.g. a tariff on wheat clearly affects the ability of flour-millers to compete on equal terms with foreigners. The ERP in this case is:

$$ERP = \frac{\text{Tariff on Output} - \text{Tariff on input}}{\text{Value Added of Industry } \textit{measured at world prices}}$$

To take a specific example. If at world prices (i.e. free trade prices) it requires £40 worth of iron ore to make £100 worth of steel, the ERP will be calculated for a 20 per cent tariff on steel and a 12½ per cent tariff on iron ore, as:

$$ERP = \frac{\text{Tariff on output (20 per cent of 100)} - \text{Tariff on input} \quad (12\tfrac{1}{2} \text{ per cent of 40})}{\text{Value added (100-40)}}$$

$$= \frac{20-5}{60}$$

$$= \frac{15}{60} = 25 \text{ per cent}$$

The rationale is that protection should be calculated as a percentage of value added, i.e. the industry's net output, so the £20 tariff (20 per cent of gross output) is equal to protection of one-third on net output. On the other hand, the firm has to pay £45 for its inputs instead of a free trade price of £40, so this extra cost acts as negative protection and needs to be deducted from the £20 tariff.

If there is a tariff on an input into an input, this is similarly calculated — does it affect the price the firm pays? Thus if instead of the iron ore tariff there were a coal tariff, it would have no effect on the price of iron ore and so no effect on the ERP of steel.

Subsidies can be added to the ERP. A subsidy of £15 per unit of steel (i.e. £100 worth of final output at world prices) adds 25 per cent to the ERP, i.e. 15 divided by the value added at world prices. Subsidies on inputs, however have no effect on the ERP being retained by the producers of the inputs. All other protective devices are similarly converted into cost penalties for foreign producers or cost bonuses for domestic producers. In the case of quotas this requires additional assumptions and is discussed below in the context of comparing tariffs and quotas.

The only remaining point about the ERP is to note that it is often negative (e.g. Oulton, 1976). If the tariff on the input is sufficiently high, this can happen even when the nominal tariff is very high. In the above example if the steel tariff were 100 per cent and the iron ore tariff 300 per cent the ERP would be:

$$ERP = \frac{100 - 120}{60} = -33\,{}^1/_3 \text{ per cent.}$$

Another quirk arises when the value added at world prices is negative; in this case the ERP is infinite by definition. This is true of some Northumberland hill farmers. However, it is perhaps simpler to take the (fictitious) case of growing tomatoes in Greenland. It would require about £600 worth of oil to heat greenhouses that would produce tomatoes that could be bought in Holland for £100. The total cost of inputs might be £800. In this case the industry's value added would be -£700. However a 900 per cent tariff on tomatoes would raise the price in Greenland to £1000 and make it profitable to produce them there. (The cost figures are approximately accurate, the tariff is fictitious.)

3.3 The Case for Free Trade

Anglo-Saxon economists have traditionally been advocates of free trade, unlike their continental European *confrères* who have usually been protectionist. Sometimes advocates of free trade have been so hysterical that it obscures the respectable and soundly based tradition of protectionist argument. For example, Hirst (1911) wrote:

> If those who made the war had been allowed to make a tariff, the greatest shipping broking and banking centre of the world would have been not only shaken but shattered. *Grass would have grown in the port of London and in the streets of the City.* (p. 72)

Samuelson's standard text states:

> 'No fair-minded reader who takes the trouble to think the matter through can fail to see how shallow are most of the economic arguments for tariff protection. The only obvious exception is the infant-industry argument. (p. 703, 10th edition)

Even this passage is less strident than the equivalent in earlier editions. It is therefore worthy of note that the US, Germany and Japan all became great economic powers when pursuing highly protectionist policies, and some argue their success was because of protection.

The original case for free trade was a natural extension of the argument in Chapter 2. Once international trade was shown to be beneficial, any restriction was taken to be undesirable. A more modern version of the argument uses the paretian welfare argument for a competitive economy. (There is no difference between the argument for permitting domestic trade and for foreign trade.) Any restriction on trade will produce a distortion that interferes with one or other paretian criteria. Figure 3.1 shows this argument, in the diagram used in the previous chapter. The production possibility frontier is PF, the consumption possibility frontier CD. If there is free trade, market forces will operate such that consumers equate the marginal rate of substitution with the world price, so consumption will be at X, where the indifference curve is tangential. Protection is designed to distort choice, through an alteration of price or otherwise, to reduce imports and increase the consumption of domestic goods. If world prices are unchanged, consumers will finish up at some point with consumption of x between the autarkic point A and X, shown as Y on Figure 3.1. Y is, by definition, on a lower indifference curve than X and so inferior to it. Free trade is a potential pareto gain compared to protection but it will only be an *actual* pareto gain if there is:

Figure 3.1: The Effects of Protection

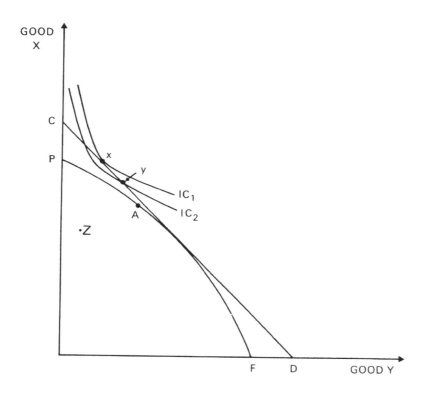

1. full employment;
2. indifference to the distribution of income (or lump sum transfers to ensure an optimal distribution);

In addition the argument implicitly assumed:

3. fixed world prices;
4. a static economy.

The major protectionist arguments depend upon a relaxation of any of these assumptions.

3.4 The Case for Protection

The major economic arguments for protection stem from a relaxation of the assumptions necessary to show the optimality of free trade. In most cases there is a free trade counter-argument which reveals that protection would be the best attainable state rather than an ideal state.

3.4.1 Unemployment

If an economy would otherwise have unemployment, there may be a case for protection. In Figure 3.1, if the economy were at point Z, then protection would be desirable if it moved the economy to Y (even though X would be better still). The free traders have always argued that there must be a better way of ensuring full employment, e.g. by monetary or fiscal policy (in this case X would be attainable). Protectionists have always denied that this is necessarily so. Here the full employment case for protection will be analysed in two forms, the macroeconomic and microeconomic one.

The macroeconomic argument is either the Keynesian foreign trade multiplier or a monetarist argument that a balance of payments surplus will increase the money supply and so income. This latter argument goes back to Mun and the other mercantilists derided by protectionists since Adam Smith. The argument is, however, perfectly valid. The only question is, can economic expansionism be secured by more orthodox means? In some cases it argued this as impossible. It might be that all the excess demand would be spent on imports. Alternatively the excess demand would produce a balance of payments deficit which was unacceptable or unsustainable. The balance of payments is considered below in Chapters 6 to 8 and 10. However, as the macro-protectionist argument is now the major one used by advocates of import restrictions, it cannot be ignored in this context. The UK Labour Party's 'Alternative Economic Strategy' is entirely based upon this (see p. 99 below). Keynes, otherwise a life-long free trader, endorsed this protectionist argument in 1930 (Keynes (1930)).[1]

One problem with the macroeconomic argument for protection is that it represents an attempt to export unemploynent, unless the 'paradox of imports' (p. 103 below) applies. However, protectionists are rarely concerned with the welfare of other nations. Even an ultra-nationalist must take note of the danger of retaliation, which may simply lead to a reduction of employment and trade in all countries — the vicious cycle of 'beggar-my-neighbour' policies allegedly seen between the wars. (The importance of it depends upon how instrumental the US Smoot-Hawley tariff of 1930 was in triggering the European slump.)

The microeconomic employment case for protection starts with the obvious point that a tariff can increase the demand for labour in a specific place or industry. A tariff on steel in the US would raise employment in Pennsylvania. This is only relevant if there is no better way of raising Pennsylvanian employment. Effectively this is so if the shadow wage, or opportunity cost of labour, is less than the market price. This may be so. To take a much cited example, shipbuilding in the UK. Most shipbuilding workers are over 50 years of age and have no other job opportunities; they live in depressed areas and retraining or moves to the south-east are ruled out as too expensive (economically or socially). In this case their opportunity cost is low, possibly zero. Hence protection which led to their being employed would almost certainly improve resource allocation.

There are two free trade counters to this:

1. The general point that a subsidy would be preferable to a tariff – although this is still protection. If the opportunity cost of a Newcastle boilermaker is £20 and the wage rate £100, then a subsidy of £80 to the employer is optimal. This is true in principle; the point is discussed in the comparison of tariffs and subsidies, section 7 below.
2. Moreover, this argument is very easy to misapply and, like most citations of market failure, opens a Pandora's box of dangers. Virtually anyone can use a variant of this shadow price argument to justify protection. This is true but the theoretical argument remains.

3.4.2 The Distribution of Income

Tariffs will normally increase the income of those who produce the protected good and almost invariably increase their relative income. This desire to change the distribution of income is probably the main reason for the imposition of tariffs, at least in Australia and the US. Moreover, this is the main rationale of the CAP, i.e. a desire to increase the economic welfare of farmers albeit at the cost of others. In terms of Figure 3.1, X may be pareto preferred to Y, but the distribution of income at Y may be less socially desirable than at X. The extreme paretian would argue for a lump-sum redistribution of income and the maintenance of free trade (for a definition and discussion of 'lump-sum' transfers see p. 49 below). However, lump-sum transfers may be impossible or politically infeasible. In this case redistribution by protection may be the best available policy.

3.4.3 World Prices and the Terms of Trade

The free trade case assumes that a nation is unable to influence world prices, i.e. that the terms of trade are exogenous. It may be that by reducing the quantity it imports, a nation can reduce its input prices and so make itself better off. (This argument is also analysed on pp. 43ff below.) This is illustrated in Figure 3.2. The protectionist policy lowers the price of imports in terms of exports and so allows a new consumption possibility frontier, at least over a limited range. It may be that producing at P_2 and consuming at W is better than P_1 and X_1 respectively. In an extreme case it may be that consumption of both goods rises, if the increase in domestic production exceeds the fall in imports (imports must fall, otherwise there is no possibility of the terms of trade improving).

A tariff which ensures the maximum welfare gain from changing the terms of trade is called an 'optimum tariff'. This does not mean the tariff which produces the most favourable terms of trade – the gain caused by an improvement is after a point offset by the loss in consumers' surplus caused by lower consumption of the good. The optimum tariff allows for 'optimum retaliation', that is other countries will retaliate if it pays them to but not out of spite. The optimal tariff with retaliation is unlikely to be the same as without.

No protectionist argument has been so deeply analysed as the terms of trade one. It is not without relevance to the real world. The UK's import policy used to have a significant effect on the price of most raw materials and US policy still does. Classic examples are UK imports of New Zealand lamb and US purchases of coffee. The EEC has a major impact on world food prices. Nevertheless, in practice the terms of trade agreement would rarely seem to be relevant to the debate about protection.

3.4.4 Dynamic Arguments

The analysis used to justify free trade assumes that production possibility frontiers are fixed. It may be that if production of one good were increased, then 'learning economies' or some other dynamic factor would shift the production possibility frontier outwards over time. The benefits of this, appropriately discounted, could outweigh the short-term costs of protection. This is called the infant-industry or young economy agrement. Free traders counter argue that a subsidy might be

Figure 3.2: Terms of Trade Gain

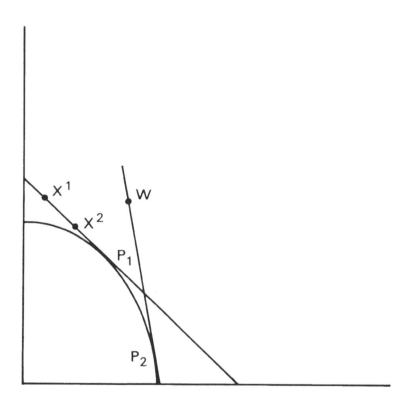

Extreme case: original consumption is X_2 and final consumption is at W so consumption of both goods has risen.

preferable or that tariffs may induce continued inefficiency. The longer-term effects of tariffs are very contentious. Tariffs may provide a secure shelter that permits long-run development, as in nineteenth-century Germany. They may protect an outdated, inefficient and complacent industrial structure, as in France until World War II.

3.4.5 Other Protectionist Arguments

There are a variety of other protectionist arguments that merit brief examination:

Countervailing Power. This is an argument that tariffs are necessary as bargaining counters in tariff negotiations. In other words, a classic deterrence argument with the usual problems this entails.

Non-economic Goals. The title for this category of arguments is misplaced since all of them amount to a statement that an industry's existence or output render an externality not captured in market prices, but the usual tag will be used. It is argued that certain industries are desirable because they render an economy or nation less dependent on others — usually used for defence-related industries, e.g. steel or shipbuilding, but often extended to cover a wide range of output especially in the field of energy. 'A gentleman needs a necktie, a nation an airline,' as a cynical American put it. A more sophisticated variation of this is to reduce foreign trade as a percentage of income to make a nation less susceptible to the world trade cycle — or less dependent on the income from a single export. A related set of arguments concern the desirability of trading with one group of nations rather than another either to show hostility to the latter or to foster friendship with the former. The counter agreements are the usual 'subsidy' or 'slippery slope' propositions. The latter has some force, given the range of industries which European governments seem to feel essential to national pride, ranging from computers to banking via aircraft production and soft drinks (the French government felt dependence on Coca-Cola derogatory to French culture).

Revenue. This argument is that all taxes distort but some tax is necessary so a tariff may be less objectionable than alternatives.

Dumping. This is a complex argument that if a foreign country subsidises its exports ('dumping'), it is right to impose a tariff. This was used to justify Britain's first modern peacetime departure from free trade in November 1919. It became very controversial in 1982 because the US government threatened to impose 'anti-dumping' duties on European steel — the subsidy in most cases is that the state owns the industry and permits enormous losses.

The argument often seems to be as much ethical as economic — *unfair* competition is wrong rather than harmful. Dumping *per se* is not undesirable for the importing country; e.g. arguably France has 'dumped' champagne in the UK, or did until the UK joined the EEC. No one could argue that the UK would have gained from a higher champagne price. The extreme free trader would argue that one should snap up cheap imports and use domestic labour to produce something else, but this is usually impracticable. Hence the pros and cons of dumping are hard to assess. The short-run opportunity cost of domestic production is often very low when faced with subsidised imports, especially in a recession. In this case the economic case for an anti-dumping duty is established; otherwise the argument is ethical not economic.

Note

1. Keynes marked his conversion by citing his early classic statement of the free trade position:

It will be fairest, perhaps, to quote, as an example, what I wrote myself. So lately as 1923, as a faithful pupil of the classical school who did not at that time doubt what he had been taught and entertained on this matter no reserves at all, I wrote: 'If there is one thing that protection can *not* do, it is to cure Unemployment . . . There are some arguments for Protection, based upon its securing possible but improbable advantages, to which there is no simple answer. But the claim to cure Unemployment involves the Protectionist fallacy in its grossest and crudest form.'

4 COMMERCIAL POLICY II: THE EFFECTS OF PROTECTION

4.1 The Effects of Tariffs

The effects of the imposition of a tariff on a particular good are best examined within the framework of the 'tariff triangle' diagram, Figure 4.1. This diagram in its simplest form requires a number of assumptions, which will be relaxed later.

1. the home market would otherwise be perfectly competitive, or at least have price takers on both sides;
2. the market for the good always clears by price; often omitted, this is necessary for any partial equilibrium comparative static analysis — including all supply and demand analysis.
3. the economy is a small one, i.e. no action by the country can influence world prices.

In Figure 4.1, HS is the home supply curve, as always this is also the industry's marginal cost curve. D is the home demand curve for the product (assumption (1) is required to permit these curves to be drawn). As the economy is a small one, it faces a perfectly elastic supply curve at the world price (WP). Foreign suppliers are prepared to offer unlimited quantities for sale at this price but will never charge less. Hence, with free trade, domestic producers must charge WP — any more and they sell nothing; any less and they are irrationally sacrificing profit to no purpose. Consequently the intersection of the perfectly elastic world supply curve (WP) with the (home) demand curve determines home consumption, Q_{CF} and with the home supply curve, domestic production, Q_{PF}. Imports are the difference between these, i.e. $Q_{CF} - Q_{PF}$.

Having established the free trade equilibrium, it is now possible to compare it with the equilibrium after the introduction of a tariff, either *ad valorem* or specific. The tariff raises the domestic price by the full amount of the tariff because the supply curve is still perfectly elastic but at (WP + T) where T is the tariff. Domestic producers are irrational to charge less than (WP + T) but unable to charge more than this because of the unlimited quantities being offered at this price, i.e. the foreign supply price plus the tariff. In fact the purchasers and suppliers

Figure 4.1: The Effects of a Tariff

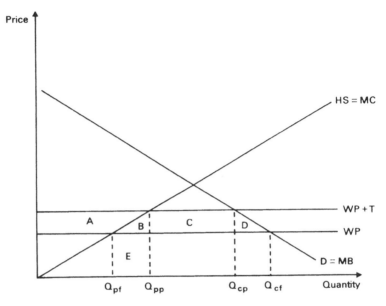

are in exactly the same position as before except that the price is higher. Domestic output rises from Q_{PF} to Q_{PP}, i.e. there is a move along the home supply curve. The higher price reduces (domestic) demand to Q_{CP}. Imports are, therefore, $Q_{CP} - Q_{PP}$.

It is now possible to establish the welfare effects of a tariff by the familiar 'area analysis' or surplus analysis using Figure 4.1. The calculation is set out in Table 4.1. Consumers' surplus falls by (A+B+C+D) because of the higher price. Producers' profits rise by A — their revenue rises by (A+B+E) but their costs rise by (B+E); the total cost is the area under the marginal cost curve, hence the cost of producing $(Q_{PP}-Q_{PF})$ is B+E. The tariff revenue accruing to the government is C; imports times tariff. Thus a tariff lowers community welfare by (B+D) and transfers A from consumers to producers and C from consumers to the government. The social cost (B+D) is a representation of the case for the potential pareto superiority of free trade. However, the income redistribution might well represent the objective of the tariff.

The two areas of social loss 'B' and 'D' are usually referred to as the 'production effect' and 'consumption effect' respectively. B is called the production effect because it is the excess of the cost of

Table 4.1: The Effect of a Tariff

	Gain (+)	Loss (–)
Consumers		– A – B – C – D
Government	+C	
Producers	+A	
Society		– B – D

domestic production (B+E) compared to foreign production (E); implicitly this assumes the world price equals the marginal cost of production. 'D' is the 'consumption effect', because it is that portion of the reduction in consumers' surplus caused by lower consumption rather than higher price.

The above is the basic analysis of the effect of a tariff. It is now possible to extend the analysis by relaxation of the assumptions made above. The easiest to relax concern the structure of the domestic market. So long as the tariff is not prohibitive, even a sole purchaser or supplier has no market power. This analysis is developed further, p. 50 below, where tariffs are compared with quotas which can create monopoly. Hence only minor modifications are necessary to Figure 4.1 to show the cases of a sole domestic purchaser or supplier. The sole domestic purchaser in fact merely requires the relabelling of the demand curve as the marginal benefit curve; there is no demand curve with a monopsonist. The demand curve is always the MB curve anyway so this generalisation affects none of the analysis. The sole domestic supplier is equally simple. There is no longer a supply curve, merely a marginal cost curve. WP and (WP+T) represent the suppliers' marginal revenue curve – so long as the tariff is non-prohibitive. Hence, for a non-prohibitive tariff all the above analysis still holds. A prohibitive tariff reduces the analysis to the elementary microeconomic supply and demand diagrams and the normal comparison of competition and mono-monopsony or monopoly can be made. With a prohibitive tariff, there are no imports and so no tariff revenue.

The terms of trade case is more interesting and is illustrated in Figure 4.2. The crucial difference is that the world supply curve is upward sloping at WS. To simplify the diagram, the HS and D curves have been replaced by a single excess demand or demand for imports (DM) curve. This is equal to home demand less home supply. It is obviously more elastic than either HS or D since it shows the *sum* of the responses of supply and demand to a change in price. A change in the 'consumers' surplus triangle' represents the net change in both consumers' surplus and profits, i.e. (B+C+D) in Figure 4.1. Under free trade

Figure 4.2: A Tariff Improves the Terms of Trade

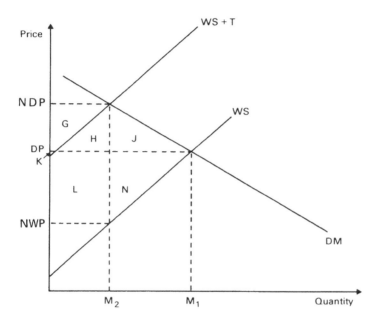

the demand for imports is M_1 and both world and domestic price are equal to DP. The tariff shifts the supply curve by T, upwards to (WS+T) (here T is specific) so the domestic price rises to NDP and imports fall to M_2. The new world price is NWP; the analysis is, of course, the most elementary of tax analyses, as in Lipsey (1979), Chapter 11.

The welfare analysis, set out in Table 4.2, is that consumers and producers together lose (G+H+J). The tariff revenue is (G+H+K+L), M_2 times T. Hence the net welfare gain is (K+L) − J. Thus there may be a net gain to the country improving the tariff by improving its terms of trade. World suppliers lose (K+L+N) so the tariff imposes a cost on the world as a whole of (J+N), the Marshallian triangle. This analysis has therefore confirmed that, on p. 33 above, a tariff must reduce world welfare but may benefit the country imposing it.

Table 4.2: Welfare Gains and Losses of a Tariff Which Improves the Terms of Trade

	Gain (+)	Loss (−)
Producers and Consumers		− (G − H − J)
Government	+G + H + K + L	
Country imposing tariff		− J + (K + L)
Producers in the rest of the world		− K − L − N
World		− J − N

4.2 The Metzler Paradox

Under some conditions the imposition of a tariff leads to a *fall* in the domestic price of the good. In other words, foreign suppliers reduce their price by more than the amount of the tariff. This is called the Metzler paradox (Metzler, 1949). This arises because of the effect of the tariff on the income of the foreign producers. This decrease in income reduces their consumption of their own good such that there is a shift in the world supply curve. Examples are rare; Ghanaian cocoa in the 1960s and New Zealand lamb being the most plausible. This case is shown in Figure 4.3 when the new equilibrium is reached; the diagram is a modified version of Figure 4.2. The WS curve has shifted from WS to WS^N. The consequence is that the domestic price *falls* from DP to NDP and the world price from DP to NWP. Imports rise from M_1 to M_2. Consumers and producers together gain (A+B+C); actually of course consumers gain more than this and producers lose. The tariff revenue is (D+E+F+G+H) so the overall effect is highly favourable to the tariff-improving country.

The effect only arises if:

1. the country is large;
2. the exporting countries consume large enough quantities of the good to generate an income effect on the world supply curve;
3. the income effect is large enough to offset the effect of the tariff.

These conditions will only be met when the elasticity of the world supply curve is sufficiently low and the propensity of the exporters to consume the good is sufficiently high; the formal conditions necessarily involve an elasticity of less than one. The paradox is rare and is more useful in highlighting the 'income effect' which is likely to arise for many raw materials, although not enough to offset the size of a tariff. Such effects have also been generated by the CAP; Third World producers of food and New Zealand being those whose income has suffered.

Figure 4.3: The Metzler Paradox

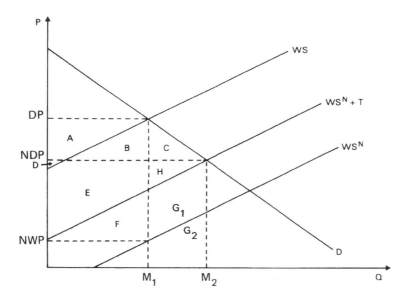

4.3 Tariffs and the Income of Producers

It was argued above that one of the major objectives of protection was to enrich those who produce the protected good. This effect was clearly shown in section 3.5. However, there are circumstances in which the imposition of a tariff actually lowers the income of those producing the good. Two of these have been mentioned *en passant*.

4.3.1 If the ERP Is Negative

This is arguably a theoretically trivial but practically relevant consideration. A tariff, or other protection, is often introduced as part of a whole
schedule of tariffs so an industry may suffer negative protection. UK
beef farmers have argued that the CAP works in this fashion since its
effects in raising the price of cattle food outweigh the apparent protection. This 'danger' was always in the front of the minds of those design-
ing US tariffs especially the McKinley tariff (1890) and Dingley tariff
(1897). They devoted painstaking care to ensure that no producer lost
out as a result of a Tariff Act or at least no producer interest associated
with the Republican Party.

4.3.2 When the Metzler Paradox Applies

Obviously if a tariff lowers the domestic price, the domestic producers
will lose revenue.

Barring these cases, the argument concerns what is usually called the
Stolper-Samuelson Theorem (1941): that protection will raise the real
income of the factor(s) used intensively in producing the protected
good. The theory is usually presented in a two-good, two-factor model
in which the result concerns the effect on real wages of protecting a
labour-intensive industry. It is much more relevant to consider the
theorem in an 'n factor' world in which the intensive factors are those
specific to an industry. Protection of textiles would, when the theorem
held, raise the income of both textile industry shareholders and workers
skilled in crafts specific to the textile industry. However, on simple
assumptions, it would not affect, or would even reduce, the incomes of
either unskilled workers or workers with general skills (e.g. typists)
employed in the industry.

Their employment might rise but the effect on the demand for
general labour would be so small that wages would not rise. In practice,
given labour immobility and the geographical concentration of
industry, protection would probably raise the wages of all workers.

The partial analysis in section 4.1 seemed to show that tariffs would
raise the income of the producer, so it may seem that Stopler-
Samuelson is self-evident. In fact, the 'general equilibrium' factors
which may affect the validity theorem stem from the fact that those
producing the good may lose as consumers. *If the producers do not
consume their own good, the theorem is necessarily valid.*

Moreover *a tariff must raise both the money income and the share
of national income going to the producers.* However as prices are
higher, and national income lower, this does not establish that their

real incomes are higher. In measuring *real* incomes there is, as usual, an index number problem because the tariff changes relative prices. It can be shown that *producer incomes rise when measured at free trade prices* but not necessarily at the new prices. Bhagwati (1959) argues that the result in this case depends upon:

1. whether tariffs are prohibitive (*prohibitive tariffs necessarily raise producer income*);
2. income elasticies of demand (with unitary elasticities, the theorem is more likely to be upheld);
3. whether the elasticity of *foreign* demand for imports (EF) exceeds the domestic propensity to consume exportables (c) — *if EF > c, the theorem is necessarily true*;
4. the nature of production functions;
5. the precise definition of factor intensity;
6. whether factor intensities are reversible.

Altogether Bhagwati produces 14 cases by combining variants of these; in eight the effect of protection on producers' real incomes is indeterminate. Batra (1973) claims to show that an alternative sufficient condition is that the tariff on the output of an industry exceeds that on all its inputs. (This claim is not universally accepted.)

In conclusion it needs only to be said that protection will almost always raise producer real incomes; but the literature is a reminder that the apparently obvious should never be accepted without question.

4.4 Tariffs and Subsidies

The argument cited above that a subsidy always imposes lower welfare losses and so is preferable to a tariff is one example of the general paretian argument for subsidies as a means of achieving goals. In the case of tariffs, the free trader argues that one should ascertain the goal of protection and minimise the cost of achieving it. This will be by a subsidy rather than a tariff; free trade writers often regard a subsidy as non-protectionist although it is a different form of protection, even if theoretically it produces fewer distortions.

If the goal of protection is to raise producers' incomes, a cash transfer can achieve this without a welfare cost. Of course, the income effect of the subsidy may reduce the industry's output, but this does not matter so long as the goal is to raise the producers' overall standard of living. If a belief that hill farmers desire larger incomes is held, then if hill farmers choose to take the benefit as leisure rather than goods a subsidy's objective has still been achieved (at least on paretian criteria). If the objective is to raise the industry's output, e.g. for strategic reasons, a subsidy will avoid the 'consumption effect' but not the 'production effect'. This can be shown in Figure 4.1; instead of a tariff, a subsidy of T per unit would produce a parallel shift in the home supply curve such that output rose from Q_{PF} to Q_{PP}. Consumers are better off by (A+B+C+D) than with a tariff and the producers are in exactly the same position. The government pays a subsidy of (A+B) (i.e. T times Q_{PP}) instead of receiving a tax of C so it is worse off by (A+B+C). Hence a subsidy has a welfare gain of D compared to a tariff. (There is a loss of B, compared to free trade.) This demonstrates that a tariff is inferior to a subsidy as a means of stimulating output. The argument is generalisable to show that a subsidy is the minimum cost method of raising output.

Unfortunately there is a fatal flaw in the argument for subsidies they have to be financed. The naive paretian argument assumes that they are financed by 'lump-sum' tax. A lump-sum tax is a tax that has no substitution effects although it may — probably would have — income effects. However, it is impossible to think of a practicable, let alone equitable, lump-sum tax. Taxes on potential earnings, Tinbergen's IQ tax and other schemes have been proposed but no one believes they are politially feasible and very few that they are practicable or just. To argue that the author of this book could have earned more writing romantic fiction instead and so he will be taxed on what he could have earned avoids any distortion of my choice about what to write. It is impossible to think of any other argument for it or any means of determining the maximum I could earn.

Hence subsidies have to be financed by taxes with distortionary effects or by inflation. In either case one must make a second-best comparison of the distortion caused by a subsidy and its associated tax with that caused by a tariff. The tariff may very well be the better means of increasing output or income transference. The whole debate is really one about political economy and some argue for subsidies because they are more overt and so more likely to arouse opposition and so less likely to be introduced or continued without good reason. Other arguments concern equity — if the EEC wishes to raise the income of Breton farmers, it is unfair and arbitrary to do it at the expense of butter consumers rather than of taxpayers generally.

4.5 Tariffs, Quotas and Competition

The effect of a tariff and a quota are relatively easy to compare using Figure 4.1. So long as the assumptions are valid, i.e. a small economy, markets clearing by price and atomistic markets, there will always be a tariff whose effects are equivalent to any quota.

A quota of $(Q_{CP} - Q_{PP})$ would have exactly the same effect as the tariff (T). If only this quantity of imports were available, price would rise to (WP+T), production rise to Q_{PP} and demand fall to Q_{CP} just as with the tariff. The only difference concerns area C, which is government (tariff) revenue in the tariff case. In the quota case it is a rent which accrues to the quota holder who is allowed to buy at WP and sell at (WP+T). This right may be auctioned by the government in which case it receives the revenue and there is no difference from the tariff case. It may be allocated to the foreign producer(s) who thereby acquire a valuable right. In fact it is possible for the foreign suppliers to do better out of protection than with free trade in this case. The right to sell a small quantity at a high price may very well be more profitable than competition which enables the sale of a large quantity at a low price. The most notorious (and much analysed) example of this is the US sugar quota. (The earliest analysis is Cater (1965), pp. 17-20 and pp. 199-204.) The right is more often parcelled out amongst domestic residents. In the US an almost unbelievable system of oil quotas provided their holders (the oil majors, Shell, BP, Exxon, etc.) with what was close to the proverbial licence to print money from 1953 to 1971. The restrictions on imports maintained the US price of oil well above world levels. A quota holder was permitted to purchase oil in the Middle East at $1.80 and resell at the US price of $3.45 (1971 figures). Both the US examples illustrate cases of the use of quota rents to buy off potential opposition to a protectionist policy. Quotas can finally be allocated to friends of the government — Elizabeth I practised this as well as the state trading monopoly. This is common in much of the Third World today and is often associated with various forms of corruption.

If the small country assumption is relaxed, big differences emerge between quotas and tariffs (Falvey, 1975)). For example, the Metzler paradox cannot occur with a quota. The terms of trade gain with a quota is in general less than with a tariff, although it depends upon how quotas are allocated and upon foreign market structures.

The most dramatic difference between tariffs and quotas occurs when there is a sole domestic producer. The analysis is illustrated in

Figure 4.4: Quotas and Monopoly

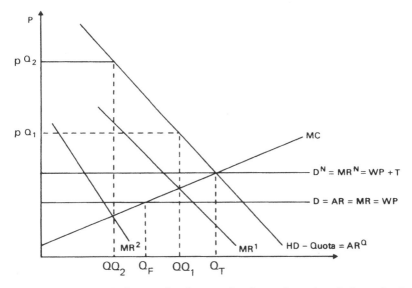

Figure 4.4. With free trade, the supplier is a price taker facing a horizontal marginal (and average) revenue curve at WP. Equilibrium output is, therefore, Q_F. A tariff has the effect of shifting the marginal revenue curve to (WP+T) but the supplier is still a price taker so MR is still equal to AR, the MR, and demand, curve is horizontal. Equilibrium output rises to Q_T (and price to WP+T). A quota, however, converts the latent market power of the sole supplier into actual monopoly power. At each price, the supplier will be able to sell (home demand - quota). This gives him a downward sloping demand curve. This demand curve (and AR curve) will pass through (Q_T, WP+T), i.e. the demand curve created by the quota whose effects would be equivalent to a tariff of T under perfect competition. At price (WP+T) the supplier can sell Q_T when imports are equal to the size of the quota. This is true whether imports are determined by a quota and price determined by the supplier or the price by the tariff and the quantity by the supplier. However, as the supplier is a price setter (monopolist), marginal revenue is no longer equal to average revenue. All that is known is that:

1. the derived demand curve (HD - quota) is more elastic than HD itself; the consequence of a leftward parallel shift of any demand

curve;

2. MR is less than AR.

The relevant marginal revenue curve could be either MR_1 or MR_2 in Figure 4.4.[1] In the MR_1 case output is Q_{Q1} and price P_{Q1}. Price is higher than in the tariff case and output lower but output is higher than in the free trade case. If MR_2 is the relevant marginal revenue curve, output will be Q_{Q2} and price P_{Q2} – i.e. output is less than the free trade case, as well as the tariff case.

In general the following are true:

1. A quota will lead to a price at least as high as with the equivalent tariff. The price will be higher unless the domestic industry is atomistic, and the economy is small.
2. A quota will lead to a domestic output no higher than the 'tariff equivalent' case. The output will be lower unless the domestic industry is atomistic and may even be less than with free trade.
3. A quota is certain to increase the income of producers and is almost certain to lead to a larger increase than for a tariff.

4.6 Tariffs and State Trading Monopolies

A state trading monopoly is capable of exploiting any terms of trade gain that might accrue to a nation; by restricting purchase they can reduce price if faced with an upward sloping supply curve. In fact it can act as a price discriminating monopsonist and so secure even greater gains than a tariff could; with a tariff all foreign suppliers receive the same price (see Gowland (1982(b)) for a discussion of price discriminating monopsony, pp. 183-4). State trading monopolies are usually used as a part of an overall *dirigiste* policy in which the allocation of imports is used as a key tool of planning and control. The monopoly may also seek to avoid a balance of payments problem by insisting on barter by paying for its imports directly with goods. The Nazi regime in Germany were experts at this tactic on occasion; e.g. insisting on discharging their import bill with aspirins (in 1939 they forced armaments on a surprised Yugoslavia). The communist states of Eastern Europe have copied the Nazis. The major exponents of state trading monopolies to improve the terms of trade were the post-war UK Labour government. In 1947, 1948 and 1949, 64, 61 and 58 per cent respectively of imports were state purchases (Ady's figures: Worswick and Ady (1954)). Because the purchases affected world prices, it is impossible, as Ady points out, to estimate the precise gain or compare it with the losses of consumers' surplus caused by lower consumption and less choice. The various special features of a state trading monopoly make it impossible to compare simply with tariffs, but in principle the effect would be exactly the same so long as the monopoly selected the quantity of world imports so as to maximise profits, so long as the atomistic assumption was valid and a uniform price was paid for imports. In many ways a state trading monopoly is similar to a quota, so that differences emerge in a world of uncertainty. A government commits itself to price with a tariff and to quantity with a quota but neither with a state trading monopoly. Hence the analysis presented above could not distinguish the three in the basic case where HS and D are taken as given. The theoretical case for state trading monopolies is impeccable, but both their antecedents and history justify extreme mistrust of their practical implementation. Profit maximisation is unlikely to be the goal of a state trading monopoly and corruption, favouritism or sheer inefficiency are likely to be prevalent even if worse sins are absent.

Note

1. For any demand curve, there can only be one marginal revenue curve of course but the demand curve could be such that either MR_1 or MR_2 is such. For completeness, the diagram should show alternative demand curves but this is not done to avoid rendering the diagram even harder to follow.

5 CUSTOMS UNIONS

5.1 Some Concepts

The best known of customs unions is the European Economic Community, or Common Market, founded by Germany, France, Italy and the Benelux countries in 1957 by the Treaty of Rome. In 1973 the UK, Denmark and Ireland joined, followed by Greece in 1981. Spain and Portugal are due to join by 1984 and Turkey may also join by 1990. Like its predecessor, the German Zollverein of the nineteenth century, the EEC has attempted to grow into something more than a customs union, but with much less success to date. The EEC has been copied without very much success by a variety of bodies in the Third World. However, before analysing customs unions, it is necessary to define them and some other superficially similar groupings of nations.

A *free trade area* is a group of nations who agree to remove all tariffs (and at least some other non-tariff barriers to trade) on trade amongst themselves. The best-known example is the European Free Trade Area, EFTA, founded under British auspices in 1958, which included, besides the UK, the Scandinavian countries and some other countries such as Portugal, Switzerland and Austria unable or unwilling to join the EEC. (Austria, for example, is constrained by treaty from membership of organisations like the EEC.)

If, in addition to forming a free trade area, the nations agree to impose a common external tariff, then a *customs union* has been formed. Its essential characteristic is therefore that its members agree on a common trading policy towards the rest of the world. Whereas, although both members of EFTA, the UK permitted unrestricted import of food but Denmark had a very protectionist policy until 1973, both had to adopt the same policy after they joined the EEC.

There are various types of customs unions but the differences are minor and mainly concern the division of the tariff revenue generated by the customs union. It may be spent centrally, as by the EEC, divided amongst the members according to a formula (the Zollverein) or kept by the country into which imports arrive. The latter is the most obvious but problems arise when imports destined for one member pass through another's territory; many of Gemany's imports enter the EEC through Antwerp. It would not be acceptable to Germany if the import duty on, say, sherry consumed by Germans were to be received by Belgium. Disputes over the allocation of customs revenue were one major factor in the break-up of the East African Customs Union (Tanzania, Kenya and Uganda) established in colonial times by the British.

There are three other types of economic association which usually involve even closer union than a customs union, although the concepts are less clearly defined. They are:

1. a *tax union*, in which the members agree on a common tax system;
2. an *economic union*, in which the members agree on common policies on such matters as regulation and, in some definitions, macroeconomic policy;
3. a *monetary union*, in which there is either a common currency or an unbreakable link between two or more currencies (Belgium and Luxemburg form a monetary union as the UK and Ireland did from 1921 to 1978).

5.2 Trade Diversion and Trade Creation

Customs unions have always induced something close to schizophrenia in economists because they combine elements of free trade, traditionally the *beau ideal* of most economists, and discriminating tariffs, an equally long-lived *bête noire*.

Free traders have always wished to see equal treatment of all imports. This is enshrined in GATT, see p. 3 above. Indeed, so strongly do some free traders feel about this point that the free trade Liberals resigned over this issue from national government in September 1932, after having accepted a general tariff in January. Yet the effect of the UK joining the EEC has been to violate this ideal. To illustrate this point, the UK car market after entry to the EEC will be considered. German cars were then allowed tariff-free entry to the UK and allowed to compete on absolutely equal terms with British cars. In other words, there had been a move towards free trade. On the other hand, until 1973 the same tariff was paid on both German and Japanese cars and in all respects they were treated alike. After entry to the EEC, Japanese cars paid a (common external) tariff of 10 per cent whereas German cars entered duty free. Hence, Japanese imports were being discriminated against, compared with German ones. This is as clear a violation of free trade principles as the free competition of German and British cars is a realisation of them. So what should be the attitude of the free trader, as virtually all economists were in, say, the 1950s?

Economists have tried to answer the question by dividing the effects of a customs union into good and bad with an almost Manichaean zeal. The first to do this was Viner (1950). He did this by inventing the concepts of *trade diversion* and *trade creation*, to capture the bad and good aspects of the effect of a customs union. Viner was only interested in the impact of a customs union on the location of production, so his analysis was based on three simplifying assumptions which will be relaxed in turn in the following three sections:

1. Fixed proportions in consumption, i.e. a fixed ratio of consumption of each good to all others. This means that in partial equilibrium analysis all demand curves are perfectly inelastic.
2. Constant returns to scale.
3. All the countries forming a union are small and the resulting union is small, i.e. the terms of trade cannot be influenced by the members either prior to or after the formation of the union.

Viner's analysis incorporating these assumptions is presented in Figure 5.1. The diagram is a modification of the 'tariff triangle' introduced on p. 42 above. Prior to the union, the world price of the good is WP. A tariff T is imposed so the domestic price is (WP+T). At this price Qc is consumed. Domestic production is Qp1. Imports are Qc − Qp1, so tariff revenue is (A+B).

A customs union is then formed with another country (or countries) which can produce the good at a price PP, higher than the world price but lower than the world price plus the new common tariff (CT). (For simplicity it is assumed that the new tariff is T, otherwise a new line WP+CT can be added to Figure 5.1.) If the partner's price (PP) were to exceed WP+CT or were equal to WP, the discrimination would have no effect so the case illustrated is the only interesting one. To take a plausible example, if a German portable colour television were £105 (excluding retailer's profit and tax) and a Japanese one £100, and the tariff were 10 per cent, the illustrated case would arise. Without the discrimination, imports would be from Japan; with it, from Germany.

After the union, consumption is still Qc but domestic output falls to Qp2 and imports are now Qc−Qp2 but all come from the partner instead of the rest of the world. The effects of the change, by the usual method of analysis, are:

Figure 5.1: Viner's Analysis

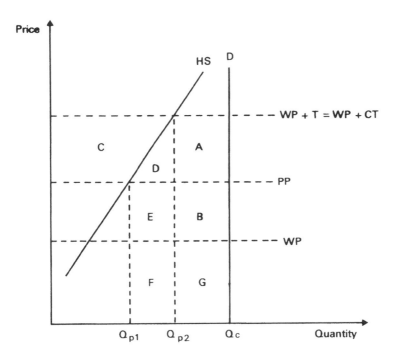

Trade created = $Q_{p2} - Q_{p1}$
Trade diverted = $Q_c - Q_{p2}$

1. the government loses the tariff revenue (A+B);
2. the producers lose profits of (C), their revenue falls by (C+D+E+F), their costs by (D+E+F);
3. consumers gain (A+D+C).

The social gain is therefore (D - B).

Viner then introduced his concepts of trade creation and diversion. He argued that trade of Qp2 - Qp1 had been *created*; imports had replaced higher-cost domestic production. Qc - Qp1, on the other hand, represented the quantity of imports for which demand had been *diverted* from a low-cost to a higher-cost producer. The gross gain D was the gain from trade creation, the gross loss B was similarly attributable to trade diversion. These welfare effects represent the differences in the costs of production so long as WP and PP are marginal (or average) costs. (Qp1-Qp2) costs the partner (E+F) to produce compared to (D+E+F) for domestic producers, hence D is the gain from trade creation. Similarly B represents the difference between the partner's cost of producing Qc - Qp1 (B+G) and the world cost of production (G). If PP and WP are marginal costs curves (or, as for a horizontal marginal cost curve, MC= AC, average cost curves), B and D represent losses to the world. If they are not, merely to the society which joined the union; in this case more information is needed to calculate the effects on the partner country and the rest of the world.

5.3 Consumption Effects

The first of Viner's three assumptions to be relaxed was (a), the fixed proportions in consumption assumption. This was originally relaxed by Gehrels (1956) who argued that the consequent consumption effect was bound to be positive. Gehrels used a general equilibrium framework to produce this result but it is more easily studied in a partial equilibrium framework, Figure 5.2. This is just the Vinerian diagram except that the demand curve is no longer vertical. Now demand rises from Qc1 to Qc2. In consequence there is a further increase, H, in consumers' surplus; this 'consumption effect' is a further benefit of the union.

Lipsey, however (1957)(a)(b), 1960, 1970), showed that this consumption effect could go either way. Moreover, in some cases a consumption effect might produce welfare benefits in the absence of Vinerian trade creation — trade diversion need not be all bad! Lipsey's general equilibrium argument is somewhat complex, but the basic notion, that the substitution of French wine for New Zealand lamb can have a good or a bad effect on the consumer's welfare, is intuitively appealing. The reason why the consumption effect can be negative does, in fact, depend upon what is happening to the quantities of other goods consumed (and the consequent change in consumer's surpluses).

Lipsey analysis is best seen in the proof of the apparent paradox that a trade diverting customs union can be beneficial: to quote Lipsey (1957b, p. 63, in Robson (1972)):

Country A might gain by entering a customs union whose sole production effect was to divert her import trade from lower to higher

Figure 5.2: Consumption Effects

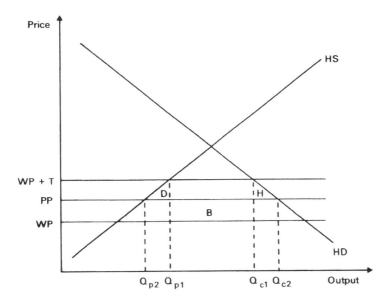

cost sources of supply.

The above conclusion may not have an immediate common sense appeal. Yet the explanation is easily seen with the help of a diagram.

The key feature of this diagram is shown in Figure 5.3. This uses a consumption possibility frontier between home produced goods and the imported good. Originally, this consumption possibility frontier is AB. Because of the tariff, consumers were not at their optimum (D); instead they are forced to the sub-optimum point 1 — see p. 34 above. The customs union changes the consumption possibility frontier to AC, reflecting the higher cost of imports, but consumers are no longer constrained to a sub-optimum, instead 2 is attainable. As drawn, 2 is clearly preferable to 1 — being on a higher indifference curve. If, however, the original consumption point had been 3, the consumers would be worse off, even though the consumption of the imported good has risen (from Q_3 to Q_2), so 'H' on Figure 5.2 exists, but it has been outweighed by the loss of surplus on the reduced consumption of other goods.

Figure 5.3: Lipsey's Analysis

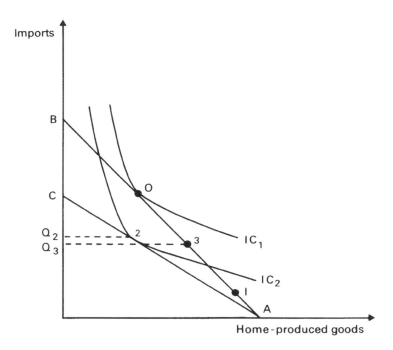

5.4 Increasing Returns to Scale and X-efficiency

That there were substantial gains from the economies of scale produced by a customs union was frequently used as an argument for British membership of the EEC prior to 1973. It was frequently linked with arguments about X-efficiency; the proposition being that the UK economy needed a good shake-up to reduce 'X-inefficiency'; the 'cold shower' or 'cold douche' argument of Harold Macmillan. Krauss (1972) cynically, but fairly, views these arguments as economic rationalisations for politically motivated decisions (p. 420) and points out the polemical value of an argument which

has become very popular both because of the large numbers it produces and because its nebulous and long-run character makes it particularly difficult to refute. (p. 432)

Krauss also points out that the evidence cited rested upon 'no theoretical rationale' in the one case and upon the weird assumption that the supply curve is the *average* cost curve, instead of the orthodox *marginal* cost curve, in the other. This preamble is necessary to explain why so much attention has been paid to what might otherwise seem to be trivial and rather pointless fields of research.

The basic proposition of the 'economies of scale' advocates that it may be better to concentrate production in an inefficient area than to produce partly in a high-cost and partly in a low-cost area (Melvin, 1969; Bhagwati, 1971). Otherwise, the economies of scale would be achieved in any case, so it is only in these circumstances that economies of scale provide an argument for a customs union.

Given that the partner country will produce a given quantity of the good anyway, it may be cheaper to produce it all there, even though at all levels of production the partner is less efficient than an alternative

Figure 5.4: Increasing Returns

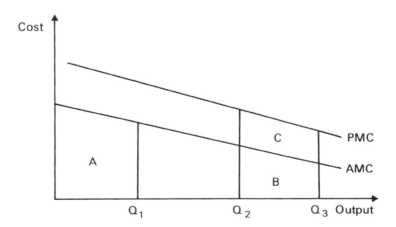

producer. Figure 5.4 reproduces this case. Partner's marginal cost curve PMC is at all levels higher than the alternative producer's (AMC). Partner will produce $Q2$ whatever else happens. The country joining the union wishes to import $Q1$. Is it better to import it from the alternative (or produce it oneself if the domestic production is the alternative) with a resource cost of A or to import it from the partner? The cost of production in the partner country is (B+C), where Q3 – Q2 = Q1. (B+C) is less than A so it is desirable to produce in a high-cost area. To use Williamson's terminology, there is a 'cost reduction' effect from concentration of production which may outweigh the 'trade suppression' effect of switching production from a low- to a high-cost area.

5.5 The Terms of Trade

Viner assumed for simplicity that both the customs union as a whole and all its members individually were small, i.e. they were unable to influence world prices. This assumption was relaxed by Viner himself later in his pioneer study (1950) and he has been followed by a host of others (see Krauss (1972)). The EEC has without doubt had a large effect on the world price of many goods, especially agricultural ones. For example, part of the CAP, see p. 68 below, has involved increased production of (beet) sugar. This, and other import restrictions, has greatly reduced world sugar prices. In consequence, the remaining imports of sugar by the EEC are much cheaper. Such effects are potentially very large, although as with all protective policies which aim to improve the terms of trade, the gains are often not realised. The beneficiaries of protection usually seek, successfully, to restrict the inflow of imports below the level which could maximise the terms of trade 'welfare' gains for their country as a whole. In fact, *pace* Pearce (1970), tariffs are rarely designed to redistribute income internationally but rather within a country. Terms of trade effects are usually a byproduct of tariffs. In any case the analysis of them is straightforward; there is no difference between the analytical tools used in the customs union case and those used in Chapters 3 and 4 above.

The problem which does arise is in deciding whether the effects are in some sense desirable. This quickly enmeshes the analyst in that notorious quagmire of compensation tests and other problems of paretian welfare economics. The concepts of welfare economics can be used in the context of the EEC, see for example Gowland in Dosser, Gowland and Hartley (1982). Nevertheless, it is probably wiser 'merely' to compute the effects of the EEC sugar policy on French farmers, UK consumers, British refiners and Australian and Jamaican producers, not to mention scores of other groups. To try to weigh these gains and losses to arrive at an overall welfare analysis is futile. Of course most people, including economists, would come to a conclusion (probably hostile to the CAP) on the basis of their value judgements but it is merely specious scientism to try to present this conclusion as a piece of economic analysis.

5.6 Some Conclusions

The orthodox theory of customs unions has been subject to a number of savage criticisms. However, none of them destroy the validity of the theory but merely stress that care must be taken in using the theory and in specifying the purposes for which it is to be used. The orthodox theory remains a useful tool; perhaps more useful than the 'new theory' discussed in 5.7 below.

The first criticism is that too much attention has been paid to the question whether 'trade diversion' could ever be a good thing. This debate often becomes a question of semantics, especially as outside the original Viner model it is often not clear to which category some changes should be assigned. However, the fact that many of the arguments have been produced within this framework does not mean that they are not useful in their own right, for example as presented above or by Krauss (1972).

The next criticism is that the 'general theory of the second best' renders any search for general conclusions vain. This nihilistic view is well founded as far as it goes. Much customs union theory is essentially piecemeal welfare economics of the sort that Lipsey and Lancaster (1956) sought to attack. It is consequently subject to the problem that an apparent welfare gain may not be a real one. (Similarly if there are 327 conditions for a welfare optimum, the achievement of 323 may not be an improvement on 322 or even none.) The indictment, however, implicitly assumes that the objective of the literature was, or should have been, to provide general conclusions about customs unions. Instead, as Lipsey made clear, and after all he was the co-discoverer of the second best, the literature was an attempt to find concepts useful in analysing what is probably the classic 'second-best' problem (1957b, p. 63 in Robson (1972)). Moreover, the literature has provided a framework for empirical analysis (see for example Krauss's survey).

The third proposition has been that the macroeconomic effects of customs unions are much more important than the resource allocation (microeconomic) effects discussed above. To take the simplest example, the increased imports whose welfare effects were applauded above may cause a balance of payments deficit which has to be cured at a much greater cost than the benefits of higher imports. This is again valid but could be applied to all microeconomic analysis. (Similarly, why bother with examining the cost effectiveness of any government expenditure? Just consider its effect on inflation and unemployment.) It is necessary to analyse the macroeconomic effects of a customs union as Godley *et al.* (1980, 1981) and El-Agraa and Jones (1981) have done. This analysis is fairly straightforward. However, the problem of deciding what would have happened otherwise is virtually insurmountable. If it is accepted that the British balance of payments would have been stronger in 1976 if the UK were not a member of the EEC, how, if at all, would Mr Healey have changed his view on the need for public expenditure cuts?

The final criticism is that customs unions, especially the EEC, have been created for political not economic reasons. This is incontravertible. Cooper and Massell have argued that there could never be an economic case for any customs union. As this is closely linked to their 'new theory' of customs unions, this view is discussed below. However, even if it were valid, it does not demonstrate the futility of orthodox theory. If a politically motivated act has economic consequences, it is necessary to examine them. This, at a minimum, will make it possible to calculate the economic cost of the policy. This may be the end of the analysis, or one may seek to try to calculate the political benefit and compare the two. To reduce the argument to a specific example, one should seek to calculate the economic consequences of membership of the EEC for the UK, even if they are adverse, and even if it were the case that no adverse economic costs would lead the UK to leave the Common Market. Even if this decision were correct, the calculation would be nevertheless important.

Hence, while all the criticisms of the orthodox theory are right in that they raise points of importance, they are wrong in that the orthodox theory is both valid and useful.

5.7 The New Theory of Customs Unions

Cooper and Massell (1965a, 1965b) sought to produce a new theory of customs unions for two reasons. One was the perceived defects of the orthodox theory (see 5.6 above) and the need to bring a political dimension into the analysis. The other was a belief that the orthodox theory was too much centred on the EEC, whereas, it then seemed, a large number of customs unions and/or free trade areas would develop in the Third World, e.g. LAFTA (Latin American Free Trade Area) and the East African Union mentioned above. With the exception of a small grouping of the statelets of Central America, none of these unions has proved successful or long-lasting; all are either defunct or moribund. However, the new theory reveals as much about the failure of these schemes as it does about their foundation.

Cooper and Massell argued that there could never be a purely economic case for a customs union. They showed that all of the benefits of a union could be achieved by a unilateral non-discriminatory tariff reduction. They then divided the effect of a union into the tariff reduction effect and a 'pure trade diversion' effect. This had achieved Viner's goal of dividing the effects of a customs union into a free trade and a protective effect (see the discussion in Krauss (1972), p. 417). However, the analysis did not show, as Cooper and Massell implied, that economic goals were not the objective, or a justification for, a customs union. It did show that a customs union could not be a first-best policy but it could still be a second-best policy. To take a specific example, in the France of the 1950s, no unilateral tariff cut was possible because no government that proposed it would have survived for more than a few days. Membership of the EEC was a feasible policy option, however. Hence a comparison of these two policies does not show that there was no economic case for French membership of the EEC. It could have been the best *possible* economic policy. Moreover, other gains as part of the EEC bargain could have outweighed the cost of 'pure trade diversion' (given the benefits to French farmers at the expense of German and Italian consumers, they probably did).

The constructive part of Cooper and Massell's analysis, the new theory itself, offers insights into Third World unions however. The key proposition is that 'two can do what one cannot', the objective being industrialisation. The underlying presumption is that Third World countries seek industrialisation as the goal of their development policy to avoid dependence on the West. However, economic independence is too expensive for any one country to achieve but a neighbouring group of countries could achieve independence. It might be that, of a group of five, A produces chemicals for all five; B steel; C cars (using B's steel) and so on. This desire for independence as a group undoubtedly inspired the abortive customs union. Equally, however, most Third World countries would rather be dependent on a far distant West, or East, than a neighbour. In the mid-1960s Kenya preferred links with the USA and the UK to ties with Tanzania and Tanzania preferred ties with China to a close relationship with Kenya. Similar examples abound. Hence it is not surprising that few such unions were long-lasting.

5.8 The Common Agricultural Policy

The EEC's common agricultural policy, CAP, is both the major achievement of the Common Maket and in most eyes its greatest shame. The CAP dominates the EEC's budget, being responsible for over 70 per cent of EEC spending, and in no other sphere of activity has the goal of a common policy achieved by common means been so successful. On the other hand, the CAP is certainly economically inefficient, arch-protectionist and does much both to impoverish the Third World and to embitter relationships between the EEC and the USA; not the best of achievements to be credited to the European ideal. The origins of the CAP are complex and go back to Pflimmin's green plan of 1949. Its most important features are a combination of high protection, usually in the form of quotas, and a guaranteed price for domestic producers; there are in fact 31 different variants of the CAP for different categories of product. An unfortunate side effect of this policy has been the reduction in efforts to modernise agriculture by most of the members – see Williams (1971) for a discussion of the changed attitude of the French government to milk producers in 1959-62, pp. 111-13. However, economic analysis of the CAP has to assume that the structure of the industry would be the same with and without the CAP.

Analysis of the CAP by Marshallian welfare area analysis is relatively straightforward and can best be illustrated by dividing the problem into two, *viz*. the effect of the quotas on the UK and the effect of the guaranteed price on the EEC as a whole. The results are presented here for a composite good, i.e. food, for which empirical data and results are taken from a variety of sources, mainly Godley (1980, 1981) and the EEC publications cited in Dosser, Gowland and Hartley (1982), Chapter 9. In the case of the UK a three-way comparison is appropriate (Figure 5.5) to compare the CAP with both free trade and with the pre-1971 'deficiency payments' system (between 1971 and 1973 an interim scheme was in force in preparation for UK entry into the EEC). The pre-1971 system was a subsidy whereby farmers were paid a guaranteed price less the average price received by all farmers (so as to maintain incentives). Thus, three prices are relevant: the world price, the UK guaranteed price, about 25 per cent higher than the world price, and the CAP price, about 90 per cent higher than the world price. A com-

Figure 5.5: CAP: Impact on the UK

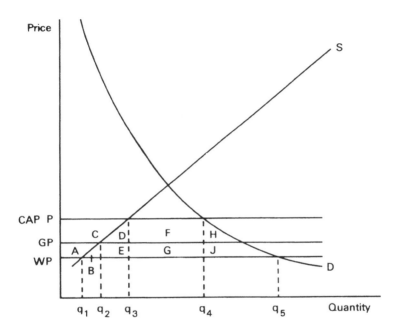

parison of free trade and the UK system is simple as domestic consumption is q_5 in both cases but domestic output rises from q_1 to q_2. Farmers gain A (revenue rises by $A + B + K$, but costs rise by K). The government pays out $(A + B)$ as a subsidy to the farmers; $(A + B)$ was in practice variable but averaged about £300 million in the late 1960s. Hence the consequences of the UK system were to impose a social cost of 'B' (the production effect); to benefit farmers at the expense of taxpayers and to reduce imports by $(q_2 - q_1)$. The effect of the CAP was to raise price to CAP P so domestic consumption fell to q_4 and domestic output rose to q_3. There is no tariff revenue as the protection is by quota so the only relevant effects are on producers and consumers. Compared to either free trade or the old UK system, consumers lose $(A + B + C + D + E + F + G + H + J)$, about £3000 million in 1980. Producers gain C compared to the UK system (£1000 million) and $(A + C)$ compared to free trade. The government gains under the CAP (compared to the subsidy system) by not having to pay out the subsidy, i.e. $(A + B)$. Adding all the relevant areas up, the social cost of the CAP is $(D + E + F$

+ G + H + J) compared to the pre-1971 system. This area was equivalent to about £1500 million in 1980. The cost of the CAP is even higher in comparison to free trade, by 'B'.

Figure 5.6: CAP: EEC as a Whole

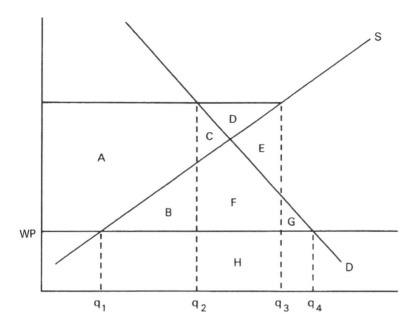

However, the total cost of the CAP is still higher because the payment to the EEC to finance the guaranteed price system has to be added. This is about £1000 million, so the total cost to the UK of the CAP is about £2500 million, about half of which is paid in foreign exchange. The derivation of this payment is shown in Figure 5.6, the food market for the EEC as a whole. D is the demand curve by EEC citizens for food, less the quota permitted by the CAP (if any). A further consequence of the CAP is that consumers pay more for this but this effect is not illustrated. The rest of the analysis is standard, except that output at the CAP price exceeds EEC demand. The EEC is committed to purchasing this excess supply at the price CAP P. EEC demand is q_2 compared to q_4 under free trade so consumers lose (A + B + C + F + G). Farmers sell q_2 to consumers but their remaining output $(q_3 - q_2)$ is bought by the EEC, through the appropriate agency.

Farmers, therefore, gain $(A + C + D)$. The EEC has purchased $(q_3 - q_2)$ of food for which it has paid $(C + D + E + F + H)$. It has to store it — the famous butter mountain, wine lake, etc. It may dispose of it in various ways. The most commonly used has been to sell the surplus at less than WP to the USSR but the range of methods of disposal is truly ingenious. The simplest method for analytical purposes is to assume that it is sold at the world price — the best from the CAP point of view and in some metaphysical sense its value. In this case the loss to EEC governments would be $(C + D + E + F)$, of which the UK share is the £1000 million referred to above. The total welfare cost of the CAP is $(B + C + E + G + 2F)$; the double appearance of F is anomalous but reflects the double cost involved in buying from a higher-cost producer and then being prevented from consuming the good.

The CAP is a rather mundane topic upon which to conclude analysis of customs unions. In fact, it is appropriate in that the message of the theory of customs unions is that there are no general rules, that all results have to be painstakingly derived. This complements the history of the EEC which reveals that hard bargaining by nation states with (enlightened) self-interest is not the destruction of the European ideal but the only means by which the ideal can be salvaged — if indeed it can be.

6 THE TRADITIONAL BALANCE OF PAYMENTS THEORY

6.1 Balance of Payments Theory: An Introduction

In the next three chapters various alternative methods of analysing the balance of payments are presented. The different theories seek to explain different aspects of the balance of payments, so they are to a considerable extent complementary rather than competitive. The elasticities, or traditional, approach seeks to explain the balance of trade; the Keynesian theories (Chapter 6) the current balance; the monetary theory (Chapter 7) the overall balance (the meaning of the balance of payments and of these concepts is explained in sections 6.2 and 6.3). The theories are complementary in another sense. The traditional theory is a microeconomic theory of adjustment in the goods market; the Keynesian theory a macroeconoimic theory in the goods market and the monetary theory a theory of disequilibrium in the money market. Balance of payments analysis needs to comprise all these elements but it is often more convenient to have three separate tools of analysis rather than a general model incorporating all three. Of course, 'after we have reached a provisional conclusion by isolating the complicating factors one by one we then have to go back on ourselves and allow, as well as we can, for the probable interaction of the factors among themselves. This is the nature of economic thinking.' As this comment of Keynes, which was endorsed by Friedman, suggests, this is the standard approach in economic analysis to a potentially complex problem (Keynes (1936), p. 297, cited by Friedman in Gordon (1974), p. 150).

6.2: Some Concepts

The balance of payments is strictly an accounting term used to describe a record of all of the transactions between one country and the rest of the world. As in all accounting records, transactions are recorded in two ways so that (unless mistakes are made) the total calculated from each method must be the same, i.e. the account must balance. Alternatively, the total derived by one method can be subtracted from that derived by the other. The result of this subtraction must be zero. As a consequence of such accounting conventions, *any* balance of payments must balance. A balance of payments problem is, accordingly, a problem about *how* the balance of payments balances. In principle a balance of payments could be constructed for an individual, a company or an area just as easily as for a country. It is a crucial feature of any balance of payments that it is a record of cash inflows and outflows. Companies frequently produce such statements which are a key tool of modern management. Instead of being called a balance of payments they are called either a cash flow account or a sources and uses of funds statement.

To illustrate the nature of a balance of payments, Table 6.1 shows the sources and uses of funds of an imaginary student. Version A simply lists his sources of funds and how he has used them. However, we might decide to group transactions which seem similar. Thus his sources of funds might be grouped into income and borrowing; his expenditure into that which involves the acquisition of an asset and the rest, i.e. current expenditure. One can also regard the use of funds as a negative source and so arrive at version B. This grouping is arbitrary. For example, one might have classed the purchase of books as a purchase of assets, with the car, rather than current expenditure with the alcohol, rent, etc. The choice of headings is also arbitrary, for example one might alternatively have divided sources into public sector, family and corporate sector. This arbitrariness is common to all balance of payments accounts.

One might then group some sources and some uses of funds having something in common. For example, the borrowing and car purchase might be regarded as having something in common with each other, as both are capital transactions while income and the current expenditure can be grouped as current transactions. This grouping is again arbitrary or rather should be a consequence of the purpose for which the account is to be used. No grouping is 'right' or 'wrong'. It is merely more or less useful. The balance of payments statistics used in the UK reflect the CSO's views of what is the most useful method of presentation; this view has changed several times in the last 30 years.

The final presentation has two features of considerable importance.

1. Whilst the total of the account must be zero, it is possible, indeed likely, that each section will show either a net contribution to the student's funds or a net drain on them. These are called either surpluses or deficits respectively.

Hence the student has a current transactions balance of payments

Table 6.1: A Student's Balance of Payments

A		Sources of funds			Uses of funds
S1	Grant	£1500	U1	Rent	£1000
S2	Income from		U2	Food	£ 990
	vacation jobs	£1000	U3	Books	£ 10
S3	Borrowing	£1000	U4	Alcohol	£ 500
	from bank		U5	Other recurrent	£1000
S4	Borrowing	£ 500		expenditure	
	from parents		U6	Purchase of car	£1000
		£4000			£4000
B			**Net source (use −)**		
B1	Income		£2500 (i.e. S1 + S2)		
B2	Borrowing		£1500 (i.e. S3 + S4)		
B3	Current expenditure		− £3000 (i.e. U1 + U2 + U3 + U4 + U5)		
B4	Purchase of asset (car)		− £1000 (i.e. U6)		
			000		
C	Current transactions (B1 + B3)		− £ 500		
	Capital transactions (B2 + B4)		+ £ 500		
			000		

deficit of £500, because his current expenditure exceeds his income.

2. Any balance of payments deficit means that some category of transaction has made a net contribution to the individual's funds. *An increase in one's holdings of assets is a balance of payments deficit* because it involves the use of funds. Borrowing is a surplus because it entails the acquisition of funds.

Both features are true of all balance of payments accounts. They must *balance* in the sense that the final total must be zero. However, they can be divided into components, such as current and capital, which must sum to zero. These are almost certain to show either a surplus or a deficit. These surpluses or deficits may be viewed as policy problems. In practice, current transactions deficits are often so regarded. Indeed in the UK from 1945 to 1972 they were viewed as the major problem of economic policy. Nevertheless, it is worth stressing that it is only components of the balance of payments which can show deficits or surpluses; the overall account must balance. Thus a balance of payments problem is really a problem of the composition of the balance of payments.

6.3 The UK Balance of Payments

Exports and imports are the two best-known transactions with the overseas sector and comprise those sales to foreign residents (exports) and purchases from them (imports), which are included in the national income accounts. However, the usual method of presenting the UK balance of payments both subdivides these categories and includes several others.

The UK balance of payments is divided in two main sections: the current account, which showed a surplus of £3206 million in 1980, and the capital account which showed a deficit of £2790 million (an item grouping errors and omissions, called the balancing item, ensures that the account balanced). The current account in turn is subdivided into:

Table 6.2: The UK Current Account, 1980

Visible trade			
		(£m)	
Exports		47,389	
Imports		− 46,211	
Visible balance		+ 1,178	
Services			
	Credit	Debit	Balance
General government	397	−1,188	−791
Sea transport	3,816	−3,681	+135
Travel	2,965	−2,757	+208
Finance	n/a	n/a	+1,595
Other	4,826	2,180	+646
	15,809	11,621	+3,285
Interest, Profit and Dividends			
	Receipts	Payments	Balance
General government	943	1,598	+655
Private sector (including public corporations)	7,261	6,644	−617
Transfers			
General government	958	2,790	−1,832
Private	793	1,083	−290
Invisible: Consolidated			
Credits		25,764	
Debits		23,736	
Invisible balance		+2,028	
Current Balance		+3,206	

6.3.1 Visible Trade

This item represents trade in goods, of which £47,389 million were exported and £46,211 million imported in 1980. This was only the eighth year since the end of the Napoleonic wars when exports of goods exceeded imports, although similar surpluses were earned in 1981 and 1982 for which complete figures are not available.

6.3.2 Invisible Trade

'Invisibles' comprise three items; trade in services, interest profit and dividends and transfers.

6.3.3 Services

Of these travel is the best known and shipping and finance are the largest. A Briton taking a holiday abroad is importing in just the same way as if he/she purchases foreign goods and consumes them in the UK. A British insurance company selling a policy to an American is exporting in just the same way as a seller of aircraft. Altogether in 1980 services showed a surplus of £3285 million, most of it earned by the City.

6.3.4 Interest, Profit and Dividends

This item, which showed a small deficit in 1980, reflects income received from foreign loans and investments and income paid to foreign investors in the UK, whether holders of UK securities or real assets (such as Ford). Normally the private sector earns a large surplus but the public sector makes large payments, so the net figure is small.

6.3.5 Transfers

This item includes all those current transactions which are, in effect, gifts, since the person paying the money receives nothing in exchange (at least directly). This item showed a deficit of £2122 million in 1980. Part of this represented private transfers – gifts to relatives abroad, charitable donations and so on. However, the bulk represented government transfers of which contributions to the EEC were the largest, over £1500 million, net of refunds.

The capital account includes real investment, or *direct* investment, in land, factories, etc. and *portfolio* investment in securities, shares, bonds, etc. Most of this investment is long term but there are also very large quantities of short-term capital transactions. Some, both official and private, are loans designed to finance the purchase of current goods and services, but large quantities of short-term deposits are made both in and by the UK only in response to the attractiveness of the deposit. This means that there are often very large movements of capital when interest rates change or when there are fears that a currency's value will fall (see p. 133 below). The capital account also includes official financing transactions such as changes in the reserves. The government holds a large stock of foreign currency which is used for various purposes, such as to influence the exchange rate (see p. 160 below). This stock is called the reserves and an addition to it − a purchase of foreign currency by the government − is a deficit, because it represents a use of funds. The official transactions are usually presented as the item needed to meet the 'balance for official settlement' or 'total currency flow'.

The current account, plus all capital transactions other than the official financing ones, is often called the *overall* balance. If the short-term capital investments described above are excluded, it is called the basic *balance*. Of course items in different sections of the balance of payments may be related. If an aeroplane is purchased from an American firm it will usually arrange a subsidised loan as part of the deal. The aircraft would appear in the current account, the loan in the capital account.

6.4 The Elasticities Model

The traditional approach to the analysis of the balance of payments is embodied in the elasticities model. This model seeks to explain the balance of trade, i.e. exports and imports, by a microeconomic approach which focuses on the choice between domestic and foreign goods. The quantity of UK imports is determined by UK residents choosing to buy foreign, rather than British, goods and services and exports by foreign residents making the opposite choice. As in all elementary (partial analytic) microeconomies, it is assumed that price is the main determinant of this choice. Thus the relative price of British and foreign goods and services will determine the quantities of each purchased; of course, this is only true when a number of other factors are held constant; when these are not constant, the defects of the theory discussed in section 6.5 arise.

Hence the theory is based on the premise that exports and imports are determined by relative prices. The relative price of British and, say, American goods is determined both by their absolute prices and by the exchange rate. To take a specific example: a china beaker costs £1 in York. Its American equivalent costs $3 in New York. The relative price of the two depends on the exchange rate. If the rate were $1.50 = £1, the American beaker would cost £2 and be more expensive. Hence, Americans would import beakers from York. On the other hand, if the exchange rate were $3, then both would cost £1 and no trade would take place. If the rate were any higher, it would pay Britons to import beakers from New York, for example if the rate were $6 the sterling price of the American beaker would be 50p. Thus the elasticities model argues that the quantity of exports and imports will depend upon domestic prices, foreign prices and the exchange rate.

Before continuing with the theory, it is worth noting that there are two alternative links between these three besides the elasticities model. One is the *purchasing power parity* theory. This argues that it is the exchange rate which adjusts, so that prices will be the same in both countries. Hence, in my example, the exchange rate will be $3 so that the £1 and the $3 it buys will both purchase the same quantity of goods, for example one beaker. A second, more modern argument is that the world price and the exchange rate determine domestic prices. In the above example, if the exchange rate were $2, then the sterling price of an American beaker would be $1.50. In this case, no UK producer has any reason to sell at any price less than £1.50, nor can he sell at any price above £1.50, so his price will be £1.50. This is an extension of the 'small country' assumption used, for example, in the tariff analysis above.

Relative prices can change either as a result of a change in the exchange rate or of a change in absolute prices, both domestic and foreign. These are often combined into an index of competitiveness. UK competitiveness will improve, in practice, if UK prices rise by less than foreign ones or if the exchange rate falls. When the exchange rate changes so that the pound buys less dollars this is called a depreciation. In some circumstances this change can be brought about by official action and is called devaluation (see p. 41 below). According to the theory, an improvement in competitiveness must lead to a rise in the *volume* of exports or a fall in the *volume* of imports (or both), i.e. demand curves slope downwards. However, one is interested in the *value* of exports, as well as the *volume*. For example, if five beakers were sold at 50p each instead of three at £1 each, then one would probably think that this was a *fall* in exports from £3 to £2.50, i.e. in value, not a rise from three to five beakers, i.e. in volume. To calculate the change in value, one needs to know the price elasticities of exports and imports; hence the name of the theory. Export revenue will rise (in pounds) if the elasticity exceeds unity, and so on as in elementary price theory.

The essence of the theory is embodied in the famous Marshall-Lerner condition:

> an improvement in competitiveness will improve the balance of payments if and only if the sum of the price elasticities of demand for imports by residents and of exports by non-residents exceeds unity (ignoring the negative signs of the elasticities).

Improvement in the balance of payments is taken to mean a smaller (current account) deficit or a larger surplus. Usually an improvement in competitiveness is achieved by a variation in the exchange rate so the condition is often stated using depreciation or devaluation instead of change in competitiveness. The crucial feature of the condition is that it is the *sum* of the elasticities which must exceed one, not each elasticity separately. Hence it is possible for both exports and imports to be price inelastic but for the condition to be satisfied, e.g. if both elasticities are equal to (–) 0.7.

It is necessary to explain in some detail why this is so. The simplest way to do this emphasises that the balance of payments can be measured in either foreign currency or domestic currency, hereafter dollars and pounds. An improvement in UK competitiveness, in this case a depreciation of sterling, will mean that the dollar price of exports falls and the sterling price of imports rises, whereas the sterling price of exports is unchanged and so is the foreign currency price of imports. This is because the change in the exchange rate has not affected the price measured in the relevant domestic currency but it has affected the price in the other currency.

If the balance of payments is measured in *sterling*, the following is true. The sterling price of exports is unchanged (even though foreigners pay less in their own currency) so the value of exports cannot fall; in fact it is almost certain to rise as volume will rise unless the elasticity is equal to zero. This assumption, however, will be made. If the export elasticity is zero, the value of exports will be unchanged. In this case, the change in the value of imports will determine what happens to the balance of payments. As the sterling price of imports has risen, the sterling value of imports will fall so long as their elasticity of demand exceeds one. In other words, *a depreciation*, or rather improvement in competitiveness, *will lead to an improvement in the balance of payments so long as the import elasticity exceeds one, even if the export elasticity is zero*.

If the balance of payments is measured in foreign currency, the converse argument is true. The price of imports in dollars is unchanged so their value cannot rise. (In fact, as the sterling price is higher, it is almost certain to fall.) If the import elasticity is zero, the value will be unchanged. In this case, the effect of the depreciation on the balance of payments will depend upon the effect of the lower foreign currency price of exports. It is obvious that there will be an increase in the value of exports so long as the export elasticity exceeds unity. Thus, *even if the import elasticity is zero, a depreciation will improve the balance of payments if and only if the export elasticity is greater than one.*

It is necessary to make a drastic simplifying assumption to derive the Marshall-Lerner condition from the two italicised propositions above. This is that the balance of payments is initially in balance. In this case an improvement in the balance of payments in either sterling or dollars implies an improvement in the other. Therefore, *either* an export *or* an import elasticity greater than unity is a sufficient condition for a depreciation to improve the balance of payments, even if the other is equal to zero. Moreover, if the balance of payments is in balance, i.e. exports are equal to imports, then an import elasticity of (-) ½ will have exactly the same impact on the balance of payments as an export elasticity of (-) ½ (as the one will reduce imports by as much as the other will increase exports). Hence if both elasticities are equal to (-) ½, the effect will be the same as if either is equal to one and the other to zero. The same is true of any other pair of elasticities which add up to one. Hence, so long as the sum of elasticities exceeds unity, then an improvement in competitiveness will improve the balance of payments, i.e. the Marshall-Lerner condition. However, to show this a number of simplifying assumptions have been explicitly and implicitly made. The deficiencies and limitations of Marshall-Lerner are considered in the next section and all stem from these. However, the basic theory is simple: *relative prices (competitiveness) determines the balance of payments, with an improvement in competitiveness leading to an improvement in the balance of payments so long as the Marshall-Lerner condition is satisfied.*

6.5 The Deficiencies of the Marshall-Lerner Condition

6.5.1 Balanced Payments Assumption

The first of the limitations of the Marshall-Lerner condition stems from the assumption that the (current account of the) balance of payments is in balance initially. Otherwise the condition is neither sufficient nor necessary for an improvement in competitiveness. This seems a very restrictive assumption as the balance of payments is very rarely in balance and, almost by definition, never so when there is a balance of payments problem. However, this is less restrictive than it seems, as in this case the Marshall-Lerner condition is replaced by the alternative sufficient condition that the *weighted* sum of the elasticities should exceed one, with the weights proportional to the value of exports and imports. In effect the simple Marshall-Lerner condition is equivalent to the proposition that an unweighted, or equally weighted, sum of the elasticities should exceed unity.

A further complication arises because it is possible for a balance of payments to improve in foreign currency but not in pounds or vice versa. For example, if the original deficit were £400 million and the exchange rate $2 = £1, the deficit would be $800 million. If after a depreciation to $1 = £1 the deficit were £600 million or $600 million this could be viewed as an improvement (in dollars) or a worsening (in sterling). The minimum necessary condition is slightly different according to which currency the deficit/surplus is measured in.

Nevertheless, whilst the Marshall-Lerner condition itself is no longer appropriate, there is always an amended elasticity condition which avoids the drastic balanced payments assumption.

6.5.2 Aggregation, Practical Problems and Elasticity Pessimism

The analysis in section 6.4 implicitly assumed that there was only one good exported and imported. This is clearly absurd; the UK exports and imports several hundred thousand different goods. However, even with two goods the aggregation problem would arise; in some ways it is a variant of the index number problem.

If the UK imported two goods, one with an elasticity of (-) 0.1 and one with an elasticity of (-) 0.6, what elasticity is relevant to the Marshall-Lerner or similar formulae? Clearly one needs some weighted average of 0.1 and 0.6, but there is no correct set of weights. The relative volume, or value, of imports (or consumption?) offer some possible answers but each level of income and price offers a different answer. In theory there is no solution to the aggregation problem. In practice, national income-based data are used as if they applied to a single good.

Perhaps more seriously, the plethora of goods makes it very hard indeed to estimate elasticities at either the level of the aggregate or at that of the individual good. It is virtually impossible to calculate the correct relative price. All the usual econometric problems are present (see p. 14 above). Hence it has proved difficult to estimate whether or not the Marshall-Lerner condition and its variants is satisfied. However, the evidence suggests that 'elasticity pessimism' may well be justified, that the values may be very low indeed, or at least so close to a sum of unity that it is not clear whether or not the condition is fulfilled (see Appendix).

6.5.3 Supply Side Factors

The Marshall-Lerner condition implicitly assumes that all supply elasticities are equal to infinity or, to put it less formally, that there are no supply constraints on the volume of trade. This is a serious limitation, and so a major justification for the absorption approach in which these are central (see Chapter 7). It is very unlikely that British producers could increase their output by very much in response to an increase in foreign demand. Almost certainly, they would choose to increase price as well as, or instead of, output. In addition, there is evidence that the state of the domestic market influences behaviour in the export market. In other words, whilst Marshall-Lerner implicitly assumes a perfectly elastic supply curve which is more or less stable, in the real world the supply of UK exports is neither stable nor very elastic.

There are two approaches to this problem; one is to try to expand the condition to include supply elasticities. Unfortunately the resulting conditions are horrifically complex and no two advanced textbooks seem to agree on what the condition would be.[2] Moreover, one should accept that elasticity analysis is about demand and incorporate this into a broader analysis. So many factors are left out by Marshall-Lerner, including any other impact of changed competitiveness on the domestic economy, that this seems to be the better solution. Marshall-Lerner can never provide a complete balance of payments model, but it is still of value (see section 6.6 below).

6.5.4. Income Effects

The major factor missing in the elasticities analysis is income effects; they are implicitly assumed away (i.e. it is partial analysis). So the Marshall-Lerner condition assumes that the income elasticity of demand for *all* goods is zero. This is so implausible that it has led to the development of the alternative macroeconomic models of the balance of payments, discussed in Chapters 7 and 8. The sort of mechanism ignored by Marshall-Lerner includes such processes as:

1. a change in relative prices increase exports,
2. the increase in exports generates an increase in income;
3. the higher level of income leads to more imports.

This latter increase in imports can be such that there is no improvement in the balance of payments despite the rise in exports.

The following example, using the elementary multiplier-accelerator model of 'A' level and first-year macroeconomics courses, illustrates the potential impact of income effects. In a simple economy:

$X = 100$ $M = 0.2Y$
$I = 100+0.3Y$ $T = 0.1Y$
$G = 100$ $S = 0.1Y$ (where X = exports, etc.)

As can be easily calculated, the equilibrium level of income is 3000. As imports will, therefore, be 600, there will be a balance of payments deficit of 500.

For simplicity it will be assumed that the price elasticity of demand for imports is 0, but that a 5 per cent devaluation, or other improvement in competitiveness, will lead to a 500 per cent increase in the level of exports. In other words, the Marshall-Lerner condition is satisfied many times over (the sum of elasticities is over 30). After the devaluation

$X = 600$ (and all the other variables as above)

The new equilibrium level of income is 8000. Imports are now 1600, so the balance of payments deficit is 1000. In other words, although the Marshall-Lerner condition is satisfied, an improvement in competitiveness has led to a doubling of the deficit.

The above example suggests that one needs to look at two distinct influences on the balance of payments:

1. the impact of a change in competitiveness on the balance of payments if income were held constant. This change (hereafter B) is given by the elasticities model: this was the increase in exports (500) in the above examples but could also include a fall in the average propensity to import.
2. the rise in imports generated by the higher level of income. The second of these is equal to the marginal propensity to import (m) multiplied by the change in income. Hence one must calculate the

change in income. This is equal to the multiplier times the increase in injections, as in any Keynesian system. This increase in injections is B (the change in the balance of payments holding income constant). This can be checked by re-examining the example above, where it can be seen that the increase in exports is the injection which raises income from 3000 to 8000. Hence, to set it out more formally, the total effect of a change in competitiveness is equal to

$$= B - B.m.k$$

where k is the multiplier (Bmk gives the generated rise in imports)

$$= B (1 - mk).$$

As B will be positive for an improvement in competitiveness so long as the modified Marshall-Lerner condition is satisfied, then additional conditions can be derived. If $mk > 1$, then the generated effect on imports outweighs the change implied by the Marshall-Lerner condition. However, so long as $mk < 1$, then an improvement in competiveness will lead to an improvement in the balance of payments. This consideration of income effects produces two conclusions; the additional condition to complement Marshall-Lerner and the idea that changes in competitiveness influence income. The latter will be considered further in the next section and in Chapter 10.

Table 6.3: Effect on Balance of Payments of Exchange Rate Changes

	Change in balance of payments	Change in exchange rate (%)
USA (1977-9)	+ $ 16 bn	− 11.3
Japan (1977-9)	− $ 9 bn	+ 15.9 '
Germany (1977-9)	− $ 6 bn	+ 13.3
Italy (1974-8)	+ $ 6½ bn	− 31.2
UK (1974-7)	+ $ 21½ bn	− 25.8
UK (1977-9)	− $ 5 bn	+ 9.1

Source: Allen, W.A. 'Exchange Rates and Balance of Payments Adjustment — General Principles and Some Recent Experiences', *BIS Working Paper No. 3.*

6.6 The Value of Marshall-Lerner

Opinion is divided about the relevance of Marshall-Lerner, or competitiveness, to the balance of payments. On the one hand, some economists believe that competitiveness is a major determinant of the balance of payments; for example Allen's estimates shown in Table 6.3. On the other hand, the doyen of British economics, Johnson, could write:

> It should be emphasised that the analysis of the effects of a devaluation is *completely* independent of *any* critical magnitude condition applying to the elasticities of international demand. The relevant stability condition is . . . monetary theoretic' (Johnson, in Frenkel and Johnson, p. 275)

> The familiar elasticity condition (sum-of-the-elasticities-of-demand-greater-than-unity) . . . is completely irrelevant. (*Ibid.*, p. 281)

However, it is clear, that the elasticities approach in general, and modified Marshall-Lerner in particular, can be relevant to the analysis of inflation and unemployment. The full argument is developed below, p. 138 , but both 'competitiveness' and 'exchange rate' are regarded as having their major impact, possibly their only impact, on the level of domestic income. Thus a depreciation is seen as a way of reducing unemployment and an appreciation of reducing inflation. Hence the income effect, whose size does depend in part on Marshall-Lerner analysis, is not an unwelcome by-product but the object of the policy. In November 1982, the Labour Party's Shadow Chancellor, Peter Shore, advocated a 30 per cent depreciation of sterling as a means of reducing unemployment. Similarly, exogenous changes in competitiveness have also been sought, e.g. by incomes policy, as a means to reduce unemployment. In some models, e.g. the Bank of England one (Bank (1979)), such effects are of crucial importance.

Appendix A: Price and International Competitiveness

Most presentations of international trade theory implicitly assume that price is the major influence on potential purchasers and that trade theory should therefore concentrate on showing why prices might differ between different countries, to establish the existence or optimality of trade. Similarly, balance of payments theories concentrated on the impact of price on volume. Strictly, these analyses need not imply that the price elasticities of international trade are high but most writers and students assumed they were until the 1950s when efforts to estimate them commenced. These results were alleged to show 'elasticity pessimism' in that the elasticities were smaller than anticipated — about 1.5 to 2. In the ensuing 30 years estimates of elasticities have become ever lower, so the current consensus is that elasticities are unitary or less.

There are a large number of major problems that must be surmounted before elasticities can be estimated. The first is the poor quality of the data. It is symptomatic of the poor quality of the data that measured world exports are 5 per cent less than world imports, even though one would expect the bias to be to underestimate imports since smuggled goods often appear in export statistics but never in import data, by definition. Moreover, it is very hard to calculate which price is relevant to which goods especially when aggregate data is used. Even where reliable data is available researchers have faced virtually all known econometric problems in their work. Technicalities aside, the major problem has been to isolate the effect of price changes from those of the other factors at work. Usually estimation of price elasticities has been by regression analysis using time series data.

A particular problem facing international economists has been the estimation of lagged relationships. It is usually argued that past as well as present prices should influence trade flows. This is partly because of *contractual commitments*. If someone agreed to buy x tons of coal per year from the UK for ten years in 1977, they would be influenced by 1977 prices (and their expectations) but deliveries will continue until 1987. Hence UK coal exports today would depend in part upon 1977 prices as well as today's. Another reason is *delivery lags*. There is often a substantial gap between the placing of an order and the delivery of a good. The observed flow is of deliveries but presumably the relevant price which influenced the decision was the one prevailing when the order was placed.

The techniques needed to estimate such lagged relationships are complicated, but the crucial problem is that one can estimate a short lag with a low elasticity or a higher elasticity but one which takes years to work through. Statistical methodology cannot satisfactorily determine which is right. The UK Treasury model of exports at one time had a high elasticity (of - 1.6) but a 26 quarter lag. Critics argued that this strained plausibility. In brief, empirical estimation of the effects of trade flows has been successful in showing that elasticities are not high but not successful in establishing how low.

Appendix B: Marshall-Lerner and Income Effects — a Diagrammatic Presentation

A demand curve shows the relationship between price and the desired quantity purchased. The change in total revenue in equilibrium when price changes depends upon the elasticity of the demand curve. It is, however, possible to use instead the concept of an expenditure function — i.e. price times quantity — and to show how this changes when price changes. This is shown in Figure 6.1 (a). When elasticity is greater than unity this slopes downwards and vice versa. The same can be done for the balance of payments which represents expenditure on imports net of exports. This can be negative, i.e. there can be a surplus. Hence, Figure 6.1 (b) shows the effect of changes in the relative price of imports on net expenditure on imports, i.e. on the balance of payments, when GDP is constant. So long as the (modified) Marshall-Lerner condition is satisfied, this will slope downwards from left to right — and this is the relevance of the condition.

If income were constant, a rise in the relative price of imports would improve the balance of payments, e.g. a depreciation that raised the relative price of imports from p_1 to p_2 would improve the balance of payments by AB. However, AB is an injection which necessarily increases income and so shifts the expenditure function from E_1 to E_2, as more is demanded at each level of income and price so expenditure rises. The shift may be such that the total effect on the balance of payments is negative, positive or zero. The shift is AB. MPM. multiplier (k) as on p. 82 above, so it is easy to see that there will be an improvement only if MPM.k $<$ 1. (NB when there are no income effects MPM = 0, so MPM. k equals zero.)

Notes

1. The use of the word 'traditional' is open to the question 'What tradition?', especially in view of the alternative tradition cited by Frenkel and Johnson (1976, Chapter 1). Nevertheless, the word traditional is a useful description of the mainstream textbook orthodoxy of the 1950s and 1960s.

2. The most comprehensive incorporation of supply elasticities was by Stern (1973). His formula required that

Figure 6.1: Marshall-Lerner

a) Expenditure functions

b) Marshall-Lerner satisfied

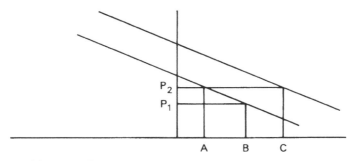

c) Income effects

$$X \; \frac{\Sigma x - 1}{1 + \dfrac{\Sigma x}{Sx}} \; + M \; \frac{\Sigma m \left(1 + \dfrac{1}{Sm}\right)}{\dfrac{\Sigma m}{S m} + 1} \; > 0$$

for a depreciation to improve the balance of payments where X and M are the initial values of exports and imports, Sx and Sm the supply elasticities and Σx and Σm the demand elasticities of exports and imports respectively.

Table 6.4 summarises his results.

Table 6.4: Stern's Results

	Demand elasticities	Supply elasticities	Effect on: Terms of trade	Balance of trade
1	Both high and sum 1	Both high	Moderate worsening or improvement[a]	Improvement
2	Both high and sum 1	Both low	Improvement[b]	Improvement
3	Both low and sum 1	Both high	Worsening	Worsening
4	Both low and sum 1	Both low	Improvement[b]	Improvement[b]

Notes: (a) depends on whether the product of the supply elasticities is greater or less than the product of the demand elasticities; (b) if supply elasticities are sufficiently small in relation to the demand elasticities.

7 KEYNESIAN BALANCE OF PAYMENTS THEORIES

7.1 The Absorption Model

The original Keynesian balance of payments theory was the absorption model developed by Alexander, of the IMF, in the early 1950s. As in all Keynesian models, the balance of payments, on current account, is analysed as a macroeconomic phenomenon in the goods market. The (current account) balance of payments will necessarily equal the difference between aggregate domestic output and aggregate domestic expenditure (with a surplus if output is larger and vice versa). This conclusion follows from a manipulation of the basic national income identity, which is that there are three ways of measuring national income: income, output (O) and expenditure (E), of which only the latter two are relevant here.

$$O = E \qquad (7.1)$$

The expenditure is defined as the sum of consumers' expenditure (C), investment (I), government expenditure (G) and exports (X) less imports (M).

$$E = C + I + G + X - M \qquad (7.2)$$

(7.2) can be substituted into (7.1) to give

$$O = C + I + G + X - M \qquad (7.3)$$

(7.3) can be arranged as

$$X - M = O - (C + I + G) \qquad (7.4)$$

This piece of manipulation is the absorption approach. Alexander called $(C + I + G)$ absorption rather than the more usual 'total domestic expenditure'. The implication of the approach is simple. One should not seek to explain the balance of payments directly, rather one should look at the determinants of output and total domestic expenditure and the balance of payments will be automatically defined as a residual. Competitiveness, the exchange rate and any other factor will matter only in so far as it influences either TDE or output. These effects may be substantial or small but, critically, they may be apparently perverse. A devaluation will increase expenditure, and may even reduce output (or output may already be at a maximum). In this case, a devaluation would worsen the balance of payments, irrespective of the size of elasticities.

It is important to realise how neatly the absorption model complements the elasticities approach. The traditional approach ignored supply side effects (6.5.3) and income effects (6.5.4). The absorption approach looks only at these two effects. The two approaches can be combined. It is also interesting to note that two of the basic implications of this approach, but not the conclusion, are included in the most elementary textbooks. It is common to see statements like

1. deflation can improve the balance of payments.

2. devaluation can improve the balance of payments but only if it is 'made to work' by deflation. (Strictly, this assumes that output is fixed.)

However, the obvious conclusion is not drawn.

3. the balance of payments can only be improved if there is deflation. ('Recognition of this point may be regarded as the fundamental contribution of the absorption approach though none of the authors cited seems to have appreciated all its implications' (Johnson, in Frenkel and Johnson (1970), p. 59).)

These three statements, and the many qualifications to them, are all drawn from the absorption model, as will be demonstrated. (1) is very simple. Deflation lowers TDE so it will improve the balance of payments. However, it will reduce output as well, so the improvement in the balance of payments will be less than the reduction in expenditure. As the absorption approach is the open economy version of the Keynesian model, this is usually illustrated by an analysis in which output is demand-determined. In this case output is $X + (1 - m)(C + I + G)$, where m is the marginal propensity to import, i.e. output is that which is necessary to satisfy export demand plus the part of home demand not spent on imports. In this case the fall in output is $(1 - m)$ times the fall in expenditure; exports are taken to be exogenous. This fall in output is obviously less than the fall in expenditure (unless m is negative). The improvement in the balance of payments is m times (the fall in expenditure).

In effect, a reduction in (C + I + G) automatically reduces imports and so improves the balance of payments. This conclusion is perhaps obvious and the analysis simplistic, but like so many other obvious facts, it took economists to point it out! (In such models, it is necessary for m to be less than 1 otherwise the model is unstable; this is not demonstrated as the model is only illustrative and it is difficult to see how m could exceed 1, so long as other influences are properly specified.)

The next statements, (2) and (3) above, are very easy to demonstrate. *So long as output is fixed*, an improvement in the balance of payments must be accompanied by a reduction in expenditure. Even if output can rise, it is necessary to ensure that output rises by more than expenditure. In both cases, any impact of a devaluation will be negated by income effects — as in the example in Chapter 6 — unless expenditure is controlled by deflationary policies. Absorption analysis can be used to demonstrate this formally and to put into the appropriate framework statements made at a more elementary level. This is not its sole merit as it is a very flexible framework into which almost any analysis can be put. One of the most common and useful involves the concepts of 'expenditure switching' and 'expenditure reducing'. These would be better named 'output switching' and 'output reducing'. The balance of payments can be improved by either

1. a reduction in expenditure (absorption), without a fall in output (expenditure switching);
2. a reduction in expenditure accompanied by a fall, albeit smaller, in output (expenditure reducing).

Both of these possibilities follow from the basic equation (7.4) above, as do alternatives involving a *higher* level of output, which are usually eliminated from the analysis as impracticable. Policies are usually classified into these two categories by use of analysis based on the elasticities approach. Depreciation, for instance, is classified as expenditure switching. Broadly, a policy is expenditure switching if it would improve the balance of payments if there were no income effects. This, of course, is precisely the question answered by the elasticities model.

In brief then, the absorption approach focuses on the key factors omitted from the traditional approach and provides a general framework of analysis. This can be extended as in the next section, the Mundell model. Precise policy conclusions usually require additional assumptions, as in the fascinating special case of the New Cambridge school (7.4 below). The greatest single virtue of the absorption approach, however, stems from its very existence; the idea that the balance of payments is a macroeconomic variable.

7.2 The Mundell Model

Robert Mundell has been one of the great pioneers of international monetary economics over the last 25 years. The model which bears his name is only one of his many contributions and certainly he no longer thinks it an accurate description of reality, if he ever did. Nevertheless, the Mundell model is important for a number of reasons. One is that UK governments according to its logic from 1951 to 1967. Indeed, one of the reasons for its development was to explore the implications of their actions and those of many other governments who pursued similar policies. Another, more important reason is that it introduces the key concepts of external and internal balance which are central to all advanced Keynesian macroeconomic theory. Moreover, it incorporates the capital account into Keynesian analysis. Finally, the model serves as an introduction to the formal theory of policy making.

The modern theory of economic policy was largely invented by Tinbergen. He showed that a government could achieve as many *targets* as it had instruments available to do it. His whole approach was based on these concepts: that a government manipulates instruments, such as tax rates, so as to achieve targets, such as the level of employment. No government can achieve more targets than it has instruments; this follows from elementary algebra. It is basically the same as the proposition that one can solve n simultaneous equations for n variables. Rather controversially, Tinbergen and his followers went on to argue for *assigning* one instrument to each target. Unfortunately this rule may lead to extreme policies. For example, an assignment rule might be that the budget deficit is increased whenever unemployment is above target and interest rates whenever inflation is above target. As a higher budget deficit would lead to more inflation and higher interest rates to more unemployment, both the budget deficit and interest rates would be raised in order to offset the effect of the other. Tinbergians would argue that so long as the targets were achieved the level of the instruments would not matter, but few others agree. The framework can be extended to incorporate either a cost of changing an instrument or even the notion that a variable can be both a target and an instrument. Nevertheless assignment remains controversial. The relevance of this debate to the present purpose is that the Mundell model implied an optimal assignment and, more important, was drawn up within the Tinbergian target-instrument framework. Many of the more sophisticated models which have followed have continued in this tradition.

Mundell suggested that a government has two instruments: the rate of interest (r) and the level of government spending (G) (or budget deficit). It has two targets: an optimal level of income, the internal target, and a balance of payments target, the external target.

The internal target might be full employment or more generally the level of nominal income which produces the least undesirable combina-tion of unemployment and inflation. Within any conventional macroeconomic framework (e.g. IS-LM) this can be achieved by a large number of combinations of r and G. These combinations are plotted as BB in Figure 7.1, which has interest rates on one axis and G on the other. As, *ceteris paribus*, higher interest rates would reduce income and so require a higher level of G to offset this, BB is upward sloping. Each point along BB represents a combination of policies which will achieve the optimal target level of income. BB is called the internal balance line. As one moves to the right along BB, the increase in G is just enough to offset the increase in r and so keep income at its optimal level. All points to the right of BB imply that a policy has been chosen such that either interest rates are lower or government spending higher than is needed to generate the target level of income. Hence income will be above its target level so there will be excess inflation. Similarly all points to the left of BB imply excess unemployment.

Mundell's model of the balance of payments was in two parts:

1. A model of current account. A higher level of G, or a lower level of r, worsens the current balance because the higher level of income means that more is imported, as in 7.1 above.

2. A model of the capital account. Capital flows are assumed to be interest-sensitive. Thus a higher rate of interest will produce capital inflows.

Governments are assumed to be interested in the sum of these two, a balance of payments definition akin to the balance for official settlements. A higher rate of interest will improve both the current and the capital accounts while a higher level of government spending will worsen the current account. Accordingly, various combinations of r and G will generate the target balance of payments which may be an exact

Figure 7.1: Internal Balance

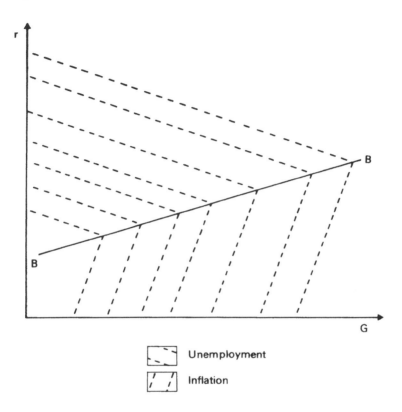

balance or a planned surplus or deficit. These are plotted as FF in Figure 7.2; FF is called the external balance line. Like the internal balance line this is upward sloping — as one moves rightwards along FF, the adverse effect of a higher G is offset by a higher r. A combination of policies represented by a point to the left of FF will produce an excess surplus — since either interest rates are higher or government spending is lower than is necessary for the target (or both). Similarly, any point to the right of FF represents a policy combination which will produce a deficit.

It is necessary to combine Figures 7.1 and 7.2, but to do this one needs to know their relative slopes. FF is the shallower of the two; this follows because interest rates influence balance of payments in two distinct ways. The resulting diagram — Figure 7.3 — shows the outcome

Figure 7.2: External Balance

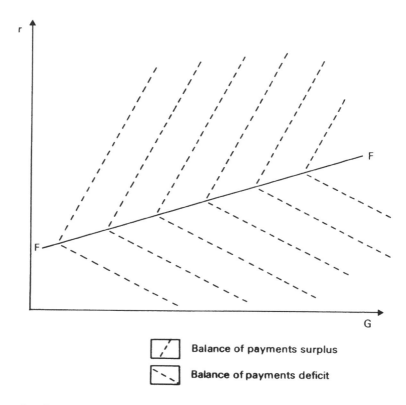

Balance of payments surplus

Balance of payments deficit

of policy options for both external and internal balance; this diagram is often called a Swan diagram after its inventor. The shaded area represents policies which produce an excess surplus and (excess) inflation, etc.

The aim of the Tinbergian approach is to produce crude rules that can be applied in the uncertain real world. The assignment which will work, *so long as BB is steeper than FF*, is:

1. assign G to the internal balance, i.e. increase G if there is excess unemployment and reduce it if there is excess inflation;
2. assign r to the external balance, i.e. reduce r when there is an (excess) surplus and increase it when there is an (excess) deficit.

Figure 7.3: Swan Diagram

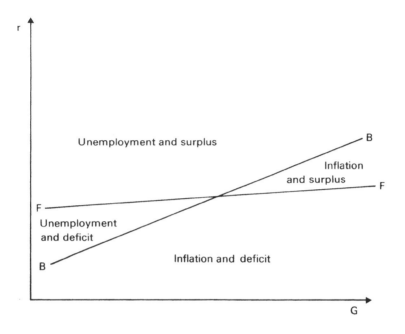

An example of the working of this rule is shown in Figure 7.4. It will also be assumed that the government gives priority to the internal balance. Say the economy starts at (1) with unemployment and a surplus. The goverment increases G to eliminate unemployment and so (2) is reached where unemployment has been eliminated. The government now reduces r to eliminate the surplus; (3) will therefore be reached. At this point, however, there will be inflation, so G has to be reduced. This process continues but the path is convergent to the optimum. Of course the government could use both tools simultaneously, in which case the path is less tortuous, for example (2A) is reached not (2).

As mentioned above, this policy was used in various countries in the 1950s and 1960s, especially the UK, so it is worth mentioning the defects of the model. The first is that governments are not — and cannot be — indifferent to the capital and current accounts. A £300 million current deficit and a £300 million capital inflow are not the same as a current account balance. If for no other reason the continual

Figure 7.4: Convergence to Equilibrium

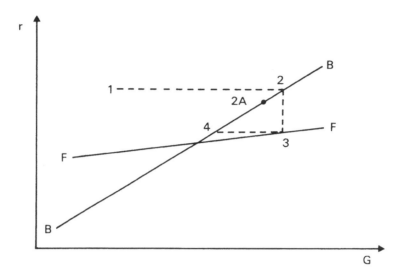

rise in overseas debts — since capital inflows are, after all, borrowing — will mean that interest payments mount and so a new deficit is created. More important, foreign wealth holders will not be prepared to go on lending in such circumstances; they may even withdraw their original loans. Finally, there is a theoretical problem — it should be the *change* in interest rates which induces the inflow not the level. The argument for this postulates stock adjustments by foreign wealth holders. In less high-falutin' language, foreign companies and banks look at interest rates and decide how much to put in each country. If interest rates were, say, 10 per cent in the UK, they might decide their optimal holdings were £15,000 million. If rates are increased to 11 per cent, this might rise to £16,000 million, so there would be an inflow of £1000 million. Unless rates rise again, there would be no further inflow as the foreign holders are already in equilibrium. The UK government learned all this the hard way, by bitter experience in 1965-7.

Besides its historic interest, however, the Mundell model has proved fruitful as a base for more advanced work which has used these key concepts: *external balance; internal balance; assignment*. Whether for good or ill is a moot point. One such development is analysed in the next section: an open economy IS-LM model.

7.3 An Open Economy IS-LM Model

The IS-LM model is usually presented as either a closed economy model or as a pseudo-open economy version. In the latter case 'sterilisation' is assumed, i.e. balance of payments surpluses and deficits are not allowed to influence the money stock, as well as the obvious addition of exports and imports to the withdrawals and injections of the IS curve. As always one can have real income, prices or nominal income on the horizontal axis, in the first two cases price and real income respectively are held constant. It is simplest if prices are held constant, so this will be assumed here.

The first addition to the model is an explicit consideration of the

Figure 7.5: An Open Economy IS-LM Model

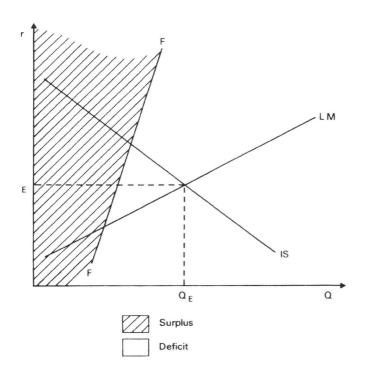

balance of payments. The easiest way to do this is to add an external balance line (FF) to Figure 7.5 representing levels of income and interest rates which generate a balance of payments equilibrium. If one is interested only in the current account it is possible to argue that FF should be vertical — with exogenous exports and fixed price, imports should depend only on income, hence only one level of income will generate equilibrium. Alternatively it could slope backwards — if interest is paid on foreign deposits a higher rate of interest causes a deficit. Usually, however, a Mundell model upward sloping curve for the overall balance is used. Although real income, not government spending, is on the horizontal axis, the same arguments apply, as G influences the balance of payments through Y. Any point to the right of the FF curve represents a deficit (higher income and so more imports) and any point to the left a surplus. Obviously FF could be to the left or right of the equilibrium level of Y and r, Y_E, r_E, i.e. there could be either a surplus or a deficit when the goods and the money markets are otherwise in equilibrium. In Figure 7.5 the initial deficit case is assumed — though as the argument is symmetric the reader can easily work through the alternative of an initial surplus.

The initial deficit reduces the money supply so the LM curve shifts to the left (Figure 7.6). A deficit reduces the money supply in a variety of ways. The simplest are

> 1. if the government supplies foreign currency to residents to purchase imports, this operates exactly like an open market operation;
> 2. the ownership of bank deposits may be effectively transferred to foreigners to pay for imports, e.g. if I write a cheque to pay for French wine and the French supplier keeps a deposit with a UK bank. (Foreign-owned deposits are excluded from UK definitions of money.)

The economy will continue with a deficit and a falling money supply until the LM curve has shifted to LM_E at which point, in equilibrium, the level of income has fallen to Y_N, interest rates having risen to r_N and the balance of payments balances.

Alternatively, the government may seek to shift the FF curve, as in Figure 7.7, so that income does not fall. In principle this can be achieved by a devaluation (so long as the modified Marshall-Lerner condition is satisfied). In practice there are problems with the use of the exchange rate, discussed below in Chapters 9 and 10, but in the simple fixed-price case no such problems exist. A depreciation will improve the

Figure 7.6: The LM Curve Shifts

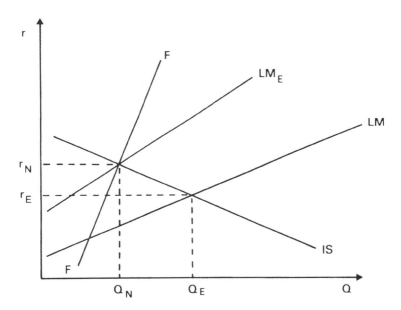

balance of payments at each level of income. Hence it increases the level of income consistent with the balance of payments equilibrium for a given interest rate, i.e. FF shifts rightwards. The authorities have three instruments in this model: money supply, government spending and exchange rate. Thus they can achieve three targets; income, interest rates and balance of payments. Suitable manipulation will make the realisation of any economic goals possible within this model. The real world example is not so amenable, as will be discussed in Chapter 10.

7.4 The New Cambridge School

The New Cambridge School have been exceptionally influential in the UK in that they have almost single-handedly been responsible for the revival of the *macro*-economic case for import controls as a major feature of debates about economic policy. They have to a large extent formulated the economic policies of the 'Tribune' group of the Labour party for almost a decade. The Labour Party's current (1982) official policy. the 'Alternative Economic Strategy', is heavily influenced by

Figure 7.7: Devaluation

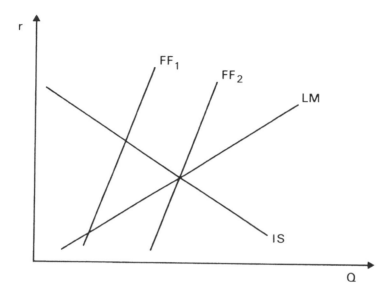

their ideas. In fact the armoury of the New Cambridge economists includes weapons of analysis besides their balance of payments theory. However, none is as well known or as elegant in its derivation of apparent paradoxes from a simple model. Their model seeks to explain the overseas sector's financial surplus. This is the current account plus any purchases of real assets. If a country has a balance of payments deficit on current account of £300 million but non-residents had purchased £100 million of land, antiques (and any other real goods *not* currently produced) from this country, the overseas sector's financial surplus (and the relevant balance of payments deficit) would be £200 million. Transactions in existing real assets are small relative to exports so they will hereafter be ignored, but it is worth noting that X, M, S, T, G and I all have a very slightly different meaning from the standard definition.

As the New Cambridge model is a special case of the absorption approach, it also starts with the national income identity but in this case it is more convenient to use the injections equals withdrawals formulation (in nominal terms):

$$S + T + M = G + X + I$$

Alternatively, a diagrammatic formulation can be used (see appendix). This can be rewritten as

$$(S - I) + (T - G) + (M - X) = 0$$

or as

$$(X - M) = (S - I) + (T - G) \qquad (7.5)$$

The New Cambridge School turns this into a theory of the balance of payments by showing that $(S - I)$ and $(T - G)$ are both determined independently of $(X - M)$ and of each other. Indeed, both are exogenous to this model:

$$(S - I) = k \qquad (7.6)$$

The original version of the model said that $(S - I)$ was a fixed amount, that is the private sector had a fixed *net* level of saving. This would arise in an elementary model if the MPC = 1 and investment were exogenous. In fact, by citing econometric evidence, New Cambridge argued for a marginal propensity to *spend* of one, i.e. if incomes rise by £1 then consumers' expenditure and investment together would rise by £1, e.g. with a MPC of 0.7 and a marginal propensity to invest of 0.3. Later the model was modified to permit credit policy to have an exogenous effect on $(S - I)$. Later still the model was further relaxed but the original assumption still captures the spirit of the model.

$$(T - G) = \bar{F} \qquad (7.7)$$

The economy can be analysed as if the budget deficit $(\bar{F})$, strictly the public sector financial deficit, were exogenous and fixed by the government. This follows from the 'par tax' system. The details do not matter, save to say that both (7.6) and (7.7) are highly controversial. However, if these are accepted, then New Cambridge results follow automatically.

If (7.6) and (7.7) are substituted into (7.4) the crucial result is

$$(M - X) = \bar{F} - k \qquad (7.8)$$

The overseas sector's financial surplus, the balance of payments deficit, is equal to the budget deficit less the constant net saving k. In other words, as F is a policy weapon, by manipulation of F the government can achieve any balance of payments deficit or surplus it wishes. Moreover, this is the only way it, or anybody or anything else, can influence the balance of payments. Hence manipulation of F is both necessary and sufficient to determine (M - X).

Keynesian models basically find two formulae for a variable and then determine the equilibrium level of income (Y_E) as the only value which satisfies both, e.g. to take the simplest case

$$S = I \text{ and } S = 0.1Y$$
If $\quad I = 100 \therefore Y_E = 1000$

The equilibrium level of income is calculated as the only possible level at which saving can equal the exogenous level of investment and 0.1Y simultaneously. The New Cambridge model similarly determines income but uses two formulae for (M - X).

Exports are exogenous to the model, being determined by world trade, relative prices and similar factors. Thus they will be written as $\overline{X}$. New Cambridge have an import function with a unitary income elasticity and a zero price elasticity. Neither are very crucial to the model, although the first simplifies matters as the average propensity to import is equal to the marginal propensity, m. If the price elasticity were unity then the value of imports (M) would be a constant proportion (m) of Y, i.e. M = mY. As the New Cambridge estimate is O however, this means that the *volume of imports* (Q_m) is a constant proportion of the volume of output (Q), i.e.

$$Q_m = mQ$$

To get the value of imports it is necessary to multiply both sides by the price of imports, P_m. Thus

$$M = Q_m P_m = mQP_m \qquad (7.9)$$

It is more convenient to replace Q by $(\frac{Y}{P})$; as Y (nominal income) is equal to Q.P (the price level), hence $Q = \frac{Y}{P}$. Hence (7.9) becomes

$$M = mY\frac{P_m}{P}$$

$(\frac{P_m}{P}$ is the terms of trade and illustrates the impact of changing relative prices on the value of imports.) So,

$$M - X = mYP_m - \overline{X} \qquad (7.10)$$
$$P$$

(7.10) can be combined with (7.8) to give

$$F - k = mYP_m - \overline{X}$$
$$P$$

After rearrangement, this gives the equation for the equilibrium level of income:

$$Y = \frac{F - k + \overline{X}}{m} \left(\frac{P}{P_m}\right) \qquad (7.11)$$

This strange-looking equation is in fact the 'multiplier equation' in an unfamiliar guise — the analogue of $\dfrac{I}{MPS}$ in the elementary model. $(F - k + \overline{X})$ is (net) injections. 'm' is the marginal propensity to withdraw. If the import function can be influenced income will alter — but not the level of imports. This is the 'paradox of imports', similar in all respects to the 'paradox of thrift'. Returning to the example used above

$$S = 0.1Y \quad I = 100 \quad Y_E = 1000$$

If people save a higher fraction of their income, income falls but saving is unchanged, at 100, e.g. if the savings propensity doubled

$$S = 0.2Y \quad I = 100 \quad \therefore Y_E = 500$$

This is the traditional paradox of thrift.

Variations in the savings function could be used as a tool of economic policy to influence income. For example if the government could reduce saving to either

$$S = 0.05Y \quad \text{or} \quad S = 0.1Y - 100$$

income would double to 2000 and saving remain at 100.

In an analogous fashion the New Cambridge analysis uses import controls to reduce the level of imports at each level of income. This will increase income but leave the actual total of imports unchanged.

Similarly, devaluation is advocated as a means of improving the balance of payments at each level of income, even though it will not improve the balance of payments since the improvement at each level of income is exactly offset by the imports generated by the higher level of income. The advocacy of the use of exchange rate or import controls to increase income has been a feature of Keynesian analysis since Keynes's *volte face* on the tariff question in 1931. Indeed, the 'foreign trade multiplier' is a standard analytical tool. The New Cambridge contribution is the 'paradox of imports' (and a passionate advocacy of import controls). New Cambridge analysis   presents an apparently bizarre reversal of assignments – the *internal* weapon (the budget deficit) is used to determine the *external* target (balance of payments) and the *external* instrument (import controls) the *internal* target, the level of income (and so employment). This is because import controls influence income but not the balance of payments while the budget deficit influences both income and the balance of payments. By the application of comparative advantage, import controls are used to influence income and the budget deficit the balance of payments. (Just as a doctor who is an expert typist would employ a mediocre typist (with no medical expertise) to type his letters in the elementary textbook example.)

New Cambridge analysis is open to criticism on three counts:

1. the validity of the assumptions concerning (S - I) and (T - G);
2. the danger of retaliation – even though the *level* of imports is unchanged the composition is not, hence foreign governments might take action to reduce UK exports,
3. the long-term damage that protection could do to the UK economy.

In addition, the forecasting record of the New Cambridge school is hotly debated. None of this matters very much for the present purpose. The New Cambridge school provide an interesting example of Keynesian balance of payments analysis and a coherent presentation of the macroeconomic case for import controls and devaluation.

Appendix : A Diagrammatic Presentation of the New Cambridge Model

It is possible to represent the basic results of the New Cambridge school in a number of different ways. An algebraic method was used in the text, p 101 above, and so a diagrammatic method is used here. There are several alternative diagrammatic presentations which can be produced by a modification of one or other of the basic macroeconomic diagrams such as the IS-LM model or the 'Samuelson cross' national income diagram. The method of showing the key results of this school used here is therefore not unique but has the virtue of simplicity. This representation combines the Samuelson cross method of determining rational income with the alternative injections and withdrawals version of the elementary Keynesian model. The basic model is shown in Figure 7.8 (a) of which the upper half of the diagram shows the determination of the equilibrium level of national income (Y_1) where (planned) output is equal to planned expenditure, i.e. where the expenditure function $(C + I + G + X - M)$ intersects the 45 line. The lower half of the diagram shows the level of injections and withdrawals, the equilibrium level of income being where planned injections $(X + I + G)$ equals planned withdrawals $(S + M + T)$. It is, however, more convenient to modify this condition to $M = X + I + G - S - T$. Imports (M) are a function of income so this is shown by the upward sloping line (as the version of the New Cambridge school used here has the MPM = APM at all levels of income, this is a straight line through the origin). The composite $(X + I + G - S - T)$ can be regarded as independent of income so this is horizontal. At the equilibrium level of income (Y_1) imports (M_1) will be equal to $(I + G + X - S - T)$ as shown.

If government spending is increased, this acts as an injection into the system such that income rises. In the upper half of the diagram (Figure 7.8 (b) there is an upward parallel shift of the expenditure function by the amount of the increase in G (in this case ΔJ) such that income rises from Y_1 to Y_2. The same result can be seen in the lower half. $(X + G + I - S - T)$ shifts upwards by ΔJ and at the new equilibrium level of income (Y_2) imports are M_2. $M_2 - M_1$ is necessarily the same as J, since otherwise the equilibrium condition would be violated. Hence imports have risen by exactly the same amount as G. As exports and taxation are unchanged, a rise in the budget deficit $(G - T)$ causes an identical rise in the balance of payments deficit $(M - X)$. The same diagram shows that an exogenous change in exports has no effect on the balance of payments. The rise in exports is also an increase in injections so a rise of ΔJ in exports will cause income to rise from Y_1 to Y_2 and imports from M_1 to M_2. As ΔJ is necessarily equal to $(M_2 - M_1)$, imports and exports rise by the same amount so the balance of payments is unchanged.

In the case of import controls, expenditure on domestically produced goods $(C + I + G + X - M)$ is higher at each level of Y so the expenditure function shifts upwards (the nature of the shift depending

Figure 7.8: The New Cambridge School

a) The basic model

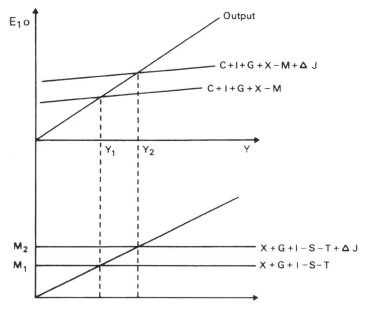

b) An increase in injections

on the form of the control; here both MPM and APM are lower but are still equal to each other). Income rises. In the lower half of the diagram the effect of the controls is to shift the import function, to show that less is imported at each level of income. In equilibrium, imports are still equal to M_1, i.e. to $X + G + I - T - S$. Thus, the balance of payments cannot have improved. A depreciation of sterling would produce both the exogenous change in exports and the shift of the import function, so both analyses would have to be combined but the result would be unchanged — i.e. a higher level of income and an unchanged balance of payments.

8 THE MONETARY THEORY OF THE BALANCE OF PAYMENTS

8.1 Introduction

The monetary theory of the balance of payments, also known as international monetarism, emphasises the financial aspect of the balance of payments, as its name implies. Every transaction is financed in some way or other, usually by the use of money. Hence one might analyse either the financial aspect or the real aspect. Take a primitive tribe whose only transactions with the outside world are the sale of skins for money and the purchase of salt. A balance of payments deficit means that it is receiving a greater value of salt than the skins it is selling. This is the real or goods market aspect of the deficit which is analysed by Keynesian models. Alternatively one might analyse the monetary aspect; it is paying out more money than it is receiving. This is analysed by the monetary theory. A complete analysis must take account of both real and financial factors, so neither Keynesian nor monetary analyses can be complete in themselves. The Keynesian analysis, moreover, is an analysis of *flows* – flows of goods that are traded, and of income. The monetary analysis is an analysis of *stocks*, especially the money stock. Again, as a complete analysis needs to look at both stocks and flows, Keynesian and monetary analyses are complementary as much as competitive. Indeed modern theorists, whether self-styled monetarists or Keynesians, use models which are hybrids of the original international monetarist and Keynesian models. A final preliminary is to note that the monetary theory seeks to explain the overall balance of payments whereas absorption sought to explain the current account. It is possible, therefore, that both are right. This is especially so as the monetary theory puts great emphasis on the capital account – as one of its advocates, Minford, once put it: 'the capital account is King' (when acting as a discussant at the 1978 Money Study Group).

8.2 Domestic and International Monetarism

It is useful to begin an analysis of the monetary theory of the balance of payments by contrasting orthodox and international monetarism.

The latter is an offshoot of the former but nevertheless denies the parent doctrine's main conclusions. This section first presents orthodox monetarist analysis and then shows how the international variant deviates from it.

First of all the behavioural assumption is made that individuals wish to maintain a fixed ratio between

1. their holdings of money (M);
2. their expenditure (or income, at an aggregate level the two are the same), i.e. the price level (P) times the volume of output (Q);
3. their holdings of assets other than money. This is the *value* of asset holdings, i.e. their price of assets (P_a) times the quantity (Q_a), i.e. in symbolic form, the demand for money is such that

$$M \propto PQ \propto P_a Q_a$$

If this equilibrium is disturbed individuals and companies will seek to regain it by disposing of (seeking to rebuild) their money holdings. In consequence PQ and $P_a Q_a$ will alter.

For example, suppose the government reduces the quantity of money, the following will ensue:

1. the government reduces the money supply;
2. the private sector is in consequence in disequilibrium because its money holdings are less than demand; so
3. individuals in the private sector seek to rebuild their money balances by

(a) cutting expenditure, both current and on assets, and

(b) selling assets.

Firms will behave similarly and may also cut stocks of final output. In consequence

4. there will be excess supply of both goods and assets. By normal microeconomic analysis
5. either the price or the quantity of both goods and assets falls.

Depending on supply elasticities, P may fall and Q remain unchanged or vice versa; more likely both will fall. Similarly either or both P_a and Q_a will adjust, though as some Q_a is fixed (Rembrandts, in theory (!) and land) price adjustments are more likely.

This continues until PQ and $P_a Q_a$ have both fallen by the same amount as the original fall in M.

International monetarism accepts this as far as (4) but then substitute

5a. foreign buyers appear and buy all the excess supply at the pre-viously prevailing price (the small economy assumption). Hence there is no change in price or output, or the volume or value of assets. Similarly, if the government increases the quantity of money, foreigners supply enough goods and assets to meet the consequent excess demand without price or quantity adjustments.

The foreign purchases (supply) of goods and assets produce a balance of payments surplus (deficit). This surplus (deficit) necessarily causes a negative (positive) overseas impact on the money supply such that the money supply returns to the original level. This story contains the key feature of the international monetarist story: *a balance of payments surplus or deficit is only temporary because it reflects disequilibrium in the money market.*

An alternative method of analysis looks at the identity

$$\Delta M \equiv DCE \pm 0$$

where 0 is the overseas influence on the money supply. The debate is about what causal pattern, if any, links these variables. Orthodox analysis — both Keynes's and Friedman's — argues that DCE and 0 determine M. DCE and 0 may and probably interact. They will do so if, as both Keynes and Friedman advocate, governments pursue sterilisation operations. However, the key feature of orthodox analysis is that M is determined by DCE and 0. Moreover, M influences income, either directly or indirectly, via changes in interest rates. Any impact of DCE or M on the balance of payments is only via the effect on income and interest rates. This is set out schematically in Figure 8.1.

The monetary theory of the balance of payments, in stark contrast, is that 0 adjusts to D and ΔM. ΔM is determined by the demand for money which is exogenous (as income is invariant), DCE by official policy. Hence 0 is the variable which adjusts to the difference between the demand for money and the (domestic) supply of money, DCE is equal to the change in this domestic supply.

To summarise, in both domestic and international monetarism, the crucial feature is the demand for money relationship (8.1). However in domestic orthodox monetarism it is income which adjusts to ensure the equality of the demand for and supply of money. In international monetarism, it is the balance of payments. Thus, the fundamental

Figure 8.1: Orthodox and International Monetarist Analysis

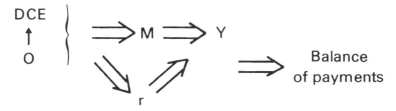

The orthodox model

International monetarism

monetarist proposition of a direct link between money and nominal income disappears.

8.3 The Exchange Rate and the Analysis of the Balance of Payments

The foregoing analysis presented the essence of the monetary theory of the balance of payments as a temporary feature of stock disequilibrium in the money market. In this section this analysis will be extended to incorporate the exchange rate and to produce a modified model more relevant to large and medium-sized economies.

In section 8.2 the exchange rate was effectively fixed. This followed from the assumption that foreigners would buy all assets at prevailing prices. This included assets denominated in domestic currency; in the simplest case, non-resident demand for pound notes was perfectly elastic at, say, $1.75. This assumption will now be relaxed. Instead non-residents will be assumed to have a perfectly elastic demand for UK real assets and goods at a price *in dollars*. However, their demand for financial assets, denominated in sterling, will depend on the exchange rate. This assumption is more plausible than the one used in section 8.2 and so is used by most international monetarists, 'almost invariably' as the founding father put it (Johnson, p. 153, of Frenkel and Johnson).

In this case some slight modifications have to be introduced into the story above. The new story continues:

5b. The excess supply of goods and real assets is still purchased by foreigners but non-residents do not purchase all the financial assets offered. In consequence the exchange rate falls.

6. The fall in the exchange rate leads to a rise in domestic prices.

7. The real value of the money supply falls (alternatively because P and P_a have risen the demand for money rises). So, as the *nominal* quantity of money need not fall to the original level, merely the *real* level, the equilibriation of money supply and demand is achieved in part by a rise in price as well as by a balance of payments deficit (and a fall in price as well as a surplus for an initial reduction in the money supply).

This analysis can be illustrated by Figure 8.2. The domestic producers of a good are necessarily price takers because it is a small

Figure 8.2: A Change in the Exchange Rate

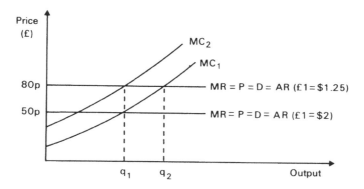

economy. Hence, the domestic producers of widgets face a horizontal marginal revenue curve. This will be at the world price divided by the exchange rate. If the exchange rate is $2 = £1 and the world price of widgets is $1, the world price of a widget, expressed in sterling, is 50p

($1 ÷ 2). The UK producers can sell as much as they like at 50p but not at any higher price, because they are 'small'. Hence, they face a horizontal marginal revenue curve at 50p. Hence, in Figure 8.2, with marginal cost curve mc_1 a typical firm's output will be q_1. When the exchange rate changes, the marginal revenue curve will shift. If the exchange rate falls to $1.25, the new world price of a widget, expressed in sterling, will be 80p, i.e. the world price in dollars divided by the exchange rate (1 ÷ 1.25). Thus the firm will face a new higher marginal revenue curve, at 80p. The new equilibrium output is q_2 and the equilibrium price is 80p. However, all costs including wages will rise by the same amount so ultimately the marginal cost curve will shift from mc_1 to mc_2 and output will fall to q_1. The analysis of the cost curve shift is considered in detail on p. 142 below. Here all that is relevant is that it is optimal for every firm to raise its prices so monetary expansion raises the price level through its effect on the exchange rate.

This result is closer to orthodox monetarism in that a rise in the money supply does lead to a rise in prices. However, the mechanism is different and there is no proportional (or even fixed) relationship between money and nominal income or prices. The validity of international monetarism depends on the validity of the premise that foreign purchases/supply will always equilibriate both goods and asset markets at the previously prevailing dollar price. This is necessarily true for a small economy — indeed it defines a small economy as in the microeconomic analysis of tariffs (p. 41 above). It is equally necessarily wrong for a large economy. Hence the theory is applicable to Luxemburg but not to the USA. The problem is that most economies are neither large nor small; Germany, the UK, Australia, Japan are all medium-sized. Perhaps the best solution is to treat such countries as facing an elastic but not horizontal supply curve in which international monetarism is relevant as a polar case.

Further complexities can be introduced to analyse medium-sized economies. One is that the change in the exchange rate may induce shifts between real and financial assets. The effect is likely to be to reduce the effects of a change in the money supply. The other is that there may be short-term effects from the change in exchange rate, i.e. the rise in output from q_1 to q_2 in Figure 8.2. Some analysts feel that this has been important in the UK in 1980-81 when, it is argued, a rising exchange rate caused unemployment.

In this modified form, the international monetarist doctrine is still that a balance of payments surplus or deficit is a temporary phenomenon caused by money market disequilibrium. The addition is that disequilibrium will also influence exchange rates and so prices (and possibly employment in the short term). The influence of the exchange rate on the economy is discussed further in Chapter 10. However, the international monetarist message is clear. Monetary policy will have a direct effect on the balance of payments and on the exchange rate. The impact, if any, of monetary policy on prices and output will be through this channel. These propositions have been very influential in the last ten years, although the consensus position would be 'a major effect of monetary policy is through the exchange rate' rather than 'the only . . .'.

Most international monetarists, e.g. one of the founding fathers, Dornbusch (e.g. 1980), are prepared to accept much more substantial modifications of the simplistic model. Notably income need not be exogenous, as in 8.2, nor need everyone be a price taker, as above. The balance of payments will still be the difference between the domestic supply (DCE) and demand for money. However, both DCE and the demand for money, as well as income and interest rates, are all endogenous. One way of analysing such models is:

$$0 = \Delta \text{ Demand for money} - \text{DCE} \qquad (8.1)$$

(a positive 0 implying a surplus on the balance of payments)
The change in the demand for money can be replaced by the demand for money function, i.e. the changes in wealth (W), output (Q), prices (P) and interest rates (r) which change the demand for money. Thus (8.1) becomes (using a linear demand for money relationship)

$$0 = \Delta (a + bW + cQ + dP - er) - \text{DCE} \qquad (8.2)$$

DCE can be replaced by its definition: PSBR + Δ bank lending Y (ΔBLP) - Δ private lending to public sector (ΔPLG) and to the non-bank private sector, and the first part rewritten to give

$$0 = b\Delta W + c\Delta Q + d\Delta P - e\Delta r - (\text{PSBR} + \Delta \text{BLP} - \Delta \text{PLG})$$

or

$$0 = b\Delta W + c\Delta Q + d\Delta P - e\Delta r - \text{PSBR} - \Delta \text{BLP} + \Delta \text{PLG} \qquad (8.3)$$

(8.3) can be used to analyse the impact of anything on the balance of payments, e.g. public spending, taxation and interest rates, and the result simply compared to the absorption approach. Some changes are very simple in their effect. An exogenous change in wealth (e.g. the discovery of oil in the North Sea) improves the balance of payments as wealth holders have a higher demand for money which the overseas sector satisfies. An exogenous change in income (e.g. when the oil is brought ashore) similarly improves the balance of payments by affecting the demand for money (and in no other way). This highlights a critical difference between the absorption and monetary approaches. In the Keynesian approach an exogenous increase in income will worsen the balance of payments, unless caused by an increase in exports. The monetary approach says it will improve it, irrespective of cause. Thus, for example, a shift in the consumption function or marginal efficiency of capital schedule (or an induced increase in house-building that does not involve extra government spending of lower interest rates) will improve the balance of payments for an international monetarist and worsen the current account for a Keynesian. For the Keynesian the argument is simple; a higher level of income will raise the level of imports. For the international monetarist, a higher level of income increases the demand for money and so causes a temporary disequilibrium in the money market. Demand for money is less than supply so the private sector rebuilds its money balances by sales of goods and assets to the overseas sector, i.e. by a balance of payments surplus. McCloskey and Zecher, in Frenkel and Johnson (1976), p. 368, highlight this difference and try to show that the empirical validity of the monetary theory is thereby demonstrated for the gold standard period, when rises in income seem to have been followed by improvements in the balance of payments (gold inflows). Some changes are rather more complex in that they may increase both the demand for and supply of money. For example, an increase in public spending in a recession would increase the PSBR and (DCE) and so worsen the balance of payments by increasing the supply of money, but this would partly be offset by the higher demand generated by the higher level of income. In many cases, the analysis yields ambiguous results unless special assumptions are made.

To conclude the monetary theory of the balance of payments has enriched balance of payments theory by

1. Stressing the importance of stocks in balance of payments theory.
2. Emphasising the monetary counterpart to a balance of payments surplus or deficit and the consequent need for explicit analysis of the demand for and the supply of money.

3. Emphasising the role of the exchange rate as a transmission mechanism for monetary policy (see Chapter 10) and the likelihood of direct links between monetary policy and the balance of payments.

8.4 Devaluation and the Monetary Approach

Depreciation of the currency, or the policy weapon of devaluation, influences the balance of payments in the monetary approach only in so far as it effects either the demand for money or DCE, the change in the domestic money supply. This effect in principle could go either way and in general is likely to be small.

The simplest monetary approach to devaluation is, using the model presented in 8.2: the rise in the domestic price level reduces the *real* value of money holdings. There is a consequent reduction in expenditure and sale of assets both because of (Pigou) wealth effects and to reattain equilibrium by rebuilding money balances. In consequence there is a balance of payments surplus in the short-term. Kuska (e.g. 1972) was the first to make this aspect of the theory clear but Johnson popularised it and summarised is as follows: 'devaluation is equivalent to domestic credit contraction; its function is to deflate domestic real balances and thereby to cause domestic residents to attempt to restore their real balances through the international commodity and security markets' (in Frenkel and Johnson (1976), p. 165). It is interesting that this involves the opposite requirement to the traditional approach wherein domestic inflation reduces the effectiveness of a devaluation, here it is essential.

This 'beneficial transitory effect on reserves and the balance of payments' (Johnson, a few pages later) 'can be offset or neutralized by a variety of factors, such as the rise in interest rates which may also be caused by devaluation'. DCE itself may be affected by the devaluation, for example, if government expenditure is maintained in real terms the PSBR may rise. Obviously the PSBR could fall if higher prices increase tax yields. The flow demand for public sector debt is likely to fall at least in the short term. The demand for credit may rise; it almost certainly will to finance increased (nominal) stocks. In general, depreciation sets off many mechanisms and so the outcome is complex and depends upon how domestic monetary policy operates. There is no clear definition of a neutral policy and so one cannot say, *a priori*, what the *ceteris paribus* effects of devaluation are on DCE.

8.5 The Determination of the Exchange Rate

One of the features of the modified international monetarist model presented in 8.2 was that the exchange rate was endogenous, whereas in both Chapters 6 and 7 it was exogenous. Of course, the rate is endogenous in the sense that rate is determined within the foreign exchange market but official intervention can and does occur in this market such that exogenity may not be an unreasonable assumption (as with interest rates). The foreign exchange market is analysed in Chapter 9 and official intervention in Chapter 11. However, it is useful at this point to list the market forces which might influence the exchange rate, or determine the cost of official intervention. In any securities market, the basic forces determining supply and demand are rates of return and expected price change but the schedules may be shifted by exogenous economic factors. Moreover expectations are likely to be influenced by economic theories and variables. The economic factors are:

1. *interest rates*, because they are an influence on the rate of return on investments in one currency rather than another;
2. *domestic credit expansion*, following international monetarist analysis;
3. *relative prices* (i.e. inflation compared to the world level), either directly (purchasing power parity theory) or because of the influence on the balance of payments (traditional theory);
4. *government spending* (or the PSBR) as the determinant of the balance of payments on current account within the Keynesian models;
5. *the trade balance or current account balance* because they affect the supply and demand for currencies directly and a change in the exchange rate might be needed to induce the offsetting effect on the other parts of the balance of payments.

9 THE FOREIGN EXCHANGE MARKET

9.1 Some Concepts

The foreign exchange market is a market in which currencies are bought and sold; many people use it to obtain currency for a holiday. Thus francs are traded for pounds and pounds for dollars and so on. The price of one currency in terms of another is called the *exchange rate*.[1] If one currency is traded against two others, there is an implied exchange rate between the latter, called the *cross rate*. If the pound is traded for two dollars and a dollar for two Deutschmarks, this implies a cross rate of four DM to the pound. If this cross rate differed from the actual sterling-DM rate, then *arbitrageurs* would intervene to profit by the discrepancy and, of course, in the process remove it. The market in currency for immediate delivery is called the *spot* market. There are also *forward* markets in which an agreement is made to exchange currency at a specified price on a particular date, both price and date being fixed when the agreement is made, irrespective of any future fluctuations in exchange rates. Forward markets, discussed below in sections 9.2 and 9.4, are of great value to both traders and speculators (see also p. 182). A *speculator* is a person who hopes to make a profit by correctly predicting a change in exchange rates. If the forward rate is £1=$1.70 for delivery in three months' time and the speculator expects the rate then to be $1.50, he can sell forward sterling. He commits himself to delivering, say, £100,000 in three months' time, knowing that he will receive $170,000 in exchange. If he is right about the exchange rate, he will be able to buy the £100,000 in the spot market for $150,000 and so make $20,000 profit. If he is wrong, he might make a very large loss.

Traders are only involved in the market as a necessary consequence of their other activities, e.g. an exporter or a holiday-maker. Because they need to transact with residents of other countries they need to obtain foreign currency or to dispose of it to meet obligations in the UK. These traders can insure themselves by a suitable forward contract. Imagine a student who has planned a holiday in the US in September which will cost her $1000. She intends to work in July and August to finance this holiday but will be paid in sterling. She does not know how much she needs to earn to pay for the holiday unless she uses the forward market. If the rate were \$2.50, £400 would be enough; if it were \$1.50, £600 would be needed — and both rates have been seen recently. Hence the student does not know how much work she needs to do. If, however, she buys \$1000 forward at say \$2=£1, she commits herself to delivering £500 on 1 September knowing she will receive the \$1000 in exchange. Hence she knows how many hours of dishwashing she needs to do to ensure her holiday. This transaction is often called 'hedging'; the student has hedged what would otherwise be her bet on the exchange rate.

Economic analysis of the foreign exchange market makes extensive use of these three categories — the trader, the speculator and the *arbitrageur* — who take certain profits and, in doing so, reduce market irregularities. However, in the real world the same agents often engage in all three. Moreover it is often impossible to decide into which category a transaction falls, even with complete knowledge of the agent's position. A failure to hedge might be viewed as speculation; if one normally hedges it is, since behaviour has been changed in the hope of profiting from a change in exchange rates. If Ford of Detroit sell pounds forward, are they protecting themselves against a fall in the dollar value of their sterling asset (Ford of Dagenham) or speculating? The categorisation of foreign exchange transactions has often proved fruitful but it can be carried too far. In the last resort, every dealer is a utility maximiser and, usually, a profit maximiser; further description is superrogatory.

Governments have usually intervened in foreign exchange markets to influence the exchange rate. The methods of doing this are discussed below, p.152, but the arguments for and against intervention are discussed in this chapter. This debate has usually taken the form of a discussion of the case for fixed and floating rates. The problem with this is that there are many varieties of each and many of the arguments used in the debate only apply to a particular exchange rate regime, not to floating rates or to fixed rates generally.

The usual definition of a *floating rate* system is that it is one without the (fixed) par value that characterises a *fixed rate* regime. The *par* value of a currency is the rate at which the authorities in a country have committed themselves to buy and sell their currency. The best examples of this are the gold standard and the Bretton Woods system. However their differences are greater than their similarities. The gold standard was really only effective between the UK and the US. Both countries were committed to maintaining a rate of \$4.88665=£1; strictly both committed themselves to buying and selling their own currency for gold at a fixed price but these prices implied an exchange rate. The exchange fluctuated a little around the parity, between the so-called gold points, because it was not profitable to sell dollars for gold, ship the gold across the Atlantic and buy. pounds or vice versa unless the deviation from the parity were large enough to cover shipping, insurance and interest rate costs. (The latter arose because no interest was earned on the gold while it crossed the Atlantic.) Bretton Woods was an attempt to imitate this system by an agreement that each country would declare a par value against the dollar and keep the actual rate within 1 per cent of this. However, the par value could be changed by the government of the country and hence the system produced very little of the stability of the gold standard. At least, after 1896, there was no speculation under the gold standard (and very little intervention) as the rate was genuinely fixed, hence there was no conceivable gain from speculation. Under Bretton Woods, there was massive speculation, effectively betting on a change of par value (see p. 128 below).

Thus it is necessary to define exchange rate regimes carefully and to be equally careful in ensuring that the arguments for and against them are really applicable to the regime being considered.

Free floating is a system in which the authorities never intervene (and in which no one expects them to intervene). This is unknown; the nearest example is the Austro-Hungarian-Russian exchange rate between 1889-1914, although even here there was some indirect intervention, e.g. via the famous Russian Bear Squeeze of 1891 on the rouble-franc rate.

'Dirty floating' is a system in which the rate is managed by the authorities without a par value. Hence the rate is under official influence but the authorities are not committed to any particular form or amount of intervention. Examples include the sterling-dollar rate from 1931-9, August-December 1971 and since June 1972. Obviously there may be very heavy or very light intervention. The authorities may virtually peg the rate or allow it almost total freedom. This is usually described in terms of the cleanness of the float; very dirty floating or a fairly clean float would describe the two situations above. Linguistic purists would rightly say that these terms both mix metaphors and overstrain them, but the terms seem to have stuck.

A *fully fixed* exchange rate regime is one in which the rate:

1. has a par value;
2. this parity is fixed forever;
3. participants in the market believe it to be fixed forever.

The closest to this is the sterling-dollar rate from 1876 (the crime of '76) to 1914, the gold standard era, but for most of this period maintenance of the gold standard was a major US political issue. In 1893-4 it appeared that the US might be forced off it by heavy speculation; eventually a loan on usurious terms from the Morgan Bank enabled the US to maintain the parity. In 1896 and 1900, the breaking of the link with gold and sterling was the major campaign plank of Bryan, the Democratic presidential candidate, who did not want to 'crucify mankind on a cross of gold'. Hence (3) was certainly not true until 1896 and (2) was in doubt. (There was also a group of countries, the Latin Monetary Union, partly on the gold standard, the so-called Limping gold standard.)

The rarity of free floating and fully fixed exchange rates needs to be stressed because of the fact that many arguments apply to these extremes and not elsewhere. 'Discipline', 'certainty' and the absence of speculation are all advantages of fully fixed but not of *semi fixed* exchange rate regimes, e.g. adjustable parity schemes. The best known of these was Bretton Woods, see above. The gold exchange standard, 1925-31, was very similar.

There are also systems in which the par value is adjusted from day to day, e.g. the *crawling peg*, used by Brazil from 1967. In this the parity was a weighted, moving average of past actual values. 'Wide bands' was a strange scheme, apparently designed to combine the worst of both dirty floating and Bretton Woods by having par values but 10 per cent fluctuation on either side (see p.167 below).

Finally, in terminology, the EEC has sought to produce a variety of schemes to link its members' currencies in an (adjustable parity) semi-fixed scheme: the European Monetary Union (1972-5) and European Monetary System (1979-). These and their partial failure have produced a menagerie of groupings – including snake (all nine), mini-snake (or DM bloc) (Germany, Holland, Sweden, Denmark, Austria (sometimes) and Belgium), worm (Benelux), mini-worm (Belgium and Luxemburg). It is not clear who gains by such a proliferation of jargon except financial journalists anxious to show off and publishers of dictionaries of financial slang.

9.2 The Interest Parity Theory

The interest parity theory was first promulgated by Keynes in 1923 (Keynes, 1923). It is a theory concerning the relationship amongst four variables: the spot exchange rate, the forward rate, the domestic interest rate and the foreign rate. It is extensively used for a variety of purposes, see for example Sohmen's argument below and the final paragraph of this section.

The theory is one of arbitrage, i.e. it argues that if investors are offered a costless, riskless profit they will take it. The consequence will be the ultimate elimination of the opportunity, since one or other price will adjust in response to the investors' activity. If good x is on sale in town A at 20p and town B at 30p and it costs 5p to ship the good between A and B, *arbitrageurs* can profit by buying in A and selling in B. The increased demand in A will tend to drive price up and the increased supply in B to reduce price until the gap is 5p. (A final possibility is that the increased demand for transport facilities raises the transport cost but the equilibrium differential is the transport cost.)

The interest arbitrage calculation is as follows where:

R^N = the New York interest rate paid on deposits or loans in dollars

R^L = the London interest rate paid on deposits or loans in sterling

F = the forward exchange rate

S = the spot exchange rate

(F and S are both expressed as dollars per pound.)

Initially it is assumed:

S = \$2 F = \$1.96 (for one year ahead)

R^N = 10 per cent p.a. R^L = 12 per cent p.a.

If \$1000 is invested in New York, the return is \$1100 in one year's time. Alternatively, the \$1000 can be converted into £500 and invested in London, in which case the return will be £560 in one year's time. It is not clear whether £560 or \$1100 will be more attractive in one year's time, but the investor can *cover* himself by a forward transaction. He can sell £560 forward and guarantee himself a return of \$1108 = 80 (560 times the forward rate of \$1.96). Hence it is preferable to invest dollars indirectly by the triple transaction of a spot transaction, a sterling deposit and a forward sale than directly. Hence investors will do this. If the rate were \$1.90, the return would be \$1064, so the dollar deposit would be preferred.

Someone wishing to invest, say, £1000 in sterling faces a similar choice. He can invest directly in sterling and receive \$1120 in a year's time or convert the sterling into dollars (\$2000), deposit them (to receive \$2200) and cover himself by selling forward the resulting dollar return, to receive £1111.11. With the rates as set out above, he would prefer a direct deposit. However, if the forward rate were $1.90, the indirect deposit would accrue to £1162.63 and would be preferred to the direct deposit.

Substituting general for specific values, the return on the indirect deposit is $\dfrac{S(1 + R^N)}{F}$ The rate of return on indirect deposits can be calculated for any period – e.g. one day, one month, three months – as well as for the hypothetical year used in the examples above. An investor considering a sterling deposit will compare R^L with $\dfrac{S(1 + R^N)}{F}$ and invest accordingly, in either a direct or an indirect deposit.

The gap between the two returns is called the *covered differential* and is a major determinant of capital flow; when it is positive, funds flow into London and vice versa. Some investors might compare the *uncovered returns* (R^L and R^N) but most will look at the covered differential, because they would otherwise bear an unnecessary risk.

The equilibrium condition is that the two covered returns are equal and the covered differential is equal to zero, i.e.

$$R^L = \frac{S(1 + R^N)}{F} \qquad (9.1)$$

This can be generalised to any pair of currencies and any foreign and domestic interest rate, in which case the condition for equilibrium is

$$R_H = \frac{S(1 + R_F)}{F} \qquad (9.2)$$

where R_H = the domestic and R_F the foreign interest rate.

It is useful sometimes to set out the equilibrium difference between the rates in which case (9.2) can be transformed into

$$R_H - R_F = S - \frac{F - S}{S} \qquad (9.3)$$

$\dfrac{F - S}{S}$ is the difference between spot and forward rates expressed as a percentage of the spot rate. $\dfrac{F - S}{S}$ is called the *forward premium* (and $\dfrac{S - F}{S}$ the *forward discount*). When there is a forward premium the forward rate exceeds the spot rate and vice versa. The theory is sometimes stated in terms of the forward discount and premium, e.g. that R_H should equal R_F plus the forward discount or R_F less the forward premium.

Keynes went on to argue that the equilibrium condition would be satisfied because the volume of arbitrage funds would be infinite. If the covered differential were not zero, either all investors would prefer an indirect to a direct sterling deposit if $RL < \frac{S(1+RN)}{F}$, or all would prefer an indirect to direct dollar deposit, if $RL > \frac{S(1+RN)}{F}$. However, in addition to these there could be a large quantity of pure arbitrage transactions. Returning to the original example (with S = $2, F = $1.96, RN = 10 per cent and RL = 12 per cent) the investor could invest $1000 and receive $100 interest, or convert (to £500), lend in sterling (and guarantee £500) and sell £560 forward to guarantee a return of $1108 = 80 which would give him $108 = 80 interest. However, the investor could alternatively borrow $1000 and incur an obligation to repay together with $100 interest. He could then convert, lend sterling and sell forward to guarantee the same return as before. The $1108 = 80 would enable him to repay the loan and the interest and have a return of $8.80 on an investment of zero. Indeed, he has every incentive to do this, since it is a riskless, costless profit. In fact, he might as well borrow $1 million and multiply his profit. In principle there will an infinite quantity of arbitrage transactions so long as the forward rate were $1.96. If the forward rate were $1.90, then there would be a similar incentive to borrow pounds, convert and buy sterling forward. If an *arbitrageur* borrowed £1000, he would have to repay £1120. His £1000 would be converted into $2000. Thus he would be able to invest it to obtain $2200 in one year's time. If he sold at £1.90, this would guarantee a return of £1157.88. Hence he would clear £37 = 88p on an investment of zero. Again, with an infinite return there is an incentive to operate on an infinite scale.

In theory there should therefore be an infinite quantity of arbitrage to ensure that Keynes's interest parity theory is satisfied. In practice there always used to be a large, but variable margin such that a purchase of sterling matched by a forward sale always offered a better return than a dollar investment. It was always puzzling why this was so (see Gowland (1979), p. 61), especially after the growth of Eurocurrency market, since the theory held in these markets. This often created a margin of 2 or 3 per cent in favour of an investment in Euro- rather than domestic sterling. This was still more puzzling since the deposit was with a different branch of the same bank. Exchange control, in principle, could not explain the observation since it did not apply to external holders of sterling, some of whom neither arbitraged Keynes-style nor even switched funds from Lloyds of London to Lloyds of Paris. However, as the differential virtually disappeared after the abolition of UK exchange control in November 1979, the paradox presumably stemmed from this.

The theory, that $R^F - R^H = S + \dfrac{F - S}{S}$, is used to explain any of the interest rates, spot rates and forward rates by different economists since, of course, if any three are given, the fourth follows *a fortiori*. Some economists have argued that domestic interest rates are fixed in this way, using a 'small country' assumption. R^F is the world level of rates, S and F being market or exogenously fixed so the domestic authorities have no choice but to accept the implied level of domestic interest rates; they are too small to influence world rates. Other theories explain why interest rates influence exchange rates, and how governments can use interest rates to influence them (see p. 156 below). Keynes himself argued that a government willing to fix the forward premium (discount) at the appropriate level could then have both the exchange rate and the interest rate of its choice. No one denies that a government could fix either, but Keynes argued that the forward rate could be an extra instrument and so ensure the fulfilment of an extra target. Finally the theory can be used to derive the forward rate or to show the profitability of offering forward cover. This is Sohmen's argument, p. 131 below.

9.3 Fixed and Floating Rates

The remainder of this chapter is devoted to an analysis of the arguments used for and against different regimes of exchange rate management. It is remarkable how many of the arguments start with an *a priori* assumption that governments are necessarily incompetent. However, some deduce from this that they should be constrained by fixed rate, others that they should be denied any power to influence exchange rates, let alone to determine them; Rueff (1967) and Friedman (1953) being the leading advocates of these two views. This is typical of much of the analysis in two ways. On the one hand, a lot of the argument is politico-economic rather than narrowly economic-theoretic. Obviously it is not necessarily the worse for this, indeed 'political economy' is the only satisfactory way to approach exchange rates but it contributes to the second feature of the literature, the number of two-edged arguments used.

The oldest argument for fully fixed rates is the need for *'discipline'*. Rueff used to be the leading advocate of this (e.g. 1967) but it is now mainly used by the American liberal 'New Right', e.g. Brennan and Buchanan (1975). The argument is that governments are naturally prone to overspend and so create inflation. *With fully fixed exchange rates, governments cannot inflate.* At worst the budget deficit leads to a balance of payments deficit whose absorptive and monetary effect is to avert the inflation. In a closed economy a government can create inflation either by increasing demand for goods relative to supply (Keynesian analysis), in which case, as an open economy, the deficit means that foreign supply (imports) exceeds foreign demand (exports) so the inflationary outcome is avoided; or, alternatively, government spending is financed by money creation which is inflationary (monetarist analysis). In this case, the balance of payments deficit leads to a countervailing fall in the money supply through a negative overseas impact. At best the need to maintain the fixed rate prevents the government from spending. At worst the inflationary effect is averted by a system of fully fixed exchange rates. There are a number of problems with this argument. To seek to constrain a government is normally regarded as an anti-democratic attitude in the UK and by many US commentators. Buchanan *et al.* however, would argue that it is democratic to constrain a government because in this way the electors' wishes prevail against those of utility-maximising bureaucrats. Buchanan would argue that any written constitution constrains a government and that he merely wants to add an economic constraint to the political constraints of the US Constitution, especially the Bill of Rights. Perhaps to quote the old text book cliché, the US Constitution is Republican but not Democratic, but that it is eminently reasonable to be undemocratic about such matters as freedom from arbitrary arrest. Whether freedom from inflation should be similarly sacred is a complex question of political theory which is beyond the scope of this book. However, even if the *'discipline'* argument is acceptable on philosophic grounds, the argument can be stood on its head by the *autonomy* argument. This is that a government needs a floating rate to permit it to manage its economy. This is sometimes put as the argument that governments should be able to inflate if they want to, or, more optimistically, have the power to avoid unemployment. Equally often, however, the argument comes from hard-line monetarists (e.g. Friedman (1953) and Friedman and Roosa (1961)). They argue that governments need to be able to determine the money supply so as to keep it either constant or growing at 2 per cent p.a. This power is denied to governments under fully fixed rates. The Rueff-Buchanan school are ready to accept an exogenous rate of inflation, determined by gold production or other countries' actions, since rigid exchange rates constrain everyone to the world average. Friedman wants to aim at price stability. Hence the hard-nosed Right can agree on their analysis but not the conclusion. It can never be clear whether a rigid exchange rate or a monetary rule is preferable, as, for example, Buchanan admits.

More seriously still, once one leaves the world of fully fixed rates, the arguments are no longer clear-cut. This affects those anxious to equip governments with the power to manage economies just as much as those anxious to constrain them. Once there is the opportunity of changing the parity, discipline can be evaded. Furthermore, there is no way that a government can be forced to keep for ever the rigid system – it can always break away, although constitutional provisions may restrict it, or simply not support the exchange rate and leave its opponents to work out how to force it to obey the law. Overseas factors influence governments in various ways:

1. their pure economic effect – e.g. the effect of the exchange rate on inflation;
2. through the need to obey the rules of the game of the international monetary system;
3. through the electorate's reaction to, say, a change in the exchange rate.

One can find examples of when a semi-fixed system has constrained a government through those mechanisms; the best known is the UK in 1964-7 (see Beckerman (1972)). Equally, however, overseas factors constrained the Labour government in 1975-6, albeit in a different way under dirty floating. The Heath government evaded all constraints under both semi-fixed parities and dirty floating to expand the money supply by 60 per cent in 27 months, the era of 'Barberism'. (For all the above, see Gowland (1982a) and references therein.)

In summary, 'discipline' and 'autonomy' depend much more upon the workings of the political system and upon personalities than upon exchange rate regimes, e.g. Germany has had very low and Italy high inflation since 1948, irrespective of the exchange rate regime.

One argument can be dismissed immediately; this is the argument that freely floating exchange rates will ensure that the *balance of payments is self-righting*. The analysis in Chapters 6 to 8 showed that depreciation may not eliminate a (current account) deficit or vice versa, largely because of income effects. The balance of payments is a macroeconomic variable and so cannot be influenced solely by microeconomic means. This point, like all the analysis in Chapters 6 to 8, emphasises the strongest argument for some official intervention in the foreign exchange market which is that *the exchange rate has such an effect upon the economy, especially upon inflation and unemployment, that no government can renounce intervention.* Even Friedman agrees that withdrawal from the foreign exchange market should be the capstone of a *laissez-faire* policy, not the initiation of it (in his debate with Roosa, 1967). The scope for, and role of, exchange rate policy is further considered in Chapter 10.

If it were accepted that some intervention is necessary, it would still be necessary to consider what form of regime is best. Ruling out the fully fixed system, one has to choose between dirty floating and adjustable parities. Two arguments are relevant: one in favour of and the other against dirty floating. The argument for dirty floating is that, because of *one-way options*, it is impossible to maintain even a temporary, fixed parity (or at least prohibitively expensive). The problem arises because, with adjustable parities, there are usually only the possibilities that an exchange rate will remain unchanged or move in one known direction, i.e. a symmetric distribution is impossible. Throughout the 1960s it was clear that the UK would never change its parity upwards, nor Germany downwards: there was only a one-way option Hence most of the risk of speculation disappeared. The sterling exchange rate was $2.79 in September 1967 and a calculation could be made of the losses from speculation if the rate were to remain unchanged and this be compared with the likely gain if there were a devaluation. This ratio could then be compared with the (subjective) probability of devaluation. There was no risk of (upward) revaluation so the speculation was attractive. For example, in September 1967, the authorities were effectively offering odds of 5-1 against a devaluation within three months. Understandably, this proved so very attractive that when the bet won (in November 1967) the UK taxpayers had to bear the very heavy loss of £356 million; more than the entire cost of higher and further education in 1967-8. With the growing size and sophistication of international capital markets and especially the Eurocurrency market, see also p. 183 below, the costs would now be many times larger. Indeed there is so much cash in the world's financial markets that it may be impossible to maintain a fixed parity or even a preferred level of exchange rate (see the discussion of the US's position in November 1979, p. 174 below, in which it is argued that even the US could not maintain the dollar's international value against the weight of market forces, even if they chose to).

Unfortunately this argument is not incompatible with the view that *floating rates have been inflationary*, for the world as a whole. There are a number of reasons why this may be so.

One group of arguments relies upon expectational factors, e.g. the argument of Machlup in Classen and Salin (1976). The author once summarised this view as follows:

> To the extent that a world inflationary psychology has now developed, inflation in one country intensifies inflationary expectations there and elsewhere, and thus renders it harder for any one country to fight the tide. It seems reasonably clear that floating rates reduce the barriers to the spread of inflation from one country to another and make it harder for one country to resist the climate of world inflation (as for example, West Germany, Belgium, Holland and Switzerland did in the mid-60s).
>
> (Gowland and Pakenham (1974))

A simpler argument relates floating rates and inflation by use of the ratchet argument that cost decreases are not as deflationary as cost increases are inflationary. Thus, if in the spring the pound falls against the mark, UK prices tend to rise but there is no counterbalancing fall in German prices. In the autumn the pound may recover, producing a rise in German prices but no fall in UK ones. Hence the fluctuations in exchange rates have left exchange rates at their original level but raised prices in both countries. For a full discussion of the relationship between exchange rates and domestic price, see section 10.1 below.

The nature of most of the arguments considered so far in this section has been such that firm conclusions were difficult to derive and rigorous analysis often had to give way to politico-economic speculation. The next two arguments, by contrast, are hard economic ones: uncertainty (9.4) and destabilising speculation (9.5). Some conclusions are then drawn (9.6).

9.4 Uncertainty and Exchange Rates

One of the longest-running arguments for fixed rates is that floating rates induce an extra uncertainty which reduces the volume of world trade. This reduction, moreover, involves an inefficient allocation of resources, since the reduction has been caused by an incentive to view two goods or markets differently simply because of their location.

This argument arises because international trade will apparently mean that at least one agent will have expenditure in one currency and receipts in another and so has an extra uncertainty about the value of his income. If Rowntree of York are considering whether or not to sell Yorkie bars in New York they will have to consider consumer demand, production costs and so on just as they would if they were selling Yorkie bars in Edinburgh. In addition, however, they must face the problem that Americans will pay for the bars in dollars, whereas Rowntree pay wages in pounds. With (fully) fixed rates this would not matter as Rowntree could easily calculate how many pounds their expected dollar revenue would buy. If exchange rates fluctuate they will not know the return in pounds from any given level of sales. If the dollar is higher than Rowntree expect, they will have an unexpected bonus, but if it is lower, their profits may be wiped out. If, as is conventional and reasonable, risk aversion is assumed, then Rowntree will dislike this extra factor that could affect profits and so will be inclined not to export when they otherwise would. Rowntree may not face the uncertainty themselves but someone will. For example, Rowntree may be paid in pounds by a US wholesaler. However, he will then have sterling expenditure and dollar receipts so he will be biased to purchase Hershey's products instead of Rowntree's.

This uncertainty about the value of export receipts, or the cost of imports, will act as a deterrent to trade that would improve the world's allocation of resources, or so the fixed rate proponents have argued since, at least, Ricardo. It is important to note, however, that it is an argument in favour of *fully* fixed rates. With adjustable parities there is a small probability of a large change in exchange rates. With dirty floating, there is a very high probability of a smaller change in exchange rates and a much smaller probability of a large change. It is not clear which would induce the greater uncertainty. Under Bretton Woods the American wholesaler's calculations might be: 'Unless there is a devaluation we will make £1 million more from Rowntree's than Hershey's products; if there is a devaluation we will make a loss (and would be £2 million better off with Hershey's). There is a 10 per cent chance of devaluation.' Under dirty floating, they might be 'We will be between £½ million and £1½ million better off with Rowntree's bars unless the exchange rate changes by more than 10 per cent. There is only a 1 per cent chance of that.'

In this example the wholesaler would be more likely to buy (British) imports under dirty floating since the risk of a catastrophic change in rates is much smaller even though uncertainty is greater in some sense (at least by conventional measures). It would be easy to construct counter examples, but in fact what matters in all cases of uncertainty is whether it can be insured against and at what cost. If there is a market in which insurance is available against the risk, then uncertainty itself will not reduce trade, only the insurance premium will. Sohmen (1969) argued that uncertainty about the value of receipts or expenditure would disappear if there were forward exchange markets. Moreover, because of the interest parity arbitrage described in 9.2, there would always be forward exchange markets.

Sohmen's first argument is incontrovertible. If Rowntree are able to sell forward dollars, or the American importer to buy forward sterling (the same transaction), there is no more risk to selling in New York than Edinburgh and no more risk in buying British than American chocolate bars. A forward sale or purchase can guarantee that receipts and expenditure are in the same currency. If Rowntree expect to sell one million Yorkie bars at 10 cents each, they can sell $100,000 forward and ensure a return of, say, £50,000 and compare this with the prospective return from selling the chocolate in Edinburgh and with the cost of making it, both of which are sterling outlays. Many uncertainties remain but none bias the choice towards one market rather than the other. If forward markets exist and are not used, the implication is that the uncertainty does not affect business decisions.

Sohmen's next proposition is more controversial, although theoretically impeccable. It is probably best to illustrate it with a specific example. If (American) dollar interest rates are 15 per cent p.a. and sterling (British) interest rates are 12 per cent p.a. and the spot rate is $2, the equilibrium forward rate is $2.054 (approximately). Sohmen's argument is designed to show that there will be a forward market, because it is risklessly profitable to offer forward cover. If a dealer were to offer to supply forward pounds at $2.1 and buy them at $2 for one year ahead, he would make a profit (of 10 cents) on any matching transactions — if Rowntree bought £1 million forward (i.e. sold $2.1 million) and Ford sold £1 million sterling forward (i.e. bought $2 million dollars) he would make $100,000 (which he could also take as £46,379 or as a mixture of pounds and dollars). If, instead, his book does not match — say he has contracted to supply £1 million forward — he can still guarantee a profit. He has contracted to pay out £1 million and will receive $2.1 million. If he borrows $1.8 million he will have to repay $2,070,000 ($1.8 million he borrowed plus $270,000 interest).

For $1.8 million he can buy £900,000 and invest it so that he receives £108,000 interest. Hence his borrowing, conversion and lending operation will leave him with an obligation to pay $2,070,000 and receipts of £1,108,000. This means that when he has paid out £1 million and received $2.1 million on the forward contract, he has a net profit of $30,000 and £8000 on an investment of zero. (He could obviously adjust the transaction to take all his profits in dollars, all in sterling, or various other combinations of them.)

More generally, so long as it is possible to borrow in one currency and lend in another, then, so long as there are spot exchange markets, it will always be possible to offer forward exchange at a riskless profit. Hence, Sohmen argues, forward exchange markets will always exist. (If they did not, hedging could be done on a home-made basis by a suitable borrowing, conversion and lending operation.)

Moreover, competition should drive the forward rate towards the equilibrium (i.e. someone else has an incentive to buy forward pounds at $2.01 and sell them at $2.09 and so on until the abnormal profit is eliminated). Sohmen's analysis makes two assumptions:

1. There is no default risk; the *arbitrageur* needs to be sure that no one defaults otherwise he is in terrible trouble. In practice, with large companies and large banks he can conduct all three transactions in complete safety.
2. The *arbitrageur* can borrow and lend in dollars at the same interest rate. If not, the difference between them adds a transaction cost, discussed below. In practice, banks are virtually the only dealers in forward exchange, because the margin between their borrowing and lending rates is so much less (perhaps negative!) than anyone else's.

The first problem with Sohmen's argument is that there is not a complete set of forward markets, especially for the far distant future — and after all if Rowntree were thinking of building a factory to supply New York they might want to sell dollars forward ten years ahead. As one commentator puts it: 'Do they work? Usually but not always . . . [sometimes] the market stops functioning just because it's a market' (Smith, 1982).

However, with the growth of Eurocurrency markets, many more forward markets exist than used to be the case. Of course, governments may not permit their residents to use the markets even if they exist, but legalisation of such transactions is the best way of removing the exchange rate uncertainty implied in international trade. For example, 'foreign currency surcharges' were at one time a common danger of booking a foreign holiday for UK residents, until the Bank of England permitted the package holiday industry to use the forward market, in 1978.

A more serious problem with the simple analysis above is that it ignores transactions costs. The arbitrage transaction will increase costs – if only by a few phone calls. Hence forward cover may always be available, but at a cost. This transaction cost will inhibit international trade in the same way as more obvious transport costs.

However, it makes it possible to assess alternatives, like 'dirty floating' and adjustable parities in terms of the effective cost of forward cover. *Ceteris paribus*, the uncertainty argument is an argument for the regime where forward cover is cheapest. In fact dirty floating involves a cost about three times that of adjustable parities. Of course, this is not a decisive consideration but the uncertainty argument can be reduced to an argument about the cost of removing it – and this is measurable.

9.5 Speculation

Arguments about speculation are either arguments for fully fixed exchange rates or, more relevantly, concern the case for some intervention by governments in foreign exchange markets. There would be no speculation if exchange rates were truly fixed for ever. However, this is obviously irrelevant to the real world since, even if a fully fixed system were introduced, it would be many years before all participants became convinced that rates would never change. More relevantly, it is alleged that if governments did not intervene, speculators would carry out transactions that would produce undesirable movements in exchange rates. In particular, speculation might be destabilising, that is, it might lead to larger fluctuations in the exchange rate than would otherwise occur. This would be an argument against free floating. Destabilising speculation would not in itself justify one system of intervention rather than another and does not provide an argument for 'fixed' against 'floating' rates in general. Indeed the reverse could be true, since adjustable parities encourage speculation by providing one-way options.

Friedman (1953) argued that destabilising speculation was impossible and that the effects of speculation would be desirable. His argument has been extended to defend speculation in all markets, invoking a tart comment from Galbraith that it was like a harlot arguing that she was a good cook (Galbraith (1953), p.137). Friedman argues that speculation will only persist if it is profitable. In any case unprofitable speculation is unlikely to be harmful; why worry if imports and exporters, or even *arbitrageurs*, gain at the expense of speculators? In fact losing speculation can persist, e.g. financed by profits from other income or by new inflows of funds, in the case of, for example, a pension fund. In fact it is quite likely that it would, since a few speculators would profit even if most lost and this would almost certainly ensure that speculation remained popular – as with any other form of gambling. (See Gowland (1982a), pp. 149-51 for a discussion of a similar problem.)

Nevertheless, Friedman's premises are acceptable. Speculation is not necessarily harmful and it would only be if there were profitable, destabilising speculation that serious problems would arise. Speculation will be profitable only if the average buying price is less than the average selling price. Such speculation will tend to iron out price fluctuations, not accentuate them.

This argument is simplest when there is a trend value of the exchange rate and the actual exchange rate varies around this trend. If speculators enter the market, they can profit by buying when price is below trend and selling when it is above but, in this case, they will increase demand relative to supply and so increase price when price is below trend; and reduce demand relative to supply, i.e. be net suppliers, when price is above trend and so reduce price. Hence, they will tend to bring the price closer to the trend.

They can profit in other ways, e.g. by buying when price is a long way below trend and selling when it is closer to trend, but all will move price closer towards the (equilibrium) trend value. Perfect speculation would ensure that the actual value was always equal to the long-run trend value. Effectively, some rational expectations models assume that this is the case.

Friedman's argument is incontrovertible so long as two assumptions are valid:

1. *The long run value of the currency is independent of short-term fluctuations in the exchange rate.* In the context above, this would mean that the trend was independent of any fluctuations round it. More generally it would mean that any speculator-induced deviation from equilibrium was not permanent. For example, if short-selling speculators drove the pound down from $1.80 to $1.20, they would necessarily lose when the rate rebounded. However if $1.20 became the

new equilibrium rate, they could cover their short sales and so profit. In this case the speculator-dominated market would have a totally different path of exchange rates from the path that would otherwise prevail and might be more or less variable. If exchange rates influence the rate of inflation, Friedman's assumption is not valid.

2. *The market is stable in the technical sense.* In Friedman's two-equation model, the stability condition is that the slope of the demand curve is less than that of the supply curve; it automatically is, of course, if the demand curve is downward-sloping (i.e. negatively sloped), and the supply curve upward-sloping. In the foreign exchange market there are both theoretical arguments and empirical evidence which suggest that the demand curve for currency might be upward-sloping in the short run. However, the more serious objection to Friedman's assumption is that his model is over-simple and that a more sophisticated model is necessary. In the multi-equation models of the foreign exchange market that have been devised, stability conditions are more complex and are by no means *a priori* valid.

Technical instability could justify intervention by itself. If a deviation from equilibrium will lead to an exchange rate that moves further and further away from the equilibrium path, the case for intervention seems very strong. The counter-argument is that rates do not either explode upwards or drop to zero — but this is not decisive because intervention is the norm.

Hence whilst Friedman's argument is valid on its own terms, it is, nevertheless, not clear that destabilising speculation is *a priori* impossible. Considerable efforts have been made to see whether destabilising speculation exists but the overall results have been inconclusive. This may be because destabilising speculation sometimes exists and/or is profitable and at other times does not.

In any case it is probably true that destabilising speculation is caused by official intervention, whether or not it would otherwise occur. The argument is simple. The classic act of a destabilising speculator is to buy when price has risen and sell when it has fallen. Official intervention often seeks to 'smooth' the market, to narrow the day-to-day movement of rates. This may justify destabilising speculation — the speculator can calculate: 'The pound has risen 2 cents and the Bank of England has probably intervened to stop it rising by more (a smoothing operation), so without the intervention it would have risen 4 cents, so I will buy as it is more likely than not to rise the other 2 cents tomorrow.'

If the destabilising speculation that occurs in the real world is (even partially) caused by intervention, it is impossible to determine whether it would occur without such intervention. Hence, one cannot say whether or not destabilising speculation justifies intervention. This conclusion may seem a little inconclusive and in a sense it is, so conclusions are usually formed by more fundamental views. It cannot be shown that intervention is either necessary or unnecessarily harmful. Hence, the question becomes one of how well markets are likely to work.

9.6 Some Conclusions

In the author's opinion, no government should, or even could, renounce intervention in the foreign exchange market because of the impact of exchange rate variations on the economy. Only the US is exempt from this and, even there, as the economy becomes more open it is less immune to the effects of exchange rate variations on employment and prices. As the exchange rate will not produce balance of payments equilibrium by itself, it is better used as a tool of domestic policy, at least partly. Even if it is accepted that quasi-constitutional devices are needed to curb public spending, a rigid exchange rate seems an indirect and ineffective method of achieving it; a direct limit on government spending or a balanced-budget constitutional rule seem both more likely to work in practice and likely to achieve the goal of the 'discipline' school. (Ignoring all other considerations, if public servants know that issuing public sector pay cheques is a criminal offence in some circumstances, it gives both those who issue and those who receive the cheques an enormous incentive to see that the circumstances do not arise, i.e. the budget remains balanced or that public spending is below its ceiling.)

Because of 'one-way options', dirty floating is inevitably the only interventionist regime that is practicable and it may well be optimal for the 1970s and 1980s even if more choice were available. Uncertainty can best be reduced by ensuring that forward markets operate as widely and cheaply as possible and that their services are well known to potential beneficiaries. It is, however, perhaps best to end this chapter by stressing how maladroit official intervention in foreign exchange markets has often been, e.g. that by the UK in 1975-6. If there is a case for freely floating rates it is (the familiar argument) that while markets may fail, official intervention is costly and often ineffectual.

Note

1. The UK convention is to define exchange rate as the number of units of foreign currency obtained for each unit of domestic currency, e.g. x dollars per pound. In the US the convention is to define the exchange rate as the number of units of domestic currency required to purchase one unit of foreign currency, e.g. pence per dollar. The two are the reciprocal of each other.

10 THE EXCHANGE RATE AND ECONOMIC POLICY

10.1 Introduction: The UK 1974-82

Balance of payments theory was considered in Chapters 6 to 8 and the exchange rate in Chapter 9. This chapter seeks to integrate the analysis of these four chapters so as to extend the analysis and, especially, to highlight the main considerations which influence economic policy in medium-sized open economies such as the UK. In apparently paradoxical contradiction to the conventional wisdom of the 1960s, modern theories suggest that the main determinant of the balance of payments is domestic macroeconomic policy, especially the level of government spending, and the level of domestic credit expansion on which it is the major influence. On the other hand, the exchange rate is important primarily as an influence upon the level of employment and the price level.

The simplest of such models is the one which seems to have had most influence upon the UK government. This is the proposition that the exchange rate is inversely related to the level of nominal income, i.e. price times output. A depreciation will increase nominal income. *Ceteris paribus*, this should increase output and so should reduce unemployment, even though the rate of increase of prices will rise. An appreciation will contrariwise reduce nominal income below the level it otherwise would be and so reduce inflation, even though unemployment will rise. Indeed, the conventional unemployment-inflation trade-off presents itself most clearly in the UK in the context of exchange rate policy.

The relationship between the exchange rate and nominal income can be established by either elementary monetarist or basic Keynesian analysis. The monetarist analysis is that the exchange rate directly influences the money supply through the overseas impact on the money supply − see Gowland (1982a), pp. 47-8, for a detailed explanation of the mechanism involved. A change in the money supply necessarily causes an equivalent change in nominal income in the orthodox monetarist model. The Keynesian mechanism is that the balance of payments is improved at each level of income, hence planned injections (X + I + G) are higher relative to planned withdrawals (S + M + T) at each level of income. Therefore the equilibrium level of nominal income is higher.

This analysis was shown on p. 88 above and, in a special case of the mechanism, in the examination of the New Cambridge school on p. 99 above. These propositions about the inverse relationship between nominal income and the exchange rate make it possible to explain both the gyrations of UK exchange rate policy over the last decade and a major difference between Mrs Thatcher's economic policies and those advocated by Peter Shore as part of Labour's 'Alternative Economic Strategy'.

The Labour government of 1974-9 sought a high exchange rate to reduce inflation whenever incomes policy was unsuccessful (1974-5 and 1977-8) and a lower rate to reduce unemployment whenever it seemed that incomes policy was curbing inflation (the early part of 1976). The Labour government's use of the exchange rate as an instrument of fine-tuning was controversial. In 1974-5 wages were soaring and unemployment was low, so the government sought to hold the exchange rate up as an anti-inflationary device. This was not too difficult because of the aftermath of the 1973 oil crisis which meant that OPEC funds poured into London. Nevertheless, it added to the pressure on corporate liquidity which so frightened Mr Healey as to produce the dramatic U-turn of the November 1974 Budget. In the early part of 1976, with a successful incomes policy and rising unemployment, the government sought a lower exchange rate to reduce unemployment. However, the attempt was disastrous in that it produced an uncontrollable and humiliating sterling crisis as the downward pressure on sterling accelerated. In 1977-8, a higher rate was at least tolerated both to reduce monetary growth and to assist a faltering incomes policy. Other more minor changes in exchange rate strategy were common. In fact, it sometimes seemed that the exchange rate was the only instrument of fine-tuning that this government permitted itself to use. The execution of the policy was marked by some very strange, indeed apparently illogical, dealing tactics (Gowland (1982a), p. 168). Moreover, the exchange rate seems at least as open as any other instrument of policy to the conventional criticisms of fine-tuning. Indeed it may be even harder to use the exchange rate in an excessively active fashion than other instruments because of the effects on the expectations of those who deal in foreign exchange. In general, UK experience in this period confirms that while the exchange rate is a potentially useful tool of economic management, considerable care is needed in implementation and it is no easier to use than conventional monetary and fiscal instruments.

A similar verdict of 'controversial, imaginative but incompetently executed' may well be history's verdict upon the exchange rate policy of the present Conservative government in the UK, which seems to have regarded the exchange rate as a transmission mechanism for its monetary policies (see Gowland (1982a), p. 186). The government's hope was that the effect of the exchange rate, both directly and via its effect on the money supply, would help to squeeze corporate liquidity and soreduce corporate spending, in particular to reduce the wage bill by reducing the wages per employee (below the level they otherwise would be). Some effect on output was anticipated, but it was believed that much of the effect of monetary policy would be on prices. Instead, corporate spending was also reduced by reducing employment and by reducing stock levels. In addition companies borrowed heavily from banks to offset the squeeze on their liquidity and so thwarted the objective of monetary restriction. Moreover, the reduction in stocks and in the numbers employed ensured that more of the remaining effects of monetary policy were on output than on price. This use of the exchange rate as both an instrument and transmission mechanism of monetary policy has been highly controversial – see Gould *et al.* (1981) for a savage partisan critique. Nevertheless, the policy was logically planned and reflected a keen awareness of the impact of exchange rates on the domestic economy. Moreover, there is some support for the policy in the Bank of England's model of the economy in which exchange rates are the main transmission mechanism of monetary policy (Bank (1979)). The execution of the policy was, however, much less imaginative than the design.

In 1981-2, as the level of unemployment rose, the goverment became less enthusiastic about a high exchange rate and a slow drift down of the exchange rate was tolerated and even welcomed in some quarters. The issue became very topical in early December 1982. The pound came under very heavy pressure (and lost abut 7 per cent of its value, in terms of foreign exchange, in a week). This was partly inspired by an article in the *Sunday Times* (5 December), alleging that the government's Chief Economic Adviser wanted a depreciation to reduce unemployment. By coincidence, in the same week, the Shadow Chancellor unveiled Labour's economic policy, of which a key element was a 30 per cent depreciation of sterling to reduce unemployment. Mrs Thatcher responded with a speech (Friday, 10 December) in which she re-avowed her opposition to a lower exchange rate because it would mean a higher level of prices.

10.2 The Small Economy Model

Besides the indirect effect of the exchange rate on prices and employment considered above, there may also be direct effects. The simplest of these direct effects can best be analysed in the context of a small economy (see p. 112 above). This stems from the undoubted fact that a change in the price of competing goods will change the behaviour of the suppliers. If the price of Fiats and Renaults rises, BL are likely to take the opportunity to raise the price of their cars. The only question is by how much; there is no conceivable microeconomic theory which would deny some increase, although the traditional analysis argues that the effect is trivial. In a small economy where domestic producers are price takers at the world price, the analysis is simple, as all domestic producers face a horizontal marginal revenue curve at the world price expressed in the domestic currency, i.e. the dollar price divided by the exchange rate. When the exchange rate changes there will be an equivalent (but opposite) change in the price level, such that a 1 per cent appreciation will lead approximately to a 1 per cent fall in domestic prices. The mechanism is simple and is illustrated in Figure 10.1(a). This shows the cost and revenue curves for a typical producer of a good, say, leets, of which the world price is $1. Initially, the exchange rate is $2 = £1 so producers of leets face a horizontal marginal revenue curve at 50p (which is also their average revenue and demand curve), i.e. at the world price expressed in sterling. If the exchange rate falls to $1 = £1, the marginal revenue curve shifts upwards to £1 ($1 divided by the new exchange rate), but is still horizontal. The equilibrium price is now p_2 (£1) instead of p_1 (50p) and output has risen from q_1 to q_2 so presumably the firm is employing more workers. Hence the representative firm will raise its output, employment and price. As the same diagram illustrates every firm in the economy, the result can be generalised to a rise in aggregate output, a higher rate of inflation and a lower level of unemployment. This analysis led, in the 1960s, to a discussion of profit elasticities because, in the case of a small economy, the analysis had to concentrate on the effect of a change in profits on output and so on the balance of payments, rather than examine the impact of changes in relative prices. This concept can easily be incorporated into the absorption approach; in which case depreciation could increase output, as well as expenditure.

This 'small economy' case, however, ignores the fact that a change in the exchange rate will affect costs. For an individual firm, costs can be divided into wages, purchases from abroad and purchases of domestic

Figure 10.1: A Small Economy

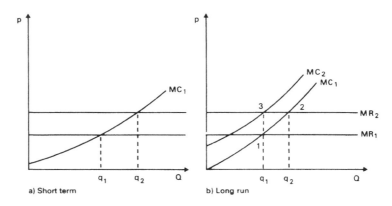

a) Short term

b) Long run

Depreciation increases output only in the short term

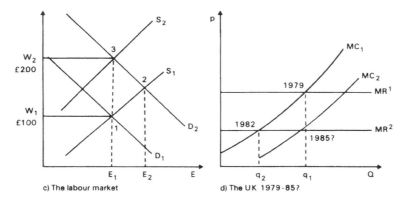

c) The labour market

d) The UK 1979-85?

inputs. However, by familiar national income analysis, the latter costs can in turn be decomposed until all costs are either wages or purchases of imports. The domestic currency price of imports will rise *pari passu* with the depreciation and so shift the marginal cost upwards. If all costs were outlays on imports, the marginal cost curve would shift from MC_1 to MC_2 in Figure 10.1(b) such that the output fell to the original level. This shift would occur because the upward parallel movement in the marginal cost curve would be exactly the same as in the price level. Thus, there will only be a long-term increase in output if wages rise by less than the price of imports, i.e. by less than the price level. This is a restatement of Johnson's proposition discussed above (p. 113) that devaluation has to reduce real wages if it is to improve the balance of payments. However, unless there is money illusion, on conventional assumptions, wages will rise by the same amount as prices. If the supply of labour is a function of real wages, it will shift upwards following the rise in prices, as from S_1 to S_2 in Figure 10.1(c). The demand for labour is a derived demand and will shift outwards from D_1 to D_2, following the shift of the marginal revenue curve in 10.1(a). The shifts are such that wages will double (for the hypothetical halving of the exchange rate) and employment will return to the original level, E_1.

Hence, as wages per worker rise by the same amount as imports, Figure 10.1(b) represents the long-term reaction of the firm producing leets to a depreciation from \$2 = £1 to \$1 = £1. The firm's equilibrium moves over time from 1 to 2 to 3 on both 10.1(b) and 10.1(c) such that it originally charges 50p, produces q_1 and employs E_1 workers at £100 per week each. In the short term, the depreciation raises output to q_2 and employment to E_2 as well as price to £1, so (generalising) the higher price level has induced more jobs. However, the final equilibrium has q_1 output and E_1 jobs, so there is a doubling of wages and prices but no change in real magnitude. This can be generalised to a trade-off between a short-term unemployment and a permanent rise in employment of the type hypothesised by Friedman (for different reasons, see Gowland (1982b), Chapter 4). The Labour Party's argument for a 30 per cent depreciation could be presented within this framework but Peter Shore would no doubt argue that an incomes policy would be able to prevent wages from rising by as much as import prices.

This model can also be used to present the London Business School analysis of the UK economy, 1979-85, Figure 10.1(d). The effect of an appreciation is the mirror image of that of a depreciation. Thus, in the short term, the rise in the exchange rate in 1979-80 led to a fall in output and in inflation, i.e. the economy's position in 1982. However, in the long term (1985?), output will recover to its trend level. The London Business School, as a matter of prescription, seem to feel that the short-term output cost is excessive relative to the long-term inflation gain; at least their media presentations have argued that the exchange rate rose by too much in 1979-80. In this respect international monetarists then felt that Mrs Thatcher was over-restrictive, whereas orthodox monetarists felt that monetary growth was excessive. The 16 per cent fall in the UK exchange rate in the last three months of 1982 was equally controversial.

10.3 Exchange Rates, Wages and Prices in a Large Economy

In a large open economy there will still be a direct relationship between the exchange rate and the price level. There is no doubt that a depreciation will have an effect on the overall price level. Imports are a component of final demand, so as a depreciation, barring very strange circumstances, must increase the price of imports in domestic currency, it must increase the domestic price level. If imports are 40 per cent of final demand, a 10 per cent depreciation increases prices (GDP deflator or RPI) by 4 per cent, using a base-weighted price index. The controversy is about the effect on the prices of domestically produced goods. The change in the price of competing goods will also lead to a change in price as in the small economy, but in a more complex fashion. The demand curve for the products of most domestic firms will be downward sloping. A depreciation (appreciation) will shift this outwards (inwards), but not necessarily by a parallel amount nor necessarily the same amount for each firm as in the small economy. Nevertheless, the direction of change is the same.

An equally simple result can be derived for oligopoly in which case either price leadership or conscious parallelism will lead to a similar matching of domestic to international price, so long as one (or more) importers are price leaders. Alternatively, the devaluation may act as a signal for a price change in more complex models. It is often argued that oligopolies require some signal before all firms are confident that rivals are likely to imitate a price increase. Depreciation is an almost perfect signal.

It is clear that a depreciation will raise the cost of imported inputs; raw materials, semi-manufactured and other intermediate goods. This rise in costs, shifting marginal cost curves to the right, will lead to a rise in price almost irrespective of assumptions about market situations and elasticity. The exception involves a bizarre (and probably illogical) combination of extreme cases, including perfectly inelastic demand and zero income elasticities. However, the rise in costs is unlikely to lead to a rise in prices by an amount equivalent to the depreciation. Costs rise by (the proportion of imported inputs to total costs) times (depreciation), i.e. only by a fraction of the depreciation. Prices themselves will rarely rise by as much as costs.

The cost effect could interact with the demand effect above to produce a price rise as large as, or even larger than, the depreciation. To obtain a substantial independent cost effect, however, it is necessary to make additional assumptions. The best way of showing a *pari passu* cost effect is to use a 'cost-push' model of inflation in which trade unions bargain for real wages and can ensure that any rise in prices is matched by an equivalent rise in wages and in which firms pass on all cost increases, i.e. some form of mark-up pricing. In this case there will be an effect on domestic prices from both the rise in costs and the rise in price of imported final goods. Either would be sufficient to ensure a rise in prices equivalent to the depreciation. For simplicity each effect will be analysed separately, although they interact. If imports are 20 per cent of final consumption, then a 10 per cent depreciation will raise the price level by 2 per cent. This will lead to a rise of 2 per cent in wages which (as for simplicity it is assumed that there are no imported inputs) will lead to a rise of 2 per cent in the price of domestically produced goods, i.e. 1.6 per cent on the price level (domestically produced goods are 80 per cent of final consumption). Wages rise by 1.6 per cent and so on until wages and prices are both 10 per cent higher. More generally, if imports are $\frac{1}{z}$ of final consumption, prices rise by $(\frac{1}{z}.d)$ where d is the depreciation, then wages by $(\frac{1}{z}.d)$, prices by $(1 - \frac{1}{z})$ $(\frac{1}{z}.d)$, wages by this amount and so on. The eventual change in prices is the sum to infinity of a geometric series, whose initial term is $(\frac{1}{z}.d)$ and whose common ratio is $(1 - \frac{1}{z})$. This sum is d. Alternatively, if all of $(C + I + G)$ is domestically produced, but imports are $\frac{1}{y}$ of costs and wages, therefore $(1 - \frac{1}{y})$ of costs, then prices rise by $\frac{d}{y}$, wages by $\frac{d}{y}$, prices by $\frac{d}{y} (1 - \frac{1}{y})$, etc. Here the sum to infinity is again d. In fact both effects work together, but prices and wages will both rise by the same amount.

Similar results which do not rely on a cost-push model can be generated by a relationship between expected inflation and past change in prices, i.e. the standard modern model of inflation introduced by Friedman (see Gowland (1982b), Chapter 4). In this case the depreciation, by increasing the price level, raises inflationary expectations and so, *ceteris paribus*, both wages and prices. Depending upon the nature of the expectations formation mechanism and any second-round effects, prices may rise by less than, as much as, or more than the depreciation. Indeed a devaluation could set off persistent inflation, as Laidler and Parkin (e.g. 1975) argued that the 1967 devaluation in the UK did.

Both the cost-push and expectations approaches may involve assumptions about trade union behaviour, although they can be derived from competitive models as well. Indeed, it can generally be argued that the response of trade unions to the rise in prices is crucial to the analysis of the effects of a devaluation. *If trade unions ensure that real wages remain constant a devaluation cannot increase competitiveness* and all prices must rise by the amount of the depreciation in large economies just as they do in small ones. Similar results follow if labour markets are competitive so long as the supply of labour is a function of real wages. It has therefore frequently been argued that *devaluation or depreciation can influence competitiveness only if there is money illusion* (see p. 142 above), otherwise the depreciation will change behaviour in such a way that it generates equal rises in all wages and prices.

Attempts have been made to deny this, but none are very convincing. One argument is that trade unions (or atomistic workers) might accept a change in the exchange rate as a signal that real wages must fall. It has also been agued that an incomes policy would prevent the rises in wages predicted by economic analysis. The snag here, even ignoring historical evidence to the contrary, is that, if trade unions will accept a reduction in real wages, the gain in competitiveness will be achieved anyway and it is impossible to see why it should be easier to negotiate an incomes policy with a depreciation than without; common sense suggests the reverse. After all, a rise in the price level is not the ideal accompaniment to an incomes policy.

In general then, it seems that a depreciation will have a substantial direct effect on prices which will probably bring about at least as large a price rise as the depreciation. There are two important qualifications to be made: one is that the effects of an appreciation may not be as anti-inflationary as the effects of a depreciation are inflationary, and that, as a depreciation may bring about a short-term gain in competitiveness, successive, and increasing, depreciation might secure a permanent gain — at the price of accelerating inflation. France pursued such a policy with some success between 1949 and 1958 (excepting the period of Pinay's premiership). Timing is considered further in section 10.5 below.

Nevertheless, analysis of a large economy reinforces the small economy conclusions about the trade-off problem inherent in exchange rate policy. A decision about the optimal exchange rate reflects the valuation of the short-term level of employment against the long-term level of inflation.

10.4 The Scandinavian Model of Inflation

The analysis above did not distinguish between traded and non-traded goods, that is goods which do and do not face international competition. Obviously the distinction is over-simplified but it can be argued that the response of a chemical firm and a restaurant to devaluation is different, although cost-push and wage factors are common to both. A lot of modern research has gone into the analysis of such effects. One offshoot of this is the so-called Scandinavian model of inflation. This is a two-sector model of the economy in which there is a traded goods sector and a sheltered sector. The traded goods or open sector is subject to international competition and is a price taker at the prevailing world price. The sheltered sector, comprising non-traded goods and the public sector, sets wages according to the prevailing level in the traded goods sector and prices. Its prices are merely a mark-up over costs.

In this model, a depreciation leads to a *pari passu* increase in prices in the traded goods sector. As factors are paid their marginal revenue product in the open sector, wages will rise by the same amount. As prices and wages in alternative employment have both risen, there is an increase in wages in the sheltered sector. This leads to an increase in sheltered sector prices and so to further wage increases. A wage-price spiral ensues until wages and prices have risen by as much as in the open sector. The practical relevance of this model is questionable. The author is a sceptic, but it is presented both because it is a further example of the impact of exchange rates on the economy and because it shows how easily one can combine parts of different models to produce an allegedly more realistic whole: the open sector is an international monetarist model and the sheltered sector is a pure cost-push model.

10.5 The 'J' Curve Model

There are two reasons for analysis of the 'J' curve model. One is that it extends the analysis of the previous sections in considering the interrelationship between domestic prices and the exchange rate. Further, it is an explicitly dynamic model of the balance of payments. The absorption and traditional theories were only comparative static models of equilibrium and, while the monetary theory was a model of disequilibrium, it was certainly not dynamic. The model is set out in Figure 10.2 which traces the movement of the balance of payments over time. The path approximates to the letter 'J' − hence the name of the model. The model is basically a dynamic version of the traditional elasticities theory; it does not incorporate income or monetary effects, but it does incorporate the direct effects of 10.1 above. The times cited are from former versions of the Treasury model (see Gowland (1979), pp. 51 and 73).

Figure 10.2: 'The 'J' Curve

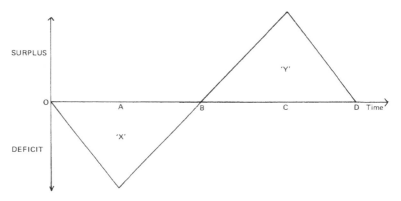

At time O the government devalues or provokes a depreciation of its currency. Initially the balance of payments worsens, the deterioration continues until 'A', about three months in the case of the UK. The reason for this deterioration is that in the short term volumes are fixed, by contractual or other relationships. Morever it is assumed that most, if not all exports are invoiced in the currency of origin. (This seems to be a valid assumption, see Williamson, Wood and Carse (1980).) That is, UK exports are priced in sterling, German exports (UK imports) in Marks, etc. Together, the two factors mean that the sterling value of exports is fixed (so the foreign currency value falls). The foreign currency value of imports is also fixed, so the sterling value rises. Thus, whether the balance of payments is measured in sterling or in a foreign currency, it deteriorates because, as the short-term elasticities are taken to be zero for contractual or other reasons, the Marshall-Lerner condition is not fulfilled.

After 'A', the balance of payments improves as volumes adjust to the new relative prices, at least if Marshall-Lerner is satisfied. After 'B' the effect is positive. ('B' is at about nine months according to those who estimated 'J' curves for the UK.) After a while, however, the rises in costs, expectations and the rest start to erode the gain in competitiveness. Hence the improvement reaches a peak at 'C' (15 months). Thereafter, the balance of payments deteriorates until at 'D' (27 months) it is back to its original level. However, while the long-run effect on the balance of payments is zero, there is an effect on the reserves (or UK holdings of overseas assets). From O − C, a cumulative deficit of X was experienced, compared, that is, to the position if there had been no depreciation. From C − D a surplus of Y was experienced, again compared to the no depreciation position. Thus there has been a net improvement in the cumulative current balance of $(Y - X)$; $(Y - X)$ could be negative but this is unlikely if the estimates of 'A', 'B', 'C' and 'D' cited above are accurate.

This 'J' curve model is special in that it assumes an exact relationship between depreciation and increases in domestic prices; e.g. the Laidler-Parkin argument is denied. It also assumes that trade flows respond faster to price changes than trade unions. It is possible to produce variants of 'J' curves in which effects are permanent and usually negative, or in which the balance of payments is always worse than if there had been no depreciation (see Gowland (1979), p. 50). Either would increase the instability of the foreign exchange market and justify intervention (see p. 135 above). An optimist could use 'J' curve analysis to justify a devaluation every 15 months; the balance of payments would always be better after the first nine months; but he or she would need nerves of steel since a slight miscalculation or variation in the parameters of the model and the balance of payments would always be worse.

10.6 Devaluation and the Terms of Trade

The terms of trade are the opportunity cost of imports in terms of exports, that is their relative price measured in the same currency. There has been much debate about the effect of depreciation of the currency on the terms of trade. The argument depreciation reduced real income by worsening the terms of trade was advanced as an argument against devaluation in the 1960s in the UK (see Beckerman (1972), p. 16). It has been advanced as an argument in favour of tariffs rather than devaluation as a device to improve the balance of payments that the former improves and the latter worsens the terms of trade, and that this difference outweighs any welfare effects of a tariff.

The effect of a devaluation or any other depreciation on the terms of trade depends upon the effect of the depreciation upon the domestic price level and the price of exports. If the price of all domestically produced goods including exports rises by as much as the (domestic currency) price of imports, there cannot be a change in the terms of trade. In the case of a small economy, by definition unable to change its terms of trade, a depreciation necessarily raises export prices (and domestic import substitutes) by the amount equivalent to the depreciation. In the case of a large economy, a depreciation, according to traditional analysis, necessarily worsened the terms of trade, by lowering the foreign currency price of exports leaving the foreign currency price of imports unchanged (or increasing the domestic currency price of imports leaving export prices constant). More modern analysis as predicted above suggests that while this is possible it may be only a short-term phenomenon.

10.7 Optimal Currency Areas

The relationship between exchange rates and unemployment led to the concept of an optimal currency area largely pioneered by McKinnon, e.g. in Cooper (1969) pp. 223-36. The subsequent literature may often seem arcane but it has been usefully applied both to the EEC and in analysing regional policy. The concept is based on the valid notion that, in effect, fully fixed exchange rates create a common currency. If two currencies are fixed for ever and are believed to be fixed for ever, there is no difference between holding one and the other. It is simply a matter of convenience, like a decision whether to have five one-pound notes or one five-pound note. Hence, an argument for a'world-wide fully fixed exchange rate regime is an argument for a common world currency. The optimal currency area literature seeks to find criteria to decide what is the right area within which there should be a common currency, or fixed exchange rate. This might be wider than or smaller than existing nation states. McKinnon based his criteria largely on factor mobility. Exchange rates should be fixed within the area within which factors are immobile. Since then wider criteria have been developed.

It is argued that regional problems have been aggravated or even caused by over-large currency areas. The north-east of England, or Puerto Rico, might have less unemployment if they had their own currencies. Separate currencies for the 'snow' and 'sun' belts might have reduced the adjustment costs experienced in the US since 1970 by the faster growth of the latter relative to the former. If a region has a balance of payments deficit with the rest of the country, this will cause unemployment. If the area were able to reduce its real wages, or if labour were mobile, then the unemployment would be eliminated by an inflow of capital and/or an outflow of labour. In practice neither happens for obvious reasons and the cumulative process of deflation and balance of payments deficits continues — so it is argued — for centuries. If the north-east region could devalue the Tyneside pound against the London and Yorkshire pounds, this might, according to one's preferred theory, achieve all or any of the following: reduce real wages; eliminate the deficit; boost real income in Tyneside. In any case it would eliminate the problem. Within a nation state separate currencies are impossible, but it has been argued that labour subsidies might be a substitute for devaluation. 'Surplus' regions suffer unnecessary inflation in consequence of an inappropriate link, since the surplus earned by the south-east will lead to inflation by the inverse of the reason why Tyneside's deficit causes unemployment.

The argument is relevant to those currency unions which transcend national boundaries. In January 1979 the Republic of Ireland broke the link with sterling which had existed since 1921 because it believed Irish economic problems would be eased (a £600 million douceur from Germany and the EEC commission may also have influenced this action). According to the *Economist* (10 August 1982) powerful forces within Luxemburg wish to break the link with the Belgian franc; in this case Luxemburg is a net exporter but suffers (Belgian) inflation in consequence. Critics of the EEC's desire to create a common currency believe it would cause mass unemployment outside the 'golden triangle' (Paris basin, Ruhr, Rhine Valley and possibly that part of northern Italy near the Transalpine tunnels).

Note

1. For larger depreciations, the equivalent, or *pari passu*, increase in prices is not the same as the depreciation. If the exchange rate falls from $2 = £1 to $1 = £1, this is a 50 per cent depreciation, but the sterling price of American goods will double, because $1 is worth £1 instead of 50 cents. Thus the appreciation of the dollar is 100 per cent for a 50 per cent depreciation of sterling. An equivalent rise in prices is by the amount of the appreciation of the foreign currency (dollar) not the depreciation of the home currency (sterling), i.e. by the amount by which the price of foreign goods rises in sterling.

11 INTERNATIONAL FINANCE

11.1 Introduction

International finance is concerned with the mechanics of international transactions. Thus, in Chapters 9 and 10 there was a discussion of the goals of foreign exchange policy but in this chapter (11.2) the means of intervention are considered. Much of international finance is concerned with loans, so the availability of credit to nations, and the size of their reserves, is the crucial issue in international finance (11.3). This leads to a discussion of the demand for reserves (11.4). In Chapters 12 and 13 specific institutional arrangements are discussed, broadly the public sector ones in Chapter 12 and the private sector in Chapter 13.

11.2 Methods of Speculation and Intervention

Speculation and intervention have been discussed above but there was no consideration of how speculation or intervention are executed. Speculation can be defined as any transaction designed to yield a profit in the event that the exchange rate changes in the direction predicted by the speculator. *En passant*, such a transaction is no more irrational or wicked than any other profit-maximising act. Intervention is any operation carried out by a government designed to lead to a level of exchange rate different to that which would otherwise occur. Strictly and logically, a tariff, exchange control or even alterations in long-term interest rates, taxation and monetary policy might be called means of intervention, since they should all influence the exchange rate through the balance of payments. However, they are not conventionally thought of in this way so in this discussion intervention will be restricted to devices which will affect the exchange rate without any change in the basic or overall balance of payments, current account plus long-term capital. Most of the means of speculation parallel those of intervention. This arises in part because intervention is designed to reduce (or offset the effect of) speculation and also because in a sense intervention and speculation are the same thing, but with different motives and executed by different agents.

Both speculation and intervention can occur in the *spot market*. The speculator sells his holdings of the currency whose value he expects to fall and buys that which he expects to rise. He will normally choose to invest the proceeds in a bank deposit or other security denominated in the relevant currency. This procedure has obvious disadvantages. It is impossible to speculate 'against' a currency not already held. However certain you are that the lira will fall against the dollar, you cannot profit from this belief by spot market speculation unless you hold lira to sell. Moreover, the amount of speculation is limited to the speculator's wealth and, in practice. to his holdings of liquid assets. A company is unlikely, may be unable to, sell some of its UK assets merely to speculate against the pound. It is ludicrous, for example, to imagine Ford selling Dagenham because they wish to engage in foreign speculation. In general then, spot market speculation is rigid, limited in extent and, therefore, not very common.

As a means of intervention, there are similar limits to the use of the spot market. A government, or its central bank, can use its foreign exchange reserves to buy its currency or sell some of its own currency in exchange for foreign currency and thereby influence the price, i.e. the exchange rate. In practice such transactions usually involve either the purchase or sale of dollars. In the 1960s, by convention all intervention was in dollars; a convention very occasionally breached. Since 1970, the scale of intervention involving third currencies has grown, but it is still fairly small. The authority considering how to intervene faces restrictions similar to the speculator. It may not have very large foreign exchange reserves and it may not wish to use them. A large part of its reserves could be in currencies against which its exchange rate is at the desired level, so a sale would be undesirable. Alternatively, it might be viewed as an unfriendly act by the central bank of the currency concerned. If the UK is engaged in intervention to support the pound, a large sale of sterling by the Belgians to support their franc would not be very welcome. Central banks, on the whole successfully, seek to maintain good relations amongst themselves and so would not normally act in this way. A central bank/government could borrow the strong currency in order to sell it, but there are problems in doing this so alternatives are sought whenever possible. Obviously a central bank does not face any restriction on the amount of its own currency it sells; it can always create more. Nevertheless, this will lead to expansion of the money supply, which could easily wreck its monetary policy as the German, Swiss and UK authorities have all discovered. So, there are practical limits; in theory the money-creating effects of intervention can be sterilised by an equivalent offsetting open market operation. In practice sterilisation is rarely a viable operation.

Hence the authorities and the speculators would prefer an alternative forum for their operations. The most obvious is the *forward market*. The speculator can sell forward and profit, or lose, by any subsequent change in exchange rates. If, on 1 January, a speculator sells £1 million sterling forward for, say, delivery in three months.at, e.g. $1.75, he is committed to delivering £1 million on 31 March. In exchange he will receive $1.75 million. If the spot exchange rate is $1.60, he can buy £1 million for $1.6 million and so make a profit of $150,000. (On the other hand, if the rate is $1.80 he makes a loss of $50,000.) The main problems of forward sales are the rigidity imposed by the fixed date of the contract and the fact that forward discounts are often very large on weak currencies, i.e. those expected to depreciate. The latter problem can be such as to eliminate any possibility of speculative profit — a 6 per cent forward discount is common, 10 per cent not unknown. The other disadvantage is that the contract can be exercised only on the named day. The spot exchange rate in the above example might be $1.70 on 28 March but $1.75 on 31 March so the speculator cannot profit, although right in his belief that sterling would fall. He might, if the spot and one-week forward rates (for simplicity) were both $1.70 on 24 March, either:

1. borrow $1.7 million spot and buy £1 million. He has then secured a profit of £50,000, less interest paid on his dollar loan plus interest he may receive on £1 million for a week;
2. buy £1 million forward for a week and so match his obligation to deliver £1 million on 31 March with a receipt of £1 million. His dollar obligation of $1.7 million is less than his dollar receipt of $1.75 million, so his profit is secure.

Both these are clumsy, however, and may not always be possible; there is no eleven-day forward market, for example. In this respect a forward market is less flexible than a *futures* or *options* market in which the right to buy or sell at a prescribed price on a specific day is traded. The right to buy £1 for $1.70 is worth 10 cents if the spot rate is $1.80, so, if on 1 January one expects a rate of $1.80 on 31 March, it would be worth paying 5 cents for the right to buy at $1.70. If in February the spot rate is $2, it should be possible to sell the option or 'future' for 15 or 20 cents. However, financial futures only came into existence in the mid-1970s, pioneered in Chicago, and the market was on an insignificant scale until 1980 and is still of limited scope. A private individual might be able to satisfy his requirements in this way but a large multi-national company could not and in any case transactions costs in this market are fairly substantial.

Central banks do not deal in futures but forward market intervention has been very common, following, but not necessarily because of, Keynes's prescription (1923). The argument for forward market intervention depends upon the existence of interest *arbitrageurs* (see p. 122 above). The basic *modus operandi* is to induce *arbitrageurs* to buy or sell your currency, since this secures the benefits of spot intervention without costs. A higher forward premium (or lower discount) will lead to increased demand for the currency and a lower forward premium (or bigger discount) to a reduced demand. *Ceteris paribus*, this change in demand should ensure a changed spot rate. These arguments will be illustrated by an example. Originally the interest parity condition is satisfied, with the dollar interest rate (RN) at 10 per cent, the sterling interest rate (RL) at 12 per cent, the spot rate at £1 = $2 and the one year forward rate £1 = $1.964. Both direct and indirect (see p. 121 above) investments in dollars yield 10 per cent and in sterling 12 per cent. The UK authorities now offer forward contracts in unlimited quantities at $1.98 = £1, i.e. they offer to agree to buy sterling offered in twelve months' time at $1.98. If an *arbitrageur* borrows $2 million he will have to repay $2.2 million in one year's time. He can convert the $2 million into £1 million and invest it so as to receive £1.12 million. If he sells £1.12 million forward he will receive $2,217,600. Hence he would make a net profit of $17,600. To obtain this he has taken advantage of the authorities' forward sterling purchases but, crucially, *he has bought £1 million of spot sterling*. This should raise the exchange rate until a new equilibrium is reached at about $2.017 = £1, when the interest parity condition is again satisfied. Hence, the authorities can influence the exchange rate without engaging in any spot transactions themselves.

Keynes ingeniously pointed out that this operation was costless if carried out on a sufficiently large scale. If the authorities peg the rate and then offer unlimited forward cover so as to maintain the rate for ever, they will never lose; indeed they will often make a large profit. In the above example, if by intervention in the forward market the rate is held at or above $2, then the authorities forward transactions yield a profit of over 2 cents per pound of transaction since they will buy in twelve months' time for $1.98 a pound worth at least $2. Unfortunately this Keynesian argument depends upon a virtually unlimited and successful operation. If the authorities chicken out or change their mind about the optimal rate, the cost can be staggering, for example if the rate cannot be held or if $1.80 becomes the optimal rate. In the real world, for example, nearly all the Bank of England's £356 million losses in 1967 were the result of forward market operations. The experience led a prominent central banker to say that Keynes's theory was like doubling up on black at roulette; it was theoretically impeccable but his nerves were not up to it. A further and crucial disadvantage of forward market operations is that they reduce the cost of forward market speculation, by reducing the forward discount on weak currencies and increasing the premium on strong ones.

Hence the forward market is not an ideal medium for either speculator or central bank. Therefore most speculation is now carried out via the overnight money markets. If a speculator borrows overnight in sterling, converts the proceeds into dollars and invests them in the overnight inter-bank dollar market, this offers an opportunity of profit if sterling depreciates, but involves the loss of the difference between the sterling interest rate and the dollar interest rate. Nevertheless, this loss is usually much lower than a comparable forward discount. This method is much more flexible than a forward contract, as one may renew the forward borrowing and lending daily. Thus the speculator has the chance to 'close out' his position on any day simply by not lending or borrowing for a further period.

Intervention by the authorities in the overnight inter-bank market is the most common technique, at least in the UK. By various devices, the authorities can engineer a squeeze in this market and force the interest rate up, often to over 100 per cent (see Gowland (1982a), p. 108). This directly raises the cost of speculation, since the speculator pays a higher rate on his borrowing. This is in marked contrast to forward market intervention which lowers the speculation costs. More importantly, the authorities will induce *arbitrageurs* to buy spot sterling (or sell it if the inter-bank rate is lowered). This time it is the domestic interest rate term in the parity equation which is raised and again the spot rate responds to arbitrage purchases, which should restore eqilibrium.

The last method of speculation, called '*leads and lags*', consists of deferring payments due to be made in a currency which is expected to depreciate (and accelerating them in one expected to appreciate). In this case a profit is made because, if the weak currency falls, the cost of paying one's bill is reduced. If one is due to pay £100 in June, when the exchange rate is $2, and actually pays in September, when it is $1, an American saves $100. Similarly a Briton due to pay $100 in September saves £50 by paying in June. Many holiday-makers practise this before going on holiday. If anyone purchases marks a few weeks in advance of a German holiday, or hangs on to marks for a few weeks after their return, they are hoping to profit from an exchange rate change. Similarly, if a purchase of lira for an Italian holiday is delayed until the last minute (or sterling travellers' cheques taken to Italy), this is a perfect example of lagging.

11.3 The Optimal Level of International Liquidity

The concept of international liquidity is not a very precise one but it has two main aspects:

1. the quantity of reserves held by all the world's central banks and/or governments;
2. the credit facilities open to them whereby they can borrow additional foreign currency.

Opinion has been sharply divided about whether the quantity of world liquidity has been inadequate. The largely Anglo-American school who believe that liquidity has been inadequate have proposed a variety of schemes to make available much easier and more extensive borrowing or to create extra reserves. The mechanism is sometimes complex but, in principle, international money can be created just as easily as a central bank can create domestic money. The other school believes that too much liquidity is already in existence and that the excess has produced very adverse effects.

The inadequate school have usually argued that liquidity is inadequate by using one of the following arguments:

1. *Liquidity is insufficient to finance international trade. In extremis*, someone wishes to buy something from, or sell something to, a non-resident but cannot because it is impossible to finance the transaction. Evidence of actual transactions that are not carried out because of a shortage of foreign exchange are rare but, in any case, usually it is assumed that (1) follows from either (2) or (3).
2. *Nations cannot finance (current account) balance of payments deficits*. The argument is that some nations, e.g. Britain in the 1960s or countries in the Third World, would like to have balance of payments deficits on current account but cannot borrow enough to have

them. Hence, they have to eliminate them in an unpalatable fashion. A variation of this is that they cannot finance a sufficiently long adjustment period. It might be optimal to eliminate a balance of payments deficit over five years, but if insufficient credit is available it may have to be eliminated in three years in a sub-optimal fashion.

3. *World liquidity has grown less fast than international trade.* This argument is that world liquidity is needed to finance world trade and that it has grown less quickly than world trade.

The counter argument starts by arguing that conventional measures of international liquidity are misleading because they take no account of the growth of the Eurocurrency market (see Chapter 13 below). Moreover, they then launch an all-out onslaught on the arguments of their opponents. The centrepiece of their argument is that *the insufficiency school has revived all the fallacies of the 'real bills' doctrine and so ignored all Keynesian and monetarist insights into economic behaviour.* The 'real bills' doctrine was the domestic equivalent of arguments (1), (2) and (3) above and was refuted by Ricardo in the early nineteenth century. No one tried to defend it in the UK after about 1850 nor in the US after the establishment of the Federal Reserve. The 'real bills' doctrine was that credit was insufficient if real transactions could not be financed, i.e. if there were insufficient credit for the 'needs of trade', to use an alternative term sometimes favoured by this group. The similarity to argument (1) above is obvious. Variants on (2) and (3) were also used by 'real bills' advocates; e.g. individuals and firms could not finance their deficits (e.g. investment plans that exceeded income) and that the money supply and/or volume of credit should grow as fast as nominal income. *The argument of the excess school is based on an application of very elementary macroeconomics to the world as a whole*, so it is best analysed by looking at the domestic case and then considering its wider application.

It is easy to refute the 'real bills' doctrine, that credit should always be available to finance a real transaction. A simple example concerns two bidders for a unique antique vase at an auction; a slightly unusual auction in that negotiations with bankers take place between bids. A bids £100 but B, who has only £50, can then legitimately approach his bank and say, "If you lend me £60 I will be able to buy the vase for £110.' This is a real transaction, so the loan is desirable according to the 'real bills' doctrine. A, with £100 cash, can then put exactly the same argument for a £20 loan to enable him to buy the vase for £120.

Then B could request a larger loan and so on *ad infinitum*. The only effect of easy credit is to drive the price of the vase ever higher. At all times one party is unable to finance a real transaction. More realistic examples are easy to construct, whereby loans to purchase goods drive the price of the good up. A real-world case is the UK housing market in 1972-3; see Gowland (1982a), pp. 128-34.

The monetarist therefore argues that the existence of a real trans-action is irrelevant to whether a loan is desirable. What matters is its effects upon the level of price and output. This is best measured by the quantity of money. Argument (3) is relevant here but clearly the money supply can grow less quickly than nominal income and still be infla-tionary, e.g. Germany in 1922-3.

The argument can be restated in a Keynesian style by looking at proposition (2) about the finance of deficits. A desire to run a deficit on current account means that the nation wishes to demand more goods than it supplies. If desired deficits exceed desired surpluses, there will be excess demand for goods which would mean a rise in price (or out-put). It is impossible for excess demand to be satisfied without a change in price and loans which create excess demand may be inflationary. The Keynesian version is even simpler. A planned surplus is a planned (net) withdrawal; a planned deficit is a planned (net) injection. Actual injec-tions will equal actual withdrawals. If plans are inconsistent, income will adjust to make them consistent. Hence, if planned deficits exceed planned surpluses, someone will have to change their plans. The plans may be changed by a lack of credit (as the deficiency school argue) or by a higher level of income. Whether it is desirable to extend credit depends upon whether the change in income is desirable.

Hence the 'excess' school argue rightly that the quantity of inter-national liquidity should be judged on macroeconomic criteria. A higher level of liquidity would increase world inflation but could also increase world output and employment. Opinions differ about whether the world balance of inflation and unemployment has been right or wrong and, in particular, about the extent to which inflation in the 1960s has caused unemployment since. The arguments are extensions of domestic macroeconomics and are left to the reader to resolve for himself or herself.

Some debates on world liquidity have been *ad hominem*. Germans, who would lose by inflation, have argued that the economists from the deficit nations (US and UK) have argued for policies which would bene-fit their own nations and vice versa. Polemics apart, this illustrates the genuine conflict of interest; the level of liquidity will be too high for a nation with a planned surplus when it is far too low for a nation with a planned deficit. A higher level of prices will put the costs on the former, a lower level of output on the latter.

Other arguments about the quantity of liquidity concern its distribution, both between different countries and different types of liquidity. The argument about distribution is that the overall quantity may be right but that some nations have too large a proportion of the world's liquidity and some too little. This is particularly relevant to Third World countries, who certainly have very little liquidity. However, the problem is one of insufficient wealth, income and resources rather than liquidity *per se*. Easy credit is not necessarily of much value to a poor nation; it may actually intensify its problems. These countries are not so much short of foreign currency as of the goods it could buy; an important distinction.

The argument about types of liquidity is more complex in that the same facts lead to opposite conclusions. There is an argument that, at least on occasions, an excessive proportion of world liquidity was in the form of dollars and that most nations held more dollars than they wanted. One group argued that the effective quantity of international liquidity was very much reduced. Comparison could be made with an internal bank failure. If a bank fails, its notes and deposits are worthless and an expansionary monetary policy is needed to deal with the problem.

The hard money school argued the reverse, citing Gresham's law, that international liquidity needed to be restricted. Nations would attempt to get rid of 'bad money' and would hang on to 'good', as Gresham argued, so only bad money would circulate. The attempt to dispose of bad money (dollars) would be inflationary. Restoring value to 'bad money' by a tighter US monetary policy was essential to the health of the system (see e.g. Smith (1982)).

11.4 The Demand for Reserves

The argument in 11.3 was that (domestic closed economy) macroeconomics should be applied to the world as a whole. In particular, elementary monetarist and Keynesian analysis was applied to the optimum quantity of liquidity. The logical extension seems to be to estimate a demand-for-reserves function so as to generate a world LM curve. Machlup has argued (1969) that the effort is pointless since the 'cloakroom theory' suffices. This is that nations will always want more reserves. The demand is for the previous level plus a small increase (the name is from an analogy with a woman who irrespective of the number of dresses in her wardrobe (cloakroom) would like one more). Less cynical economists have tried to estimate demand functions based on the conventional demand for money; Clark (1970), for example, attempted to apply a Tobin-Baumol model to the problem.

Utilising demand-for-money theory, one can group variables that might influence the demand for reserves according to the level of income/transactions; the return forgone by holding reserves and the rate of return on reserves, the opportunity cost and benefit of holding reserves.

1. *Income/Volume of transaction*
   (a)   GDP
   (b)   level of imports
   These are both straightforward.

2. *Rate of return on competitive assets*
   (a)   rate of return on real assets
   If a nation did not hold reserves it could use them to buy capital goods.
   (b)   rate of return on consumption
   As in (a), but the imports could be consumed. In this case the opportunity cost is the loss suffered by consuming later rather than now, the social rate of time preference (see Henderson (1969)).
   (c)   the rate of return on portfolio investment in the US
   (d)   long-term interest rates
   Any of (a) to (d) could be relevant depending upon what is perceived to be the alternative(s) to holding reserves.

3. *Rate of return on reserves*
   Reserves yield two benefits. The simplest is that they can earn interest if invested in a suitable medium, in practice this is
   (a)   US Treasury bill rate
   (b)   Eurodollar deposit rate
   (a) and (b) are comparable to the interest which is paid on bank deposits; the 'own rate'.

   The other benefit is that reserves can enable a nation to avoid having to deflate to remove a (current account) deficit. This benefit depends upon the cost of eliminating a deficit and its frequency.

4. *The marginal propensity to import*
   The cost of eliminating a deficit depends upon the marginal prospensity to import (MPM) since, in absorption theory, a deficit is eliminated by a change in expenditure equal to the reciprocal of the MPM times

the deficit (if the MPM = 0.2, a £500 million fall in expenditure is needed to reduce imports by £100 million).

5. *The variance of imports and/or exports*

If the long-run levels of exports and imports are equal, then short-run fluctuations in them will cause deficits. These are measured by such measures of dispersion as the variance.

Much work has been done to see which if any combination of these twelve variables best explains the observed pattern of reserve holding. The results are somewhat mixed but on the whole well-fitting functions have been discovered. It seems that the balance of payments variables (4 and 5) are relevant to the developed countries but not to the Third World. This suggests that Third World countries eliminate deficits by quantity controls (quotas, etc.) and do not use reserves to finance deficits. On the other hand, the transaction variables are relevant to Third World countries but not to the developed world. This suggests that the Third World Countries, or their citizens, do not have access to the sophisticated banking system which eliminates the need for transaction balances. Nevertheless, all such conclusions have proved to be of a tentative and preliminary nature.

12 THE INTERNATIONAL MONETARY SYSTEM

12.1 History

There are three major aspects to any international monetary system:

1. the exchange rate regime;
2. arrangements for co-operation between nations, in practice usually between their central bankers;
3. arrangements for loans to be extended to nations, either by other nations on a bilateral basis or multilaterally through an international agency.

Any analysis must concentrate on these, whether historical or descriptive or prescriptive. Analysts may also wish to differentiate between the way the system works and the formal mechanism, rather as constitutional scholars since Bagehot have distinguished the 'efficient' from the 'dignified', the reality from the formal system.

The modern history of the international monetary system starts with the Bretton Woods conference of 1944, which was a major part of the Anglo-American efforts to 'reconstruct' the world which also led to the formation of the UN, GATT and, at a domestic level, the National Health Service. Bretton Woods led to the establishment of the system which bore its name. The exchange rate regime was to be one of flexible parities, a semi-fixed system, described above, p. 120. The parities were to be adjusted in the event of 'fundamental disequilibrium' after a process of international consultation. In practice, this was a dead letter and the 'efficient part' of Bretton Woods was an informal understanding that par values would not be changed very often nor without an effort to avoid the change. In other words devaluation would not be an 'easy' or 'costless' option. The system was often called the dollar exchange system, as the parities were set in terms of dollars. Although this convention was a reflection of US dominance, it paradoxically meant that the US could not devalue without breaking the system up.

International co-operation would be effected through two new institutions, the International Monetary Fund, IMF, and the International Bank for Reconstruction and Development, always known as the World Bank. As wags have always been fond of noting, the World Bank was a fund and the IMF a bank. The World Bank existed to make loans, on commercial terms, for development projects initially in Europe but later almost exclusively in the Third World. It has been very successful as has the soft-loan affiliate it spawned, the International Development Association, IDA. However as these two bodies are peripheral to the monetary system they will hereafter be ignored.

The IMF was also to serve as the body through whom loans were to be made. As the IMF is still of major importance, its structure and the peculiar mechanism by which it extends credit is described below in section 12.2. This system was established at the end of World War II. However, the practical workings of the system were dominated until 1957-8 by three related 'brute facts'.

12.1.1 American Dominance

This was the era of overwhelming US military supremacy and economic dominance. To a very considerable extent the US ran the world, with occasional assistance from Bevin over the Marshall plan, or deft obstruction from Attlee (Korea) or Eden (Indo-China) designed to avert war. The UK was still a major power but no other Western nation counted. The IMF has always reflected the reality of power, so it was in some sense a front-man for the US Treasury which provided the dollars it lent. The co-operation within the system was provided by American leadership and loans were, in effect, made by the US — whether through the Marshall plan and later variants, or the IMF.

12.1.2 The Dollar Shortage

This reflected (12.1.1); every nation but the US faced a balance of payments problem, or at least constraint, and the dollar was universally demanded and in short supply.

12.1.3 Restrictions on Transactions

This was a consequence of (12.1.2). Bretton Woods was supposed to involve convertibility of currencies, that is a French holder of sterling could change his pounds into dollars or marks. In practice even external convertibility was restricted until the late 1950s and savage restrictions on the movement of capital and goods were imposed — and enforced. In 1947 the US forced the UK government to make sterling convertible but the experiment was abandoned after five weeks and the ideal forgotten for a decade (see Worswick and Ady (1954) for the restrictions and the events of 1947 — chapters by Balogh (22), Sargent (23-4) and Ady (25) — and Dalton (1960) provides a detailed, vivid and illuminating description of the 'crisis' of 1947). These restrictions were associated with more restrictive policies on trade, see p. 30 above.

With a neatness rare in history all of these features disappeared in 1957-8 and a fundamentally different world monetary system arose. The US balance of payments swung into deficit on current account and the dollar shortage disappeared. The major European currencies all became convertible against the dollar and each other, at least for non-residents. In some places important steps towards convertibility had been taken earlier – e.g. the UK govenment's decision to support the transferable sterling exchange rate in 1955, but the major steps occurred in a brief period in 1957-8. US dominance did not disappear overnight but was slowly eroded by the reemergence of Germany under Adenauer, by growing Soviet might and by the steps taken towards a united Europe. Nevertheless, in 1957-8, the Russian sputnik dented US prestige; the EEC was founded and de Gaulle came to power in France, resolved to end American domination of Europe. In consequence central bank co-operation after 1957-8 was to take place against a background of conflicting interests and views between the US and continental Europe with a declining UK caught uneasily in the middle.

The major arguments arose over the persistent US and UK deficits. The dollar served as an international medium of exchange under Bretton Woods and sterling was still an international currency for historic reasons. Hence, US and UK current account deficits were financed by the creation of large quantities of dollars and pounds which the rest of the world had to accept. In effect as the creators of (international) money, the US (and to a lesser extent the UK) could behave like a domestic government. If it ran a deficit, this could be financed automatically by money creation. The consequence might be inflation but, whereas there are some checks on a government (e.g. elections), the German and French governments felt powerless to stem the flood of dollars and pounds.

The German-French complaints concerned the following.

12.1.4 Seignorage Profits

Money creation is highly profitable; a bank note costs about 5p to print but the issuer obtains goods in exchange worth, say, £10, depending on the note's denomination. This profit is called seignorage and, although the mechanism was complex, the US and UK benefited in a similar fashion. This especially irked the French as much of the seignorage profit was used to buy European assets. Authors grumbled about 'the American challenge' which would make American industry in Europe the world's third great power (Servan Schreiber (1969)). In essence, the French complaint was that the US was acquiring valuable assets in exchange for worthless pieces of paper and the UK was living beyond its income and settling its debts with worthless paper.

12.1.5 Inflation

In addition to the loss of real resources, the excess creation of liquidity led to inflation, see p. 158 above; or at least so the Franco-German group argued. The US and UK argued, of course, that unless they ran deficits liquidity would be inadequate so unemployment would rise.

However, the seignorage profits enjoyed by the US and UK were not costless. In principle they were liable to buy their liabilities back in either gold (for the US) or dollars (UK). Neither had anything like enough liquid assets to pay their liabilities. The US and UK had enjoyed bankers' profits but had avoided the bankers' responsibilities. The problem caused international tension when, in 1965, France announced its intention of refusing to increase its dollar holdings; any increase would be exchanged for gold at the $55 per ounce price fixed by President Roosevelt in 1935. The UK balance of current payments was in apparently permanent deficit, despite half-hearted deflation by the Wilson government in 1965-6. The US balance of payments was adversely affected by the Vietnam war from 1965 onwards. Finally, the growth of the Eurocurrency market was putting pressure on the adjustable parity system as the difficulty and the cost of maintaining fixed parities grew. However this was a minor factor until after 1968 (see below, p. 176).

Various 'band aids' were applied to the system. Large loans were extended to the UK who had to agree to repay in foreign currency; the end of seignorage profits. Large quantities of short-term sterling liabilities were in effect turned into medium-term foreign exchange liabilities by the Basle guarantees (see Blackaby (1976) especially p.3: 1-2 for details).

An ingenious scheme designed to solve several problems was the introduction of 'Special Drawing Rights', in 1967. These were linked in value to a so-called basket of currencies, an SDR is worth x cents and y pence and z pfennigs, etc. They were a form of international money created by the IMF and distributed amongst its members pro rata to their quotas, see below p. 169, approximately their wealth. This had various, inconsistent aspects to it:

1. Seignorage profits were distributed amongst all governments, not

restricted to two (US and UK), nor pre-empted by banks, as with Eurocurrency creation;

2. liquidity was increased, as the US and UK wanted;

3. SDRs were to *replace* dollars and sterling at least in part as the international medium of exchange.

(2) and (3) were apparently inconsistent, as some supporters believed they were increasing the quality of liquidity while others believed they were changing its composition with a view to reducing the total. If the IMF created world money, creation was expected to be less than if the US and UK created it.

These palliatives could not restore viability to the Bretton Woods system and it collapsed between 1967 and 1972. The collapse was marked by a series of events. First of all, the UK government was forced to devalue the pound in 1967. Then, in 1968, the London gold pool was suspended. This gold pool, supplied largely by the US, had kept the price of gold at $35 per ounce, the price fixed by Roosevelt. Thereafter, there was a free market price of gold which was to fluctuate wildly but was substantially higher than $35. The latter remained the official price (until it was raised to $42 in 1971) at which gold was valued in central banks' books. The official price became of less and less relevance throughout the 1970s. The devaluation of sterling and the suspension of the gold pool were body blows to the tottering Bretton Woods system but the knock-out punch was delivered by President Nixon in 1971. He announced a formal devaluation of the dollar which raised the official price of gold to $42 an ounce. More importantly his August measures (aptly called Nixon's Shokku by the Japanese) ended the system of semi-fixed exchange rates and introduced a period of dirty floating; convertibility of the dollar was suspended. An attempt was made to revive the Bretton Woods system by the Smithsonian agreement of December 1971, described by President Nixon as the 'greatest event in the history of the world'. This agreement produced a new set of parities and amended the Bretton Woods rules to permit fluctuations of 2 per cent on either side of the par values. The new scheme did not survive the UK government's decision to float in June 1972 and by March 1973 all the major currencies were floating. Henceforth, the exchange rate regime was to be one of dirty floating, modified by the regional schemes for adjustable parities of the EEC (see p. 173 below).

Attempts were to be made to restore adjustable parities during the 1970s. In particular a committee chaired by Sir Jeremy More proposed the 'Outline of Reform'. This proposed a 'wide bands' scheme of exchange rates which was effectively Bretton Woods with fluctuations of 10 per cent either side of parity rather than 1 per cent. This was rejected at the Kingston meeting of the IMF in 1976, because it was felt to incorporate the worst features of both Bretton Woods ('one-way options') and of 'dirty floating' (large short-term fluctuations). The committee had felt that it combined the flexibility of dirty floating with the advantages of fixed parities, not least for the IMF's internal workings.

The international monetary system had to adjust to the shock administered by OPEC's price increase of November 1973, see p. 6 above. The system required very little modification. IMF lending was expanded by the special facilities, discussed below, and by increasing 'quotas' so as to permit greater conventional lending, see below. The increased importance of the OPEC nations was recognised by an adjustment of power within OPEC. OPEC nations held very large balances with, mainly, New York and London banks. Some of these were 'Eurocurrencies', i.e. external holdings, but they were mainly 'domestic deposits', i.e. dollars deposits with New York banks or sterling ones with UK banks. The only institutional change was a series of gold auctions which started in 1975. The IMF had run short of hard currencies and solved the problem by auctioning its gold (on one occasion in the late 1960s the IMF found that it had only Australian dollars and Venezuelan bolivars available). Gold auctions solved various problems an attracted diverse support, because

1. they expanded the IMF's liquid resources;
2. the US viewed it as a step towards demonetising gold;
3. because of (2), the IMF could realise its gold holdings held in New York without it seeming to show a lack of confidence in the US;
4. some European and Arab states thought the auctions increased the role of gold in the international monetary system — the IMF (and central banks) had not dealt in gold since 1968 — and moreover some of them wanted to buy, or let their citizens buy, the gold;
5. as the gold was on the IMF's books at $42 and was sold at market prices a profit ensued which was handed over to the IDA for lending to Third World countries; this received their support for the scheme;
6. the gold price was to some extent managed by the timing of the sales.

A large number of grandiose reforms were proposed in the late

1970s, all involving some combination of the gold standard, fixed parities, the creation of more SDRs (either to replace dollars already held or to increase Third World reserves or just to enable the IMF to lend more) and the creation of new international assets, often linked to commodity prices.

It seems safe to predict that nothing will come of them nor of any other reform ideas floated − such as the one proposed in September 1980. 'Dirty floating' and the so-called 'era of ad hoc' are here to stay.

12.2 Institutions

12.2.1 The IMF

The international monetary system is based upon 'dirty floating', but it remains to describe the institutional arrangements for co-operation and international lending. The IMF plays a key role under both heads. The IMF currently has over 140 member countries, comprising virtually all Western countries, most Third World countries and a few communist states such as Hungary. The internal organisation of and orthodox lending by the IMF is based on the quota assigned to each country. As each quota was originally fixed in terms of its own currency par values are needed to facilitate easy comparison and so that adjustments can be made at convenient intervals. Voting within the IMF is weighted by quota. For most decisions an 80 per cent majority is needed. This requirement gives the US a veto since its quota is over 20 per cent of the total. No other country at present has a veto, although the UK used to have one but various groups of countries can combine to block schemes. The IMF employs several thousand international civil servants headed by a managing director. They are supervised by a board of 20 directors, who are usually represented by deputies since the directors are either finance Ministers, such as the incumbent UK Chancellor, or central bank governors. The five largest quota holders have a director automatically. The big five have always included the US and the UK. Saudi Arabia is a recent entrant to this elevated status. The remaining members of the IMF are grouped into 15 blocs who each elect a director (invariably from the largest quota holder of the group) and an alternate from the second largest quota holder. This arrangement is remarkably stable; even when two members of a group are at war with each other the system operates smoothly.

Quotas are also the key to the IMF's conventional lending and the structured constraints placed upon nations in exchange for funds. Each nation was originally required to lodge a sum equal to its quota with the

IMF and to increase the deposit whenever its quota was increased. Twenty-five per cent of this must be paid in either gold or dollars, the remainder in one's own currency. In fact Switzerland paid all of its quota in gold and the US, of course, paid all of its in dollars, so the gold and dollar holding was over 25 per cent. A simplified case for a two-country IMF will be used; the two countries being A and B whose currencies are called αs and βs, 1α and 1β each being worth 1 dollar. A's quota is 100,000 so it pays over 75,000 αs and \$25,000. Country B's quota is 200,000 so it subscribes 150,000 βs and \$50,000. Hence the IMF holds 150,000 βs, 75,000 αs and \$75,000.

Countries borrow from the IMF by making drawings, that is they exchange their currency for foreign currency. In the example B draws \$10,000 and 20,000 αs giving 30,000 βs in exchange. The IMF now holds 55,000 αs, 180,000 βs and \$65,000. The crucial calculation is: what is the IMF's holding of each currency as a percentage of the quota? In the example, the holding of A's currency is now 55 per cent of quota, B's 90 per cent. Once the percentage exceeds 75, the country is said to have drawn a tranche, these being divided into bands as follows:

75-100	gold tranche
100-125	first credit tranche
125-150	second credit tranche
150-175	third credit tranche
175-200	fourth credit tranche

IMF holdings of a member's currency are not allowed to exceed twice its quota. The gold tranche may be drawn without condition other than the payment of interest (currently 6¼ per cent) on the amount by which the holding exceeds 75 per cent of the quota. However, it is necessary to obtain IMF consent before each credit tranche is drawn. This is always conditional, the conditions being expressed in a 'letter of intent'.

Before discussing the nature of the conditions, two points are relevant to the working of the system. One is that the IMF obtains its funds interest free and earns two lots of interest on them. When the UK drew foreign exchange from the IMF in 1967 and 1977, the IMF received sterling which it invested (in Treasury bills) and in addition the UK paid interest because the IMF's holding of sterling exceeded its quota. In general the IMF charges interest on the currency it supplies but receives interest on the currency it receives in exchange. The other point is that most of the 'loans' are repaid by drawings by other nations. In 1969 New Zealand drew a large quantity of sterling from the IMF, thus repaying the UK's loan. In the example if at a later stage A draws 30,000 βs, in exchange for 30,000 αs, then IMF holdings of βs are now 85 per cent of A's quota but holdings of βs are down to 75 per cent of B's quota, so B's 'loan' has been repaid by A's transaction.

The conditions for a drawing are usually set out in a letter of intent. The conditions are usually stiffer as each successive tranche is drawn. These conditions vary considerably. In many cases a country has to agree to adhere to IMF rules, especially on convertibility and multiple exchange rates. IMF rules require that a currency be freely convertible at least for non-residents. Multiple exchange rates were invented by Schacht in Germany in the 1930s; he had over 300 of them. There are different rates for different transactions; a well-known one is the preferential rate available for tourists to Eastern Europe (preferential compared to the even less favourable official rate). The more publicised conditions concern domestic policy. Targets are invariably set for DCE and frequently for public spending or the PSBR, but never for monetary growth. Monitoring devices are used to see that these are met, ranging from a bi-annual visit to an adviser in the Prime Minister's office.

It is, however, necessary to emphasise the political reality behind these targets. They usually represent not scientific calculation by disinterested experts but the outcome of political bargaining. The IMF and the world financial system still reflect the nineteenth-century notions that the community of nations has a right to tell the individual nation what to do and that the view of the community reflects the view of the strong. The IMF reflects the reality of financial and economic power in a way that Palmeston would have understood. When the UK borrowed from the IMF in 1976, the crucial negotiations were those between the US and UK governments (the talks were prolonged because of the need to talk with the incoming (Carter) as well as outgoing (Ford) administrations). The very light conditions imposed on the UK reflected US policy, not the opinions of the international civil servants of the IMF. After the Portuguese revolution, Germany provided Portugal with funds and set the conditions, but it suited both Portugal and Germany to use the IMF as an intermediary. It is easier politically to say 'the IMF says we must raise taxes' than 'country X says we must'. It is also easier for the strong to use the IMF as a front-man. The IMF fulfils many useful functions but, like any body involving nation states, its functioning involves political processes.

Since 1973 the IMF has made a number of more straightforward loans, that is, it has borrowed and lent without going through the rig-marole of quotas, drawings and so on. The first such loans were the 'buffer stock' and oil facility of 1973. The latter was almost entirely borrowed by the UK and Italy and was small ($1.3 billion) relative to the deficits caused by OPEC price increases. The former was used only to finance buffer stocks in tin and rubber. The largest was the Witeveen facility, $16 billion, named after the then IMF managing director. $16 billion was raised because no amount either smaller or larger could be raised, as each country's contribution was conditional on others' and only $16 billion satisfied all the conditions, or so the story went. At the time of writing, Sir Geoffrey Howe was seeking to raise funds for another such facility, in his capacity of chairman of the IMF.

12.2.2 The BIS

The Bank for International Settlements (BIS) is nominally a relic of the interim arrangements established after World War I with such picturesque quirks as shares which pay neither interest nor voting power but are among the ultimate status symbols in the banking community. In fact the institution acts as a forum for central bank co-operation through the monthly meetings held in Basle. These arrange co-operative acts in domestic and international policy, seeking a common reduction in interest rates. On several occasions BIS meetings seem to have sought to produce across the board interest rate reductions so as to stimulate economies without changing exchange rates. BIS meetings frequently arrange large loans. The UK government borrowed $3 billion in November 1964 and $5.2 billion in June 1976. Basle meetings arranged the conversion of liquid sterling balances into illiquid foreign currency ones in the late 1960s. The range and scope of action taken at BIS meetings is enormous, but there are two major problems in describing it. One is that the system is as informal and flexible as possible and one cannot describe a structure that does not exist nor explain the rules of a body without them. Moreover, the BIS is merely the agency of international co-operation and in one sense one is recording the fact that central bankers have co-operated since the 1920s to keep the international monetary system functioning. Such co-operation is a vital part of the system but by its nature not easily describable.

As an institution the BIS collects statistics and carries out research. Its main corporate function, however, is that it manages the reserves of some countries. By switching these from, say, US Treasury bills to bank deposits or vice versa these have the effect of open-market operation on the world banking system.

12.2.3 Swaps

Swaps, frequently arranged at BIS meetings, are a device whereby one central bank lends to another. The 'loan' is effected by an exchange of currencies, e.g. the Bundesbank giving the American 'Fed' DM 2 billion in exchange for $1 billion. These are prearranged so that a central bank knows that it has x billion available to supplement its reserves. The prob-lem is that the lender risks monetary expansion when its currency is used to buy up some of the other currency, e.g. if in the above example the 'Fed' used its DM 2 billion to buy dollars to support the exchange rate, the effect would be an expansion of the German money supply. The 'swap' does nothing to diminish the costs of spot intervention, p. 152 above, but it may make it possible. Moreover, the use of 'swaps' involves an explicit decision about the cost of intervention. If, as in 1978, the Germans felt that the DM was overvalued against the dollar they could have intervened themselves. However, if they had they would have acquired dollars which they felt might depreciate in the medium term. An unsuccessful forward market intervention would have been even more costly. If the Germans supplied the US with marks by a swap and the US intervened, the US would bear these costs.

12.2.4 The EEC

The EEC has sought to produce a system of fixed parities amongst its members. This was intended to produce more integration amongst its members' economies but probably confuses ends and means and inter-feres with private sector integration – see Dosser, Gowland and Hartley (1982), pp. 19-20, 102-4. That exchange control between members has been introduced as a step towards union strikes all but the Euro-fanatic as bitterly ironical.

The first such scheme was the European Monetary Union, introduced in April 1972. This was to restrict movements of member and prospec-tive member currencies to within 1¼ per cent of parity, about half the Smithsonian divergence (hence the name 'snake in the tunnel'). The UK left the system within six weeks and neither Italy nor Ireland joined. The French left the group in 1973 in all but name so the snake really became a DM bloc, reflecting German economic power and the depend-ence of economies like the Netherlands or Austria upon it (see p. 121 above).

In a triumph of political reality over economic sense, the EEC decided to try again in 1978. It has been argued that the consequent European Monetary System (EMS), which came into force on 1 January 1979, was an accident, in that d'Estaing, the French President, proposed it assuming that some one else would veto it. Certainly French participation was opposed by many French employers (CNPF) unions (CGT), bankers and economists. The EMS sought to restrict movements amongst the six full members (the EEC less the UK, Ireland and Italy) to within 3 per cent of parity and with the two associates (Ireland and Italy) to 6 per cent.

The system also included a European Currency Unit (ECU), which was equal to x centimes, y pence, z pfennigs, etc. (the proportions vary over time). A currency's rate against the ECU was calculated. If this fell out of line remedial domestic policy was required; e.g. in May 1979 Belgium was the first country whose currency fell below its ECU limit so it raised interest rates. The EMS also includes some reserve pooling, the Monetary Co-operation Fund. The EMS has been kept in existence only by frequent parity changes at great cost to its members, in that it provides 'one-way options' on occasion. It has achieved nothing except its survival as a token of co-operation. Its history has shown some amazing ironies. When the pound-punt (Irish pound) bank was broken on 1 January 1979, informed opinion was unanimous that the punt would rise against the pound and several billions of Irish securities had been bought by 'smart' investors to anticipate the gain. In fact within twelve months the punt had fallen 25 per cent. Problems had been caused for the EMS by an over-strong pound, whereas one reason the UK had not joined was a fear that the pound would be too weak to stay in.

12.3 The System in Action: A Case Study

This section presents a description of a particular episode in international monetary history designed to illustrate some of the points made in Chapters 9-11 about the impossibility of fixed parities and the problems faced by those who operate the international monetary system. Throughout 1976-8 the dollar was depreciating especially against the Swiss franc and the Deutschmark. At the end of 1975 the dollar was worth 2.62 Swiss francs and 2.65 DM, at the end of 1977 only 1.98 and 2.09 respectively. At the end of October it had fallen to 1.49 and 1.74, a loss of about 40 per cent of its value in under two years and 25 per cent in nine months. This fall reflected a mixture of lack of confidence in President Carter, fears about US oil imports and the US balance of payments deficit and a belief that Miller, the 'Fed' chairman, was expanding the US money supply too quickly. The German government, international opinion, reflected in the *Economist, The Times,*

Le Monde, etc, and Wall Street opinion, reflected in the *Wall Street Journal*, argued that President Carter should do something to defend the dollar. In particular the German authorities urged him to take action to transfer the costs of intervention to the US authorities; the Germans were buying dollars to hold the DM rate down but had no more confidence in the dollar than the speculators and did not wish to buy any more of this depreciating asset. The view was typical in its mixture of political and economic factors.

In November President Carter succumbed to the pressure, but it is much easier to see why he resisted earlier than why he gave in then. The cost of depreciation is mainly added inflationary pressure but this would be small, because its imports are so low relative to US GDP. Depreciation benefits producers, at the expense of consumers, and it is universally agreed that producers are much stronger than consumers in the US political system (see e.g. Cater (1965)). Finally the US had available only about $30 billion of short-term assets, $10 billion of foreign exchange and $20 billion of gold (not all of which could be sold for legal and practical reasons). It could borrow perhaps $30 billion, $20 billion of 'swaps' and $10 billion from the IMF, although this would have impaired the IMF's ability to lend to others. In November and December the 'swaps' were doubled to $40 billion. Against this, US short-term liabilities were $700 billion and another $600 billion of short-term claims were denominated in dollars in the Eurocurrency market and extra dollars could be created to sell to the US for harder currencies. Nevertheless Carter and Miller, by a mixture of borrowing and raising US interest rates, were to influence foreign exchange markets by a package of measures announced on 1 November; at the end of the month the dollar was worth 1.73 Swiss francs and DM 1.93. In 1979 the Soviet invasion of Afghanistan and the appointment of the monetarist Volcker to the 'Fed' were to have the effect of changing sentiment around so that the dollar became a very strong currency. The political dangers to Germany, let alone Switzerland, of a Soviet move against Afghanistan seemed remote to most readers of the *Guardian* but the desire for a safe haven in a troubled world is a major factor in foreign exchange markets. The foreign exchange market and the entire international financial system are a fascinating complex mixture of politics and economics. No student of international monetary theory, nor author of a textbook, should ever forget the nature of that which he or she seeks to analyse.

13 THE EUROCURRENCY MARKET

13.1 Introduction

There are two sorts of banking transaction, those carried out in the native currency and Euro ones. The dollar is the native currency in the USA, the pound in the UK and so on and traditionally nearly all banking transactions were executed in the respective native currency of the bank accepting a deposit. In recent years, however, more and more banking transactions have been Euro ones, that is involving banks in accepting deposits or making loans in a currency which is not native to them. A typical Eurocurrency transaction would involve an Arab depositing dollars with a London bank or an Italian borrowing Deutschmarks from a French bank. The precise definition of the Eurocurrency market has been a matter of some debate (see Gowland (1979), pp. 65-6) but the underlying concept is of an active banking market outside the country which issues the currency concerned. The Eurodollar market is the largest of the Euromarkets but there are Euromarkets in virtually all the European currencies. Many of the Eurobanks and dealing centres are located in Asia and currency never changes hands, so the name is potentially misleading.

There are two facts about the Eurocurrency market which dominate all analysis of it: its phenomenal size and incredible growth rate. In 1960 the market was about $2 billion. In 1980 it was about $1500 billion, including inter-bank transactions and $1100 billion net of them, i.e. there were $1500 billion of deposits in the market of which $1100 billion were held by firms, individuals and governments and $400 billion by banks. This is nine times the size of native currency banking business in the UK (on a comparable basis) and equal to 120 per cent of the US money supply.

The Euromarket is conventionally assumed to have been founded in 1927, although strictly medieval bankers were Eurobankers, but its period of phenomenal growth started with the changes in the world financial system in 1957-8 especially the end of the dollar shortage and the introduction of convertibility for European currencies (the history of the market involves major roles for Stalin, Hitler and, in some versions, the Mafia; for a detailed account, see Gowland (1979), pp. 69-72, for a brilliant, racy account Smith (1982)).

The nature of the market is such that it is almost totally beyond the control of any central bank, or any other official body. A transaction can be 'booked' in any country, so, for example, a German lending dollars to a Spaniard in London might record the transaction ('book' it) in Singapore; effectively all he would do is make the loan by giving the Spaniard a cheque drawn on a Singapore bank. Thus, attempts by any one country to control the market would merely push the market to another centre. No international body can, or is likely to, exercise control over banking, so the banks in the market are totally free of any prudential requirement. Moreover, banks in this market borrow short and lend long on a grand scale; in June 1982 only 15 per cent of deposits were for more than one year against 87 per cent of loans. All banks borrow short and lend long but rarely in so spectacular a fashion. Domestic banks are subject to various forms of control to minimise the risks they (and their depositors) run: licensing, ratios or deposit insurance (see Gowland (1978), pp. 97-101). In addition, central banks in practice accept a responsibility to cover the deficiency of any defaulting bank by one means or another. No such protection is available when a Eurobank crashes, e.g. the Bank Ambrosiano group collapse in 1982. The Italian authorities accepted a responsibility to protect the customers of its domestic banking business but not of its Eurobanking subsidiary (a Luxemburg company). Eurobanks have lent heavily to some sovereign borrowers whose repayment prospects are doubtful (Poland, Argentina). In practice, such debts have usually been rescheduled, i.e. the borrower is given longer to pay but the bank's balance sheet shows the asset as if it were beyond reproach.

In the mid-1970s, the conventional wisdom was that worries about the stability of the Eurobanks were misplaced, e.g. Crockett (1979), so the author's fears (Gowland (1979), p, 68) seemed alarmist in comparison. By 1982, orthodoxy had swung to the other extreme, and for example Mr Healey was not alone in his warning of a total collapse of the world banking system (*The Times*, 9 September 1982). By contrast, my views now seem almost Panglossian in their complacency. Nevertheless, it still seems to me (as in 1979, p. 68) that the system does not have the 'potential of a credit Anstalt to trigger a world depression (as was alleged to have happened in 1931) but it embodies considerable risks'. To deny the risk seems as foolhardy as it is ill-founded to produce apocalyptic visions of the collapse of the world financial order. In the second half of 1982, for example, careful management by the IMF and the US Federal Reserve System avoided the problems caused by a loss of confidence in the system. The costs included an easing of US monetary policy so the operation was neither costless nor impossible.

Many Eurobanks have been imprudent, but it may be that such risks are an inevitable byproduct of banking. The Eurobanks, like the domestic US banks, have proved very flexible and rendered the world great service in such activities as recycling OPEC surpluses, i.e. in accepting deposits from OPEC members and their citizens and on-lending them to those purchasing oil. The dangers arise from the absence of a central bank rather than the behaviour of the Eurobanks *per se*. Rather similar considerations apply as do to the analysis of US banks in the nineteenth century and Temin (1976) has argued that the costs imposed by unregulated banks and the occasional failure may not be as great as is conventionally assumed.

Finally, the Eurocurrency market is a very capitalistic institution, whether for good or ill. The Eurobanks normally put their responsibility to depositors and borrowers and the opportunity to earn profits far above adherence to the spirit of (national) government regulations. Often this means that the banks shelter the (rich) victims of oppression, as with the Jewish victims of Hitler in the market's early days. Sometimes criminals are sheltered but, much more importantly, facilities are provided to enable large companies to minimise tax or to evade exchange control. The market has probably been highly beneficial despite its drawbacks, but any analysis of it must acknowledge that it is capitalism, red in tooth and claw, with all its faces acceptable and otherwise.

13.2 Models of the Eurocurrency Market

Any model of banking has to start with the proposition that by lending a bank can create a deposit and that each loan must create a deposit (or equivalent liability of a bank) (Lipsey (1979), p. 378; Gowland (1982a), pp. 21-5). The basic problem is not to explain the growth of banks but to explain the limits to deposit creation. A naive student of elementary banking models might wonder why banks do not loan infinite amounts, despite the usual qualification about the difference between an individual bank and the banking sector. There are two basic approaches to this problem of explaining the constraints on loan and deposit creation; the multiplier approach and the profit maximisation approach, called the 'new view' of money, although it goes back at least a century to Bagehot and arguably to such fifteenth-century authors as the author of the *Mirror of Banking*. These explanations are the basis of alternative models of banking.

The 'multiplier' approach is based upon the idea that banks have to, or will be forced to choose to, maintain an approximately fixed proportion of reserves to deposits. Elementary textbooks often start with a seventeenth-century goldsmith who receives deposits in gold. He has to maintain, say, a 10 per cent reserve to meet repayments. Hence, if he gets a new deposit of £100 in gold he will retain £10 and loan out £90. The £90 is redeposited with him and he keeps £9 and loans £81, the £81 is redeposited and so on *ad infinitum*. In the end, his balance sheet shows liabilities of £1000, deposits, and assets of £1000 made up of £900 of loans and £100 of gold. The influx of £100 of gold has allowed a multiple expansion of deposits of the inverse of the reserve ratio (i.e. ten) times the inflow. Multiplier models extend this analysis in some ways, e.g. to allow leakages into other assets (Gowland (1982a), p. 59ff.). Nevertheless, the basic principle is retained, banks will behave in such a way that the total size of their assets (or deposits) will be in (more or less) fixed relationship to their holdings of reserve assets and that a change in the available quantity of reserve assets is both sufficient and necessary to explain changes in bank assets and loans. In some cases (Germany, the USA, Australia) the reserve holding is imposed by law but the multiplier school argue that even where legal restraints are missing, as in the Eurocurrency market, the banks will impose a ratio on themselves. In particular, this school has sought to explain the growth of Eurocurrency markets in this way by arguing that the balance of payments deficits, especially US ones, have provided the reserve assets which both permitted and caused growth.

The profit-maximising school of thought, to which the author belongs, believes that multiplier analysis is irrelevant to modern banking. Banks holdings of reserves will vary so much in both size and composition that there is no fundamental reserve ratio. It is true that banks must hold some cash but there is no fixed minimum, and the actual percentage is very low. Banks need only $1/4$ or $1/3$ per cent cash so the credit multiplier would vary between 300 and 400 and would be both unstable and move inversely with the size of deposits, so that there would be no relationship *at the margin* between deposits and reserves (in the elementary example above, the goldsmith might hold £100 of reserves, whether his deposits are £1000 (and the ratio 10 per cent) or £2000 (and the ratio 5 per cent)). Crucially to this approach, banks can always obtain reserve assets so it is *deposits which determine reserves, not vice versa.* The constraint upon banks is the balance sheet one that they must induce depositors to hold deposits equal to the size of their loans (less any owners' capital). Hence, what matters is the marginal cost of increasing deposits compared to the marginal revenue derived from increasing loans (marginal cost includes the cost of the necessary increase in reserves, if any) so multiplier analysis is a special case of the 'new view', where this cost is infinite. Of course, the theory can be extended from pure profit maximisation to include risk, managerial goals and so on. The 'new view' therefore explains the growth of the market by looking at the demand for loans and the supply of deposits and the exogenous factors which have shifted these schedules (e.g. US monetary policy in the 1960s, below, or the OPEC price increase of 1973). From these marginal cost curves and demand curves for the banking industry can be derived so output (i.e. deposits and loans) can be determined by using the usual apparatus of microeconomics, either competitive or monopolistic.

There has been a long debate about which of the two approaches is more relevant to the Eurocurrency market (see Makin's paper in Stem *et al.* (1976), pp. 357-62 for a brilliant summary of the early stages and Johnston (1981, 1982) for a later analysis). It is clear that the argument will have to be resolved empirically since *a priori* either might be right. Friedman and Schwartz (1963) showed conclusively that the US banking system could be explained by multiplier analysis prior to 1914 whereas Goodhart (1972) showed that, in the same period, the UK system could not. Indeed, the UK banking system has never been explicable by multiplier analysis, see Gowland (1982a) pp. 11-12 and Chapter 3. Plausibility and the currently available evidence suggests that the 'new view' is right, but the debate is not over yet.

In any case it is necessary to explain the inter-relationship between domestic and Euro-banking. Both schools of thought can do this but the analysis is less awkward with the 'new view'. All Eurocurrencies are perfect substitutes for each other, because as the interest parity theory holds in this market so one can always invest in a deposit in currency A directly or indirectly via a deposit in currency B and a forward purchase of A for B and receive the same return. Domestic and Euro-deposits of the same currency are substitutes for each other and so are loans. Hence, the cost of borrowing in the US is one of the factors determining the demand for Eurodollar loans – just as the price of raspberry jam is a factor explaining the demand for strawberry jam. Similarly the return on domestic dollars influences the desire to hold Eurodollar deposits. In the 1960s, this substitutability was the main factor determining the growth of the market since the US authorities both restricted the rate of interest paid on bank deposits in the US (regulation Q), thereby making Eurodollar deposits more attractive and forced a lot of borrowers from the US domestic market to the Euromarket (see Gowland (1979), pp. 70-1 for details). Faced with a simultaneous rightward shift of both the marginal cost curve, because of the former, and marginal revenue curve, the market grew. As Euro- and domestic markets are always substitutes, the growth of the Euromarkets has served to integrate world money markets.

To summarise this section, there are two alternative theories of the Eurocurrency market; the multiplier approach and the profit maximisation or 'new view' model. The role of reserve assets is debatable but it is clear that the 'new view' is right in emphasising the adaptability of banks in grasping various opportunities presented to them by chance or official blunders over the years. The story of the market shows innovative capitalism in its most striking form.

13.3 The Impact of a Unified Capital Market

To a very large extent the growth of the Eurocurrency market has integrated the world's money and credit markets. The most immediate impact of this has been to increase competition in banking throughout the world. In the 1950s banking was a cartelised industry with small groups dominating the industry in each country (or region, in the USA), usually working in close accord with the relevant central bank. The desire of each cartel to raid the others, and willingess of members of a cartel to compete abroad but not at home, was a major cause of the growth of Eurocurrency business. Equally, however, the growth of Eurocurrency business has played a large role in smashing the cosy cartels of the 1950s. The change is most marked in wholesale business (large transactions) but there is now much more competition even in retail business than in the 1950s.

The integration of banking has had a large effect upon all industry and services. More or less, all large firms compete in the same market for funds and can invest their spare resources in the same market. It is difficult to overstate the role of the integration of banking in integrating economic activity more widely. It is impossible to isolate the role of Eurocurrency markets from that of cheaper transport and trade liberalisation in promoting a more unified world economy since 1950 but the effect of banking has not been the least of the factors involved. Moreover, a substantial percentage of world trade is financed by Eurocurrency market transactions (see Gowland (1979), p. 68).

The effect of the growth of Eurocurrency markets on economic policy has been pervasive but not particularly uniform. The *simpliste* argument is that an integrated financial system will deprive a nation of any autonomy in the conduct of its monetary policy. This argument is based upon a presumption of almost perfectly elastic capital flows with respect to interest rate changes, so if the authorities seek to change interest rates they will be unable to do so as the rest of the world creates the open economy equivalent of a horizontal LM curve which pegs the interest rate at the world level. If the target is a monetary one, similar problems apply because, although the authorities can change DCE, the change in DCE will involve a change in interest rates which will induce a capital flow, such that the overseas impact on the money supply exactly offsets the effect of the change in DCE. Direct controls, such as credit ceilings, can be circumvented by Eurocurrency trans-actions, as in Italy in 1969-70. More sophisticated analyses qualify this by pointing out that the argument implicitly assumes a constant ex-change rate. Otherwise it is possible to control the money supply, or the interest rate, so long as the exchange rate is allowed to adjust to the appropriate level. For example, a higher interest rate can be maintained so long as the exchange rate is so high that is is expected to fall by the amount of the differential (i.e. if dollar rates are 10 per cent, sterling rates can be 15 per cent if and only if the pound's value in terms of dollars is so high that is is expected to fall by 5 per cent so as to equate the return measured in dollars from both currencies). Hence, the standard conclusion, e.g. derived in Mundell (1968), is that if capital markets are integrated (perfect capital mobility) then a government can control any one of the money supply, the exchange rate and the rate of interest, but only one of them. The UK government in 1977-8 and 1979-81 seemed to face this choice and resolved to control the money supply (see Gowland (1982a), pp.160 and 190).

The theoretical answer to the dilemma for a government wishing to control both money and exchange rates is Keynes's solution discussed above, p. 124. This is to use forward market operations so as to control both the exchange rate and a domestic target (money or interest rates). However, this is not practicable because of the enormous scale on which forward contracts might have to be extended and the consequent scale of possible losses. The alternative answer is to insulate the domestic economy from the market by (both inward and outward) ex-change control. This was advocated by the UK House of Commons Treasury Committee in 1980 but has been successfully used only by the German authorities with the Bardepot. This, when imposed, required any German firms or individuals borrowing from abroad (i.e. including a bank taking a deposit) to lodge any percentage specified by the Bundesbank with the Bundesbank at an interest rate of the Bundesbank's choice. The sting of this device is the negative interest rate — down to minus 10 per cent. Ruthless enforcement enabled the German authorities to use this device to insulate the domestic mark banking market from the Euromarkets. This sort of exchange control requires a political will and availability of means of enforcement that few governments possess. Another fundamental effect of the Eurocurrency market on economic policy is that a nation with a balance of payments deficit need no longer deflate (see Gowland (1979), p. 72).

The sheer size of the Eurocurrency market has meant that fixed exchange rates of the Bretton Woods type can no longer be maintained, see p. 130 above. The consequences of the change to dirty floating are as far reaching as they are incalculable. One is that world inflation has probably been higher than it would otherwise have been. If this is so, it has reinforced the direct inflationary effects of the market. These arise because the Eurocurrency has caused, or at least been the agent of, a massive expansion of world credit money and liquidity. In this way, the Eurocurrency market has had an immense effect upon the world but it has been so pervasive that it is impossible to isolate its effects. Indeed, it is, in principle, impossible, since it is necessary to know how central banks and governments would have acted in the absence of the market. Otherwise it cannot be determined whether Eurodeposits and loans have been additional to, or replacements for, domestic ones.

To conclude, analysis of the Euromarkets puts the economist in the position of a historian in 1500 trying to assess the significance of Columbus's discovery of America. It is clearly very important, but it is not yet clear exactly why nor what the future effects will be.

A GUIDE TO FURTHER READING

There are three excellent advanced textbooks which can be recommended. In approximately ascending order of complexity, these are Sodersten (1980), Kindelberger and Lindert (1978) and Grubel (1977). In addition, there are a number of useful specialist textbooks: Findlay (1971), Shone (1972) (pure theory), Michaely (1977) (commercial policy) and Crockett (1979) (international finance). References to these are omitted below.

Pure Theory (Chapter 2)

Clement *et al.* (1967) sets out the issues comprehensively. Johnson (1958) is still a very useful guide to the complexities of the subject, as is Pearce (1970, Book II). Batra (1973), Chapters 3 to 5, is very difficult but even more rewarding.

Commercial Policy (Chapters 3 and 4)

Johnson (1971) is extremely comprehensive. On specific topics the following are recommended: Batra (1973), Chapter 9, on the effective rate of protection; Bhagwati (1969) on the effect of protection on producers' incomes; Bhagwati and Ramaswami (1963) on domestic monopoly; Falvey (1975) on tariffs and quotas.

Customs Unions (Chapter 5)

Krauss (1972) is a superb survey article which explores most of the literature and puts it into context. Robson (1972) is a well-chosen collection of articles, including the classic Viner (1950), Lipsey (1957a) and Cooper and Massell (1965a). Lipsey (1970) and El-Agraa and Jones (1981) provide comprehensive surveys for the mathematically oriented. Those interested specifically in the EEC should consult Swann (1978), Dosser *et al.* (1982) and El-Agraa (1980) in approximately ascending order of complexity.

Balance of Payments Theory (Chapters 6 to 8)

On the conceptual and statistical material, the (annual) *Guide to the Official Statistics* published by the CSO lists a huge range of sources and explains what the official statistics are. However, the annual *UK Balance of Payments*, HMSO, presents all the major items and explains their meaning. The best summary of the orthodox theory is still Haberler's paper, reprinted in Cooper (1969), pp. 107-34.

The best summary of the Keynesian approach is Johnson, reproduced in Cooper (1969), pp. 237-56 and in Frenkel and Johnson (1976), pp. 46-64. Mundell's model can be found in Mundell (1968) along with many other extensions of his approach. Chapter 8 (also in Frenkel and Johnson (1976), pp. 64-92) is an alternative open economy IS-LM model to the one above. The standard exposition of New Cambridge is by Cripps and Godley (1976); for further analyses see Gowland (1982b), pp. 71-6, Crystal (1979) and Cuthbertson (1979). For the overseas impact on the money supply see Gowland (1982a), pp. 43-9.

The standard exposition of the monetary approach is Frenkel and Johnson's compilation (1976); of especial value are Chapters 6 and 11 (by Johnson) and the introductory piece by the editors. At a more advanced level Dornbusch (1980) is the best available presentation of what is a moderate or modified monetarist stance. A relatively simple sympathetic presentation is by Crystal (1979) and a comparable, more hostile analysis is Cuthbertson (1979). Hahn (1977) and Currie (1976) contain criticism at a much more advanced level.

Exchange Rates (Chapters 9 and 10)

The best piece upon the merits of fixed and floating rates is the debate between Friedman and Roosa (1967). Johnson (1969) is still a classic if polemical piece. For those who prefer an attempt at balanced judgement to elegant advocacy, Gowland (1979), Chapter 2 is available.

The effect of the exchange rate on the economy is considered briefly in many places but rarely comprehensively. Mundell (1968) and Rhomberg (1978) are perhaps the best available.

International Finance (Chapter 11)

Williamson (1973) is a first-class summary of the international liquidity literature. Grubel's survey article (1971) is an ideal complement to it.

The International Monetary System (Chapter 12)

Gold (1970) is a first-rate guide to the IMF. The history of the international monetary system is reviewed in several excellent books of which Tew (1982) is perhaps the best.

The Eurocurrency Market (Chapter 13)

Crockett (1979), Chapter 12, and Gowland (1979), Chapter 3, provide useful introductions to the Eurocurrency market. Stem *et al.* (1976) is still the best available advanced material together with Johnston (1983) and Dreyer (1980).

BIBLIOGRAPHY

'Adam Smith' (Goodman, G.J.W.) (1982) *Paper Money* (UK edition), Macdonald, London

Balassa, B. (1963) 'An Empirical Determination of Classical Comparative Cost Theory', *Review of Economics and Statistics*, vol. 37 (August)

Baldwin, R.E. (1971a) *Non-Tariff Distortions on International Trade*, Brookings Institution, Washington DC

Baldwin, R.E. (1971b) 'Determinants of the Commodity Structure of US Trade', *American Economic Review*, vol.61 (March)

Bank (1979) *Bank of England Model of the UK Economy*, Bank of England Discussion Paper No.5 (September)

Batra, R.N. (1973) *Studies in the Pure Theory of International Trade*, Macmillan, London

Batra, R.N. (1975) *The Pure Theory of International Trade under Uncertainty*, Macmillan, London

Beckerman, W. (ed.) (1972) *The Labour Government's Economic Record 1964-70*, Duckworth, London

Bhagwati, J.N. (1959) 'Protection, Wages and Real Income', *Economic Journal*, vol. 69, pp. 733-44

Bhagwati, J.N. (1969) *International Trade: Selected Readings*, Penguin, Harmondsworth

Bhagwati, J.N. (1971) 'Customs Unions and Welfare Improvement', *Economic Journal*, vol. 81 (September), pp. 580-7

Bhagwati, J.N. and Ramaswami, V.K. (1963) 'Domestic distortions, tariffs and the theory of optimum subsidy', *Journal of Political Economy*, vol. 71

Blackaby, F.T. *et al.* (1978) *British Economic Policy 1960-74*, Cambridge University Press, Cambridge

Buchanan, J.M. and Brennan, H.G. (1981) 'Monopoly in Money and Inflation', *Hobart Paper 88*, Institute of Economic Affairs

Buchanan, N.S. (1955) 'Lines on the Leontief Paradox', *Economica Internazionale*, vol. 8 (November), p. 791

Cater, D. (1965) *Power in Washington* (English edition), Collins, London

Claasen, E.M. and Salin, P. (1976) *Recent Issues in Monetary Economics*, North Holland, New York

Clark, P.B. (1970) 'Demand for International Reserves: A Cross-country Analysis', *Canadian Journal of Economics*, vol. 3 (November), pp. 577-94

Clement, M.O., Pfister, F.L. and Rothwell, K.J. (1961) *Theoretical Issues in International Economics*, Houghton Miflin, New York

Cooper, C.A. and Massell, B.F. (1965a) 'Towards a General Theory of Customs Unions for Developing Countries', *Journal of Political Economy*, vol. 73, pp. 461-76

Cooper, C.A. and Massell, B.F. (1965b) 'A New Look at Customs Union Theory', *Economic Journal*, vol. 75 (December), pp. 742-7

Cooper, R.N. (ed.) (1969) *International Finance*, Penguin, Harmondsworth

Cripps, T.F. and Godley, W.A.H. (1976) 'A Formal Analysis of the CEPG Model', *Economica*, vol. 43 (November)

Crockett, A.D. (1979) *International Money*, Nelson, London

Crystal, K.A. (1979) *Controversies in British Macroeconomics*, Philip Allan, Oxford

Currie, D.A. (1976) 'Some Criticisms of the Monetary Analysis of Balance of Payments Correction', *Economic Journal*, vol. 86 (September), pp. 508-22

Cuthbertson, K. (1979) *Macroeconomic Policy*, Macmillan, London

Dalton, H. (1962) *High Tide and After: Memoirs 1945-60*, Muller, London

Dam, K.W. (1970) *The GATT*, University of Chicago Press, Chicago

Dornbusch, R. (1980) *Open Economy Macroeconomics*, Basic Books, New York

Dosser, D., Gowland, D.H. and Hartley, K. (1982) *Collaboration amongst Nations*, Martin Robertson, Oxford

Dreyer, J.S., Haberler, G. and Willett, T.D. (eds.) (1980) *The International Monetary System: A Time of Turbulence*, American Enterprise Institute for Public Policy Research, Washington and London

El-Agraa, A.M. (1980) *The Economics of the European Community*, Philip Allan, Oxford

El-Agraa, A.M. and Jones, A.J. (1981) *The Theory of Customs Unions*, Philip Allan, Oxford

Ellis, H.S. and Meltzer, L.A. (eds.) (1949) *Readings in the Theory of International Trade*, Irwin, Homewood, Illinois

Falvey, J.F. (1975) 'A Note on the Distinction between Tariffs and Quotas', *Economica*, vol. 42 (August), pp. 319-26

Findlay, R. (1970) *Trade and Specialization*, Penguin, Harmondsworth

Frenkel, J.A. and Johnson, H.G. (eds.) (1976) *The Monetary Approach to the Balance of Payments*, George Allen and Unwin, London

Friedman, M. (1953) 'The Case for Flexible Exchange Rates' in *Essays in Positive Economics*, University of Chicago Press, Chicago

Friedman, M. and Roosa, R.V. (1967) *Balance of Payments: Free versus Fixed Exchange Rates*, Rational Debate Seminars, American Enterprise Institute, Washington DC

Friedman, M. and Schwartz, A.J. (1963) *A Monetary History of the US 1867-1960*, NBER Studies in Business Cycles No. 12, Princeton University Press, Princeton

Galbraith, J.K. (1954) *The Great Crash* (English edition), Hamish Hamilton, London (also published by Pelican (1961))

Gehrels, F. (1956) 'Customs Unions from a Single Country Viewpoint', *Review of Economic Studies*, vol. 34, pp. 61-4

Glyn, A. and Sutcliffe, R.B. (1972) *British Capitalism, Workers and the Profit Squeeze*, Penguin, Harmondsworth

Godley, W.A.H. *et al.* (1980) 'Britain and Europe', *Cambridge Economic Policy Review*, vol. 6 (April), pp. 27-34

Godley, W.A.H. *et al.* (1981) 'The European Community: Problems and Prospects', *Cambridge Economic Policy Review*, vol. 7 (December)

Gold, J. (1970) *The Stand-by Arrangements of the International Monetary Fund: A Commentary on their Formal Legal and Financial Aspects*, IMF, Washington DC

Goodhart, C.A.E. (1972) *The Business of Banking 1891-1914*, Weidenfeld and Nicholson, London

Gould, B., Mills, J. and Stewart, S. (1981) *Monetarism or Prosperity*, Macmillan, London

Gowland, D.H. (1978) *Monetary Policy and Credit Control*, Croom Helm, London

Gowland, D.H. (ed.) (1979) *Modern Economic Analysis*, Butterworth, London

Gowland, D.H. (1982a) *Controlling the Money Supply*, Croom Helm, London

Gowland, D.H. (ed.) (1982b) *Modern Economic Analysis 2*, Butterworth, London

Gowland, D.H. and Pakenham, K. (1974) 'Floating Rates and Inflation', *RIB*

Monthly Review (November)

Grubel, H.G. (1971) 'The Demand for International Reserves: A Critical Review of the Literature', *Journal of Economic Literature*, vol. 13 (December)

Grubel, H.G. (1976) *The International Monetary System*, Penguin, Harmondsworth

Grubel, H.G. (1977) *International Economics*, Irwin, Homewood, Illinois

Hahn, S.H. (1977) 'The Monetary Approach to the Balance of Payments', *Journal of International Economics*, vol. 7 (August)

Hartley, K. (1982) *Nato Arms Cooperation*, George Allen and Unwin, London

Henderson, P.D. (1968) 'Investment Criteria for Public Enterprise' in R. Turvey (ed.) *Public Enterprise*, Penguin, Harmondsworth

Hirst, F.W. (1911) *The Stock Exchange*, Williams and Northgate, London

Johnson, H.G. (1958) *International Trade and Economic Growth*, Unwin University Books

Johnson, H.G. (1969) 'The Case for Flexible Exchange Rates, 1969' in 'UK and Floating Exchanges', *Hobart Paper 46*, Institute of Economic Affairs

Johnson, H.G. (1971) *Aspects of the Theory of Tariffs*, George Allen and Unwin, London

Johnston, R.B. (1980) *Banks' International Lending Decisions and the Determination of Spreads on Syndicated Medium-term Euro-credits*, Bank of England Discussion Paper No. 12 (September)

Johnston, R.B. (1981) Theories of the Growth of the Euro-Currency Market: A Review of the Euro-Currency Deposit Multiplier', *BIS Economic Papers No. 4* (May)

Johnston, R.B. (1983) *The Economics of the Euro-Market*, Macmillan, London

Kemp, M.C. (1976) *Three Topics in the Theory of International Trade*, North Holland, Amsterdam

Keynes, J.M. (1971) *A Tract on Monetary Reform*, reprinted in *The Collected Writings*, Macmillan for the RES, 1971

Kindelberger, C.P and Lindert, P.H. (1978) *International Economics*, (sixth edition), Irwin, Homewood, Illinois

Krauss, M.B. (1972) 'Recent Developments in Customs Union Theory', *Journal of Economic Literature*, vol. X, no. 2 (June), pp. 413-35

Kuska, A.E. (1972) 'The Pure Theory of Devaluation', *Economica*, vol. 49

Laidler, D.E.W. and Parkin, J.M. (1975) 'Inflation – a Survey', *Economic Journal*, vol. 85 (December)

Leontief, W. (1956) 'Factor Proportions and the Structure of American Trade: Further Theoretical and Empirical Analysis', *Review of Economics and Statistics*, vol. 31 (November)

Leontief, W. (1969) 'Domestic Production and Foreign Trade: The American Position Re-examined' in J. Bhagwati (ed.) *International Trade*, pp. 93-139, Penguin, Harmondsworth

Lipsey, R.G. (1957a) 'Mr Gehrels on Customs Unions', *Review of Economic Studies*, vol. 34, no. 65, pp. 211-14

Lipsey, R.G. (1957b) 'The Theory of Customs Unions:Trade Diversion and Welfare', *Economica*, vol. 34, pp. 40-46

Lipsey, R.G. (1960), 'The Theory of Customs Unions: A General Survey', *Economic Journal*, vol. 70, pp. 496-513

Lipsey, R.G. (1970) *The Theory of Customs Unions: A General Equilibrium Analysis*, Weidenfeld and Nicholson, London

Lipsey, R.G. (1979) *An Introduction to Positive Economics* (fifth edition), Weidenfeld and Nicholson, London

Lipsey, R.G. and Lancaster, K.J. (1956) 'The General Theory of the Second Best', *Review of Economic Studies* XXXIV, vol. 63 (October), pp. 11-32

Loeb, G.A. (1954) 'A Estrutura do Comércio Exterior da América do Norte', *Revista Brasileira de Economia*, vol. 8 (December), p. 81

MacDougall, G.D.A. (1951-2) 'British and American Exports:A Study Suggested by the Theory of Comparative Costs', *Economic Journal*, vol. 61 (December 1951) and vol. 62 (September 1952)

Machup, F. (1969) 'The Cloakroom Rule of International Reserves', *Quarterly Journal of Economics*, vol. 79, pp. 337-55

Melvin, J. (1969) 'Comments on the Theory of Customs Unions', *Manchester School*, vol. 36, no. 2 (June), p. 161-8

Metzler, L. (1949) 'Tariffs, the Terms of Trade and the Distribution of Income', *Journal of Political Economy*, vol. 57 (February)

Michaely, M. (1977) *Theory of Commercial Policy*, Philip Allan, Oxford

Mundell, R.A. (1968) *International Economics*, Macmillan, New York

Oulton, N. (1973) *Tariffs, Taxes and Trade in the UK: The Effective Protection Approach*, HMSO, London

Pearce, I.F. (1970) *International Trade*, Papermac (Macmillan), London

Rhomberg, A. (ed.) (1978) *The Monetary Approach to the Balance of Payments*. IMF, Washington DC

Robson, P. (ed.) (1972) *International Economic Integration*, Penguin, Harmonds worth

Rueff, J. (1967) *Balance of Payments*, Macmillan, London

Samuelson, P.A. (1948) 'International Trade and the Equalisation of Factor Prices', *Economic Journal*, vol. 58 (June)

Samuelson, P.A. (1966) *Economics* (11th edition), McGraw Hill, New York

Servan Schreiber, J.J. (1969) *The American Challenge*, Avon Books, New York

Shone, R. (1972) *The Pure Theory of International Trade*, Macmillan, London

Shoup, C.P. (ed.) (1967) *Fiscal Harmonisation in Common Markets*, Columbia University Press, New York

Sodersten, B. (1980) *International Economics*, Macmillan, London

Sohmen, E. (1969) *Flexible Exchange Rates*, University of Chicago Press, Chicago

Stem, C.H., Makin, J.H. and Logue, D.E. (eds.) (1976) *Eurocurrencies and the International Monetary System*, American Enterprise Institute, Washington DC

Stern, R.M. (1962) 'British and American Productivity and Comparative Costs in International Trade', *Oxford Economic Papers* (October)

Stern, R.M. (1973) *The Balance of Payments*, Macmillan, London

Stolper, W.F. and Samuelson, P. (1941) 'Protection and Real Wages', *Review of Economic Studies*, vol. 9, pp. 58-73

Swann, D. (1978) *The Economics of the Common Market* (4th edition), Penguin, Harmondsworth

Swerling, B.C. (1954) 'Capital Shortage and Labor Surplus in the United States', *Review of Economics and Statistics*, vol. 36 (August), p. 286

Temin, P. (1976) *Did Monetary Forces Cause the Great Depression?*, Norton, New York

Tew, B. (1982) *The Evolution of the International Monetary System 1945-81*, Hutchinson, London

Viner, J. (1950) *The Customs Union Issue*, Carnegie Endowment for International Peace, New York

Williams, P.M. (1971) *Politics and Society in de Gaulle's Republic*, Longman, London

Williamson, J.H. (1973) 'Surveys in Applied Economics: International Liquidity' *Economic Journal*, vol. 83 (September)

Williamson, J.H., Wood, G.E. and Carse, S. (1980) *The Financing Procedures of British Foreign Trade*, Cambridge University Press, Cambridge
Worswick, G.D.N. and Ady, P.A. (eds.) (1952) *The British Economy*, Oxford University Press, Oxford

INDEX

The
Sky at Night

About the Authors

SIR PATRICK MOORE, CBE, is a British amateur astronomer, researcher, radio commentator and television presenter, and author of over 70 books on astronomy. He is a former president of the British Astronomical Association, and co-founder and former president of the Society for Popular Astronomy. He is a specialist on observing the Moon, a Fellow of the Royal Society, and is one of Britain's best-loved and most popular television personalities.

DR CHRIS NORTH is an academic researcher at Cardiff University's School of Physics and Astronomy. His research primarily involves the design, build and operation of astronomical telescopes and instruments, though he also has a strong involvement in public outreach and education. He has worked on the Planck Satellite and the Herschel Space Observatory, and is one of the team behind Chromoscope, a popular online astronomy visualisation tool.

The
Sky at Night

PATRICK MOORE
& CHRIS NORTH

This book is published to accompany the BBC series entitled
The Sky at Night, first broadcast in 1957.

Series Producer: Jane Fletcher
Executive Producer: Bill Lyons

3 5 7 9 10 8 6 4

BBC Books, an imprint of Ebury Publishing
20 Vauxhall Bridge Road
London SW1V 2SA

BBC Books is part of Penguin Random House group of companies
whose addresses can be found at global.penguinrandomhouse.com

First published by BBC Books in 2012
This paperback edition published in 2018

A CIP catalogue record for this book is available from the British Library.

ISBN 978 1 849 90347 9

Penguin Random House is committed to a sustainable future for
our business, our readers and our planet. This book is made
from Forest Stewardship Council certified paper

Printed and bound in Great Britain by Clays Ltd, Elcograf S.p.A.

Contents

Other Worlds 285

Manned Space Exploration 311

Space Missions 343

Foreword

The Sky at Night is the world's longest-running programme with the same presenter. Every month, Sir Patrick Moore continues to extend this unique record, and I very much doubt he will ever be beaten by anyone else. The reason for *The Sky at Night*'s success is certainly Sir Patrick himself and the awesome subject that he so enthusiastically communicates.

The first programme was aired on 24 April 1957 and helped usher in the space race. Since then every possible aspect of astronomy, from comets to quasars, has been covered. Sir Patrick's good sense of humour helped him report on some unusual stories too, such as UFOs and little green men. Sir Patrick has always maintained that if an alien arrived in his garden, he would invite him into his study, sit him down and offer him a gin and tonic; a possibility I have never ruled out.

For the past ten years, Sir Patrick has invited the BBC into his home to film *The Sky at Night*. Transforming his study into the programme set you see on TV every month is nerve-wracking. There are piles of precious documents and manuscripts, not forgetting the multitude of remote controllers and spectacles. It is organised chaos and, unfortunately, it is my job to see it is all put back in the 'right' place.

Working on such a long-running programme, with such a rich heritage, has meant that milestones are being reached all the time. It seems only yesterday we celebrated fifty years of *The Sky at Night* with an edition titled 'Time Lord'. We went back in time and visited the set of the first programme, where we met a young Patrick, played by the impressionist Jon Culshaw. We also went forward in time to join Brian May, the Queen guitarist and doctor of astronomy, in his Martian observatory on top of Olympus Mons, while fellow presenter and leading astronomer Chris Lintott played cricket in a spacesuit. As I remember it, Chris blamed the thin Martian atmosphere for affecting his spin.

In 2011, *The Sky at Night* reached another landmark – its 700th programme. I have two memories from this unique show: Brian May and the Astronomer Royal Martin Rees passing each other behind the cameras, with the latter commenting he thought Brian looked just like Sir Isaac Newton; and Patrick reminiscing with 'Patrick' *c.*1982, aka Jon Culshaw. It was hard to know which Patrick to look at.

Now we are celebrating the 55th anniversary of *The Sky at Night*, and my tenth year of making the programme. It's been a pleasure, a privilege and an honour to work with such an exceptional presenter and on such a unique programme. I have many wonderful memories and look forward to gathering many more.

Jane Fletcher
Series Producer, *The Sky at Night*

Introduction

THIS BOOK BEGAN with the 700th *Sky at Night* programme – transmitted more than half a century after the first edition was broadcast back in 1957. We called for questions from viewers about things they particularly wanted to know, and the response was quite overwhelming. We had hundreds upon hundreds of questions, and we realised that put together they would make an excellent book.

Questions have been sent in by serious astronomers, by those who are just starting out in stargazing, and by those who are interested in the Universe at large. As ever, some of the best questions have come in from the younger viewers. The questions are from all over the UK, from across Europe – Ireland, France, the Netherlands, Greece – and also from Canada, the USA, even Australia. Luckily, most of them arrived on our desks in English!

When it came to answering the questions there were certain things we had to bear in mind. One of us (Chris) is a professional astronomer and cosmologist, while the other (Patrick) is an amateur whose expertise is the Moon and so would stay near home! At least it means our outlooks are slightly different. The first step was to take the questions and divide them into convenient groups, which was done by Chris. The next step was to work out who was going to answer which! Obviously, all the cosmological and technical questions were given to Chris, leaving Patrick with the less technical questions on the Solar System and the Moon. We hope we have achieved the right balance – at least you have plenty of choice.

Since the questioners have a wide range of backgrounds, the answers necessarily assume a range of pre-existing knowledge. For every question that is detailed and complex, there is another that seems much more basic. But one thing is certain – the more basic questions can in fact have the most complex answers. We have avoided mathematical formulae, as that takes us into a different realm, and we didn't feel it had any place here. This is a book we hope can be picked up, read and enjoyed by everybody.

When we were writing the book, we realised we were producing something that was in some senses rather new, and we have tried to include as many of the up-to-date results as possible, while acknowledging that astronomy is a very rapidly moving field. We hope that you will like the result. If not, let us know and we will try again!

Best wishes

Patrick and Chris

A number of different units are used to describe distances in this book, and also in astronomy in general. Here is a very brief conversion guide:

1 km = 0.621 miles

1 mile = 1.61 km

1 astronomical unit = 150,000,000 km (93,000,000 miles) [the distance from the Earth to the Sun]

1 light year = 9,460,000,000,000 km (5,880,000,000,000 miles) [the distance light travels in a year]

And finally, where we use the word 'billion', we assume its modern value of 1 thousand million (1,000,000,000).

Patrick with his 15" reflector, with which he mapped the Moon.

Observing

Naked-eye Observing

To someone who is much younger than *The Sky at Night*, how would you advise getting into amateur astronomy?

Rufus Segar (Worcestershire)

I [PM] began by reading a few very elementary books, getting the main principles into my head. I then went outdoors on a clear night and looked up at the stars. There seemed to be so many of them I did not know how to make a start on sorting them out. I always remember that the stars are so far away that their movements compared to each other are so slow they cannot be noticed over periods of many lifetimes. Consider the seven stars which make up the famous pattern called the Great Bear, or the Plough (or, in America, the Big Dipper). These stars always seem to stay in the same relative positions and so the pattern does not alter. Also, from latitudes such as Britain the Great Bear never sets.

My next step would be to take an elementary star map and start using the Great Bear as a 'pointer'. For example, the two end stars in the pattern point upwards to the North Pole of the sky, marked very closely by the star Polaris in the constellation of the Little Bear. At the other end of the

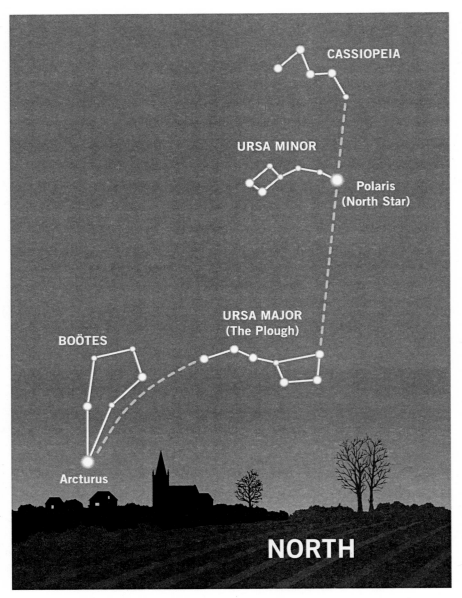

CASSIOPEIA

URSA MINOR

Polaris
(North Star)

URSA MAJOR
(The Plough)

BOÖTES

Arcturus

NORTH

The Plough can be used to find stars and constellations all over the sky at all times of the year.

Great Bear pattern, the three stars point downwards to a very brilliant star – orange in colour – which we call Arcturus in the constellation of the Boötes the Herdsman. You can see the way in which I am working, using the patterns of the constellations to navigate around the sky. In the winter skies there is another easily found constellation, Orion the Hunter, which is also invaluable as a pointer.

But before long an enthusiast is going to need something more powerful than his or her two eyes. My advice is to buy a pair of binoculars – they do not cost very much and they are of immense interest astronomically. They are able to show you the craters of the Moon, double stars, coloured stars, star clusters and many other features of the night sky.

Once you become really familiar with the binocular sky, you may start thinking about a telescope. But in my view there is one important act to take before that: join an astronomical society. There is the national British Astronomical Association, but many towns and cities have astronomical societies of their own – for example, here in West Sussex we have the South Downs Astronomical Society which serves Chichester, Bognor Regis and the whole of the surrounding area. By joining a society, not only will you make many new friends, but you will be able to exchange your ideas and observations with other like-minded people.

Another facility we have in Chichester is the South Downs Planetarium. A planetarium is a large dome with a special projector that can show the stars, giving an amazingly realistic impression of the real sky. Quite apart from this, the planetarium can do things which would otherwise mean waiting for a long time. For example, if you want to stay in England and see a total eclipse of the Sun you must wait for around 80 years, but the planetarium can provide one at any moment! There are numerous planetaria in Britain, so I recommend that you visit one.

The Sun is so bright, and yet space itself is really dark. Why is that?

Helen Adams (Southport, Merseyside)

The only way for something to appear light is for it to either emit or reflect light. There is nothing in empty space to do this, and so we see it as dark – essentially just an absence of light. By contrast, the sky is very bright during the day, though this is simply due to the atmosphere scattering light from the Sun.

The fact that space is black was one of the first pieces of evidence for the fact that the Universe does not go on forever unchanging. If that were true, then in any direction we looked we would see a star. Look a little bit off to one side and there would be another star, possibly much further away. Although light travels at a finite (if very fast) speed, if the Universe were infinitely large and had been around in the same state for an infinite amount of time then we would be able to see stars at infinite distances. Such a situation would mean that the entire sky should be bright with the light of distant stars. The fact that the sky is black indicates that there are distances so vast that light has not yet had time to reach us.

This thought, often called 'Olbers' Paradox', is normally attributed to a German astronomer called Heinrich Olbers in 1823, though he was by no means the first or last person to pose such a question. The answer came in the twentieth century with the advent of the Big Bang theory, which introduced an age to the Universe, and therefore a reason why we cannot see an infinite distance in every direction.

When I stand in the UK and face the Sun, it appears to move from my left to my right. If I am standing in Australia, does it go the other way?

Susan Coward (Athens, Greece)

Yes, it does, though only because you would have to face north to see it rather than south. In fact, it is rather disconcerting to observe the sky from further south, as many of the constellations give the impression of moving the wrong way. In fact, one of us [CN] was part of a group of astronomers who drove for half an hour in the wrong direction while in French Guiana, simply because we forgot that the Sun was then in the north, not the south. There's probably a joke about how many astronomers it takes to navigate by the Sun!

What is the difference, if any, between the night sky observed from the North and South Poles and that from a site on the Equator?

Peter J Wilde (Mansfield, Nottinghamshire)

If you are observing from the North Pole, with the north celestial pole marked by the star Polaris, the Equator in the sky would lie along the horizon. From the South Pole, the south celestial pole would be above you. At either of these positions you can only ever see half the sky, though it would rotate around in a circle. Of course, you would also have much longer nights, lasting for months, and so you would have to wrap up warm! There are a number of telescopes that take advantage of the location of the South Pole to observe particular regions. On the Equator you would, in principle, be able to see the whole sky if you waited long enough.

The stars appear to move differently when seen from different latitudes. For example, from the Equator the constellation of Orion the Hunter would in fact rise vertically in the east, pass right overhead, and set due west. I [PM] can remember standing in Singapore, which is very close to the Equator, and seeing the Great Bear in one half of the sky and the Southern Cross in the other.

Why are there no really bright stars? If you go out on a clear night, there are lots of stars but all roughly the same magnitude to the eye. Logic says there should be some really bright stars that are either so big or so close that they could even be seen during the day.

Danny Sheehan (London)

The eye is a very impressive tool, especially when properly dark-adapted. The faintest stars visible are around 1,000 times fainter than the brightest, though all are very distant. Apart from the Sun, the closest star visible to the naked eye, Alpha Centauri, is around four light years away, but is not the brightest in the sky. That honour falls to Sirius, which is over twice as distant. There are other stars which are far more luminous in their own right, but which are hundreds of light years away and so nowhere near as bright as seen from Earth. All the stars are so very distant that they appear as tiny dots of light, even when viewed through all but the largest telescopes in the world. After all, space is very big, and one light year is around 10 million million kilometres (6 million million miles).

We denote the brightness of stars on a scale called 'magnitude'. This works somewhat like a golfer's handicap, with brighter stars having lower values. Bright stars are magnitude 1, slightly fainter ones are magnitude 2 and so on. Most people can see down to magnitude 6 with the naked eye, and the more powerful telescopes in the world can see down to magnitudes of around 30. The brightest stars can have magnitudes of zero, or even negative values. For example, Sirius is of magnitude -1.5. Some of the planets in our Solar System can be considerably brighter than this simply because they are much closer, though they are simply reflecting the Sun's light. The brightest planet Venus is around magnitude -4, and is visible with the Sun above the horizon, particularly near dawn and dusk. For comparison, on this scale the Sun is magnitude -27!

Just below and to the left of the constellation Orion there is a large star which is flickering brightly. When viewed through binoculars, you can see a kaleidoscope of colours, reds, blues, greens and yellows. Can you let me know what this fantastic sight is?

Susan Thompson (Burnley, Lancashire)

That is Sirius in the Great Dog. It is actually a pure white star, but seen from Britain it is always quite low down and so its light has to come to us through a rather thick layer of atmosphere. The distortions from the atmosphere make it flicker all manner of colours. Go further south to view Sirius and it looks brilliant white.

There is a minor mystery here. Several astronomers from a couple of thousand years ago described Sirius as a red star, but there is no sign of it being red now. I'm sure there is a mistake or mistranslation – stars don't change as quickly as that.

I've often seen the International Space Station with the naked eye as it crosses the night sky. Sometimes it is very spectacular, but how can I observe it at a higher magnification? As it moves so quickly, can its movement be tracked?

Bruce Canning (Cambridge)

The International Space Station is the brightest artificial satellite in the sky, and if the alignment of the solar panels is correct it can be brighter than Venus. It does move rather quickly, however, which means catching it through binoculars or a telescope is very difficult.

The International Space Station being approached by the Japanese HTV supply ship, seen from the ground by an amateur astronomer. Ralf Vandenbergh uses a 10" telescope and an enormous amount of skill.

A pair of large binoculars may give an indication of a somewhat irregular shape, though a telescope would obviously give a better view. The trick with that, though, is to be able to move the telescope quickly enough to track it through the sky. A large field of view is well recommended. Telescopes will not have a default mode to track the Space Station, and I understand that most amateurs who image it do so by moving the telescope manually, rather than by automatically tracking its position. Images of the Space Station from amateur telescopes can be staggeringly detailed, with some showing a Space Shuttle docked!

My father observed what seemed to be a star exploding, not far from the Pole Star. It appeared, to the naked eye, to explode, and then disappear completely. Is this a common occurrence?

Miranda Taylor on behalf of Bryan Winman (Heckfield, Hampshire)

This was almost certainly a meteor coming straight towards you and exploding; it certainly was inside our Solar System and not a star. This can happen sometimes, and I agree it is most confusing.

The only other possibility is that it was some kind of artificial satellite. One family of satellites, called the Iridium satellites, have very reflective, flat surfaces. As they spin they reflect the Sun's rays down on to Earth in a beam a few miles across. These can be brighter than any star or planet for the few seconds that the reflection is directed to your location, though normally the satellites appear much fainter. Since these satellites are in polar orbits, they will appear to pass close to the Pole Star, and there is a chance that such an 'Iridium Flare' could occur nearby.

A cylindrical, green-coloured object was seen travelling fairly fast and not straight or level. It was slower and larger than a meteor. What could this have been?

Brian Cooper (Sheffield)

This sounds an awful lot like a fireball, or perhaps a satellite re-entering the Earth's atmosphere. Such occurrences are uncommon but not unheard of, and there is now a story of a fireball in the news every few months. As low-Earth orbit becomes busier, there will be more satellites in decaying orbits that will eventually re-enter the atmosphere and burn up.

Most of a satellite is destroyed when this happens, though it is possible that some parts would reach the surface. Since much of the Earth is covered in ocean, the majority of these chunks of space debris fall into the sea. If the spacecraft or satellite has the ability to control its trajectory, then the re-entry is designed such that as little as possible hits land.

The colour of the fireball would be due to the chemical composition of whatever is burning. For example, green could indicate copper. Such events are rare and normally very spectacular – you should count yourself lucky!

Telescopes

What is the best telescope for a beginner to start with, and what sort of things can be seen with it?

Peter Isles (Bristol), Sherri Smith (Basildon, Essex), Jos (Dorset), Chris Durkin (Three Legged Cross, Dorset), April Ryder (Shropshire), R Burford (Bath, Somerset), John Kavanagh (Liverpool), Robert Westacott (Ipswich, Suffolk), Roger Creed (Camberley, Surrey), Tom Clarke (Luton), George Salloway (Derby), John Heselden (Wiltshire), Andrew Meredith (Sunderland, Tyne & Wear) and James Davies (Crewe)

I will start by assuming that our beginner really *is* a complete beginner who knows absolutely nothing about astronomy. I repeat my earlier advice to do some reading and begin learning your way around the sky. An excellent tool for this is a planisphere, which shows what is visible in the sky at any time of the year and at any time of the night. There are a number of excellent pieces of software available as well. I am also very strongly of the opinion that, before considering a telescope, newcomers to astronomy should invest in a pair of binoculars. I have a very good pair of '7 x 50' binoculars (7 is the magnification and 50 is the diameter in millimetres of each of the small telescopes in the pair) – I believe they cost me £4 in a lost property office! Of course, binoculars come in many kinds, but those with bigger apertures and magnification can collect more light and show more detail.

But the questioners asked particularly about telescopes. Astronomical telescopes are of two main types: refractors and reflectors. A refractor collects its light by means of a specially shaped glass lens known as an 'object-glass' or objective lens. The light passes through the object-glass and the various rays are 'bunched up' to bring the light into focus. At the focal point an image is formed and magnified by a second lens known as an eyepiece. The eyepiece is interchangeable, and all telescopes will have several: one for low-power views, one for more detailed views, and possibly one of still higher power to use for special objects on very good nights.

My first telescope was a three-inch refractor, that is to say a refractor with an object-glass three inches across – it served me very well and still does. Obviously a mounting is all important, because a shaky mounting would mean that the object you are looking at would move around and produce a result that is of very little use. The simple tripod of my three inches is quite satisfactory.

I used to say that a refractor with an object-glass less than three inches across would be of very little use, and I advised against buying a telescope costing less than £100. Things are somewhat different now and it is quite possible to buy a useful little refractor at a cost of less than £100. It will show you a tremendous amount of detail on the Moon, it will show you the four main moons (or satellites) of Jupiter, and it will even give you a reasonable view of the lovely rings of Saturn. Of the other planets, Venus shows phases, or changes in shape, in a similar way to the Moon, although not much else can be seen there because the actual surface is hidden by Venus's dense cloudy atmosphere.

Looking out to the stars, your telescope will show you wonders of all kinds. In particular, search out the red stars, the star clusters, and the features we call 'nebulae' – Latin for clouds. Some nebulae are really gas clouds in which new stars are being formed. Other 'nebulae' are made up of stars and are themselves entire star systems, or galaxies, very similar to our own Milky Way. It will take you a long time to complete even a rough survey of the sky with your newly acquired telescope; there is so much to see! You can of course obtain a more powerful refractor

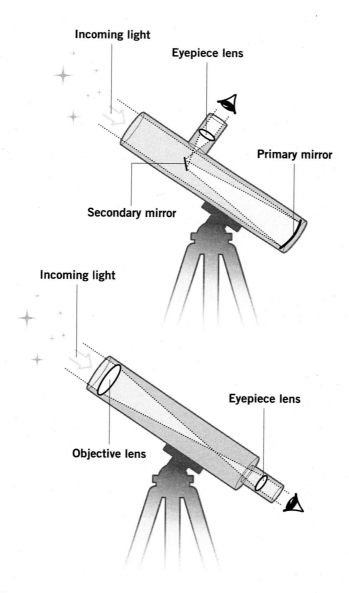

Incoming light

Eyepiece lens

Primary mirror

Secondary mirror

Incoming light

Eyepiece lens

Objective lens

Reflecting telescopes, (*top*), use mirrors to focus the light, while refracting telescopes (*bottom*) use lenses. There are many variations on each type.

with a larger object-glass, though this takes us away from the role of the absolute beginner. The larger the object-glass, the more light the telescope can collect and the fainter the objects it will show you, but using them takes more experience and it really is much better to start with something more modest.

You could also consider reflecting telescopes. The reflector collects light using a curved mirror. A popular arrangement is the Newtonian telescope, first worked out in 1668 by Sir Isaac Newton. Here the light comes down an open tube and hits the mirror at the bottom. This curved mirror reflects the light waves back up the tube on to a smaller flat mirror placed at an angle of 45 degrees. This flat mirror directs the rays to the side of the tube where they are brought to a focus, and the resulting image is enlarged by an eyepiece. In a Newtonian reflector you are 'looking into' the side of the telescope rather than along its length. There are many other kinds of reflectors but the Newtonian is the simplest. For example, a popular telescope amongst experienced observers is a Schmidt-Cassegrain telescope, which is more compact than a Newtonian, though considerably more expensive.

Now let us compare the advantages and disadvantages of these two types. A refractor has the advantage that it needs very little maintenance, and if properly cared for will last a lifetime. By comparison, a reflector tends to be much more temperamental. Generally speaking the mirror is made of glass coated with a thin layer of some very reflective material such as silver or aluminium. The mirrors have to be periodically re-coated, and this is not so simple a matter as might be expected. Against all of this, a reflector is generally cheaper than a refractor of an equivalent power in terms of the initial outlay. Today, all the world's largest telescopes are reflectors, though that is largely because it is much easier to make enormous mirrors (some of which are more than 8 metres across!) than it is to make massive lenses.

A four-inch or six-inch reflector will give endless pleasure and many amateurs now favour them. But it is certainly true that you do not need to spend huge amounts of money on elaborate equipment. A small reflector or refractor will give you the best possible start. If you do need any extra help then contact your local astronomical society because you will almost certainly find somebody ready and willing to help you.

How can I get the best possible view of the Messier objects, particularly the galaxies?

Mark Broster (Norwich)

Some of the Messier objects are decidedly elusive, and their shapes are not easy to make out. They were catalogued in the 1770s by the French astronomer Charles Messier, who was actually searching for comets – most of which look like fuzzy patches through a telescope! The Messier catalogue was compiled as a list of objects that were not comets, and most are star clusters, nebulae or galaxies.

Obviously, the larger and more powerful your telescope, the easier it will be to find them. When you have located your object, it is good practice to use 'averted vision', looking away from the actual object and using the most sensitive part of the eye – which is not in the centre. Some of the Messier objects are quite striking, such as the Whirlpool Galaxy (Messier 51), but others are much less so. Make absolutely certain that you have the right identification, and if you have the adequate photographic equipment, take a long-exposure photograph.

Could you explain the anomaly of the Blinking Nebula? I understand it is some kind of optical illusion, but how is the eye 'tricked'?

Kim Robinson (Leicester)

The Blinking Nebula is a planetary nebula, created when a dying star sheds its outer layers. The central star is still visible, and is much brighter than the surrounding nebulosity. This makes the nebulosity rather hard to see through a small telescope, as the brightness of the star simply overwhelms the eye and prevents it from seeing the more diffuse regions.

To best see the nebula, an observer has to use 'averted vision' – looking slightly away from the star, such that it can be seen in peripheral vision. Without the central star overwhelming the eye's response, the nebulosity reappears. As the eye naturally moves around the field of view of a telescope, the nebulosity appears to blink on and off, hence its name.

This technique of using averted vision is useful in many situations, since the peripheral vision is more suited to seeing fainter objects. The centre of the eye can see in much higher resolution, but is actually somewhat less sensitive.

Is it better viewing the cosmos with two eyes using binoculars or with one eye through a telescope? Are there any binocular professional telescopes out there?

Gavin Hall (East Riding of Yorkshire)

There are a number of commercially available telescopes that make it possible for the observer to use both eyes, though after all this is simply a pair of binoculars. A pair of binoculars consists of two small refractors joined together and capable of being focused either together or separately. It can be easier to observe with both eyes open, but it is much more difficult to put two larger telescopes together and still look through them with both eyes.

Of course there are some very large professional telescopes such as the Large Binocular Telescope, which can provide the resolution of a telescope of twice the diameter of the single one for less than the cost of a mirror twice the size, though the technical details become very complicated. And, since each of the two mirrors is 8.4 metres in diameter, this is certainly leaving the amateur field!

I have a three-inch (75mm) reflector telescope with a few eyepiece lenses, ranging from 20 mm to 4 mm. What can I expect to see with such lowly equipment?

Paul Boswell (Newhaven, East Sussex)

Such equipment is far from lowly, and is what many astronomers start with – both authors of this book in fact started with something very similar! A three-inch telescope is perfectly adequate for seeing a great deal of detail on the Moon, as well as the four largest moons of Jupiter and the rings of Saturn. It is also worth looking out for some of the brighter star clusters, such as the Beehive Cluster in the constellation of Cancer the Crab, the Double Cluster in the constellation of Perseus, or Messier 13 in the constellation of Hercules. These should all be visible through the viewfinder as fuzzy patches, making finding them through the main telescope much easier. And, of course, we must not forget the wonderful Pleiades, also known as the Seven Sisters. It is truly amazing to see those few stars visible with the naked eye turn into the dozens visible through a small telescope.

The Large Binocular Telescope with its twin 8.4-metre mirrors sitting atop Mount Graham in Arizona.

In terms of fainter objects, it should be possible to see the brighter nebulae, such as the Orion Nebula, and even a few galaxies, such as Messier 81, 82 and the Andromeda galaxy M31.

The best way of observing these objects is to start with the lowest-power eyepiece – that is the one with the longest focal length (in this case the 20 mm eyepiece). This will give a wider field of view, which is particularly useful for finding objects, and is generally easier to observe with. When you have found your target, switch to a lower-power eyepiece, say around 10 mm in focal length, to get a better view of your object. Be careful when changing eyepieces, as it is very easy to move the telescope during the process, and remember that you will need to refocus it. The 4mm eyepiece is really rather powerful, and you should only use this for the best observing conditions, as it will not add anything on most nights – in fact, it might even give the impression of making a fuzzier image.

What are the different eyepieces for, such as the 25mm wide-angle eyepiece?

Graham Hoare (Coventry, West Midlands)

An eyepiece is all-important in an astronomical telescope. Trying to use a good telescope with a poor eyepiece is like trying to play a record on a machine with a poor-quality needle, or watching a film through the bottom of a milk bottle! The strength of the eyepiece depends on its focal length, which is the number associated with the eyepiece, normally given in millimetres. The magnification achieved is the focal length of the primary lens or mirror (for a small telescope this is probably somewhere in the region of one metre, though it depends on the design) divided by the focal length of the eyepiece you are using. The main point here is that one cannot use too powerful an eyepiece with too small a telescope. For example, I have a very fine three-

Patrick with his 12½" reflecting telescope, which is ideally suited to observations of the Moon and planets.

inch refractor that I had when I was a boy and which I still use. Use this with an eyepiece with a power up to 100 and the results are excellent, but if I tried the power of, shall we say, 300, the resulting image would be so faint that it would be useless. Generally, the best maximum power for a telescope is about 50 per inch of aperture, and using a lower power can often give more pleasing results.

Is a motor drive on a telescope useful for a novice?

Alan Keys (Brighton, East Sussex)

A motor on a telescope is certainly useful, but it is by no means essential for a beginner.

Some motors only drive one of the telescope axes of motion, and these are for the purposes of keeping the telescope pointed at the same object as the sky rotates (though only if it has an equatorial mount and has been set up correctly). While this is a very useful addition to any telescope, it is far from essential for a beginner. It really is not necessary to buy expensive or elaborate equipment to start observing the skies.

More expensive computerised motors allow the telescope to be pointed at any target in its database. However, I always recommend learning your way around the sky first, otherwise you will find identifications difficult. I compare this to people who have been brought up using a mathematical calculator but have no idea how to carry out manual multiplication and division!

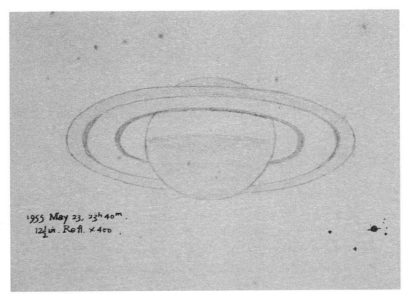

A sketch of Saturn made by Patrick in 1955 using his 12 ½" telescope.

In the twenty-first century, with advances in astrophotography for the amateur, is there still a place for sketching, and can the amateur sketcher still contribute?

Pete Mellor (Saddleworth Moor)

The answer is an emphatic 'Yes'! The sketcher can sometimes come across an unusual feature that the photographer may miss. In particular, the eye is adaptive and can take advantage of the best of the atmospheric conditions, while in contrast a long-exposure photograph will blur the image as the atmosphere fluctuates. Many astrophotographers take black and white images, using different filters to allow the assembly of a colour image. By contrast, the eye can bring out colour in the brighter objects instantly.

Quite above all this, sketching is a very good way to start observing and getting used to the sky. It requires time and patience at the eyepiece to become accustomed to the view, but this makes it an excellent way to become familiar with the sky as seen through the telescope. I suggest that you try it!

When I view images through my telescope, everything appears black and white. Why is it that images from the Hubble Space Telescope are always in glorious colour?

George Brown (Wester Ross, Scotland)

There are several answers to this. First of all, images from Hubble use colour processing, just like almost all astronomical images. Secondly, there is the sensitivity of the eye, or rather the lack of it. Objects seen through a telescope are usually very faint, and the eye is only really capable of seeing faint things in black and white. Mind you, there are some lovely coloured objects in the sky, and my own favourite is the double star Albireo (also called Beta Cygni) which has a golden yellow primary star together with a blue companion. And, of course, Mars is always red while Saturn is yellow.

I'm a Carl Sagan fan, and wondered if it is possible to see the asteroid 2709 Sagan from Earth?

Duncan Borrington-Chance (Bedfordshire)

The asteroid 2709 Sagan orbits the Sun at around twice the distance of the Earth, placing it in the main asteroid belt. Its magnitude is around 13.3, which means that it requires a large telescope to see it. It was discovered in 1982, not by Carl Sagan but by E Bowell of the Lowell Observatory near Flagstaff, Arizona. Its official name is 1982 FH, but it was named in honour of Carl Sagan, one of the leading astronomers of the twentieth century.

Astrophotography

How can I take a photo of stars, given that they move in the night sky?

Mark Bullard (London)

These are easily done with an ordinary camera capable of a long-duration exposure. Of course, the stars will come out as trails across the sky, but the results can be spectacular and the colours of the stars are often brought out very well.

Otherwise, you need a motorised drive to keep your telescope pointed in the same place, and possibly a guide scope to keep the stars in the same position in the image. This needs practice, but it is not very difficult to start getting excellent results. Much of the expertise is spent in processing the image.

Should *The Sky at Night* broadcast another 700 episodes, what photos or images could we expect to see in 53 years' time, and with what sort of clarity?

Jason Eddowes (Manchester)

It is rather difficult to look over half a century ahead. Large amateur telescopes may by then be equipped with adaptive optics, and be able to rival the best professional images of today. From professional telescopes, we may have images of Earth-like planets moving around other stars, and maybe the first stars ever born in the Universe. And, of course, we must remember that we can also expect new results from all parts of the electromagnetic spectrum.

A photograph of star trails taken by Stewart Watt from Thurso Castle over the course of 83 minutes.

Light Pollution

What is the best way to combat light pollution? Are there any tricks?

April Carlucci (London), Paul Foster (Clapham, London),
Morgan James Morgan (Twickenham, Middlesex)

Light pollution is an increasing problem. One obvious solution is to take your telescope to a really dark site as far away as possible from artificial lights, but this is not nearly as easy as it used to be and, of course, it means that your telescope has to be portable. If you are limited to towns and cities, you will really have to confine yourself to brighter objects. There are filters which you can put into your telescope either to cut out unwanted light or to allow through only the wavelengths that you want. If you have a bright street light right on the edge of your garden, the best solution may be an air gun, but unfortunately this is illegal and therefore we couldn't possibly encourage or condone it!

I [PM] do, however, know an astronomer in this country who had a bright street light beyond his hedge. One night he went out and painted it green so it gave out almost no light. As far as I am aware the local council has not yet realised that the light gives out nearly no illumination!

Where are the best places around the UK to observe, away from light-polluted areas?

John Royle (Liverpool) and Aiden Stone (Rotherham, South Yorkshire)

There are various areas that are particularly dark, such as Kielder Park in Northumberland, or Galloway in Scotland. There are other isolated areas where there is not much light pollution due to a lack of people, for example one of the Channel Islands, Sark. But all in all, the only real solution for most people is to head for the remote areas where city lights are hidden from view, and this must mean a portable telescope. You may not have to travel far – a few trees or a small hill can be enough to hide the worst of the glare from a town.

I live in an area where light pollution only allows the brightest stars and planets to be seen. If I know my location, and the position of the object in the sky, is there a way of identifying it?

Brian Armstrong (Merseyside)

For the objects that do not move in the sky, a planisphere will provide the information you require, though they can take a little getting used to. For the most part, your location within the UK will not make much difference to what is visible. An easier solution may be one of several pieces of astronomical software. For example, Stellarium is completely free to download and use and has a very simple interface.

When we are observing at night, we are in the Earth's shadow, but the Sun's rays are also shooting past the Earth in the direction we are looking. Why does this not cause any interference to the night sky?

Michael Bush (Sheffield)

For the main part, there is nothing for the Sun's light to scatter or reflect off, and so we cannot see it. However, there is a way in which it can cause interference, and there is one phenomenon that is always worth looking for. This is called the 'Zodiacal Light', and appears as a faint cone of light seen coming upward from the Sun's position, but when the Sun is below the horizon. It can best be seen after sunset or before sunrise, but the conditions have to be very good as it is very faint. It is due to the Sun's light illuminating very thinly spread particles of dust lying in the main disc of the Solar System.

Even more difficult to see is the Gegenschein, or Counterglow, which appears as a very faint patch of light exactly opposite the Sun in the night sky. It is due to light scattering directly backwards from dust located directly outwards from the Sun with respect to Earth, though I may say that I [PM] have seen it well only two or three times from England!

Radio Astronomy

It is often mentioned that radio telescopes can observe for 24 hours a day, unlike optical telescopes. Why is this so?

Chris Bond (Surrey)

A radio telescope is not affected by scattering or emission by the Earth's atmosphere, and is unaffected by cloud and mist. After all, the main thing that stops optical telescopes observing during the day is the fact that the atmosphere scatters the Sun's light so that it comes from all directions (and, of course, it is sometimes cloudy). There are other problems for radio telescopes, though, such as radio emissions from ground-based sources. For example, many radio telescopes have problems with the signals caused by emissions from mobile phones.

Over the last 50 years, more people have taken up astronomy, and there are many companies building and selling telescopes. Do you think that in the next 50 years there will be companies making radio telescopes for people to buy and set up in their back gardens?

Brian Woosnam (North Wales)

The technology in a lot of radio telescope hardware is much easier to manufacture than that in an optical telescope, but size is a problem. To be effective, the dishes have to be very large. It is possible to buy or construct a small radio telescope for a relatively low cost, and no doubt future companies will find a way around the issue of size. Perhaps in the future there will be a network of amateur radio telescopes working together, much like professional radio telescopes often do today.

The Amateur Scientist

What areas of science can amateur astronomers participate in?

Peter House (Penwortham, Lancashire), Bernard Ingram (Guildford, Surrey), James Brook (Sheffield) and Matthew Porter (Larne, Co Antrim)

Plenty! For example, amateurs are very well equipped to make observations of variable stars, simply because there are so many that the professionals can't observe them all constantly. Amateurs also observe asteroid movements and the surfaces of planets. The clouds on Jupiter and Saturn are always changing, and amateur work is invaluable for monitoring this. It has even been known for amateurs to discover supernovae in other galaxies.

In July 2009, amateur astronomer Anthony Wesley, based in Australia, was the first to observe a new dark spot on Jupiter, which he correctly identified as an impact mark. Amateurs tracked it over the course of days and weeks, and a few observations by the largest telescopes in the world confirmed that it was almost certainly the result of an asteroid striking Jupiter.

How has the role of the amateur astronomer changed over the history of *The Sky at Night*, and how do you envisage it developing over the next 50 years?

Ian Graham (Paris, France) and Martyn Hopkins (Peterborough, Cambridgeshire)

The amateur astronomer is just as important now as he or she was in the 1950s. The rapid development of technology means that amateurs

A photo of Jupiter by Anthony Wesley, which was the first discovery of the impact mark from an asteroid.

can compete with much of what professional astronomers were doing only a decade or so ago. The average size of amateur telescopes has increased, and I suspect this trend will continue. This will allow the amateurs to see fainter and fainter objects, especially when combined with whatever the future of camera technology has in store for us.

In another 50 years, perhaps amateurs will be doing serious spectroscopy, detecting the compounds and elements present in space. While this will not be able to compete with professional telescopes, perhaps the spectrographs of the future will have the resolution that normal cameras have now.

But overall the amateur astronomer will probably continue doing what he or she has always done: marvel at the wonders in the sky and continue to observe.

We are looking to establish an observatory in the Falkland Islands. Given its location in the South Atlantic Ocean, what uses can you see for amateur and professional astronomy?

Linda and Duncan Lunan (Glasgow)

As a professional observatory, the Falkland Islands could do little to compete with the tremendous facilities in Chile, just a few thousand miles away, where some of the largest telescopes in the world are located. The

Falklands are not particularly high and, being islands, probably do not have astounding observing conditions in terms of professional-quality facilities. The best observatories tend to be at altitudes of at least 2,500 metres (8,000 feet), as this puts them above the worst of the weather.

But as an amateur observatory, the Falklands could be a very useful addition to the worldwide network of amateur telescopes. There are two main advantages to setting up observatories around the globe. Firstly, there is the fact that no single location can see the entire sky well. Over the course of a year from the UK we can see the entirety of the northern sky, but only a fraction of the southern sky. We can never see below 39° south, even from the south coast, and anything below the celestial equator will never rise high above the horizon.

From the Falkland Islands, which are about as far south as the UK is north, the situation would be reversed, with the southern skies easily observable. There are very few observatories that far south, aside from a few professional observatories in Antarctica. An advantage that the Falkland Islands have is their longitude, positioned close to South America. Apart from the very tip of South America, the only major landmasses that far south are Southern Africa, Australia and New Zealand, although there are a few other islands dotted throughout the Atlantic and Pacific Oceans. This would make an observatory sited there useful for monitoring transient events, that is to say events that change in a matter of hours. If such an event occurs in the southern skies, then having telescopes at a range of longitudes allows it to be monitored continuously. Such events might include strange occurrences in the atmospheres of Jupiter and Saturn or near-Earth asteroids passing by.

Past and Future Skies

How did ancient cultures measure the motions of the stars so accurately, including the precession of the Earth's spin axis?

Ian Downing (London) and Mick Scutt (Elsenham, Hertfordshire)

Some of the most ancient astronomers were the Babylonians and Sumerians, who lived in modern-day Arabia, more than three thousand years ago. The motion of the Sun, Moon and stars would have been known since ancient times, and the constellations around the zodiac were among the first to emerge. They would have known that different patterns of stars were visible at different times, but they would not have known why. It was these cultures who were the first to notice changes. They would have noticed that some of the planets appeared to move among the stars, particularly the brightest planet, Venus. This was known to be visible in the evening or morning, and the periodicity was noticed by the Sumerians. Of course, they didn't associate this with another planet, but with the actions of deities.

The Babylonians were aware of a number of cycles, such as those that govern the appearance of the Moon, and more importantly lunar and solar eclipses. These cycles were passed on to the Ancient Greeks, who were very methodical and logical in their astronomy. The most astonishing astronomical events would have been the eclipses of the Sun and the Moon – in fact many ancient cultures were terrified of them. Due to the different motions of the Sun and Moon around the sky, eclipses seem to be very irregularly spaced, but in fact they repeat themselves over a period of around 18 years.

This period, called a Saros cycle, is the time it takes for the geometry of the Sun-Earth-Moon system to return to the same configuration. To take into account the rotation of the Earth, then one needs to use a triple-Saros, which is around 54 years. That means that if you observe an eclipse, then in 19,756 days (or 54 years, 1 month) an almost identical eclipse will be visible from the same place on the Earth.

One of the most fascinating remnants from ancient astronomy is the Antikythera Mechanism, which was built in the first or second century BC. Made from Bronze, it was found in a shipwreck off the coast of the Greek island of Antikythera in 1900. After much study it was realised that a sequence of around 30 very carefully arranged cogs could be used to predict the location of the Sun, Moon and planets on any given date. The makers presumably had no knowledge of the layout of the Solar System, and it was designed based on a geocentric model, but its accuracy is astounding. No similar device has ever been found, and it is essentially the oldest known scientific calculator.

In terms of the motions of the stars themselves, they were in general not measurable in ancient times over the course of a single lifetime. The Sun's position in the sky was well measured, and so the locations of the solstices and equinoxes could be charted. An equinox occurs when the Sun crosses the celestial equator, and its position in the sky was monitored by many ancient astronomers. It was the Greek astronomer Hipparchus who, in the second century BC, noted that the location of the Sun at equinox had changed relative to the observations of his predecessors. The discovery of the 'precession of the equinoxes', which we now know to be caused by the rotation of the Earth's axis relative to the stars, marked a turning point in precision astronomy, and the ESA satellite *Hipparcos* was named after him – the strange spelling was because it was actually called the High Precision Parallax Collecting Satellite, or HiPPParCoS.

Hipparchus took one of the first steps in removing the idea that the Earth was at the centre of all motion. He observed that the Sun moved with a varying speed throughout the year, and computed that the centre of the Sun's motion must be slightly offset from the location of the Earth. It would take over a century before scientists were able to overcome the establishment and overturn the theory that the Earth was at the centre, and establish that it moved in an ellipse around the Sun.

The Babylonians and Ancient Greeks were responsible for the first great leaps in astronomy, measuring the movements of the Sun, Moon and planets. More than two thousand years later, the likes of Nicolaus Copernicus, Tycho Brahe and Johannes Kepler made the next leap, removing the idea that the Earth was at the centre of the Universe. I [CN] would argue that we are now emerging from the third great leap in knowledge of astronomy and cosmology, becoming aware of the true scale of the Universe.

Where is the best place in the UK to see the Northern Lights?

Clive Calow (Dingley, Northamptonshire)

The only place with fairly reliable displays is Scotland. Once north of the border, displays are not uncommon, though there are not nearly so many as you get in northern Norway or Alaska. The main aim is to get somewhere really dark, and there are still places like that in Scotland.

So it's worthwhile keeping a regular watch, but don't be surprised if you have to wait for some time. If you go to a place such as Tromsø, north Norway, then you'll see the Northern Lights on most nights of the year.

How has the sky changed throughout the duration of *The Sky at Night*'s existence? Have any new objects arisen, and have there been any major changes in the position or appearances of stars or other objects in the night sky?

George Kristiansen (Upton, Lincolnshire)

Obviously, the stars and the planets don't change for periods much longer than *The Sky at Night*'s duration. We have had some comets, and one or two bright novae. Otherwise, things are very much as they were.

The most spectacular thing I've seen in *Sky at Night* times was probably the great comet Hale-Bopp, which really was a magnificent sight, and remained a naked-eye object for more than a year. I think we were all sorry when it finally bade us farewell. Never mind, it'll be back in 4,000 years!

Of course, some of the planets are always changing, notably Jupiter and Saturn. Jupiter has shown great disturbances in its belts during the last few years, and there has been a tremendous storm on Saturn. It's worthwhile keeping a constant watch.

Will stargazers of the future see star formations such as the Plough, Orion's Belt and the Eagle Nebula as we see them today?

Alan Cave (Staffordshire)

In the foreseeable future there'll be no detectable change, but of course come back in 10,000 years or longer and you'll see definite changes in the constellations. For example, the Great Bear will be distorted, as two of its stars (Alkaid and Dubhe) are moving through space in an opposite direction to the others. The stars are moving through space so slowly that the changes are very hard to see with the naked eye. Mind you, come back in a million years, and the skies will be very different.

Over time, the constellations will become distorted by the movement of the stars, and new patterns will become apparent. Even nebulae will change, as the stars in their centres form from the gas and dust, though this process takes many millions of years.

If we could go forward in time a billion years, how different would the sky look, and how many of the stars would no longer be in existence?

Stephen Andrews (Leigh, Lancashire)

Go forward as far as that and all the constellations will have changed so much that the sky will be unrecognisable. Moreover, some of our familiar stars will have changed beyond all recognition. Rigel in Orion will certainly have been through the Red Giant stage, and will probably have died in a supernova explosion. The same is true of many of the other massive stars in our galactic neighbourhood, though more stars will have sprung up in other locations around the sky.

If the Solar System were plucked out of the Milky Way and placed intact in an otherwise empty region of space, in what ways would we be poorer or richer?

Brian Wood (Cheltenham)

Well, we'd be very much poorer because we'd only see the bodies of our own Solar System. We could know nothing about the stars. In fact, our knowledge would be limited to a very small region, rather like going to London and looking no further than Victoria Station. It must be remembered that astronomy is one of the oldest sciences, with ancient civilisations continually revising and improving our understanding of the cosmos.

The Moon

Observations

I recall as a child in the late 1970s going to a friend's birthday party and seeing the Moon looking very large in the sky. I remember a lot of people commenting on how unusually big it was. What is the explanation for this optical illusion?

Chris Walling (North Wales)

In fact the low-down Moon looks no larger than the high-up Moon, but it certainly gives that impression. The 'Moon illusion' has been known since very ancient times, and it was described by no less a person than Ptolemy, the greatest of the old observers.

The cause is not as straightforward as might be imagined. Ptolemy's explanation was that when the Moon is low down we are seeing it across 'filled space' and can compare it with objects such as trees and hillocks. When it is high up there is absolutely nothing to compare it with and it does not appear so large.

One of us [PM] once produced a *Sky at Night* television programme about this, together with the late Professor Gregory. On the night of a full moon we went down to Selsey beach armed with a mirror which would show us the image of the Moon. We could tilt the mirror to match the Moon's altitude. The idea was to see whether the low-down Moon looked particularly large. We found that it did, although it was really exactly the same size. We also enlisted the help of various holidaymakers on the beach, and asked them to estimate the size of the full moon by picking up a pebble and seeing how far away it would have to be to match the size of the full moon. Everybody got it wildly wrong – next time the Moon is full try it for yourself, and you will see what I mean.

All in all, Ptolemy's explanation seems to be the correct one. The Moon illusion is very marked, but it is an illusion and nothing more.

What exactly is a 'Blue Moon'?

Paul Duff (London)

There are two answers to this, both quite straightforward. If there are two full moons in a calendar month the second is called a blue moon. This is not unusual; the Moon's synodic period (i.e. the interval between successive full moons) is 28.5 days. If a full moon falls on 1 February during a Leap Year, there is bound to be another before the end of the month 29 days later. Owing to the nature of our calendar, blue moons can also occur during other months.

Why blue? It doesn't look blue! The name is due to the misrepresentation of an article in an American journal, the *Maine Farmers' Almanac* in 1937. Why an article in an obscure periodical became so widespread is not clear – but it did, and is still being used even today.

Yet one can have real blue moons. On the evening of 26 September 1950 one of us [PM], observing from East Grinstead in Sussex, noted that 'the Moon shone down from a slightly misty sky with a lovely shimmering blueness – like an electric glimmer, utterly unlike anything that I have seen before.' The sight was not confined to East Grinstead; over the next 48 hours people in various parts of the world reported not only blue moons but even blue suns! Giant forest fires were raging in Canada; vast quantities of dust were hurled into the upper atmosphere, and it was this dust that caused the eerie effects. They lasted for almost a week.

Does the distance of the Earth from the Sun vary according to the phase of the Moon?

Matthew Craven (Rochester, England)

There is no direct connection between phase and distance, but of course at New Moon the Moon is on the sunward side of the Earth and it is then slightly closer to the Sun than the Earth is. At Full Moon the Earth is between the Moon and the Sun and is slightly closer to the Sun than the Moon is. But remember, the Moon is only about a quarter of a million miles from the Earth and the mean distance of the Earth from the Sun is 93 million miles, so these effects are not very great.

All kinds of efforts have been made to link the Moon's phases with other phenomena such as weather. I [PM] once carried out a long study trying to see if there were any link between lunar phases and the weather in my home town of Selsey, and I found absolutely nothing. I think it is fair to say that any effects of this kind are negligible.

We always see the same side of the moon, and never the dark side. If this is true, how has the Moon remained in this neutral state over millions of years? Is this coincidence or is there an explanation?

Matthew Craven (Rochester, England)

There is indeed an explanation. It is also important to talk about the Moon's 'dark side'. The Moon takes 27.3 days to go once around the Earth, or more accurately around what we call the 'barycentre', the centre of gravity of the Earth-Moon system but, as this barycentre lies well inside the Earth, the simple statement 'the Moon goes around the Earth' is good for most purposes. The Moon spins on its axis in exactly the same time; a 'day' on the Moon is 27.3 times as long as ours. The Moon keeps the same face to the Earth, but not to the Sun.

The reason is tidal friction. In the early history of the Solar System, the Moon was much closer to the Earth than it is now, but it has slowly receded. It has been in the state for a very long time – before the space age, we knew nothing about the far side of the Moon, which is always turned away from us. When it became possible to send rockets around the Moon, however, we were able to obtain information about the far side, which turned out to be just as mountainous, cratered and lifeless as the side we have always known.

All the major satellites for the other planets behave in the same way, with 'captured' or 'synchronous' rotation. By now we have complete maps not only of the near side of the Moon but the far side as well.

Orbit and Tides

Why is the Moon 400 times smaller than the Sun and also 400 times closer, making it appear the same size in the sky?

Stuart Abel (Bournemouth, Dorset)

This is pure coincidence, nothing more than that! It is a very fortunate one for us, because it means that otherwise we would not see total eclipses. People have often questioned why this should be so, but it just happens. It is also interesting to note that this situation is not duplicated anywhere else in the Solar System. If you could go to Jupiter (which you cannot!), the satellite Io would appear larger than the Sun, but not exactly the same size, so the effect of an eclipse would not be so spectacular.

In fact, if you could go to any other planet you would not find the same situation. For example, Mars has two satellites, Phobos and Deimos, but both these would appear much smaller than the Sun if you could go to Mars and look. If they passed between Mars and the Sun they would appear as small disks crossing the Sun, and such an image was captured by the Mars rover *Opportunity* in 2004.

What would the Earth be like if we had two moons?

Emma Marie Lea (Brighton, East Sussex)

It would depend on the size of the second moon, and it would probably be much further away from the Earth than our present Moon. Of course it would make its presence felt. For one thing, we would have much brighter

The Full Moon photographed by Jamie Cooper.

nights if the two moons were full at the same time. More importantly, the second moon would cause tides just as the present one does, and the whole situation would become remarkably complicated!

Of course, there are planets with several moons. Mars has two Moons, Phobos and Deimos, but these are less than 20 miles in diameter. The giant planets have whole families of moons. Jupiter has four large satellites and a whole swarm of smaller ones; Saturn has one very big moon (Titan) and several of a fair size, as well as over 60 very small ones. Uranus has four major moons, and Neptune one, though both have a number of smaller ones.

Do lunar eclipses have any effect on earthquakes? What about other planetary alignments?

Anthony Atkinson (Northallerton, North Yorkshire)

No, an eclipse of the Moon has no effect whatever upon earthquakes. There have been many suggestions that the planets may line up and cause effects upon the Earth, but these effects are so small that for all practical purposes we can forget about them.

Of course, we did have a massive earthquake off the coast of Japan after a lunar eclipse in December 2011, but this was sheer chance.

Is the Earth-Moon system a binary planet system? If not, why not?

John Stoney (Malvern, Worcestershire)

This is a particularly interesting question. The Earth and the Moon rotate round their common centre of gravity known as the 'barycentre', but the Earth is 81 times as massive as the Moon and the barycentre lies well inside the Earth's globe. The most common definition of a binary planet system is that the centre of mass must lie outside the surface of both objects, and so by this definition the Earth and Moon do not form a binary system.

There are only a few examples of true binary systems in the Solar System, the vast majority of which are asteroids. The largest and most famous of these is Pluto and its largest satellite, Charon. Charon is around half the diameter of Pluto and around one-tenth the mass, and the barycentre lies well above the surface of Pluto.

Out of the all the satellites of eight major planets in the Solar System, our Moon is the largest relative to its host planet. Although there are several satellites larger than the Moon (three in Jupiter's system, one in

Saturn's), all these move round much more massive giant planets. So the Earth-Moon system is unique and I [PM] regard it as a double planet rather than a planet and a satellite.

Why do we have two tides in a 24-hour period, when the Moon only orbits once every 24 hours?

Nigal (Conwy, Wales)

The theory of the tides is remarkably complex. On Earth, both the Sun and the Moon cause notable tides, but those of the Moon are much stronger. Imagine the whole Earth covered with a shallow uniform ocean and both the Earth and the Moon are standing still. The Moon's gravitational pull is heaping the water up on the nearest side where the force is strongest. This is all very well, but at first sight it is not so easy to see where there should be a second high tide on the far side of the Earth. It is slightly misleading to say, as many books do, that the solid globe is simply being pulled away from the water, so for a moment let us assume that we have a situation in which the Earth and the Moon are alone in the Universe, and are falling towards each other because of their mutual gravitational pulls. Taking the matter a step further, imagine that it is the Moon which is standing still, and the Earth is being drawn towards it. The point which is closest to the Moon would be subject to a greater accelerating force than the average, and so the water will bunch up around it. The result would be a high tide. On the far side, the reverse will happen. The acceleration will be less than the average, and so the water in that region would tend to be 'left behind' so bulging away and causing a similar high tide. Of course, the Earth is not falling towards the Moon, but remaining at the same distance as they both orbit their common centre of gravity (or barycentre) once every 27.3 days. In

The gravitational pull of the Moon creates tides on both sides of the Earth.

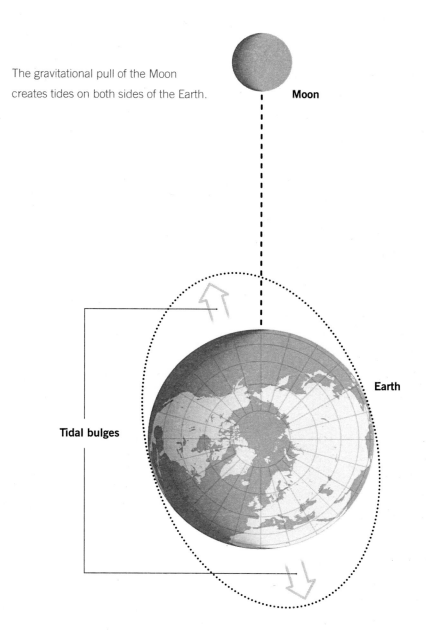

Moon

Earth

Tidal bulges

NOTE: Distance between Earth and Moon not to scale.

addition, the Earth is spinning round once in 24 hours. Obviously, the water heaps – that is to say the high tides will not spin with it, but will keep 'under the Moon'. Therefore, each bulge will seem to sweep right round the Earth once in 24 hours, and every region would have two high tides and two low tides a day.

There are many complications, but the basic picture is what we have given here. For example, if you look at the location of the Moon at high tide, you will notice that it is not directly overhead – in fact it is probably very close to the horizon. That is because the viscosity of the water causes it to be pushed ahead of the point directly under the Moon.

There are tides caused by the Sun as well and, while these Solar tides are much weaker than those of the Moon, they do have an effect. When the Sun and the Moon are pulling in the same 'sense' as full moon and new moon, the tides are strong, and we call these spring tides, although they have nothing to do with the season of the spring. At half moon, the solar and lunar tides are pulling against each other, and we have what are called neap tides.

There are tides in the land too, but these may be disregarded for most purposes because the land is solid rather than liquid, and land tides are really weak.

The Moon is receding from the Earth, but what is pulling them out of orbit?

Diane Clarke (Thamesmead, London)

I am afraid this is all a bit complicated, but we will make it as simple as we can. The crux of the matter is what is termed angular momentum. The angular momentum of a moving body around a point or axis is a measure of the amount of rotation, or spin, that it has. It is obtained by multiplying together its mass, the square of its distance from the centre of motion, and the rate of angular motion – that is to say the rate of axial rotation. According to a well-known principle, angular momentum can never be destroyed; it can only be converted. If therefore the axial rotation is slowed down, as happened in the Earth-Moon system because of tidal forces, something else had to increase, and this 'something' was the distance between the two bodies.

The process is not complete even now, because the Moon's tidal pull on the Earth is still braking our rotation. Each day is approximately 0.00000002 seconds longer than its predecessor, though there are also irregular fluctuations unconnected with the Moon. Also, the Moon is still receding from us. The rate of increase is only 1.5 inches (4 centimetres) per year, however, so that we need be in no hurry to study the Moon before it disappears into the distance!

In fact, the Moon will not go on receding indefinitely. If it could move out to 350,000 miles, it would start to draw inward again, because of tidal effects due to the Sun, and would eventually be broken up into a swarm of particles – but this will not happen, because long before the critical period both Earth and Moon will have been destroyed as the Sun swells out to become a red giant star. In the meantime, we may be sure that nothing dramatic will happen to the Moon for a good while.

How far from the Earth was the Moon 400 million years ago (early Devonian) and how high were the tides then compared with today?

David Leather (Ilkley, West Yorkshire)

At present the mean distance of the Moon is 238,000 miles (the orbit is, of course, slightly eccentric). Today most astronomers believe the Moon was caused by a giant impact on the original Earth, and initially the Moon and the Earth were very close together. Tidal friction has resulted in the recession of the Moon at the rate of 1.5 inches (4 cm) per year. The Devonian period, so called because rocks of this period are well seen in Devonshire, began about 408 million years ago, following the Silurian period, during which life was developing. At the start of the Devonian there were early land plants, together with amphibians, insects and spiders. The Devonian was a warm period, and Greenland, North West Scotland and North America were probably joined.

The Moon had receded to a distance of roughly 200 thousand miles, and went around the barycentre once in approximately 18 hours so that its days were much shorter than they are now. Because the Moon was closer, the tides were around half as high again as those of today. It took some time for these tides to become more moderate, which they did in the following period known as the Carboniferous, when the coal measures were laid down and the first reptiles appeared.

Why do we sometimes see the Moon and the Sun in the same part of the sky?

Alan Thomas (York)

The best way to explain this is to imagine that the Sun stays motionless in the sky while the Moon makes its journey around the Earth over the course of a month (actually 27.3 days). If this was so, anyone on the Earth would see the Moon and the Sun close together once every orbit. If the Moon passes directly over the Sun the result is a solar eclipse.

Of course all three bodies are moving, but we on Earth see the Moon and the Sun in the same part of the sky. It is difficult to see the Moon when it is near the Sun, but when it is further away we see it quite clearly. As the Moon moves around its orbit we see different amounts of its illuminated surface, and we call these the phases of the Moon.

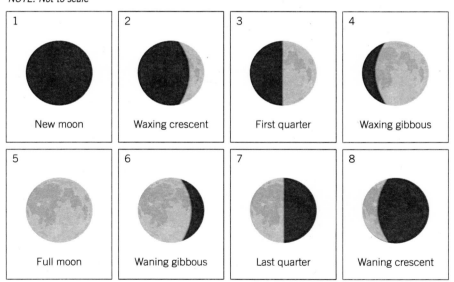

NOTE: Not to scale

1	2	3	4
New moon	Waxing crescent	First quarter	Waxing gibbous

5	6	7	8
Full moon	Waning gibbous	Last quarter	Waning crescent

As the Moon orbits the Earth different proportions of its near-side are illuminated by the Sun, causing the phases of the Moon.

Do erupting volcanoes, meteor strikes, nuclear explosions, rocket launches, etc. affect the orbit and/or speed of revolution of a planet/satellite?

Frank Ward (Leicester)

Let us begin by considering earthquakes. If they are very violent, such as the Japanese earthquakes of 2011, they can have tiny effects upon the Earth's rotation period, but these are so small that for all practical purposes they can be ignored. For example, the Japanese earthquake of 2011 shortened the length of a day by just under two millionths of a second – no need to adjust your watches! Volcanoes can also have very minor effects; nuclear explosions, rocket launches, etc. are far too weak to have any measurable effects on movement around the Sun, or the speed of rotation.

A meteor is a tiny particle which burns away in the Earth's upper atmosphere; we see it as a shooting star. It is of dust-grain size, and can have no effect at all. But in the past the Earth has been struck by much larger bodies and most astronomers believe that the Moon was formed when the Earth was hit by a body about the size of Mars. If this happens again, the results would be very serious from our point of view, but the chances of this now seem to be extremely small. In very recent times there have been bodies of considerable size which have hit the Earth such as the Siberian impact of 1908, but even this was much too small to knock the Earth out of its orbit. One might as well try to stop a charging hippopotamus by throwing a baked bean at it!

We don't often hear of Cruithne, the Earth's second 'moon' discovered in 1986. Is it still performing its irregular path in relation to the Earth, and why have there been no missions to investigate it?

Eric Hayman (London)

The asteroid called 3753 Cruithne is a perfectly ordinary asteroid, discovered in 1986 by Duncan Waldron. Is simply happens to have a rather unusual orbit. It is very small, about 3 miles (5 km) in diameter, and spins around once in 27 hours. Its brightest apparent magnitude is 15, which means that it is fainter than Pluto. I [PM] have seen it with my 15-inch telescope but not very easily.

The strange thing about the orbit is that in some ways it is similar to that of the Earth. Its average distance from the Sun is almost exactly the same, at one astronomical unit, but its orbit is much more eccentric than the Earth's, and also is tilted at an angle of almost 20 degrees. Its distance from the Sun ranges between 1.3 astronomical units and 0.6 astronomical units. This means that it seems to accompany the Earth around the Sun, and makes periodic close approaches but there is no danger to the Earth. It has been said that Cruithne follows a path relative to the Earth like a kidney bean, though it can also make close approaches to Mars.

Although the orbit appears to be related to the Earth, this pattern will not continue indefinitely; there is no real point in sending a mission to it, because we know enough about it to realise there is nothing unusual about it apart from its orbit at this present moment.

There are one or two others asteroids of the same type, such as 54509 YORP and 1998 UP1. But let's all be clear – Cruithne is an ordinary asteroid with an unusual orbit, and not a second Earth satellite. Clyde Tombaugh, who discovered Pluto in 1930, made a very careful search for minor moons of the Earth. He failed to find any, and it now seems safe to say that we have no second satellite with a diameter of more than a foot or two.

Mars has four known asteroids sharing its orbit, of which the largest is 5261 Eureka. So far as we know, Venus has none.

Eclipses

During a lunar eclipse, does the Earth cast a perfect shadow on the Moon?

Simon Franklin (Leeds)

When the Moon is eclipsed, it passes into the shadow cast by the Earth. The Earth's shadow has two parts: the 'umbra', within which the Earth obscures the entire Sun, and the 'penumbra', within which the Earth only obscures part of the Sun's disc. The edge of the Earth's umbral shadow on the Moon is very obvious; during a total eclipse the entire Moon is shadowed. An eclipse does not happen at every full moon, because the Moon's orbit is not in the same plane as that of the Earth.

When the eclipse is total, all direct sunlight is cut off from the Moon, but the Moon does not (usually) disappear completely because the light is bent or refracted onto the lunar surface by the Earth's atmosphere. Since blue light is scattered away more easily by the Earth's atmosphere, the surface of the Moon appears red. The French astronomer Danjon has given a scale for lunar eclipses ranging from 0 (very dark) out to 4 (coppery or orange red, with a bright, bluish rim). Of course all light reaching the eclipsed Moon has to pass through the Earth's atmosphere, and everything depends on the atmospheric conditions. After a volcanic eruption, for instance, a great deal of dust has been sent into the Earth's upper air, and this blocks the light onto the eclipsed Moon so that the eclipse is 'dark'.

Lunar eclipses do not have the glory of solar eclipses, and to be honest they are not important, but they are always worth watching and have a quiet beauty of their own.

Why do eclipses of the Moon only seem to occur at full moon?

Andy Parker (Leeds)

Simply because this is the only time when the Earth, Sun and the Moon are all lined up, with the Earth in the mid position. This means that only then can the Earth's shadow fall upon the Moon. The slight tilt of the Moon's orbit means that they don't occur every month.

During the last total eclipse of the Sun visible from the UK, I turned and saw a beautiful planet in the sky. I will never forget the sight, it was absolutely amazing! Why do we not hear about seeing the planets during an eclipse?

Linda Parker (Christchurch, Dorset)

When the Sun is totally eclipsed, it is certainly possible to see the bright planets and the brightest stars. But during totality, why waste time in looking at them? This is a very special occasion; so one can see the Sun's corona and prominences, and it is probably the most magnificent sight in all nature. It doesn't happen very often, though, and if you stay in Britain the last total eclipses were those of 1927 and 1999 (though in 1954 the eclipse was total very briefly over Northern Scotland). The next UK eclipses will be on on 3 September 2081, in the Channel Islands, and in 2090 in Southern Ireland and Cornwall, so if you would like to see one sooner then a plane ticket will in all likelihood be required.

If you want to search the stars and planets during totality there is no reason not to, but remember that totality ends very suddenly, and as soon

A photo of total solar eclipse, taken by Alan Clitherow from Turkey in 2006 during *Sky at Night* filming. With the full glare of the Sun obscured, fine structure is visible in the solar corona.

as the bright surface of the Sun reappears it is as dangerous as when it is not eclipsed at all. Our advice – don't bother about stars and planets; spend your time marvelling at the Sun.

The Earth is not in a circular orbit and its distance from the Sun varies. What happens when an eclipse occurs when we are at our closest to the Sun?

Paul Spencer (Worthing, East Sussex)

It is correct that the Earth's orbit around the Sun is not quite circular, and as its distance from the Sun varies so does the apparent diameter of the Sun as seen from Earth. Similarly, the Moon moves around the Earth (or, more accurately, around the centre of gravity of the Earth-Moon system), but again not in a circular orbit, so that its apparent diameter varies.

The most important factor is the Moon's variable distance from the Earth, which can range from 250,000 miles to less than 230,000 miles. If an eclipse of the Sun happens when we are closest to the Sun and the Moon is at its furthest from the Earth, the Moon doesn't appear large enough to cover the Sun completely so, if the lining up is exact, a ring of sunlight is left showing around the dark disk of the Moon. This is called an annular eclipse; the name 'annular' comes from the Latin *annulus*, meaning 'ring'. An eclipse of this kind is fascinating to watch, but not as magnificent as a total solar eclipse because neither the corona nor prominences can be seen. Is it important to remember not to look directly at the Sun through any kind of telescope during an annular eclipse, because the ring of sunlight left showing makes the Sun just as dangerous as it is when there is no eclipse at all.

Are there any other places in the Solar System where eclipses can be seen?

Chris Grey (Guildford, Surrey)

Yes, but there is no other case where the observer of the surface of another planet can see a satellite just big enough to cover the Sun. For example, consider someone standing on the 'surface' of Saturn (which, of course, cannot be done, because the surface of Saturn is gaseous). All Saturn's major moons out as far as Titan appear bigger than the Sun as seen from Saturn, so that when they pass in front of the Sun they hide it completely. In contrast, from the surface of Mars the largest Martian moon Phobos looks too small to cover the entire disc of the Sun. Therefore there is no other place where there are total eclipses as we see them from Earth, and so the Earth is the only place that solar prominences can ever be seen with the naked eye.

Formation and Impacts

Why is Earth's Moon round, when the moons of some other planets are irregular in shape, and how did it form?

Sally Ward (Brora, Sutherland)

The Earth's Moon is so large that it is 'differentiated' – that is to say it has a core and an outer shell. To develop in this way a body has to be large enough and dense enough, and some of the satellites of other planets are not. Generally speaking, any body more than 200 miles across is liable to be a globe. The gravity on the surface of such a large body is strong enough to flatten out any large irregularities.

The only major satellite which is completely irregular in shape is Hyperion, one of the satellites of Saturn. Its maximum diameter is over 200 miles, but it is of very low density. It seems to be composed mainly of water ice and only a little rock, so that it is not dense enough to be differentiated. There have been suggestions that Hyperion is half of a larger body which broke up. This is not impossible – but if so, where's the other half?

In terms of the Moon's formation, there have been endless arguments about the origin of the Moon, and even now we cannot pretend that we are quite sure.

The first widely accepted theory, proposed in 1878, was that of GH Darwin (son of Charles Darwin). The Earth and the Moon were originally combined and rotated so quickly that part of the globe broke away and became the Moon. Some later authorities, notably O Fisher, believed that the basin left by the departing Moon is now filled by the Pacific Ocean.

All this sounds plausible, but there are fatal mathematical objections. A thrown-off mass would not form a lunar-sized globe; also, the Moon's diameter is one-third that of the Earth, but the depth of the Pacific Ocean is negligible compared with the diameter of the Earth. Darwin's theory is now universally rejected.

HC Urey put forward the 'capture theory': the Moon was formed in the same way as the Earth from the solar nebula and was originally an independent planet, but after a while the two became gravitationally linked. However, this would require a very special set of circumstances, and cannot explain why the Moon is so obviously less dense than the Earth. Again, Urey's theory has been rejected.

In 1984, W Hartmann and DR Davies proposed the Giant Impact theory. This involved a collision about four thousand million years ago between the Earth and a body about the size of Mars. The cores of the two bodies merged, and debris was spread around, subsequently accreting to form the Moon. At the time of the collision, so much energy was set free that the outer part of the young Moon was melted to form a deep global magma ocean. Over the next 100 million years, the dense elements in the young Moon sank to form the core, while the lighter elements rose up and floated to make up the surface – a process known as 'differentiation'. Following this came the period of Heavy Bombardment, when both Earth and Moon were pelted by smaller bodies moving around the Sun, with a result that both were cratered. We still see the craters of the Moon but most of the craters of the Earth have been eroded by the action of wind and water, as well as the motion of the tectonic plates.

It is this theory which is now generally accepted, but there are still difficulties, and some authorities are very doubtful about it. At one stage Harold Urey commented that, since all theories of the Moon's origin were so unsatisfactory, science had proved that the Moon does not exist!

Was the Moon's orbit in the same direction as the Earth's rotation after its formation?

Chuck Atkins (Portland, Oregon, USA)

Probably but, as we have seen in other questions, we are by no means sure how the Moon was formed. If the Giant Impact theory is right, everything was rotating in the same direction, but of course it is very difficult to see just what happened when the impact occurred.

There are no other major satellites in the Solar System that move around their primaries in the direction opposite to that in which the primary is rotating, with the exception of Triton, the large satellite of Neptune; there seems no doubt whatever that Triton was an independent body in the Kuiper Belt which was captured by Neptune, and is therefore a special case. To be candid, this is really as much as we can say at the moment.

If the Moon is covered with evidence of meteorite damage, why do we not see meteorites hitting it now?

Jason Gillingham (Kettering, Northamptonshire)

We have to remember that all craters of the Moon are very old by terrestrial standards. There has been very little major bombardment for at least a thousand million years, but the Moon has no atmosphere, and so the craters produced by the impacts are still visible, whereas most of the craters that must have been formed on the Earth have been eroded away.

If there are impacts, even small ones, continuing to the present day, then they should be observable with telescopes and modern recording equipment. Flashes have been recorded, some by experienced observers, and even photographed, though we have never seen craters produced where the flashes have been seen. Also, one would expect a major impact to produce a cloud of dust which would be visible for some time before sinking to the surface, and nothing of the kind has ever been observed.

It has often been said that there are visible impacts on the Moon at times of meteor showers. There is considerable disagreement here. One of us [PM] is of the opinion that a shooting star meteor, which is of sand-grain size, is far too small to cause a flash visible from the Earth; other observers believe that we really are seeing tiny bodies impacting the Moon. The jury is still out.

Has the creation of a Moon crater ever been observed and, if so, when was the last one?

Peter Barton (Doddinghurst, South Essex)

We have never observed the formation of any large crater and, as we have noted, all the large lunar craters are very ancient. However, we have created our own craters. The lunar probes SMART-1 and LCROSS were deliberately flown into the Moon, with the impacts being imaged by telescopes around the world, as well as by satellites in orbit around the Moon. There are small pieces of rock flying through space, some of which hit the Moon, and since the Moon has no atmosphere we must expect tiny craters to be formed all the time.

There are some interesting historic reports of changes on the Moon, however, including an event witnessed in 1178. This was described in medieval chronicles by Gervase of Canterbury and, according to J Hartung (1976), the translation from the original Latin reads:

In this year, on the Sunday before the Feast of St John the Baptist, after sunset when the moon had first become visible a marvellous phenomenon was witnessed by some five or more men who were sitting there facing the moon, and as usual in that phase its horns were tilted toward the east; and suddenly the upper horn split in two. From the midpoint of this division a flaming torch sprang up, spewing out, over a considerable distance, fire, hot coals, and sparks. Meanwhile the body of the moon which was below writhed, as it were, in anxiety, and, to put it in the words of those who reported it to me and saw it with their own eyes, the moon throbbed like a wounded snake. Afterwards it resumed its proper state. This phenomenon was repeated a dozen times or more, the flame assuming various twisting shapes at random and then returning to normal. Then after these transformations the moon from horn to horn, that is along its whole length, took on a blackish appearance. The present writer was given this report by men who saw it with their own eyes, and are prepared to stake their honour on oath that they have made no addition or falsification in the above narrative.

The 'horns' to which they refer are simply the points of the crescent Moon, and what they describe seems to fit with what might be expected from a fairly large impact. In his investigations, Hartung came to the conclusion that these men may well have been witnesses to the formation of the crater Giordano Bruno. This crater is in the same area that the description identifies (near the upper tip of a waxing crescent Moon), and seems to be one of the younger craters on the Moon, estimated at around 800 years old. Its youth is indicated by its relatively bright appearance and the presence of rays emanating from it, which would be eroded over time by subsequent impacts.

The interpretation of the description is that the men, who may or may not have been experienced astronomers, saw a flash as material from the impact was illuminated by sunlight, which they interpreted as flames and sparks. The dimming of the entire crescent Moon could have been due to a shroud of dust temporarily surrounding the Moon, though it is surprising that this happened so quickly and it may have simply been clouds in the Earth's atmosphere.

Of course, the observations are probably impossible to prove. The formation of a crater would have created a shower of bright meteors in the Earth's atmosphere, something that would certainly have been of note at the time. The lack of evidence for such a shower is not promising for the hypothesis, but it is very tempting to imagine that we could have a written record of such a remarkable event.

What would happen if an asteroid crashed into our Moon rather than the Earth?

Frank Duckworth (Washington, Tyne & Wear)

If a large asteroid impacted the Moon, it would make a very large crater! This has certainly happened in the past: the huge Mare Imbrium certainly has an impact origin, for example. But the age of the Heavy Bombardment is over and, though there is no reason to suppose that a major impact will occur in the future, the Earth is properly more likely to be hit than the Moon, because of its greater gravitational pull.

It is impossible to predict when this will happen, if it ever does, but it certainly cannot be ruled out.

Is the greater cratering on the far side of the Moon due to the fact that the Earth shelters the facing side?

Andy Cook (Yate, Bristol)

The difference in cratering between the Earth-turned and far sides is due to quite a number of factors. Of course, the fact that the Earth shields

Mare Ibrium, one of the 'lunar seas', was formed by a huge impact billions of years ago and subsequently filled with lava. This volcanic material appears darker than the surrounding terrain, as clearly shown in this image by Julian Cooper.

the facing side is one, and the Moon has kept the same face turned towards the Earth since a long time ago in the story of the Earth-Moon system. Also, in those far-off days, the Moon must have had some kind of atmosphere, though this would have quickly disappeared. The interior of the Moon was also active, with vulcanism going on everywhere, and the end result is that the two sides are quite different. On the far side, there are no major seas of the type such as the Mare Imbium on the Earth-turned side. Studies of the Moon's interior have shown that the crust is significantly thicker on the far side. There are several possible explanations for this – that the difference in the tides experienced on the two faces caused the difference in structure, for example – but it is not yet clear which is right.

Recent computer simulations have suggested that the thicker crust on the far side could have formed from the impact of a second moon. This second moon could easily have been formed in the same impact that formed the Moon we see today, and it is possible that it could have ended up in a stable orbit for tens of millions of years. Eventually, however, that orbit would have become unstable and the second moon, which is assumed to be somewhat smaller, would have hit our Moon from behind (at least from our point of view). If at the time of the impact our Moon was still in the process of cooling then it would still have had a small molten mantle below the surface. The simulations indicated that the impact of a second moon could have coated the far side with the same sort of material as seen in the crust, and shifted the mantle to the near side.

While this theory would explain the observations, it is hard to prove. The material from the second, smaller moon would have cooled more quickly and therefore would appear older. The proof (or otherwise) could come from the results of the twin satellites of the GRAIL mission, which went into orbit around the Moon at the start of 2012.

Mysteries

'Lunar swirls' are found on the Moon, usually directly opposite large impact basins. Why are they still visible today when the impact basins were formed billions of years ago?

Geoff Roynon (Isle of Dogs, London)

These features are decidedly mysterious, and we do not yet have a full explanation of them. There are not many of these swirls, and it seems that they are associated with impacts which occurred when the Moon's core was still molten. There is little doubt that magnetism was involved; the Moon has no detectable overall magnetic field now, but it is likely that there used to be one when the core was still molten. It was not molten for very long, however, as the Moon's small size means that it has cooled much more rapidly than the Earth.

Conspiracy theorists tell us that the Moon landings were staged. Surely, the lunar rover and launch platforms can still be seen by telescopes on Earth?

Jason Taggart (London)

When we hear about these conspiracy theories, the instinct is to look around for men in white vans! Quite honestly, it would be more difficult to fake the landings than actually do them. What can one say about people who believe that men never landed on the Moon? If ignorance is bliss, they must be very happy.

Actually, the rover and other signs of man's activity cannot yet be seen by Earth-based telescopes because they are too small, but they have been photographed by the Lunar Reconnaissance Orbiter from lunar orbit. They are quite unmistakable. Surely these pictures should have killed the conspiracy theory once and for all? But there are some people who will never be convinced, and arguing with them is like to trying to eat tomato soup with a fork!

If there was one thing you could have an answer to regarding lunar observations, what would it be? What has had you scratching your head after all these years?

Adrian Asbury (Tamworth)

My answer [PM] is the cause of the elusive outbreaks which we call transient lunar phenomena (or TLP for short). For a long time, it was thought that these observations were faulty, probably because they were made by amateur observers, but they have also been seen by professional astronomers paying close attention to the Moon. It is almost certainly quite wrong to say TLP are due to volcanic activity. I am certain that they are real, however, and the famous French astronomer Audouin Dollfus has actually photographed them. My own theory is that the rising Sun can heat and uplift dust off surfaces on the Moon, and this is the main cause.

There are some areas much more susceptible to TLP than others, and the most famous of these is the brilliant crater Aristarchus, which is one reason why I would like a future mission to be sent there.

How likely is it that a telescope will be constructed on the far side of the Moon, and what would the benefits be?

Paul Bertenshaw (Ashby de la Zouch, Leicestershire)

There are many advantages to having a telescope on the surface of the Moon. There is no light pollution, and no atmospheric disturbance. If all goes well, and the world leaders agree to work together, this could well happen within the next decade or two. (Whether it actually will, however, is a matter of much debate.)

But going onto the far side has other advantages, too. There would be absolutely no disturbance from anything we can see from Earth and, more importantly still, the far side of the Moon would be the ideal place for a radio telescope. On Earth, radio telescopes are being increasingly disturbed by commercial and private transmissions; it was once said, by the Astronomer Royal, that 'unless something were done, radio astronomy from Earth will be limited to the entirety of the twentieth century'. This has not happened, but certainly radio astronomers would be immensely relieved to have a completely 'radio quiet' site.

Neither does there seem any crushing reason why this should not be accomplished. Landing a radio telescope on the far side of the Moon should not be a great deal more difficult than landing one on the near side. Of course, this requires full international cooperation, and we can only hope that this will be forthcoming. If it is, then we may hope that in the foreseeable future a radio telescope on the Moon's far side will lead on to all manner of new discoveries. (En passant, where better to listen out for signals coming from some remote world light years away? This may seem far-fetched, but stranger things have happened!)

The Solar System

Could you describe the sizes and distances from the Sun of the planets in our Solar System?

Tom Williamson (Northumberland)

Yes, this can certainly be done. We must remember in our Solar System there are tremendous differences in size and mass, with Jupiter, the largest planet, being more massive than all the others put together. To explore this, let us use a scale based on London. We will place the Sun just outside the Houses of Parliament at Westminster, and make it a globe 600 feet in diameter – which is a little less than the length of the Houses of Parliament. The planets can now be filled in on the same scale. First, we have Mercury at 2 feet in diameter, about the size of a large beach ball, and at a distance from Westminster of 4.75 miles. That's about as far as Hampstead Heath, or Wimbledon, so there is immediately a sense of the immense distances between the planets relative to the sizes of them and the Sun. Venus would be 5.25 feet in diameter and 9 miles away, taking us out to Croydon, or Mill Hill. The Earth is a little bigger, at 5.5 feet in diameter, and 12.25 miles away (somewhere near Barnet), while Mars is 3 feet in diameter and 18.5 miles distant (in St Albans). This puts us outside the M25 ringroad. The 'Asteroids', or Minor Planets, are tiny globes ranging from the size of a grain of sand to five inches in diameter, at an average distance of 30 miles (around the region of Slough or Luton).

MIN: Minimum distance from Sun / MAX: Maximum distance from Sun
NOTE: Distances between planets is not to scale

Sun
(Radius: 695,500 km)

Mercury (Radius: 2,440 km)
MIN: 46 million km / MAX: 70 million km

Venus (Radius: 6,052 km)
MIN: 108 million km / MAX: 109 million km

Earth (Radius: 6,371 km)
MIN: 147 million km / MAX: 152 million km

Planets

Mars (Radius: 3,396 km)
MIN: 207 million km / MAX: 249 million km

Ceres (Radius: 487 km)
MIN: 380 million km /
MAX: 446 million km

Jupiter (Radius: 69,911 km)
MIN: 741 million km / MAX: 817 million km

Saturn (Radius: 60,268 km)
MIN: 1,353 million km / MAX: 1,513 million km

Uranus (Radius: 25,559 km)
MIN: 2,748 million km / MAX: 3,004 million km

Neptune (Radius: 24,764 km)
MIN: 4,452 million km / MAX: 4,553 million km

Dwarf planets

Pluto (Radius: 1,153 km)
MIN: 4,437 million km / MAX: 7,331 million km

Makemake (Radius: 750 km)
MIN: 5,760 million km / MAX: 7,939 million km

Haumea (Radius: 718 km)
MIN: 5,194 million km / MAX: 7,710 million km

Eris (Radius: 1,300 km)
MIN: 5,650 million km / MAX: 14,600 million km

Our Solar System (not to scale!), showing the eight planets and five dwarf planets.

Jupiter, the giant of the Solar System, is larger than a house at 60 feet in diameter, and 64 miles away – about as far as Selsey or Northampton. Saturn, the ringed planet, is 51 feet in diameter and 117 miles away, reaching as far as Bristol and Lincoln. Uranus, 22 feet in diameter and 236 miles away, would be in the Lake District, while Neptune, 19.5 feet in diameter and 370 miles away, would be over the Scottish border in Edinburgh.

Beyond Neptune, we have hundreds of much smaller bodies, of which the brightest but not the largest is Pluto. Before 2006, Pluto was generally regarded as a planet but has now been changed to the status of a dwarf planet. On our scale it would be nearly 500 miles away from our central Sun. That places it at the same distance as John O'Groats in northern Scotland or, going the other way, in the south of France.

We must not forget the moons or satellites which revolve around most of the planets. Of the large satellites, the Earth has one (the Moon), Jupiter has four and Saturn one; all the other satellites are smaller. One satellite in Jupiter's system, Ganymede, is actually larger than Mercury and two other satellites, Jupiter's moon Callisto and Saturn's single large moon Titan, are very nearly the size of Mercury. Both Jupiter and Saturn also have a large collection of smaller moons. Most other satellites in the Solar System, such as the two attendants of Mars, are indeed tiny. One of the Martian Moons, Deimos, is actually less than 10 miles in diameter, and on the scale we've used here would only be about a sixteenth of an inch across (about 1 mm).

Why are there no small-sized planets, such as the size of a football?

Philip Quinn (Rugby)

There are lots of very small objects in the Solar System, but we don't call them planets. Instead, we call them asteroids. The largest asteroids are hundreds of kilometres in diameter but there are much, much smaller ones around as well.

They can be as big as boulders, or indeed as small as a football. The smaller you go, then typically the more objects of that size there are, and the Solar System in fact contains a healthy supply of tiny grains of dust.

Is it possible to get a planet as large as the Sun?

William Edwards, age 12 (Beckenham, Kent)

Planets form by accreting, or attracting, matter from a cloud of gas and dust that surrounds a star. It is possible for an object to continue accreting until its centre becomes hot and dense enough for nuclear fusion to start in its core. Nuclear fusion is what powers the Sun and provides the light we see. If an object grew so large that nuclear fusion started, then we would call it a star rather than a planet, and such a system would be become a multiple-star system. Brown dwarfs are somewhere in between stars and planets.

Why are the planets spherical?

Gerry Mooney (Birmingham) and Tony Roberts (Shoreham by Sea, West Sussex)

That is essentially because of gravity. The mass of the planet is so high that everything gets pulled down to get as close to the centre as possible. The most compact possible shape is a sphere, and anything more than a few hundred kilometres in diameter will be spherical. Of course, even the Earth is not completely spherical, as there are mountains and valleys covering its surface. These are possible because the forces pushing them up are strong enough to overcome the pull of gravity, but it's usually only temporary. For example, the Himalayan mountains were created when the tectonic plates of India hit those of Asia, forcing material up into the highest mountains on Earth. The relative motion of these plates has now ceased, and over time gravity, ably assisted by the wind and weather, will gradually pull the mountains down.

Smaller objects have a lower gravitational pull and so the mountains can be higher. The highest mountain in the Solar System is Olympus Mons on Mars. At around 25 kilometres tall, it is six times the height of Mount Everest.

If all the planets in the Solar System were formed from the same cloud of material, by a similar mechanism, why are they so different, in particular Saturn?

John A Tomkins (Skelmersdale, Lancashire)

We can split the eight planets in the Solar System into two groups. First, there are the solid, rocky planets of Mercury, Venus, Earth and Mars, and then we have the giant planets of Jupiter, Saturn, Uranus and Neptune. This is a relic of the time when the planets were forming from the disc of material swirling round the Sun.

The Sun was also forming at the same time, and in its life it went through a very energetic phase that astronomers call the 'T Tauri' phase (named after the first star observed to exhibit this behaviour, found in the constellation of Taurus). The energy released from the star blows away the gas from the inner Solar System, meaning that only rocky planets can form from the heavier elements that remain. They can hold on to thin atmospheres, some of which were created by volcanoes.

The outer planets formed in a region where there was lots of gas, and so could grow much larger.

Orbits and Rotations

Why do planets orbit their star in an ellipse, rather than a circle?

David Gay (Hull)

It's first important to clarify that a circle is simply a special case of an ellipse, specifically one that has zero eccentricity. It was Johannes Kepler who showed that objects all orbit in ellipses, rather than perfect circles, which helped to explain their movements more accurately. The orbits are very nearly circular, though, and if you drew a circle a metre wide with chalk, the Earth's orbit would deviate from a perfect circle by less than the thickness of the chalk.

Even if you found yourself with a God-given power to place the planets into perfect circles, it wouldn't last. Although the Earth's orbit is dominated by the Sun's gravity, the small tugs from the other objects pull it around a small amount. The largest effects are from Jupiter and Saturn, but even some of the larger asteroids have a measurable effect.

Whenever we see the Solar System on screen or in books, it looks very flat. Just how accurate is this and what observations led to it?

Chris Levett (Sheffield, South Yorkshire) and
Edward Wright (Skelmersdale, Lancashire)

The path of the Sun through the sky is called the ecliptic, and it has been realised for millennia that the planets follow roughly the same path through the sky. Even before it was acknowledged that the Sun is at the centre of the Solar System, rather than the Earth, the planets were known to be orbiting in the same plane.

The orbits of the eight major planets all lie pretty much in this 'ecliptic plane'. Relative to the Earth's orbit, the others are only tilted by a few degrees at most. This alignment originates from their formation, as the planets formed from a disc of material orbiting the Sun. The planets themselves, however, can be tilted at a range of angles relative to their orbits; for example, the Earth is tilted at around 23 degrees and this is what is responsible for our seasons. Uranus is tilted almost completely over on its side and Venus is flipped upside down. Most of the moons of the planets are aligned roughly with the equators of their planets, though there is more variation here than with the orbits of the planets around the Sun. For example, our own Moon's orbit is tilted at around 20 degrees to the Earth's Equator, and by around 5 degrees to the ecliptic plane, which is why we do not get solar and lunar eclipses every month.

The minor bodies of the Solar System are different. While most of the asteroids in the main asteroid belt lie in the same plane, many of the small outer bodies do not. A classic example is the dwarf planet Pluto, which lies in the Kuiper Belt – a band of relatively small icy, rocky bodies that orbit at the distance of Neptune and beyond. Pluto has an orbit that is tilted by around 17 degrees to the Earth's, though many of the other objects are more tilted. Most comets, for example, are thought to lie in the Oort cloud, a roughly spherical cloud at a great distance from the Sun (although they would have formed closer in and been sent out there by interactions with the giant planets). Many of the comets we see from Earth come from the Oort cloud, and so can have very high inclinations relative to the planets. Comet Hale-Bopp, for example, which graced our skies in 1997, has an orbit tilted by around 90 degrees.

A question from my son: what caused the planets to rotate in the first place?

Rob Manning (Fleet, Hampshire)

A very good question, which can be rephrased as 'what makes the world go round?' Contrary to what some people would have you believe, it's not money! The planets are rotating because nothing has stopped them. They formed from a disc of material orbiting the Sun. As the material collected together to form planets, the rotation of the material was carried into the rotation of the planets.

Such rotation is hard to get rid of, though forces such as those responsible for the tides can slowly stop the rotation. The tides that the Earth causes on the Moon have already stopped the Moon rotating relative to the Earth, and the same is true of most of the other moons around other planets. Given long enough, the Earth will stop rotating relative to the Sun, though before that can happen the Sun will swell to a red giant and die.

Do any planets appear to spin the wrong way?

Jonathan Sawyer (Reading, Berkshire)

Almost all the planets in the Solar System spin in an anticlockwise direction when viewed from above the North Pole of the Sun, but there are two interesting exceptions.

Firstly there is Venus, which rotates in the opposite direction, although much more slowly than the other planets. It orbits the Sun in 224 Earth days, but it spins on its axis in 243 Earth days. This means that the Sun would rise in the west and set in the east, with the time between two sunrises being around 116 Earth days.

The cloud tops of Venus as seen by the *Pioneer Venus Orbiter* in ultraviolet light as it orbited the planet in 1979.

The reason for this is not entirely clear, though there are fairly convincing theories out there. It is likely to be due to the tides created on Venus by the Sun, which would try to make its day equal in length to its year, essentially stopping its rotation. However, Venus's thick, gaseous atmosphere is far less susceptible to the tidal friction that affects solids and liquids. The rotation of the atmosphere would therefore not decrease as quickly, and it is so dense that it has enough mass to prevent the planet's rotation from stopping altogether.

It is possible that over the past few billion years of the Solar System's history the rotation of Venus has varied wildly. The same could happen to Earth though since we are further from the Sun the effect is weaker, and much smaller than the effect of the Moon on the Earth's rotation. While the tides on the Earth act on the oceans, the tides on Venus act on its very thick atmosphere.

The second interesting example is Uranus, which is tilted over at around 90 degrees – almost completely on its side! Rather than orbiting the Sun like a spinning top, Uranus can be thought of rolling around like a snooker ball. The reason for this is not entirely clear, but is suspected to be due to one or several impacts with another body.

Do the planets gradually drift away from the Sun, towards the Sun, or stay in situ?

Paul Smith (Alfreton, Derbyshire)

The planets are relatively fixed in their orbits at the present time, but this has not always been the case. The planets formed nearly five billion years ago from a dusty disc of material surrounding the Sun. The interaction of the planets with the disc caused their orbits to shift. A planet on its own would tend to move inwards through the disc, thanks to drag provided by the dust, but there can be drastic effects from other planets.

It is generally assumed that the planets formed in different places than we see them today, with the inner planets possibly forming closer to the Sun and moving out. Jupiter may have moved inwards then outwards, while Uranus and Neptune could have swapped places. Such gravitational interactions can have a significant impact on smaller bodies, perhaps even sending them flying out of the Solar System all together. In fact, some theories even suggest that there could have been five giant planets originally, but that one was booted out by the others in the early stages of the Solar System's existence.

We know that many other solar systems have giant planets like Jupiter, or sometimes even larger, orbiting very close to their star. Since these could not have formed there, they must have migrated inwards, and if this had happened to such an extent in our Solar System then the Earth would very likely not be here today. An important question is what stops the planets moving inwards. Since much of the movement is thought to be caused by interactions with dusty material in the proto-planetary disc, one factor would seem to be that they stop moving when the supply of dust is exhausted, having been used up in the formation of planets, moons and asteroids, though whether the timing of this is coincidental or not is unknown. Another possibility is that the presence of Saturn prevented Jupiter from migrating inwards any further.

In our Solar System we orbit the Sun, but does our Sun have an orbit and does this affect the Earth?

Keith Haysom (Keynsham, Somerset)

Technically speaking, the Earth does not orbit the Sun. Rather, they both orbit the centre of mass of the system, called the barycentre. Since the Sun is nearly a million times more massive than the Earth, the centre of mass of the Earth-Sun system is very close to the centre of the Sun, and so the statement in the question is a very good approximation.

But the more massive planets, particularly Jupiter, have a larger effect on the Sun. The centre of mass of the Sun-Jupiter system is actually near the surface of the Sun, and so the Sun could be thought of as rolling round a point in space once every 12 years, while simultaneously spinning on its axis every 25-30 days. It is this sort of motion that has allowed many of the planets outside our own Solar System to be detected, by looking at the 'wobble' effect they have on their parent star.

Of course, the Solar System is much more complicated than just the Sun, Earth and Jupiter, and so the motion of the Sun is rather complex. The dominant motion is due to Jupiter, but the other large planets, particularly Saturn, also have an effect.

The Sun has an orbit of its own around the centre of the Galaxy, which it completes in around 200 million years. It also moves up and down a little, which causes it to pass through the centre of the galactic disc once every few tens of millions of years. With more stars and dust clouds in the centre of the disc, there could be small effects on the Earth. For example, one theory is that such a passage through the Galactic plane would increase the chances of the Sun passing close to another star, which could send comets in from the Oort cloud. Such theories are very hard to test, not least because the Oort cloud has yet to be directly observed.

The Sun

Who was the first to realise that the Sun was just another star, like the thousands you could see in the night sky?

Bart van der Putten (Amsterdam, the Netherlands)

This is an interesting question, as it involves making the mental leap about what our own star is, but the leap was probably the other way, with people learning that the stars are similar to our Sun. The first thoughts about this are hard to find, though there are lots of myths about the deities assigned to the Sun. For the 700th *Sky at Night*, Dr Lucie Green did some digging and traced it back as far as the sixteenth century, to an Italian monk, philosopher and astronomer called Giordano Bruno.

Bruno held similar views to Copernicus, namely that the Earth went round the Sun, but he took it one step further. He believed that the Universe was infinite and that the stars were all suns in their own right, but much, much further away. He even theorised that they all had planets orbiting them. While his ideas were ridiculed at the time, some believe his contribution to have been an important step in our understanding of cosmology.

The actual proof that the stars were the same as the Sun didn't occur until the advent of spectroscopy in the nineteenth century. The German physicist Joseph von Fraunhofer discovered dark lines in the spectrum of the Sun and stars, and in 1859 Gustav Kirchhoff linked these with the absorption of light by certain elements. The fact that the Sun and stars looked similar meant that they had similar chemical compositions, and in the 1880s Edward Pickering compiled a catalogue of the spectra of over 10,000 stars.

Not all stars were found to be the same, and the classification of stars was developed by Annie Jump Cannon of Harvard College Observatory in the early twentieth century. The seven types of star that are normally used are O, B, A, F, G, K, M, remembered by the acronym 'Oh Be A Fine Girl, Kiss Me'! These are listed from hottest to coldest, and the Sun is in the middle as a G-type star. The addition of three classes of brown dwarf stars, L, T and Y, has left astronomy lecturers struggling to find a better mnemonic. If you think of one, do let us know…

Is it true that the Sun becomes four million tonnes lighter every second?

Jon Culshaw (London)

Indeed it is, purely because of the fusion taking place in its core. Every second, 600 million tonnes of hydrogen are turned into 596 million tonnes of helium. That means that 4 million tonnes goes missing every single second, and that mass is converted into energy – giving us sunlight.

But there's no need to worry about the Sun losing weight. It might be losing 4 million tonnes every second but, since it's total mass is two thousand million million million million tonnes, there's plenty left!

Over what timescale does a solar prominence actually occur: a minute, an hour, a day?

John Moore (Peterborough, Cambridgeshire)

Solar prominences are one of the most beautiful phenomena on the Sun, and possibly in the Solar System. They can stretch for hundreds of thousands of kilometres, many times larger than the Earth. Considering their vast size, they form surprisingly quickly, sometimes in as little as around a day. Once formed, they can last for anywhere from a few hours to weeks, hanging above the surface of the Sun. They are best seen by looking at 'hydrogen alpha' light, which is emitted by hot hydrogen gas, and we are able to see them from a range of different angles as the Sun rotates.

The prominences can erupt with little or no notice, however, and this is related to how they are formed. The prominences are made of hot, ionised hydrogen gas, which is suspended in huge arcs by loops in the Sun's magnetic field. The magnetic field changes and evolves over time, and if it destabilises it can suddenly change into a new configuration. The material in the loop continues to follow the field, with some falling back into the Sun and some being thrown up and away from the surface. Depending on the energy released, the material can either fall back down or be ejected out into space.

Why is the solar corona so much hotter than the photosphere?

Alison Barrett (Kettering, Northamptonshire)

The photosphere of the Sun tends to be called its surface, as that is the point beyond which we cannot see. Just above the surface is a much fainter region called the 'corona', which can be considered to be the Sun's atmosphere. While the photosphere is at a temperature of thousands of degrees, the corona is much, much hotter. What we have to remember is that the scientific meaning of temperature is not the same as what we call 'heat' in day-to-day life. Scientifically, temperature depends upon the speed the atoms move around – the quicker the movement, the higher the temperature. The amount of heat given off depends on how much stuff there is at that temperature, so we have to take density into account. Consider a firework sparkler of the kind we use on 5 November. Every spark of the sparkler is at a very high temperature, but each one carries

A view from the Solar Dynamics Observatory of an enormous solar prominence. The prominence is many times larger than the Earth.

so little heat that they do no damage if they touch your hand. Conversely, the temperature of a red hot poker is much lower, and yet we are very reluctant to grasp a glowing poker.

The atoms and molecules in the Sun's corona are moving very quickly, and this means the temperature reaches millions of degrees. But the corona is also very rarefied, thousands of times less dense than the air we are breathing. This means there is very little actual heat given off by the corona, despite the high temperature. The vast majority of the energy that makes its way to Earth is from the photosphere, and in turn that energy originates in the fusion reaction taking place in the Sun's core.

There are still many theories as to why the corona has a higher temperature than the solar surface or photosphere. It seems that magnetic events are involved, linked to the explosions on the surface of the Sun, called 'solar flares', but we do not yet have the full story.

If we could hear the sound the Sun makes, what would it sound like?

Nev French (Essex)

We cannot hear any sounds from the Sun simply because sounds audible to human hearing cannot travel through the almost perfect vacuum of the Solar System. The fact that space is not *completely* empty means that sound waves, which are simply variations in density, can travel, but at incredibly low frequencies.

Within the Sun, the situation is somewhat different as it is much denser. The Sun does vibrate as pressure waves travel through it. These have an effect on the surface of the Sun and are evident through observations of the speed at which small regions of the surface are moving towards or away from us. An analysis of the movement of the surface of the Sun can be used to deduce its interior, which is something called helioseismology. As the name suggests, this is very similar to the way in which seismologists on Earth use the propagation of shockwaves caused by earthquakes to determine the structure of the interior of the Earth.

The dominant frequency in the Sun corresponds to an oscillation with a period of around five minutes. This is the time it takes a sound wave to travel from the surface of the Sun to the centre and back out again, although since the density varies with depth the waves do not travel along straight paths. There are smaller effects as well, but this five-minute period would be the dominant sound.

So if you had an appropriate set of headphones and ears tuned to sounds thousands of times lower than those we normally hear, then you would hear a dull drone from the Sun, varying over the course of hours as the surface writhes. The tone would be around 15 octaves below middle C!

Planet Earth

Why don't the earliest sunset and latest sunrise coincide with the shortest day?

Bill Northrop (Epsom, Surrey)

If the Earth were in a perfectly circular orbit around the Sun then this would be the case. However, the Earth's orbit is not a perfect circle, and its distance from the Sun ranges from 147 million to 152 million kilometres (91 million to 94 million miles), a variation of around two per cent either way. At its closest to the Sun, called perihelion, the Earth moves slightly faster round its orbit than at its farthest, called aphelion.

We think of the Earth spinning on its axis once every 24 hours, but in fact it takes just 23 hours and 56 minutes. A solar day, which is the time from sunrise to sunrise, takes a little longer because the Earth moves around its orbit and the planet has to rotate a tiny amount more to bring the Sun back over the horizon. At perihelion, when the Earth is moving fastest around its orbit, it has to rotate a tiny amount further relative to the Sun to make another sunrise, delaying the next sunrise by a small amount. It just so happens that the Earth's perihelion is around the start of January, which is coincidentally close to the shortest day in the northern hemisphere.

The difference is small, however, and the change in sunrise and sunset times over the period in question is only a few minutes, and also depends on your location. In the period of December 2012 to January 2013, for example, the shortest day occurs on 22 December, on which day in London the sun rises at 08.04 and sets at 15.54. The earliest sunset in London is a week before, occurring at 15.51, and the latest sunrise about a week later, at 08.06. Perihelion occurs on 5 January 2013.

A similar effect occurs six months later, when the longest day in the northern hemisphere happens to coincide with aphelion, when the Earth is furthest from the Sun. Of course, we should not forget that for those in the southern hemisphere this will be the other way around as their seasons are reversed.

The Moon creates tides on the Earth, but is it possible for the other planets to have similar effects?

Christian Fisher (Fleetwood, Lancashire)

The gravitational pull of the other planets is much weaker than that of the Moon. The only other measurable tides are caused by the Sun, and are roughly half the size of the tides due to the Moon. The next largest tides are caused by Venus, but even at its closest they are 500,000 times weaker than those due to the Moon, and the effect from the other planets is smaller still. So if the tide due to the Sun and the Moon was a metre high, the change due to Venus passing closest to us in its orbit would create an additional tide of around five microns, or five thousandths of a millimetre. I think you'll agree that such a tide is completely negligible and for almost all purposes can be completely ignored!

Whose idea was it to decide to view the Earth as we do, with Australia down under, and so on?

Peter Tierney (Ireland)

That, I'm afraid, has very little to do with astronomy and more to do with politics. Most of the world maps were originally drawn by Europeans, who put Europe in the middle and at the top of the map. The poles are easy to define as the axis around which the Earth rotates, but what is much harder is the reference point in terms of longitude. Today, we measure longitude relative to the Greenwich Meridian, sometimes called the Prime Meridian. Even this convention was political, being chosen over other alternatives that passed through Paris and Antwerp.

How far does the Earth rotate in a single day? One might assume 360 degrees, but in one day the Earth travels a small distance around the Sun.

David Vickers (Wirral, Merseyside)

In one day, the Earth moves one 365th of its orbit around the Sun, which corresponds to around one degree. This means that the Earth must actually rotate by about 361 degrees to face the Sun again. The length of our day is based on the Sun, and is called the solar day. While the time between two consecutive sunrises varies throughout the year (being longer in the winter and shorter in the summer), on average they are 24 hours apart. This is distinct from the 'sidereal day', which lasts around 23 hours and 56 minutes, and corresponds to the time it takes for the Earth to rotate on its axis once relative to the distant stars. In one year, there is one more sidereal day than solar day.

Setting aside the maths for now, if the Earth had a sister planet on the exact opposite side of the Sun, is it possible that we'd have missed such a planet?

John van Dieken (Fife, Scotland)

There are a number of space probes that have travelled far enough from Earth to be able to look back at its orbit. Many of the missions to other planets have looked back at Earth's location, and so can see the point on the other side of the Solar System. In 1990, the *Voyager 1* spacecraft took a 'family portrait' of six of the planets from its vantage point six billion kilometres away from the Sun, providing an image of our own 'pale blue dot'. The *Cassini* probe has also been able to record the Earth as seen through the rings of Saturn, which is a stunning image.

But the best view of anything opposite the Earth would be provided by the two STEREO spacecraft. While they are designed primarily to observe the Sun, they are also looking at the surrounding area in order to track solar flares and coronal mass ejections. The two probes are orbiting the Sun at slightly different speeds relative to the Earth, so that one gradually pulls ahead while the other falls behind in its orbital path. Launched in 2006, their gaze has swept around until they are now almost exactly opposite each other. Their constant vigil not only allows astronomers to track material coming from the Sun, but also provides an excellent way of finding and tracking asteroids and comets. If there were anything opposite the Earth, they would definitely have seen it.

There is a gravitational 'sweetspot' opposite the Earth, just a touch closer to the Sun than the Earth, called a Lagrange Point. In principle, an object placed there would orbit exactly once a year, but it would be incredibly susceptible to perturbations from other objects, and would not stay there for long.

Does the Earth hold the record for the lowest known temperature?

Sandy (Scotland)

The coldest known natural temperature in the Solar System is actually on the Moon, near the edge of Hermite Crater near the Moon's north pole. At a chilly minus 248 Celsius, just 25 degrees above absolute zero, this makes it much colder than the equator of Pluto, which is a positively balmy minus 189 Celsius. The low temperature is due to the fact that this northerly region of the Moon very rarely sees sunlight, thanks in part to the crater walls that leave it in shadow.

The coldest place that we know of in space was at the core of the Planck satellite, which had detectors cooled down to a tenth of a degree above absolute zero, at minus 273.05 Celsius. On Earth, key parts of some ultra-low-temperature physics experiments are less than a billionth of a degree above absolute zero!

If the Sun stopped working on 1 April, how quickly would all life disappear from the Earth?

Robert Gillespie (Brighton, East Sussex)

If the Sun were to suddenly be switched off, which would certainly be an impressive April Fool's prank, there would obviously be a significant effect on the Earth. The majority of the warmth and light we receive comes from the Sun, and so it would obviously get rather cold and dark. The darkness would happen instantly, though the ground and atmosphere would retain some heat. Consider a night following a summer's day, when the temperature in the UK might only fall as low as 15 Celsius or thereabouts. It would take some time for the temperature to drop significantly, though other areas of the Earth might notice a larger effect.

The Sun has an important impact on our weather. It is the heating of the air by sunlight that creates clouds and weather systems. The effect of suddenly removing the solar heating could have drastic consequences, though since we do not fully understand the effect of the Sun on the weather when it is behaving normally, it is hard to predict what might happen were it to suddenly turn off.

Over longer timescales, we can think of the Antarctic plains, where the temperature can drop as low as minus 80 Celsius in midwinter. Certainly, the oceans would freeze and the land areas would be covered by a thick layer of ice as all the water vapour in the atmosphere would freeze out. With no heating from the Sun whatsoever, the temperatures would likely drop much lower than that. Very inhospitable, though not bad for some naked-eye observing – the skies would be clear, but you'd have to wrap up warm!

The icy temperatures would kill off almost all life on land or near the ocean's surface, probably in a matter of days or less. In built-up areas, pockets of humanity might survive, buried deep under the ice. Artificial heating and lighting might be possible for a while, but securing a source of fuel might be tricky.

The only source of energy, aside from burning fuel, would be from the ground itself. Some regions, such as Iceland, currently get much of their power from geothermal energy, and this might continue to be possible. It would certainly not be possible to maintain anywhere near the current population, creating a rather post-apocalyptic scenario.

Not all life would necessarily die, though, as there is some that does not require sunlight. There are 'black smokers' on the sea floor that are populated by a variety of life. At depths of several kilometres, the sunlight does not directly reach the sea floor, but there is a huge amount of energy supplied from these volcanic vents. This energy maintains a surprisingly advanced ecosystem which includes creatures not unlike shrimps, all of which survive solely on the geothermal energy, though they do rely on a liquid ocean which is only present due to sunlight. At the risk of some wild speculation, the heat might be sufficient to prevent small volumes of water from freezing, allowing at least the more basic life forms to survive.

Other forms of life have no direct reliance on the Sun at all, such as microbes that live deep within the rock. These microbes live a very sedate lifestyle, and it is their discovery that led to experiments which proved that some life forms can hibernate in deep space for significant lengths of time. Perhaps, if this is the case, then life might once again begin to thrive on the Earth if the Sun got turned back on.

If it were an April Fool, of course, the Sun would presumably turn back on at midday, so the main effects would be having to keep the central heating on for a little longer than normal!

What stops the Earth and Moon colliding due to their gravitational pull?

Ken Barraclough (Sheffield, South Yorkshire)

The Moon is kept in orbit around the Earth by its speed. If it were suddenly stopped dead in space, then gravity would cause it to fall towards the Earth, which would create rather a large splash! One can think of being in orbit as continually falling, but moving so quickly that by the time you've fallen a metre downwards you've moved so far sideways that the curvature of the Earth means that the ground has receded by a metre. That's easier to imagine for an astronaut in orbit at an altitude of a few hundred kilometres, but the same is true of the Moon at a distance of a few hundred thousand kilometres.

From time to time, we observe transits of Mercury and Venus across the face of the Sun. Would it be possible to observe similar transits of Earth from Mars?

Richard Allen (East Grinstead, West Sussex)

Yes, it would, though there has not yet been a telescope or camera sent to Mars that is capable of capturing the image. Mars' orbit is only tilted to the Earth's by a little under two degrees, compared with over three degrees for Venus and seven degrees for Mercury. That would make the Earth transits from Mars a little more regular than those we see of Venus, with the next one due to take place in 2084 – I wonder if anyone will see it?

Mercury, Venus and Mars

Could Mercury be the remnant core of a 'hot Jupiter' planet in the early Solar System?

Robert Jones (Staffordshire)

Mercury is an oddity because it contains such a large quantity of iron given the rather diminutive size of the planet. There have been numerous theories proposed over the years to explain this, with the most widely accepted in recent years being that Mercury may be the core of a larger planet. Such a planet could have been hit by another large object, removing much of the outer layers and leaving just the inner layers. The original planet would not have been a 'hot Jupiter' like the giant planets we see in other solar systems, but could have been a larger rocky planet not unlike the Earth.

This theory has recently been thrown into doubt, however, by measurements made by the *Messenger* probe, which is in orbit around Mercury. *Messenger* discovered that there were more volatile elements present on the surface of Mercury than should be present if the planet had been subjected to a massive impact. These elements, which include potassium, thorium and uranium, would have been removed by the high temperatures involved in the process, reacting to form other compounds.

These new measurements point instead towards the planet having formed of material with a slightly different composition from the other planets, most likely because of its proximity to the Sun. There are still a number of mysteries surrounding the origin of Mercury, but missions such as *Messenger* are starting to provide a few clues.

How has Venus managed to retain its atmosphere, despite the strength of the solar wind to which it is exposed, while Mars has lost its atmosphere?

Alex Andrews (Oxford)

To compare these two planets, it's actually easier to relate them to Earth. First, let's look at Mars, which has lost most – but not all – of its atmosphere. There are two important differences between Earth and Mars: Earth is somewhat larger and more massive than Mars, and also has a global magnetic field caused by the molten core. The larger mass helps the Earth to hold on to more gas, which might otherwise be stripped away by the solar wind coming from the Sun. The magnetic field means that the planet and its atmosphere are much better protected from the energetic particles in the solar wind. So we can understand Mars. Most of the particles don't reach the Earth's surface, and the few that get close help create the Northern Lights.

Venus, however, is a lot more difficult to understand, and we're not yet sure that we do. The planet is about the same size as the Earth but closer to the Sun, so the higher-intensity solar wind should strip off more of the atmosphere. In addition, Venus has no magnetic field, and therefore no protection – so how has it kept not just an atmosphere, but an incredibly thick one?

We believe that the reason is that the atmosphere is actually too thick, which sounds rather peculiar. On the sunward side of Venus, ultraviolet light from the Sun hits the molecules in the top of Venus's atmosphere and strips off their electrons. These incomplete atoms form an ionosphere which is positively charged, and we have one here on Earth. The difference is that Venus's atmosphere is so thick that the ionosphere creates a much stronger barrier than the Earth, and shields what's below from the Sun's radiation – without the need for a magnetic field. It's not perfect, though, and the Venus Express satellite has measured the stream of atmosphere being stripped off and pushed away from the Sun. This might not mean that Venus is going to lose its atmosphere, as it could be regenerating it. The variation of the concentration of sulphur dioxide in its atmosphere, combined with the detection of hot regions on its surface, leads to the conclusion that Venus probably has active volcanoes on its surface. The gases emitted by these volcanoes could replenish the gas that is lost to space.

The fact that we have three planets that in terms of size and mass are so similar, but which are actually so different, is very interesting. Could Earth-like planets in other solar systems actually be like Earth, or will some be more like Venus?

Why does Venus rotate on its axis in the opposite direction to the other planets?

Tim T (Nottingham)

Venus spins on its axis in the opposite direction to the other planets, though it does so very slowly. In fact, it takes Venus longer to spin on its axis than it takes it to orbit the Sun. The reason for this is not entirely clear, though there are a few possibilities.

One is that a series of impacts caused the planet to stop rotating in a clockwise sense and start rotating in this 'retrograde' manner. Another is that its thick atmosphere experiences strong tides caused by the Sun, which have caused it to stop rotating. Measurements by astronomers in the 1960s, updated by orbiting spacecraft such as *Venus Express*, have established that the atmosphere is rotating incredibly fast, taking just four Earth days to complete one revolution compared with the 243 days it takes the planet itself to rotate.

Does Mars have volcanoes?

Hannah Thomas (Basingstoke, Hampshire)

There are no active volcanoes on Mars, though there are lots of extinct examples. The most famous is Olympus Mons, which is the largest mountain in the Solar System at almost 25 kilometres high. There are also volcanoes in the Tharsis region of Mars, which can sometimes be picked out by a modest telescope thanks to clouds that appear around their peaks.

Almost all the volcanoes on Mars were formed by hotspots in the planet's mantle, causing magma to swell up and break through the surface. This also happens on Earth, though the majority of our volcanoes are caused by the movement of tectonic plates. An example of hotspot volcanoes on Earth are the Hawaiian islands in the middle of the Pacific Ocean, where the motion of the tectonic plates has lead to the creation of a chain of volcanoes.

There is no evidence of similar tectonic motion on Mars, and the planet is not largely geologically active. There is some evidence, namely the presence of methane in the atmosphere, which could indicate that there are weak geological processes still taking place today, though not powerful enough to create volcanoes.

What evidence is there that the solar wind is responsible for the loss of the Martian atmosphere?

Alex Mackie (Stirlingshire)

A number of spacecraft have visited Mars and detected a stream of ionised particles being stripped from its ionosphere. This is an upper layer of the atmosphere that contains particles that are ionised by radiation from the Sun. The solar wind can strip the particles from the atmosphere, carrying them away from the Sun. Such a flow of particles can be measured by instruments on the *Mars Express* spacecraft. The results show that Mars is losing particles from its upper atmosphere at a rate of up to one kilogram per second, with increases coinciding with increases in the strength of the solar wind.

If Mars had been a little bigger and Venus a little smaller, could we have had three Earth-like planets in our Solar System?

Karen Cappleman (Kent)

It is certainly possible that the two planets would be more hospitable if Mars were closer to the Sun and Venus were a little further away. But the distance from the Sun and the mass of the planet are not the only things that determine the thickness of a planet's atmosphere.

A larger planet can generally maintain a thicker atmosphere due to its larger gravity, and since Mars is one-eighth the mass of Venus this would seem to be a reasonable explanation. But that doesn't explain why Saturn's moon Titan, which is only slightly smaller than Mars, has such a thick atmosphere. There are clearly other processes at work than simply gravity.

The solar wind, a stream of charged particles flowing from the Sun, can strip planets of their atmosphere, which is what appears to have happened on Mars. Earth's magnetic field offers protection from the solar wind by deflecting the charged particles, but Venus has no magnetic field. Instead, it would appear that the solar wind ionises Venus's thick atmosphere to such a degree that the planet's ionosphere creates a protective barrier that deflects the worst of the solar wind.

Perhaps Venus used to have a stronger magnetic field, allowing its atmosphere to become thicker, but which died away over time. Impacts from asteroids and comets may also play a factor, since these can cause the atmosphere to be blown away. Mars, being closer to the main asteroid belt, may have experienced more impacts in its early life than Venus.

So if Venus and Mars had switched places early on in the history of the Solar System, then it's possible that we would have three more Earth-like planets, but it is also possible that they would still have ended up being inhospitable. Since we only have one solar system to study in enough detail, we shall have to wait until we have found enough that we can make a proper statistical analysis to investigate the various effects.

Jupiter

Sometimes Jupiter is described as a failed star. Is that right?

Jon Culshaw (London)

We don't think so, as we believe that stars and planets form differently. A star is a pure condensation of gas, with the pressure and density in the centre high enough to allow nuclear fusion to take place. Our understanding is that Jupiter probably has a rocky core at its centre, possibly about the size of the Earth, and that the gas accreted at a later stage.

Besides, describing something like Jupiter as a failed star is a little unfair – it would be like calling a shrub a failed tree!

How is longitude assigned to the other bodies, especially if they have a moving atmosphere?

Derryck Morton (Devon)

Assigning longitude to other bodies is actually done in a similar way to that on Earth – by picking a reference point and sticking to it. On Earth, the consensus was to use the Greenwich Meridian, while on the Moon it was the centre of the Earth-facing side. Other solid bodies have similar reference points set, even asteroids, and this is often a particularly notable crater or other unmoving feature.

Planets with rapidly changing atmospheres, such as Jupiter, are more difficult to map. The main body of Jupiter rotates in 9 hours 55 minutes, as measured by the rotation of its magnetic field. The clouds rotate at slightly different speeds, with those near the equator rotating faster than those at higher latitudes. The difference means that the cloud patterns change over the course of a rotation, and there are certainly differences if measured from night to night. To provide a consensus for observers, Jupiter is given three coordinate systems, imaginatively called System I, System II and System III. The first relates to the equatorial cloud features, the second to the clouds nearer the poles, and the third to the rotation of the planet itself (measured by the rotation of its magnetic field). While this is not a perfect solution it does provide a way for astronomers to compare notes without too much difficulty. The challenge is that to make a map one needs to know the current positions of the longitude coordinate systems relative to one another.

I understand that there are electrical storms in Jupiter's atmosphere. Would these be accompanied by sound, and if so would there be a difference in the sound that we hear on Earth?

Peter Salter (Great Yarmouth, Norfolk)

There are indeed electrical storms in the atmosphere of Jupiter, discovered in 1979 by the *Voyager 1* spacecraft. The radio waves produced by the spark were detected along with an image of flashes on the dark side of the planet. In 2000, the *Cassini* spacecraft flew past Jupiter on its way out to Saturn and took pictures of lightning storms, which coincided with the locations of storm clouds.

A lightning strike heats a column of air to tens of thousands of degrees for less than a thousandth of a second, and the resulting shockwave is what causes the sound of thunder. The frequency of the sound is dependent on the properties of the shockwave, which depend on the pressure and density of the atmosphere and on the energy released. The atmosphere of Jupiter changes rapidly with altitude, as the pressure and density both increase, and so the frequency of the sound generated would depend on your altitude. In the upper layers of the atmosphere, the sound generated would probably have a lower frequency than the sound we hear on Earth.

Thunder and lightning can have effects on an atmosphere other than making people jump and blowing up televisions. In particular, the energy of a lightning strike can have an effect on the chemical composition. Experiments have been conducted for decades, starting in the 1950s, to try to artificially create life. This was attempted by generating sparks in a prebiotic soup similar to that which existed on the early Earth. While artificial life has yet to be found, such experiments generate a surprising variety of amino acids, which make up proteins. Comparable experiments with gases similar to those found in Jupiter's atmosphere show that, while there is more energy released, the abundance of hydrogen suppresses the chemical evolution. So I wouldn't start hoping for the discovery of any floating microbes of gas-cloud creatures listening to the low rumbles of Jovian thunder.

When *The Sky at Night* started, there were nine planets and very few moons (Jupiter had 12, for example). What do you think will be the state of play in another 50 years?

Rob Johnson (Liverpool)

In 1957 there were twelve moons of Jupiter, nine of Saturn, five of Uranus and two of Neptune. Over the decades, the numbers gradually rose as telescopes became better and more observations were made. There were several jumps, for example when the *Voyager* spacecraft visited the outer planets, allowing a much closer view of the systems.

Perhaps surprisingly, more recent visits by spacecraft have not been as productive as one might imagine. The *Galileo* spacecraft did not discover any new moons of Jupiter, though the *Cassini* probe has allowed the discovery of eight Saturnian moons. The most efficient method for finding moons of the outer planets has been to conduct surveys of the regions of sky around these planets. A number teams have made discoveries, though one led by Scott Sheppard has been particularly fruitful in the last decade or so. The majority of the new satellites discovered are the so-called irregular satellites, which are often very small with diameters of a few kilometres or less, and with orbits that are significantly tilted to the equator.

There are now more than 60 known moons of both Jupiter and Saturn, almost 30 orbiting Uranus and more than a dozen around Neptune. It is likely that most of the moons of Jupiter and Saturn have been discovered, though observations of Uranus and Neptune are far less sensitive to the smaller moons, simply because of the enormous distances of these planets from Earth. It is likely that Uranus and Neptune both have sizable populations of small moons, though perhaps not quite as many as the larger gas giants of Jupiter and Saturn.

An easier way of finding these small moons may be to use infrared telescopes, which would look for their heat signatures rather than their reflected light. Infrared astronomy is still a relatively immature field, though the results of the WISE mission and at the Herschel Space Observatory indicate that it has a very promising future. In another 50 years, I [CN] would hope that large infrared telescopes would have been placed into orbit and knowledge of moons around Uranus and Neptune advanced significantly.

The rings of Saturn in springtime, illuminated edge-on by the Sun. The shadows are cast by ring particles disturbed by the passage of moons. The *Cassini* probe's observations of the rings have shown that the rings are incredibly thin.

Saturn

Why are the rings of Saturn almost entirely made up of water ice and not rocky materials?

Carl Harris (Cwmbran, South Wales)

That simply reflects the composition of the Solar System at that distance from the Sun. The outer planets have a much higher abundance of what are called 'volatile compounds', such as methane (carbon and hydrogen), ammonia (nitrogen and hydrogen), carbon monoxide (carbon and oxygen) and water (oxygen and hydrogen).

Closer to the Sun, these compounds are broken up by the young Sun's intense light and so could not condense into planets. That is why the inner planets are made of elements and compounds with higher melting points, such as metals. Since these heavier elements are much rarer, the inner planets are much smaller. It is in fact the inner planets that are unusual rather than the objects in the outer Solar System.

The point beyond which these ices can form is called the ice line, or sometimes the frost line or snow line, and it lies three or four times further from the Sun than the Earth. This places it between the orbits of Mars and Jupiter, within the asteroid belt. The easiest ice to form is water ice, with methane and other ices only forming within the atmospheres of the planets, where they are shielded from the Sun's light.

Saturn's rings are made of material which either formed from a moon that broke up, or from material that was unable to form into a moon. They are therefore made of the same stuff as the moons of Saturn, primarily of water ice with small amounts of rocky material.

Why do Saturn's rings have such a flat, circular shape?

Ellen Hartmeijer (Amsterdam, the Netherlands)

The rings are likely to have formed from one of two processes: either a moon broke up, or it was impossible for a moon to form due to tidal forces. The age of the rings has been a long-running debate, with recent evidence suggesting that they have been around since shortly after the formation of the Solar System.

Gravity causes a cloud of material to fall inwards, but the centrifugal force caused by rotation means that it stays inflated in the plane of the rotation. This is the same reason that galaxies and solar systems form discs. With particles as small as those in the rings, most being less than a thousandth of a millimetre in size, the process is much quicker.

The true thinness of the rings was discovered in 2009 during the most recent equinox on Saturn, when the rings were viewed edge-on from Earth. The *Cassini* probe, orbiting Saturn, gathered remarkable images of shadows cast by one part of the rings on another. As well as showing streams of ring particles pulled upwards by some of Saturn's moons, the images revealed that the rings are just tens of metres thick.

Are Saturn's rings perfectly circular, or actually elliptical and just very close to being circular?

Peter Williams (Carmarthenshire, Wales)

With no external forces, the orbit of small objects around a planet or star will eventually become circular. But most objects do not orbit in isolation, and that is certainly true of ring particles. The orbits of the particles are affected by Saturn's moons, pulling them into slightly elliptical orbits. The perturbing forces of the closer moons, such as Prometheus and Pandora, create waves and amazing spoke-like structures.

Is Saturn's moon Prometheus causing the distortion of the debris in the planet's outer ring?

Anne Edwards (Beckenham, Kent)

There are a number of moons that orbit close to Saturn's rings, and these are often called 'shepherd moons'. Prometheus and another small moon, Pandora, orbit either side of the F ring, which is the narrowest of the distinct divisions of the rings. Other sections of the rings have similar shepherd moons, such as Atlas which patrols the outer edge of the A ring. Other moons are the cause of gaps in the rings, such as Pan which orbits in the Encke Gap within the A ring.

The rings of Saturn are as mysterious as they are wonderful, which makes them particularly fascinating. I [CN] often think it is a shame the rings have such boring names, having simply been assigned letters in alphabetical order of discovery.

What is the cause of the hexagonal feature near Saturn's north pole?

Nigel Asher (UK)

The clouds at Saturn's north pole are dominated by a hexagonal feature, which looks surprising regular. Its origin was a mystery at first, though it now seems that it is the result of the wind speeds at those high latitudes. If there are two bands of cloud moving at different speeds then this can set up a wave-like motion. This wave just so happens to experience almost exactly six oscillations in one revolution around the planet, and so the hexagon feature is formed.

The feature requires the wind speeds to be varying in just the right way, and so such regular patterns are unusual. Laboratory experiments have shown that in different circumstances there could be a different shape there, perhaps a septagon (with seven sides) or maybe even a triangle.

Are there tides on Titan caused by Saturn's gravity? What types of sedimentary features are likely to be produced by flowing hydrocarbons on Titan?

Ben Slater (Claverdon, Warwickshire)

Titan is tidally locked to Saturn and so has one face towards it at all times, just as our Moon does to the Earth. However, there are seasons on Titan, and these create changes in the water cycle. The *Cassini* probe has seen clouds in the atmosphere as well as lakes, which are detected through their radar reflections.

The lakes are filled not with water, which is frozen at these temperatures, but of a mixture of ethane and methane. The lakes have been observed to fill up after clouds have passed and then empty again, showing that there is flowing liquid on the surface. When the liquid drains away, it will leave a sedimentary layer behind, and there are channels cut through the soggy lake beds. It seems that on Titan the lakes have beaches, though the hazy atmosphere and freezing temperatures make it a little unsuitable for sunbathing!

Why is it that gas giants have a large number of moons, while terrestrial planets such as Earth do not?

Edward Ignasiak (Enfield, Middlesex)

The moons of the gas giants almost certainly fall into two different categories. The larger ones probably formed along with the planets, such as Jupiter's large moons Io, Europa, Callisto and Ganymede. When the core of Jupiter formed out of the disc of material around the Sun, these moons would have formed at the same time. The same is almost certainly true of Saturn's larger moons, such as Titan and Rhea. Most of the other moons around Jupiter and Saturn are much smaller, and we believe that most of these would have been asteroids that have strayed too close and ended up being captured into orbit. Some of these moons are very peculiar indeed, with many having orbits that are tilted at relatively large angles, and some even orbiting backwards.

Of course, the outermost planets, Uranus and Neptune, are nowhere near the asteroid belt, so where did their moons come from? Those that didn't form in situ are probably captured from the Kuiper Belt, which is a

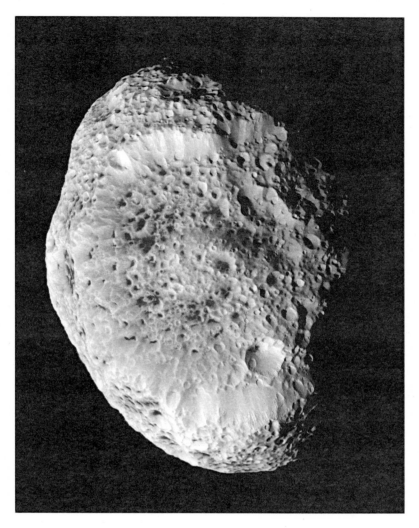

Surely one of the oddest moons in the entire Solar System, Hyperion has
a bizarre sponge-like appearance.

little further out from Neptune and contains objects such as Pluto. Beyond the Kuiper Belt there is the Oort cloud, which is populated by comets, and it's possible that some of the weirdest moons are comets that were captured as they made their way in towards the inner Solar System. Take, for example, Saturn's moon Hyperion. With such a heavily pitted surface, not unlike a sponge, it is quite clearly very different from its companions. The question is why – is it because of something that happened to it, or is it because it originated in a very different part of the Solar System?

The Outer Solar System

In spite of the very cold temperatures on the outer edges of our Solar System, how can Neptune's largest moon, Triton, generate the ice geysers first seen by the *Voyager 2* spacecraft in 1989?

Gerard Gilligan (Liverpool Astronomical Society)

This is one mystery that still remains from *Voyager*'s flyby of Neptune. The towering geysers were a big surprise but, since we only got that one brief glimpse over twenty years ago, it's very hard to be certain. We have limited amounts of additional information as well, such as the fact that it is known to have a very tenuous atmosphere, and that the surface appears to be rather young. This indicates that there may be a source of vapour, which the geysers would provide, and also that the geysers would be replenishing the surface material over time.

There are two main possibilities that are generally considered. First of all, the geysers could be created in a similar way to volcanic activity on the other planets, using energy from an internal heat source. Triton is pretty small, but there could be small amounts of radioactive material which could keep it warm. Out at this distance from the Sun, there would only need to be a slight temperature difference to create the geysers we can see. Rather than the heat melting rock, as on Earth, the heat would melt the ices on the surface – hence its name of 'cryovolcanism'.

The other option is that the Sun's light can penetrate the nitrogen ice on the surface and increase the pressure of gases beneath. In the places where the ice is thin, the gas could break through – not unlike the outgassing that occurs on the surfaces of comets to create their tails. This is supported by the fact that all the geysers seem to be clustered on the sunlit side of the Moon.

What we don't think is happening is that there is a sub-surface ocean like those thought to exist on Saturn's moon Enceladus and Jupiter's moon Europa. These oceans rely on heating due to the tidal forces between the moon and the planet, but Triton is so far from Neptune that there would not be sufficient heating to create the observed effect. All in all, a very interesting world, and one well worth visiting if we ever send a probe out to Neptune.

Is it true that Pluto has not made a full orbit since records began?

Darren Donaldson (Rosyth, Scotland)

Pluto was discovered in 1930 by Clyde Tombaugh. Orbiting between 30 and 50 times further from the Sun than the Earth does, Pluto takes 248 years to complete one revolution. It has therefore only moved a third of the way round its orbit since its discovery.

Of course, from Pluto's point of view it's made many orbits, having been touring the outer Solar System for billions of years.

Is there enough mass in the Kuiper Belt to form a real planet or two, and if so why has this not happened yet?

Chris Stinson (Nuneaton, Warwickshire)

Although there are a few large objects out in the Kuiper Belt, these are few and far between. It seems that the entire mass of the Kuiper Belt is a fraction of the mass of the Earth, probably below ten per cent. The reason that the objects have not clumped together is that when they hit each other the fragments

The dark streaks seen in *Voyager 2*'s image of Triton are thought to be caused by cryovolcanoes, or ice geysers.

simply fly apart – they are moving too fast to be brought together by their mutual gravity. Some of these fragments end up drifting into the inner Solar System, where they make up about half the comets that are discovered.

What are your thoughts on the declassification of Pluto?

Roy Jackson (Selsey, West Sussex)

Our thoughts on the classification of Pluto have no impact on anything aside from which part of a list it appears in. Whether we call it a planet or a dwarf planet, Pluto will still be there. In fact, most professional astronomers would probably say that they don't care what we call it.

The decision from the International Astronomical Union (IAU) in 1996 was prompted by the fact that we were discovering more Pluto-like objects, and that they seemed to be different from the rest of the planets. The intention was to derive a scientific definition of a planet, though this would seem to be impossible; there will always be borderline cases. Grouping Pluto in with other similar objects seems the most sensible option, and there is little use in being emotional about it.

It is worth bearing in mind that Pluto is not the first planet to be demoted in this way. When Ceres was discovered in 1801 by Guiseppe Piazzi it was classified as the fifth planet from the Sun. By 1830, the Solar System had eleven planets: Mercury, Venus, Earth, Mars, Vesta, Juno, Ceres, Pallas, Jupiter, Saturn and Uranus (Neptune and Pluto were yet to be discovered). When more objects were discovered between the orbits of Mars and Jupiter it was realised that they were all similar and as a result they were demoted to 'minor planets' or asteroids. I suspect there was somewhat less of a public outcry about the declassification of Ceres in the nineteenth century than there was of Pluto in the twenty-first.

In 1996 there were many alternative naming schemes proposed, but the final decision from the IAU was to make a distinction between the eight planets and an increasing number of dwarf planets. The official designation of a planet is now:

A celestial body that (a) is in orbit around the Sun, (b) has sufficient mass for its self-gravity to overcome rigid body forces so that it assumes a hydrostatic equilibrium (nearly round) shape, and (c) has cleared the neighbourhood around its orbit.

A dwarf planet is officially:

A celestial body that (a) is in orbit around the Sun, (b) has sufficient mass for its self-gravity to overcome rigid body forces so that it assumes a hydrostatic equilibrium (nearly round) shape, (c) has not cleared the neighbourhood around its orbit and (d) is not a satellite.

Is the surface of Sedna made of red ice?

Rebecca Taylor (Chichester, West Sussex)

We don't know exactly what Sedna's surface is made of. From observations with the Keck and Gemini telescopes it seems to be one of the reddest objects in the Solar System, but it is not completely covered with ice. Sedna orbits in a huge ellipse between 76 and more than 900 times the distance of Earth from the Sun. It has orbited alone for billions of years, possibly sent out there by interactions with other planets – perhaps even one we have yet to discover. Over time, the solar radiation has broken down the methane and nitrogen ice, creating dark reddish-brown substances called tholins.

The term 'tholin' was coined in 1979 by Carl Sagan to describe molecules that could not be identified, and originates from the Greek word for 'muddy'. The substance is not unlike tar, and in fact Sagan nearly called it 'star-tar'!

Voyagers *1* and *2* are on the verge of leaving the Solar System. What will they experience when they do so, and what lies in store for them over the next few millennia?

Ed Davis (March, Cambridgeshire)

The *Voyager* spacecraft are wonderful missions. After showing us so much about the planets and the outer Solar System, they are now exploring the very edge of the Solar System. At almost 120 times as far from the Sun as the Earth, *Voyager 1* is the most distant man-made object ever, with *Voyager 2* not far behind at just shy of a hundred times the Earth-Sun distance.

The two probes are travelling in different directions, with *Voyager 1* heading up out of the plane of the Solar System and *Voyager 2* travelling in a downwards direction. This provides in situ measurements of the very limits of the Solar System in two different directions. This region is dominated by the solar wind and the effect of the interaction between the solar wind (the constant stream of charged particles emitted by the Sun) and the interstellar wind (a similar stream flowing between the stars).

The solar wind blows a bubble round the Sun, called a heliosphere and, as the Solar System moves through the Galaxy, this bubble pushes a shockwave ahead of it, much like the bow shock of an ocean liner. The outermost region of the heliosphere is called the heliosheath, and both *Voyagers* are in this region. There are now indications that *Voyager 1* is approaching the heliopause, the point at which the solar wind is stopped by the interstellar wind. It is marked by a change in direction of the particles and also the magnetic field. It was expected that the transition would be smooth, but it appears that the region is much 'frothier' than expected, with magnetic fields coiled tightly around regions of higher and lower particle density.

The *Voyager* probes are not unduly affected by the magnetic turbulence, as it is only the sensitive instruments on board that allow the flow of particles and the magnetic field to be detected. It is expected that *Voyager 1* will cross the heliopause and enter true interstellar space in the next five to ten years. All that the mission teams have to hope for is that the nuclear power generators on board do not dwindle and fade enough to cause them to turn off the instruments before we learn all we can about the very edge of the Solar System.

Once they've passed into interstellar space, they really will be in the unknown. Neither spacecraft is targeted at a specific star, though in around 40,000 years *Voyager 1* will pass within a couple of light years of the star AC+79 3888, and in around 260,000 years *Voyager 2* will zoom by Sirius at a distance of a little over four light years. The two craft are destined to wander through the Galaxy for eternity, though in many, many millennia they may end up being caught in orbit around another star. That is, of course, unless an alien spaceship uses them for target practice!

Is there any evidence, say from the WISE mission, that in the far reaches of the Oort cloud there could be a brown dwarf or even a dim red dwarf? Could future surveys such as Pan-STARRS or LSST prove otherwise?

Alan Davis (Winchester, Hampshire)

It is still possible that there is a very faint star or planet orbiting at a great distance from the Sun, though it would have to be very faint to not be found. There have been numerous claims over the decades that 'Planet X' or a brown dwarf has been found, though none have been proved true so far. In the 1980s, the IRAS infrared satellite detected a very faint anomalous source, though Planet X was only ever one of a large number of possibilities and has since been ruled out.

Having said that, the WISE mission surveyed the entire sky at infrared wavelengths and managed to discover a new ultra-cool brown dwarf at a relatively close distance of around 15 light years. The fact that we didn't know these stars existed means that there could still be close objects which have not been found. If there is a brown dwarf orbiting near the outer limits of the Solar System, the WISE should see it, though it would only be able to detect objects with their own heat source; the reflected sunlight at such huge distances is too faint for WISE to pick up.

Asteroids and Comets

Why does the asteroid belt exist, and not another planet?

Ken Barraclough (Sheffield, South Yorkshire)

The asteroid belt is simply too close to Jupiter for a larger planet to form. With the huge gas giant so close, any larger proto-planets that started to coalesce from the rubble were ripped apart the next time Jupiter came past. What is left in the asteroid belt, however, would not form a large planet even if it could. The largest object is Ceres, which is less than a thousand kilometres across, and the total mass is equivalent to less than a thousandth that of the Earth.

Jupiter's impact on the asteroid belt may also be the reason that Mars is so small, having prevented any larger bodies from forming which might otherwise have contributed to the bulk of early Mars.

How do comets move through the sky?

Michael, age 4 (Marple Bridge, Greater Manchester)

Comets move slowly across the sky in the same way that planets do, with the Sun's gravity keeping them going round in their orbits. When they get close to the Sun, the bright sunlight starts to evaporate their surface, forming the comet's tail. This tail does not point backwards like a rocket, but instead directly away from the Sun, though sometimes they can curve round. The tail is always more impressive when the comet is closest to the Sun, when the sunlight is at its most intense.

Is it possible to estimate how many comets were needed to hit the Earth and fill its oceans with water? How much other material did they bring?

Mark Bullard (London)

The presence of oceans on the Earth sets it apart from the other planets, though their origin is not completely clear. The most widely accepted theory is that the early Earth was a hot, dry place, and that the oceans were deposited by comets or meteorites. The oceans cover more than two-thirds of the Earth's surface, amounting to 1.4 billion billion tonnes of water, or a volume of 1.5 billion cubic kilometres, which is a lot of bathtubs.

Comets seem a likely possible source. Often referred to as dirty snowballs, they are composed of rock and dust bound together by water ice, along with other frozen compounds such as methane, carbon dioxide and ammonia, all of which were common in the early Solar System. The solid nucleus of a comet is very small, with the largest being tens of kilometres across, but their diffuse atmosphere, or 'coma', can be much larger. This coma is comprised of gases that are released from the surface by sunlight, and is incredibly tenuous – the closest approach to nothing that can still be anything!

The small size of comets means that hundreds of billions of them would have been needed to supply the Earth's oceans. This sounds like a lot, and it is, but around three to four billion years ago there was a period of the Solar System's history called the Late Heavy Bombardment. Small objects such as comets and asteroids were swarming the Solar System and impacted with many of the planets and moons. Many of the craters on the Moon come from this period, for example, and most of the water delivered to the Earth by comets would have arrived at this time.

The evidence for the Earth's water having originated in comets has been attributed to the chemical composition, in particular the ratio of hydrogen to deuterium (also called heavy hydrogen). The water currently on the Earth is richer in deuterium than the material that the Earth would have formed from, and so is thought to have arrived at a later date. One source could have been comets, though the composition of the water in most of the comets studied does not match the composition of the water on Earth. The only currently known exception is comet Hartley 2, which formed in a different place to the other comets observed. While the other comets formed in the region of Jupiter and Saturn before being flung out, Hartley 2 is one of those that formed in the Kuiper Belt. It is possible that the water on Earth was delivered by comets that formed in the Kuiper Belt, rather than those that formed further in. Since only a few comets have been measured in the appropriate way the truth is not yet known.

Comets are not the only possible source; many meteorites are found to have the same composition as the oceans and so are another possibility. A big factor in the discussion is whether the composition of the Earth's oceans has changed with time, though this is not certain.

Water is not the only thing comets and asteroids provide. Recent analysis of meteorites has shown that they have complex chemistry in them, thought to originate from reactions between the basic chemicals and sunlight. Some have even been found to have amino acids and the molecules that make up DNA, though we've yet to find any alien microbes actually riding a comet!

Where does the water in comets come from?

Dave Annear (Newquay, Cornwall)

Comets are left over from the very early Solar System, and are formed of the material that made up the nebula from which the Sun and planets formed. The comets formed in the outer reaches of the Solar

System, where water ice was able to form grains. These grains accreted material and combined with rocky material to form the comets. The exact composition of the comets depends on where they formed, as those further out would have started to condense earlier. Those formed closer in would have taken longer to start condensing in the slightly warmer environment, and so have the composition of the solar nebula at a slightly later stage in its evolution.

Which comet that enters our Solar System goes farthest out into space?

Gerald Hutt (Okehampton, Devon)

Comets are split into three main groups, called short-period comets, long-period comets and single-apparition comets. Short-period comets are those that have orbital periods of less than 200 years, while long-period comets have periods ranging up to millions of years. Single-apparition comets are those that will only ever be seen once, as they are travelling so fast that they will escape the Sun's gravity.

The fate of comets is rather difficult to predict, however, as there are many other contributing factors. Their orbits are calculated by noting their position very precisely over months or years and comparing that to what would be expected due to the Sun's gravity. A complication is that comets experience other forces as material is ejected from their surfaces by the pressure of sunlight. The loss of material is relatively slow and so these forces are small, but it adds uncertainty to the determination of their orbits. A more predictable, though equally complex, problem is the effect of the other planets. Comets that pass close to the gas giant planets can be set inwards to the inner Solar System, but also outwards into interstellar space.

Take, for example, comet Arend-Roland, formally known as 'C/1956 R1 (Arend-Roland)'. This made its closest pass to the Sun in April 1957, and was the subject of the first-ever episode of *The Sky at Night*, broadcast on 24 April 1957. The predictions of its orbit put it on a slightly hyperbolic path (i.e. one that would take it out of the Solar System), though there were still some uncertainties over the non-gravitational forces.

It does not seem likely, however, that these comets actually originate from outside the Solar System. Instead, they originate in the outer Solar System and are put on escape trajectories by encounters with the planets. Comet C/1980 E1, for example, used to be on a nice sedate orbit around the Sun, taking more than 7 million years to complete an orbit. It ranged from just inside the orbit of Jupiter to more than 77,000 times as far from the Sun as the Earth. This all changed in 1980, when it came within around 30 million kilometres of Jupiter. This relatively close encounter increased its speed so much that it will never return, unless it encounters another object on its way out. This comet is the fastest-moving natural object to be discovered leaving the Solar System.

How near to the Earth would an asteroid have to pass in order to cause any adverse effect?

Gillian Ann Jackson (Bedfordshire)

Compared with the Earth, asteroids are incredibly small and there is no danger posed by one passing close to the Earth. The largest asteroid, Ceres, is less than a thousand kilometres across and just only a millionth of the mass of the Earth. The vast majority are much smaller, with many being tens of metres across or smaller.

There are thought to be around a thousand near-Earth asteroids larger than one kilometre across and at least 20,000 larger than 100 metres across.

While this may sound like a lot, it is worth remembering that the Solar System is absolutely huge compared to these asteroids and the Earth, and the chances of them hitting are very slight.

It is not unknown for asteroids to hit the Earth. Most of these are very small, and tens of thousands of tonnes of material falls to the Earth every year, primarily comprised of objects a few grams in mass. However, asteroids do not need to be particularly large to have a noticeable impact. In 1908, an object assumed to be around 30–50 metres across blew up above the Earth's surface before it hit the ground. This flattened trees over an area of 2,000 square kilometres in Tunguska, Siberia, though there were no eyewitness accounts. A similar-sized object hit Arizona around 50,000 years ago, creating a crater around a kilometre across and 200 metres deep, which is commonly called a 'Meteor Crater'.

Larger impacts can have more serious consequences, as the dinosaurs discovered 65 million years ago, but these are incredibly rare.

In July 2002, a friend and I spotted what looked like an enormous asteroid skim off the atmosphere. Would it be possible to track it down after all this time?

Scott Hamilton (London)

It is likely that what you saw was in fact a very small asteroid, or possibly a fragment of space debris, burning up in the Earth's atmosphere, rather than skipping off. If it did skim off the atmosphere, which is possible, then tracking it after many years would require very accurate knowledge of its position. The predicted orbit is very sensitive to the precise speed and direction of the object, and without these the object is impossible to find again.

Is the UK investigating Earth-crossing asteroid detection and response methods?

Robert Ince (Preston, Lancashire)

There are a number of national and international projects to monitor near-Earth objects, such as the Spaceguard project. These tend to focus on two different strategies: finding and monitoring near-Earth objects, and developing strategies for what to do should we find one.

There are now a number of telescopes that are monitoring the skies in search of such objects, a notable one being PanSTARRS. There is also a vast network of amateur telescopes which are continuing to make discoveries. Thousands of new asteroids are discovered every month, and it is now thought that we have discovered 90 per cent of the near-Earth objects more than a kilometre across.

There are a number of proposals as to the course of action to take should we discover an asteroid or comet on an impact course. Most involve trying to change its orbit, though they are likely to take considerable time to implement.

The world has certainly woken up to the threat posed by near-Earth objects, and the skies are now being monitored. It will probably take the discovery of a serious threat for significant action to be taken over plans for what to do in the event that we discover an object on a collision course.

If sunlight touching an asteroid can move it in space, has the Earth been moved by light touching its surface?

Stephen Marshall (Cramlington, Northumberland)

Sunlight can have an effect on any object it touches, though the extent of the effect depends on the object's size. Tiny grains of dust and ice are pushed away relatively easily, as seen in comets' tails, but the effect on larger objects is much smaller. The pressure caused by the solar radiation is much lower for a dark, absorbing surface than a bright, reflective one, and the adjustment of an asteroid's orbit by changing its reflectivity is one possible way of deflecting an object on a collision course.

All the large objects in the Solar System, from asteroids up to planets, have reached a balance in terms of the pressure from sunlight. Changes in solar radiation are very small, and so the outward pressure does not vary by significant amounts. A larger effect would have been present in the early Solar System, when the molecules and dust grains that would later form the Earth were being pushed outwards. Since the lighter molecules would have been pushed out more easily, you could argue that sunlight changed the composition of the Earth by removing some of the lighter elements.

Is it right that I might find small meteorites in the sludge in the gutters of our church roof, and if so how would I identify them?

Jessica Allen (Ipswich, Suffolk)

You may indeed be able to find meteorites in church gutters, as they are as likely to land on a roof as on any other area of the Earth's surface of a similar size. You might expect a meteorite to simply punch through a roof, but they can be moving surprisingly slowly.

You'll need to look carefully, though, as most meteorites are very small. The smaller ones would be easy to mistake for a bit of wind-blown dust, though larger objects would be harder to explain away with terrestrial explanations. If you do find something interesting, then the best thing to do is to send it to a local university or museum.

In 1965, I [PM] was lucky enough to find a meteorite. A fireball was seen hurtling through the skies over the UK and exploded over the village of Barwell, Leicestershire. I drove up there and asked the owner of the largest farmhouse if I could have a look around. He kindly agreed, and I found a fragment of rock protruding from the ground in a most unusual manner. The seven-inch fragment showed signs of scorching, which allowed me to identify it as a meteorite rather than any old lump of rock.

I took it to a local museum, which already had a number of fragments, one of which had entered a house via an open window and was found nestling coyly in a vase of artificial flowers! The agreement was that I would keep the fragment for display and leave it to the Science Museum in my will, which I have done. It now sits on the mantelpiece in my study.

How do we determine the age of a piece of rock, such as a meteorite?

Ingrid van Dam (Tilburg, the Netherlands)

Rocks and meteorites are aged using radioactive dating, using the decay of long-lived radioactive isotopes that occur naturally. These isotopes, such as uranium, decay to stable isotopes with long half-lives, sometimes measured in billions of years. In one half-life, half of the atoms will have decayed, and so by comparing the quantities of the un-decayed and decayed atoms the age of the rock can be calculated.

The oldest rocks found on the Earth are up to four billion years old but, since they were laid down in lava flows, the Earth must have formed before that. One problem with the radiometric dating methods is that they are 'reset' when the rock is melted again. Older ages are gathered from studies of individual crystals, pushing it back to around 4.4 billion years.

Dozens of meteorites have been aged and found to be just over 4.5 billion years old, giving an accurate measurement of when the Solar System was formed.

Magnetic Fields

Do the north and south poles of planets act the same as the poles of magnets? Would two planets on a collision path with their north poles facing each other push each other away, or are they too weak?

Les Stringer (London)

The magnetic field of a planet is much, much weaker than the gravitational field. While the fields can have effects on the tiniest of particles, such as those in the stellar wind, they have no effect on larger objects. That is because while individual particles, such as protons and electrons, have an electric charge, large objects such as planets and asteroids do not. They have almost exactly the same number of positive charges and negative charges and so are electrically neutral.

Most planets don't have particularly strong magnetic fields, as these are caused by the movement of conductive materials below the surface. On Earth, the core constantly rotates, causing the magnetic field, but Mercury and Mars have both long solidified. Venus rotates too slowly to generate enough of the dynamo effect required to create a magnetic field.

Magnetic fields can only exist with a moving electric charge, i.e. an electric current, so why is electricity not taken into account in astrophysics?

Les Fulford (Llandrindod Wells, Powys)

Electric and magnetic fields are essentially two aspects of the same phenomenon, called the electromagnetic field. A stationary charge creates an electric field, while a moving charge creates a magnetic field. Large objects such as the Earth, the Sun and asteroids are electrically neutral, and so create no overall electric field.

There can be moving charges without an overall electric charge. Consider the centre of the Earth, where the metallic core is rotating. The movement of the charges in the core creates a magnetic field, but overall the core is electrically neutral. Another example is the solar wind, which is a stream of protons and electrons being driven from the Sun. Each particle has a charge and so reacts to the fields, but since there are the same number of positive particles as negative particles, the solar wind is electrically neutral.

On larger scales, magnetic and electric fields are extremely important when we want to understand the forces on ionised gases around planets, the solar corona, the radiation from neutron stars, and the alignment of dust grains in the spiral arms of galaxies. For many bodies, however, they can be ignored for understanding what is going on.

From Beginning to End

Since the Earth is around a third the age of the Universe, how has there been time to form all the elements in nature?

Ron Sexton (Cam, Gloucestershire)

There may be many elements in nature, but they are not very abundant compared to hydrogen and helium. The Universe as a whole is 75 per cent hydrogen and 25 per cent helium, with very small amounts of other elements. The heavier elements, such as carbon, oxygen and iron, are created in the cores of stars, or when massive stars explode at the end of their lives.

The Sun is around five billion years old, so there was an eight-billion-year period of the Universe before the Sun formed. While eight billion years is not long enough for a star like the Sun to live and die, more massive stars live for much shorter periods. The first stars were probably much more massive than the Sun, living for just millions of years, and it is in these most massive of stars that the majority of the heavier elements are produced.

The Earth itself is not composed of 75 per cent hydrogen, and the most abundant element is in fact oxygen. That is because in the early Solar System the intense light from the Sun prevented hydrogen from condensing and pushed it into the outer regions. Beyond around four times the distance of the Earth from the Sun, there is much more hydrogen and the composition of the giant planets reflects this. On Earth, the chemistry is dominated by iron, oxygen, silicon and magnesium, which are some of the elements that make up most of the planet.

During its formation, the Earth became differentiated, meaning that many of the heavier elements, particularly iron and gold, sank to the centre. That left oxygen, silicon and magnesium to make up the bulk of the Earth's crust and mantle. Around 160 parts per billion (by weight) of the entire bulk of the Earth are made of gold, for example, but in the crust that decreases to one part per billion. Gold is not the rarest element in the Earth, but it has the advantages of not corroding and looking rather shiny when polished, something which has appealed to humans for thousands of years.

Which came first, the gas giants or the solid, rocky planets?

Rosemary Davis (Bristol)

The planets would all have begun to accrete out of the material in the early Solar System at roughly the same time, though we believe some formed faster than others. The exact processes involved are a matter of much debate, with some believing that the gas giants form in a way similar to stars, as clumps of gas growing from the proto-stellar disc, while others suggest that the cores formed first.

Most of the material in the Solar System is made of hydrogen, with a smaller amount of helium and relatively tiny amounts of the heavier elements such as oxygen, carbon and iron. The hydrogen would have been mainly in the form of gases, such as methane, ammonia and water, while the heavier elements would have formed dust grains that built up into larger and larger rocks.

The intense radiation from the young Sun, however, would have split the Solar System into two main regions. In the cold outer regions, the material can clump together freely, with the gas sticking to the dusty clumps and growing into small, gassy proto-planets. In the inner Solar System, where the Sun's radiation is somewhat more intense, the gas is broken down and blown outwards. That leaves just the relatively small amounts of the heavier elements in the form of dust and asteroids. The boundary between these two is called the ice line, or sometimes the frost line or snow line, and today lies somewhere in the asteroid belt.

In the outer Solar System, the gases condensed onto the surfaces of the small proto-planets and froze, helping these proto-planetary cores grow rapidly. The large quantities of hydrogen and helium increased the mass of the proto-planets and let them grow even faster, forming planetary cores several times the mass of the Earth in just a few million years. In the inner Solar System, this gas is not present, and so the planets formed more slowly, taking perhaps ten million years or so. Since there is less material in the inner Solar System overall, thanks to the removal of the lighter gases, the inner planets are also much smaller. Initially, the material would have been composed of rocks, which gradually grow in size until a relatively small number of large objects dominate. These larger ones would have merged together to form the planets we know, with most going into the Earth and Venus, while the smaller planets, Mars and Mercury, would have been made of the 'leftovers'.

The real bulk of the gas giants, particular Jupiter and Saturn, only grew when they became massive enough that they could start accreting gas from the surrounding disc, reaching their present size in ten million years or so. The real problem for scientists studying planet formation is when the ice giants of Uranus and Neptune formed. These have large solid cores, more than ten times the mass of the Earth, which could not have formed at such large distances from the Sun. Instead, the consensus is that the cores formed closer to Jupiter and Saturn, but were then flung into the outer Solar System when the gas giants started to grow even larger. It has even been proposed that Jupiter migrated inwards briefly, and that this could be responsible for Mars' rather diminutive nature.

The details of how we think the planets formed are the result of computer simulations, and depend on the initial state of the disc around the young Sun. As computers get better, the simulations become more sophisticated, and I [CN] would not be surprised if our ideas of how the planets form evolve further. As we observe many more other solar systems at a range of stages of formation, we are starting to build up a better picture of how ours may have formed, both in terms of the processes involved and the conditions that existed to begin with.

When will life on Earth end, and why?

Granville Grey (Loughborough, Leicestershire)

By far the most significant factor in the continuation of life on Earth is the Sun. We humans could blow ourselves to kingdom come and eradicate all the larger species on Earth, but even then the insects and microbes would still survive.

It seems that the key is the presence of liquid water, which is only possible in a narrow range of distances from the Sun called the Goldilocks zone. The Sun is very gradually warming up as it ages, and so this zone is very slowly moving outwards. In one or two billion years, the oceans will boil off due to the heat and the Earth will probably become uninhabitable. It is possible that some very basic forms of life will be able to survive, and the process is certainly slow enough that some may evolve to handle the searing heat, possibly by sheltering underground, though this is unlikely. The most likely fate of the Earth, however, is that it will be consumed when the Sun turns into a red giant in a few billion years. At that point, all life on Earth will certainly be unable to exist!

When the Sun turns into a red giant, it will become less massive. Does this mean that the Earth will move into a larger orbit, giving a bit of extra time before being consumed?

Ronald Mallier (Warrington, Cheshire)

The Sun will slowly lose mass as it turns into a red giant. Part of the reason for that is that it is constantly burning its nuclear fuel, converting it to energy. Every second, four million tonnes of the Sun disappears, being converted into sunlight by nuclear fusion in the Sun's core. But the Sun is really very massive, and that process has little effect. A more dominant effect is the solar wind, which will increase in strength as the Sun ages. In the last few hundred million years of its life, it will lose over a third of its mass, growing to two hundred times its current diameter.

This mass loss will cause the orbits of the planets to spiral outwards, and would seem to indicate that the Earth will escape a fiery death. However, as is so often the case, there is a catch. As the Sun expands and its surface gets closer, the tidal forces on the Earth will cause its orbit to decay and for it to spiral inwards. The spiral is likely to take just a few million years, which is short enough for it to spiral into the surface of the Sun before the star shrinks again.

Even Mars will probably not escape this fate, due to a combination of its orbit spiralling in and evaporation by the intense sunlight. Some studies indicate that even Jupiter will be partially evaporated by the ultra-luminous Sun, so even the moons of Jupiter may not be a sensible place to stop.

When the Sun is at its most luminous, the Goldilocks zone will have moved out into the Kuiper Belt, and so perhaps mankind will be living on Pluto. Of course, that won't last either because the Sun will then fade into a dim white dwarf, leaving the rest of the Solar System a frozen wasteland.

We've all been told about the fate of the inner rocky planets when the Sun dies. But what will happen to the gas and ice giants of the outer Solar System?

Baz Pearce (Bolton, Greater Manchester)

When the Sun enters its later phases of life, it will do two things. Firstly, it will grow much larger, with its surface reaching out to roughly where the Earth's orbit is now. Secondly, while its surface will actually cool slightly, the Sun will output a lot more energy – in its final stages its energy output will be around 10,000 times its current level. This is all due to the exhaustion of the supply of hydrogen in the Sun's core, meaning that it has to burn helium instead. We expect this to happen in a few billion years, and that this giant phase will last for around a billion years.

During that time, the conditions in the Solar System will be much warmer. While the inner planets will either be consumed by the Sun or become completely uninhabitable due to the heat, the outer planets will remain intact. There will probably be smaller effects, however. For example, the increased solar radiation and the stronger solar wind might blow off some of their atmospheres, while the increased temperature could change the chemistry and composition of the atmosphere.

What is particularly interesting is that the temperature on some of the moons of Jupiter and Saturn might actually become bearable for humans. This might make them suitable refuges for mankind, though the atmosphere would remain unbreathable. Once the giant phase of the Sun's life is over, however, it will dim to a tiny white dwarf, surrounded by a gorgeous planetary nebula. The Solar System will become desperately cold, and if anyone is still here that'll be the time to up sticks and find a new solar system.

Stars and Galaxies

Distances

What method is used to measure the distances to the stars, and how do we know that it is right?

Jonathan Phipps (Shropshire)

When compared to human scales, the stars are almost unimaginably distant. Even the closest star is somewhere around 40 million million kilometres (25 million million miles) away. Written out as a number, it seems even further: 40,000,000,000,000 km! Even light, which travels at a staggering 300,000 km per second (186,000 miles per hour) takes around four years to cover such a vast distance. If a jet plane could travel in space, it would take around five million years to get there. Such large distances require a new unit of measurement, and in astronomy we use the light year, which is the distance light travels in a year: ten million million km (six million million miles). It then becomes easier to say that the closest star, Proxima Centauri, is around four light years away.

We obviously can't use a ruler to measure these distances, and they're too far for laser range finders. Instead, we use a system called 'parallax', which involves measuring the position of an object from different positions. You can see the effect of parallax by staring at an object in the far distance, then holding your finger up at arm's length. While staring at the distant object, close first one eye, then the other. Your finger will appear to move, an effect caused by the fact that your two eyes are not in the same place. The effect is smaller for objects which are more distant, as their apparent position changes less, and providing you know the separation of your eyes it is possible to work out the distance to your finger.

But the few centimetres that separates our eyes isn't going to help when measuring a distance of 40 million million km. We need to go much further, and we can do if we sit and wait for half a year. In that time, the Earth will move halfway around its orbit, which puts it around 300 million km from where it started. So if we measure the position of a star compared to background objects, such as very distant galaxies, and then make the same measurement six months later, we can work out the distance to it.

This is a very simple, reliable method, but for stars the effect is very small – compared to the Earth's orbit they are still very distant. Even the closest star moves less than the diameter of a human hair held 20 metres away! The first star to have its distance measured in this way was the star 61 Cygni, in the constellation of Cygnus the Swan. In 1838, the German astronomer Bessel measured the distance to be around ten light years, which was pretty close to the distance we now measure of 11.4 light years.

In 1989, the European Space Agency launched the *Hipparcos* satellite, which measured the distances to thousands of stars, producing reliable results for stars up to around a thousand light years away. But that is only a tiny fraction of the stars in our Galaxy, which is around 100,000 light years across. To go further we need to use a different method.

The answer comes from a particular type of variable star, called Cepheid variables. These stars pulsate, and the time between their pulsations is

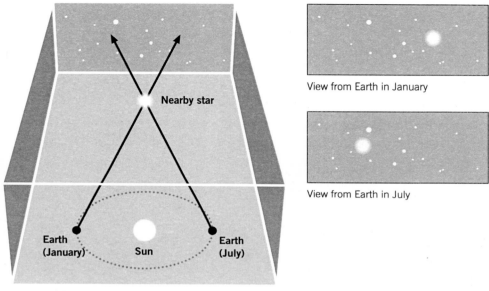

View from Earth in January

View from Earth in July

NOTE: Not to scale

The apparent motion of nearby stars due to the Earth's movement around its orbit can be used to calculate their distance.

linked to how bright they are. Once we know a star's true brightness, we can compare that with how bright it looks in the sky. Since a more distant star would look fainter than the same star if it were much closer to us, we can then estimate its distance. It was one of these types of stars which allowed Edwin Hubble to demonstrate that the Andromeda galaxy was separate from our own, and we now know that it is around 2.5 million light years away!

These Cepheid variables are a type of 'standard candle', and allow distances to relatively nearby galaxies to be measured. To measure greater distances we need to use brighter candles, and some estimates can be made for the true luminosity of the brightest stars, or even clusters of stars. This allows distances to be estimated out to hundreds of millions of light years, but beyond that even these are too faint. For the largest distances, we use the brightest standard candle we know of, which is a particular type of exploding star, or supernova. The time the afterglow of the supernova explosion takes to decay tells us its true brightness. In a similar way to the Cepheid variables and other standard candles, this true brightness is compared with the apparent brightness, from which its distance can be calculated. Using these types of supernovae, called 'Type 1a supernovae', distances of billions of light years can be measured.

To measure the largest distances, we use a property of the Universe itself. In the 1920s, Edwin Hubble showed that the Universe is expanding, and that the expansion 'stretches' the light from distant galaxies, moving it from blue towards red light. This 'redshift' is related to the distance to the distant galaxies, and allows astronomers to map out the distribution of galaxies on the largest scales of the Universe, though only by making assumptions about the structure and evolution of the Universe.

How do astronomers tell the difference between a large, bright, star far away and a smaller, less luminous one, closer?

Spencer Taylor (Rochdale, Greater Manchester)

Well, that is sometimes a difficult issue. If the distance to the star can be calculated using one of the methods discussed in the previous question, then the problem is solved. But what about where there's no such distance measure, for example with an ordinary star, similar to our Sun, that is a reasonable distance away in our own Galaxy. This is where knowledge of how stars live their lives comes in.

There is a well-understood relationship between the colour of a star and its brightness. During the bulk of their lives, when a star is described as a 'main sequence star', stars that are more massive are intrinsically brighter and have hotter surfaces. The temperature of the surface of the star is indicated by its colour, with red stars being cooler and blue stars being warmer. This means that a star's temperature can be calculated if its colour is known, and thus its true luminosity can be obtained. By comparing that to its apparent brightness, the distance can be estimated.

The situation is more complicated when stars gets older, as in their final stages of life the luminosity and surface temperature of a star can vary significantly. But having studied so many, astronomers have detailed models of what stars should look like at various points in their life, allowing them to estimate their distances. The answer is somewhat approximate, but it is normally good enough to estimate roughly where stars lie in our Galaxy.

With the aid of ever more powerful telescopes, we are observing stars and galaxies as they were millions of years ago. Do those stars and galaxies now exist in a different position in the sky?

Vince McDermott (Cheshire), Maeve C (Glasgow) and John Morgan (Northern Ireland)

Whenever we observe an object, the light we see has taken a certain length of time to travel to us. Light travels very fast, at 300,000 km per second (186,000 miles per second), which on human scales is pretty quick – it travels one foot in just a billionth of a second – but astronomical distances are very large. Consider looking at the Moon. At a distance of around 400,000 km (250,000 miles), the Moon is a little over a light-second away. That is, light takes a little over a second to travel from the Moon to our eye, camera or telescope. So we see the Moon as it was just over a second ago, and in that time it has moved around a kilometre around its orbit.

The Sun is 150 million km (93 million miles) away, which is just over eight light-minutes, so if the Sun suddenly 'went out' we wouldn't see any change for eight minutes. Of course, the Sun and Moon are on our astronomical doorstep, and stars and galaxies are much, much further away. Our closest large neighbouring galaxy, the Andromeda galaxy, is two and a half million light years away, so we see it as it was two and a half million years ago. In the intervening time, it has moved around 8,000 light years relative to the Milky Way. This sounds a lot, but when compared to the size of the Andromeda galaxy, which is 140,000 light years across, that's not far at all.

We see much more distant galaxies as they were much longer ago, sometimes measured in billions of years. In that length of time, the picture can change dramatically, with galaxies grouping into massive clusters, and merging together to form the enormous clusters of galaxies we see around us today. So while the galaxies might move around a lot relative to their neighbours, if we could see them as they are now they wouldn't appear to move in the sky much at all. After all, at such large distances, even a very large movement would only cover small angles on the sky.

Knowing Our Place

What would our Sun look like to an alien living on a planet around the nearest star to our Sun – how bright would it be and which constellation would it be in? Would they be able to detect the presence of planets?

Mr Campbell (Welling, Kent)

Alpha Centauri is, to the naked eye, the third brightest star in the entire sky, though it is not visible from the UK. This brightness is slightly misleading as Alpha Centauri is actually a triple-star system, meaning that it is actually made up of three stars in orbit around each other. The brightest star, usually called Alpha Centauri A, is a little more massive than the Sun (by about ten per cent), and about one and a half times as bright. The second star, called (perhaps unsurprisingly) Alpha Centauri B, is a little less massive than the Sun and is only about a third as bright. The third star, Alpha Centauri C is a much smaller, fainter red dwarf star, and of the three is actually the closest star to Earth – hence sometimes being called Proxima Centauri.

From Alpha Centauri, the Sun would look like a fairly bright star, but wouldn't be spectacularly bright. It would be similar in brightness to either Rigel, in Orion, or Procyon, in Canis Minor. The position of the Sun as seen from Alpha Centauri would be in the constellation of Cassiopeia, changing it from a 'W' shape to more of a '/W'.

We don't know of any planets orbiting Alpha Centauri, but if there were, would they be able to detect our Solar System? The orientation of our Solar System relative to Alpha Centauri is such that none of the planets would be seen to pass in front of the Sun. That rules out detecting any planets by the 'transit method'. The other methods for detecting planets generally involve looking for the motion of the star. The presence of the planets means the Sun wobbles, with the dominant effect being due to Jupiter. Seen from Alpha Centauri, the Sun would appear to move around by several thousandths of an arcsecond. This is within the capabilities of our most accurate measurements of the positions of stars, so if they had our current technology, the Alpha Centaurans would be able to at least detect the presence of Jupiter, and possibly the presence of a few of the other massive planets such as Saturn, Uranus and Neptune.

But the most successful method we have found for detecting planets around other stars has not been to look for the actual change in position of the star, but rather the speed with which it wobbles. The light from the star is split into its constituent colours, called its spectrum – a sort of stellar fingerprint. The wobble causes the star to move forward and backward slightly, and its speed towards or away from the observer changes the spectrum, or fingerprint, of the star slightly. Again, the motion of the Sun due to Jupiter, and possibly Saturn, would be detectable with our technology, but the other planets would be undetectable by this method.

The most recent method of detecting planets has been to directly image them. This is difficult due to the incredible brightness of the star compared with the planet. It is here that the proximity to the Sun would really help, as Jupiter would appear to be relatively far from the star, making it easier to block out the Sun's light. Jupiter would, however, be very faint, right at the limit of what can be seen with the largest ground-based telescopes even without the bright Sun right next to it.

So if aliens on a planet orbiting Alpha Centauri had the same level of technology as we do, they would be able to detect the larger planets, but the presence of the Earth would probably elude them.

Where is our Solar System located in the Milky Way?

Alec Bordacs (Long Eaton, Nottinghamshire)

Our Milky Way Galaxy is comprised of a flattened disc of stars around 100,000 light years across. Our Solar System is between half and two-thirds of the way out, around 30,000 light years from the centre. If we could see the Galaxy from above, the disc would appear to have a spiral structure, with a number of spiral arms running from a central region to the outer extremities. The particular region we're located in is often called the 'Orion Spur', which actually runs between two of the major spiral arms. It is so-called because as seen from Earth it has one end pointed towards the constellation of Orion.

Is our Solar System aligned with the disc of our Galaxy?

Robin Drake (Exeter, Devon)

The Solar System is tilted at an angle of around 60 degrees to the disc of the Galaxy. There is no reason it should be aligned to the Galactic disc, as it is so small in comparison. The other planetary systems we see around the sky are all tilted at different angles with respect to the Galaxy.

On a really clear night, and from a dark site, it is possible to see the disc of our Galaxy, the Milky Way, stretching across the skies. It runs through the constellations of Cassiopeia, Cygnus, Scorpius and Sagittarius, and is easiest to see from the UK in the spring and summer, when it passes almost overhead. It looks like a faint, misty streak across the sky, and a closer look will reveal dark lanes, which are clouds of dust blocking the light from background stars. From the southern hemisphere, the view is more spectacular still, as it is possible to look towards the centre of the Milky Way, a region which never rises much above the horizon from the UK.

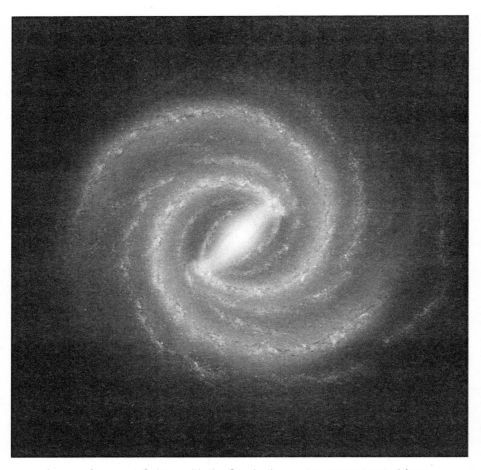

A map of our own Galaxy, with the Sun in the centre, reconstructed from measurements in the infrared by the Spitzer Space Telescope.

We know from observation that we sit in one of the spiral arms of our Galaxy, but do we know where we are in the Universe?

Tony Matthews (Newport, Gwent)

We know that our Galaxy, the Milky Way, is one of billions scattered through the Universe. They are not arranged randomly, but rather are grouped into clusters of galaxies. The Milky Way is one of three large members of the Local Group of galaxies, which also includes the similarly sized Andromeda and Triangulum galaxies, as well as dozens of smaller ones. The Andromeda galaxy is around 2.5 million light years away, and the Triangulum galaxy is a little more distant at almost three million light years. The galaxies in the Local Group are bound together by gravity, and move around each other over astronomical timescales. It is thought that the Triangulum galaxy once passed close to the Andromeda galaxy, which in turn is likely to collide with our own Milky Way in five to ten billion years.

But our little group of galaxies is tiny in relation to the scale of the Universe. We see much larger groups of galaxies, called clusters, which are normally named after the constellation they appear in. The Local Group is on the edge of the Virgo Cluster of galaxies, whose centre lies around 50 million light years away, in the constellation of Virgo. This cluster contains more than a thousand galaxies, some of which are much more massive than our own Milky Way, and on its outskirts are hundreds of groups of galaxies similar to our own Local Group.

On even larger scales, we find clusters of clusters, which are called 'superclusters'. Our local supercluster is (somewhat confusingly) called the Virgo Supercluster, because the Virgo Cluster is its largest member. But there are also groups of galaxies on much larger scales. The superclusters are arranged into great filaments of galaxies stretching for billions of light years, with enormous, empty voids in between. Such large-scale structures originated from the way the matter collapsed together in the early Universe, and have been mapped out to incredible distances.

If we include the rotation of the Earth, its speed around the Sun, and the Sun's speed around the Galaxy, how fast are we moving through space?

Shane (Devon)

The Earth's circumference is about 40,000 km (25,000 miles), so the Equator is spinning at around 1,600 km per hour (1,000 miles per hour). At the relatively high latitudes here in the UK, the surface moves in a somewhat smaller circle, and the speed is roughly half that at the Equator. At the same time, the Earth is moving around the Sun at around 30 km per second, or 108,000 km/h (67,000 mph).

The Sun is moving through the Galaxy, and completes one orbit in around 200 million years. That's a very long time, but the distance around the orbit is nearly 200,000 light years, which means that the Sun is actually moving at around 250 km/s through the Galaxy. The Galaxy itself is also moving through space, being tugged around by the gravitational attraction of nearby galaxies and galaxy clusters. For example, the Milky Way is moving towards the Andromeda galaxy at around 130 km/s (300,000 mph). But the Milky Way, Andromeda, and other nearby galaxies in the Local Group are all moving through space as well.

Working out speeds and directions on such large scales requires us to define a suitable reference point. We can't really choose another galaxy, or even a galaxy cluster, since they may well be moving as well. But there is one frame of reference we can consider to be absolute, and that is the Universe as a whole. We can measure the speed of the Solar System relative to the Universe by looking at the light from the Big Bang. This relic light, called the Cosmic Microwave Background, shows a slight increase in frequency in one direction, and a light decrease in another direction. This 'Doppler shift' is the same effect that causes a train or a police car siren to be higher pitched when coming towards you than when moving away from you.

If everything in the Universe were expanding uniformly, we should see no effect, but we measure that the speed of the Solar System through space is 370 km/s. When we combine this with the previous speeds, we find that the Local Group of galaxies is moving at a speed of 630 km/s in the direction of the constellation of Hydra. The cause of this motion is a massive supercluster of galaxies called the Norma Supercluster, towards which the Milky Way, the Local Group and even the Virgo Cluster are all being attracted.

How does our Solar System interact with particles emitted from the centre of our Galaxy?

Sean Daley (Melbourne, Australia)

Many different phenomena in astrophysics produce streams of incredibly high-energy particles, travelling at speeds close to the speed of light. These phenomena include exploding stars, or supernovae, as well as the matter circling around neutron stars or black holes. In the centre of our Galaxy there lie not only millions of stars packed closely together, but also a massive black hole, millions of times the mass of our Sun. From this extreme region of space the flow of particles is particularly high. There is a steady stream of these particles travelling through the Galaxy, making up what is often termed an 'interstellar wind'. Most of the particles are electrically charged, such as protons and electrons, and so they generally travel along the Galaxy's magnetic field which runs around the disc.

Like all stars, the Sun produces a steady stream of particles called the solar wind, though generally weaker than those from the more extreme regions throughout the Galaxy. This wind flows outwards, forming what is called a heliosphere. In some senses, this is the Sun's atmosphere, though it is incredibly vast, stretching hundreds of times further than the Earth's orbit. Eventually, the solar wind meets the interstellar wind, marking the edge of the Sun's influence. This 'heliopause' is where the Sun's own magnetic field merges with the much larger-scale galactic magnetic field. When particles travelling through the Galaxy reach this point, some are deflected away from the Solar System. In this sense, the solar wind protects the Earth and other planets from the majority of the particles, though some do pass through the heliopause and travel inwards towards the Sun. These form some of the most energetic particles known, millions of times more energetic than those created in the Large Hadron Collider at CERN.

Such particles, whether originating from the Sun or elsewhere in the Galaxy, are also called cosmic rays, and can produce adverse effects in electronics and astronomical detectors. The flow of particles from the Galaxy varies with the Sun's activity. When the Sun is more active, the solar wind is stronger and more of the galactic cosmic rays are deflected. So while we receive many more particles from the Sun during its active phase, we are also subjected to fewer of the much higher-energy cosmic rays from outside the Solar System.

Binary Stars and Star Clusters

Is it possible to have two suns in a single solar system?

Paul Foster (Clapham, London)

We know of many examples of stars which are in multiple-star systems. In fact, it's the norm, with more than half of stars being in systems with two or more stars. We even know of two sextuplet-star systems in the sky, one of which is the star Castor in Gemini.

In general, stars form in clusters, with many forming in these multiple-star systems. In many of the binary systems the two stars are relatively far apart, and it is possible to have planets orbiting one of the stars.

The stars in binary pairs tend to spiral together over long time periods, which would eventually disrupt the orbits of any planets, either sending them into highly elongated orbits or flinging them out of the system entirely. We do, however, know of some systems where a planet orbits a binary-star system.

In binary-star systems, is it always the case that one star strips mass from the other? What triggers this process and what are the final outcomes?

Lindsay Ferguson (Overton, Hampshire)

Most binary stars orbit at fairly large distances and are not disrupted by the presence of their companion star. The plasma, or ionised gas, that makes up a star is only held in place by gravity, and normally that keeps them spherical in shape – just as with the Sun and planets. Matter only moves between the stars if they are particularly close, and normally when one of them is very large.

The situation normally begins when one of the stars grows old, shedding its outer layers before finally dying and becoming a white dwarf, a neutron star or even a black hole. During this period, binary stars tend to spiral in towards each other. Things get more exciting when the second star nears the end of its life and starts expanding. In the latter parts of their lives, some stars grow to hundreds of times their original size, and if the companion object is close enough its gravity pulls the giant star into a teardrop shape with the point directed towards the companion. Beyond the tip of the teardrop, the gravity of the companion is actually greater than that of the original star, so the material starts to move over.

When it reaches the companion object, be that a white dwarf, neutron star or black hole, the stream of material is heated to immense temperatures, emitting X-rays. The smaller and denser the object is, generally the hotter the stream of transferred matter becomes. Images of other galaxies in X-rays show many points of light, almost all of which are examples of these 'X-ray binaries'.

Do the stars in globular clusters tend to 'evaporate' due to close encounters with each other? Given that dwarf galaxies orbiting our own Galaxy are torn apart, why has this not happened with globular clusters?

David Hall (Great Barr, West Midlands)

A globular cluster is a group of stars that all formed together, and which now lie in a roughly spherical ball. They are massive, typically containing tens of thousands of stars or more. While it is thought that almost all stars formed in clusters most of these were smaller, containing perhaps tens or hundreds of stars, and have since dispersed. We can see stars forming in these 'open clusters' today, and there are numerous examples in the night sky. The most famous is the Pleiades, or Seven Sisters, which is found in the constellation of Taurus. The Pleiades are relatively young, with an age measured in hundreds of millions of years, and are therefore still fairly tightly packed compared to most open clusters that we can see. Not far from the Pleiades in the night sky are the Hyades, which make up most of the 'V'-shape of the head of Taurus.

As we've said, globular clusters are much more massive, containing many more stars. The strong gravitational attraction of all the stars means that they fall into a roughly spherical ball, and look like a fuzzy smudge when seen through a small telescope. A fine example of a globular cluster that is visible from the UK is the Hercules Globular Cluster, also known as Messier 13. From further south, naked-eye observers are treated to the wonderful sight of Omega Centauri, containing millions of stars. As with most globular clusters, Omega Centauri and M13 are much brighter in the centre, as there is a greater density of stars in their core.

During the life of a globular cluster, some stars are likely to be flung out, but the gravity is so strong that most stay in the cluster. The cluster can be stretched out of shape, but the stars remain tightly bound together. Most dwarf galaxies are considerably more massive than globular clusters, though also much larger in extent. When a dwarf galaxy passes close to a larger galaxy, its outer regions are disrupted the most, but its core normally stays intact for much longer. It is even thought that Omega Centauri could be a remnant of the core of a very small galaxy that was absorbed into our Galaxy billions of years ago, and may even contain a moderately large black hole at its centre. This process is currently happening with the Sagittarius Dwarf Elliptical Galaxy, which lies about 50,000 light years from the centre of our Galaxy. Careful observations have proved the existence of a stream of stars passing round the Milky Way, all travelling in the same direction, which have been stripped off over billions of years.

Such events have taken place in the past, and this is evident from the motions of the stars. Some stars seem to move backwards around the Galaxy, and are thought to have originated from dwarf galaxies which have been absorbed. An example is a group of stars which includes Kapteyn's Star, a small red dwarf currently 13 light years away. The motion and composition of a group of 14 stars indicates that they were originally part of the Omega Centauri globular cluster.

Birth, Life and Death

We are told that stars are born out of clouds of gas, but what physics are at play to make a cloud of gas collapse in on itself to form a star when it is in a boundary-less space?

Les Fulford (Llandrindod Wells, Powys)

The physics that forms a star is, by and large, just gravity. Any sufficiently large cloud of gas and dust will start to collapse in on itself simply because of its own gravitational self-attraction. As the cloud collapses, it tends to heat up, and the increased temperature and radiation actually slows the contraction. Over time, normally tens or hundreds of millions of years, the cloud will gradually start to cool by radiating away its heat. This cooling allows it to collapse further still, and eventually it reaches a point where the gravitational collapse outweighs the expansion due to thermal energy.

As it collapses, the core of the gas cloud gradually gets denser and denser. Eventually, the pressure and density in the centre of the core becomes high enough for nuclear fusion to start. The ignition heats up the gas cloud very quickly and the object becomes a star. The mass of the star that is formed depends on a wide range of factors, such as the mass of the initial gas cloud and its composition.

When talking about the formation of new stars, reference is made to hydrogen gas and dust clouds. What makes up the dust?

Louisa (Merseyside)

Most of the Universe is made of hydrogen and helium, but there are small amounts of heavier elements as well. The most common elements are created during the life of stars, and include carbon, nitrogen, oxygen, silicon, sulphur and so on. These elements are distributed into the surrounding regions when the star puffs off its outer layers and, if it is massive enough, when it explodes in a supernova.

As these elements travel through space, they cool and collect together into small particles. The particles gradually build up until they form grains which can grow to a tenth of a millimetre in size. The most common elements – carbon, oxygen and silicon – dictate the most common types of grains, which are carbonates and silicates. There are other grains formed, made of heavier elements such as iron, but these are generally less common. A particularly easy molecule to form in space is water, using just hydrogen and oxygen. This normally exists as water vapour, but this can form grains of ice when the temperature is cool enough, and these ices help the grains stick together.

In particularly dense regions, it is possible to build up even more complex molecules on the surfaces of the dust grains. In many nebulae, such as the Orion Nebula, we have found 'organic chemicals'. We must be quick to point out that these organic chemicals are not alive in any way, shape or form, but are simply molecules containing hydrogen, carbon and oxygen, along with a few other elements such as nitrogen. Some of the most complex organic chemicals found are amino acids, which have also been found in nebulae, and on meteorites which have made it to Earth. These are important because it is very particular (and very complex) arrangements of these amino acids which form the proteins which are so important for life. The jump from the organic chemicals found in the Orion Nebula to life on Earth is a huge one, but it is important to know that the building blocks are there.

Having been thrown out by dying stars, these grains of dust and ice, along with the organic molecules, will then be present around newly forming stars. The process doesn't necessarily stop at a tenth of a millimetre, and the grains can continue to stick together, forming pebbles and rocks. It is not completely ridiculous to consider the rocky planets to be the culmination of this aggregation. Of course, that would mean that we are just complex clumps of organic molecules orbiting a star on a giant grain of dust, but that's not a particularly appealing thought!

Which star is energising the bright nebula IC434 in Orion, against which the Horsehead Nebula is silhouetted?

Anthony Simons (Sheffield, South Yorkshire)

The Horsehead Nebula is a dark cloud of dust which is only visible because it is silhouetted against the glow of gas in a more distant nebula. The more distant nebula, called IC434, is being illuminated by the star Sigma Orionis, close to one end of Orion's Belt. When viewed to its full extent, IC434 gives the impression of being a ring, centred on Sigma Orionis.

The distance to nebulae is often hard to measure and normally requires there to be an association with a star whose distance is known. Sigma Orionis is measured to be 1,150 light years from Earth, but it is possible that the visible portion of the cloud is either closer or further from Earth. With the two-dimensional view that we get, it is very hard to tell.

Why are stars not all the same size? It seems that they should all 'switch on' when they have reached a certain critical mass and core temperature. If any excess gas would be blown away when the star initially lights up, then the only stars shining in the sky would be red dwarfs, but this is clearly not the case.

Richard Chapman (Runcorn, Cheshire)

The point at which a star 'switches on' is defined by the density and temperature in the central core, and not by the total mass of the gas cloud from which it forms. When it reaches a critical temperature and density, nuclear fusion begins and the star starts to shine. At this point, the intense radiation will blow away any gas that is not tightly gravitationally bound to the star.

A single gas cloud normally forms a number of stars, and rarely collapses evenly. Some pre-stellar cores will be larger and denser than others, and when nuclear fusion starts they will be able to hold on to more matter. In any given cluster, stars with a wide range of masses are formed. There are lots of small stars, such as red dwarves, a fair number of stars with masses similar to the Sun, and a few stars much more massive.

The star R136a1, which is 256 times the mass of our Sun, was thought to be unlikely. What is the practical limit on how massive a star can be created?

Russell Aspinwall (Farnham, Surrey)

The mass of a star which is formed from a cloud of gas and dust depends on a number of factors. Firstly, the density of the cloud defines how massive a pre-stellar core can become by the time nuclear fusion begins. Once fusion starts, material that is not sufficiently gravitationally bound can be blown away by the bright radiation from the star. The ease with which material is blown away also depends on what it is made of. The first stars formed from clouds made almost solely of hydrogen and helium atoms, which cool more slowly than molecular clouds or dust, and therefore allowed larger stars to form, possibly up to a thousand times the mass of the Sun.

The material which makes up gas in our Galaxy today is more chemically enriched, and based on that it would seem that the maximum mass which a star can achieve is between ten and twenty times the mass of the Sun. This is based on computer simulations of stars forming in isolation, and it is clear that something is missing. After all, we know of stars in our Galaxy which are dozens of times the mass of the Sun. And we now know of the star R136a1 in the Large Magellanic Cloud, which is hundreds of times the mass of the Sun.

The formation of such 'monster stars' could be explained by the merging of multiple pre-stellar cores. An alternative is 'triggered star formation', where strong stellar winds from existing stars compress the surrounding material and allow the resulting dense cores to form more massive stars. Such processes are thought to be common in star clusters.

The pre-stellar cores are relatively cooled compared to stars themselves, and are best observed in the infrared. The Herschel Space Observatory has observed a number of cases of stars in the process of forming, some of which may well be examples of triggered star formation.

It is thought that the Sun was born in a cloud of gas and dust similar to the Orion Nebula. Is it possible, five billion years later, to tell which of the stars in the sky are the Sun's siblings?

Derry North (Ashby-de-la-Zouch, Leicestershire)

The Orion Nebula is the nearest example of a large star-forming region, and contains a number of very young stars. These stars will start to drift apart over time, and we see similar examples of this motion all over the sky. For example, five of the stars in the Plough are moving together through space, and are part of a group of around 200 stars which formed together 500 million years ago. These stars would once have been in an open cluster, possibly not unlike that in the centre of the Orion Nebula, but are now spread over a region around 30 light years wide.

We know that the Sun did not form along with these stars, as it is ten times older. This age means that the stars the Sun formed with will have moved apart even more, and be distributed all over the sky. As they move apart, some of the stars might have close encounters and be flung out of the vicinity. After so long, it is not thought possible to locate the Sun's siblings.

Why are brown dwarfs referred to as stars when they are not massive enough to support nuclear fusion?

Simon Lang (London)

Brown dwarf stars are stars which have a mass less than about one-twelfth that of the Sun, or around 80 times the mass of Jupiter. These stars are too feeble to allow fusion of hydrogen into helium, and therefore cannot shine brightly in the way a star like the Sun does. Once formed, they gradually contract until the matter in the centre cannot physically become any denser. The International Astronomical Union defines the lower limit on the mass of a brown dwarf to be 13 times the mass of Jupiter, which allows deuterium fusion to take place in the core. The deuterium fusion will not last for long, however, and eventually the brown dwarf will cool and fade.

The term brown dwarf was coined in 1975 by Jill Tarter, though it is somewhat of a misnomer as they would actually appear a dull red colour. The coolest brown dwarfs are incredibly cold, at temperatures of just a few hundred degrees centigrade. These are particularly hard to find, and their discovery requires observations in the infrared. We are still finding examples surprisingly nearby, and in 2011 two brown dwarfs were found at a distance of around 15 light years using observations from the WISE, 2MASS and SDSS sky surveys.

What happens to a red dwarf star when it has fused all its core hydrogen into helium, and what happens to the envelope?

Steve Bickerdike (Bedford)

A red dwarf star is less than around half the mass of the Sun, and so lives for much longer. They are small enough that the hydrogen is constantly circulated to keep the core supplied with its nuclear fuel. In fact, a red dwarf will burn hydrogen into helium for more than a trillion (i.e. a million million) years. That is over a hundred times longer than the current age of the Universe, so there are no examples of red dwarfs which have moved beyond the main part of their lives. We can, however, apply our knowledge of stellar evolution to predict what will happen.

As the hydrogen finally begins to run out in the core, the star will be producing less energy and will initially start to contract. This will heat up the core again, and increase the energy output. The delicate balance between the energy from nuclear fusion and the force of gravity pulling everything inwards means the outer layers of the star cool and expand. Unlike a star such as the Sun, the core will not become hot enough to allow fusion of helium, and when the hydrogen runs out the energy output of the star will quickly drop.

At this point, the star will collapse in on itself until the core material cannot physically get any denser, when it will only be the size of the Earth. There will not be an appreciable envelope of material remaining, as there won't be a significant stellar wind to push the gas away. This remnant of a star is called a white dwarf, and stars that result from a red dwarf will be particularly rich in helium.

Although there has not been sufficient time for any red dwarfs to burn all their hydrogen, we look forward to reporting observations of them in a trillion years or so!

Why do huge stars have a shorter life span than smaller stars?

Duane Miles (Weston-super-Mare, Somerset)

Massive stars have a much greater supply of fuel, but consume it much more quickly. This is because the temperature of the core of the star is so much higher due to its higher density. The higher rate of consumption of fuel means that the star is much brighter, and the comparison is quite striking. For example Deneb, the brightest star in Cygnus, is around 20 times the mass of the Sun but 60,000 times as luminous! The fusion process occurring in the core is essentially the same, so Deneb must be burning fuel thousands of times faster than the Sun. Stars like Deneb live fast and die young, and while the Sun will live for 10 billion years, Deneb will live for just 30 million years.

How big does a star need to be before its destruction is capable of forming a black hole?

Steven Rossiter (Barnsley, South Yorkshire)

When a star much more massive than the Sun consumes all of its nuclear fuel, it explodes in a powerful supernova. This applies to stars which start their lives at least eight times the mass of the Sun, but by the final stages of their lives they have blown off around a third of their initial mass.

During the supernova, much of the material of the star will be flung outwards, but some will re-collapse under gravity. What happens to the re-collapsing material depends on how much there is. If what collapses has a mass more than a few times the mass of the Sun it will form a black hole, while if it has less it will become a neutron star.

So the final state of a massive star depends on how much mass it has lost, both over the course of its life and in the supernova explosion itself. Typically, black holes are formed from stars which are around 35 times the mass of the Sun, of which there are relatively few.

Supernovae

How many types of supernovae are there, and what is the difference between them?

Geoff Wortley (West London)

Supernovae are characterised by numbers and letters, such as 'Type 1a' and 'Type 2', where the categories are defined by both the way the supernova brightens and dims, and also by which elements are detected in the light from the explosion. Until recently, there were just two known ways for a supernova to occur.

The first method is caused by a white dwarf in a binary-star system. If the companion is very close to the white dwarf when it enters the red giant phase, its outer layers can be pulled off by the white dwarf. If enough matter is transferred, the mass of the white dwarf continues increasing until it reaches a critical mass called the Chandrasekhar limit. At this point, a white dwarf is too massive to be stable and it explodes in a violent explosion – a Type 1a supernova. Because this always occurs at the same mass, about 1.4 times the mass of the Sun, such a supernova has a very predictable brightness. The most recent nearby supernova of this type occurred in the spiral galaxy Messier 101 which lies around 20 million light years away. It was first observed in August 2011 and was visible in small telescopes for weeks afterwards.

The second most common type of supernova explosion takes place when the core of a massive star runs out of nuclear fuel. At this point the core of the star is made mostly of iron, with layers of lighter elements on top, moving out to a hydrogen envelope. When nuclear fusion ceases, the sudden drop of outward pressure means that the gravity of the star suddenly wins and the star collapses in on itself. Such a supernova is really more of an implosion than an explosion, though much of the material rebounds off the dense core and is flung out into space. This type of supernova is normally called a 'Type 2' supernova, though the explosions of stars which have previously blown off their hydrogen envelope are called types 1b and 1c. The names were assigned before the physical cause was known, and so relate purely to the observations.

This second method of causing a supernova occurs in stars which are at least eight or nine times the mass of the Sun. If the star is greater than 20–30 times the mass of the Sun, the remaining material will be so massive that it forms a black hole. An even more massive star, above 40–50 solar masses, would probably form a black hole instantly on collapsing, producing no supernova explosion at all – though these are necessarily very hard to detect. But at really high masses, it is thought that something even more extravagant takes place.

Most supernovae show a peak in brightness followed by a slow fade, but in 2007 a particularly bright supernova was observed that didn't peak for 77 days. The star in question lay in a dwarf galaxy and had a mass around 200 times that of the Sun. The observations match the predictions of a previously unseen type of supernova, called a pair-instability supernova. In these cases, the temperature in the core gets so high that photons split into electron-positron pairs, reducing the pressure that combats the immense gravitational force of such a massive star. As the star collapses, the energy release destroys the entire star, leaving no remnant whatsoever – not even a black hole. Such massive stars are incredibly rare, but may have been much more common in the early Universe.

If it were possible to remove a small sample from a neutron star, would it be stable or would it either decay or explode?

Richard Green (Hampshire)

A neutron star is the remains of a star in which nuclear fusion has ceased, causing the star to collapse in on itself. As the matter falls inwards due to gravity, the object gets more and more dense, until the atoms are crushed together. Eventually, the material forms a neutron star, which is prevented from collapsing further by the fact that neutrons can only get so close together. These stars, which are not too different in mass to the Sun, end up being just 10–20 km in diameter – tiny when compared with our Sun's diameter of over one million km.

The density of a neutron star is not dissimilar to that of an atomic nucleus, and a teaspoon's worth of a neutron star would weigh a billion tonnes. The neutron star's state is due to its immense mass, something that a small sample would lack. Such matter would probably cease to be a neutron star and undergo a massive nuclear explosion.

Of course, this is all hypothetical, since running experiments on a billion-tonne sample would be incredibly difficult. Not to mention getting such a sample off the surface of a neutron star, where the gravity is more than ten billion times that on the surface of Earth – you'd certainly need a very special teaspoon!

What do you think of the existence of quark stars?

Sean Hopkins (Geddington, Northamptonshire)

Quark stars are purely hypothetical objects which would be denser than neutron stars, but not as dense as black holes. A quark star would be composed of quarks, sub-atomic particles which make up neutrons and protons. The formation mechanism is also purely theoretical, but they could be created when an object created in a supernova is too massive to form a neutron star but not massive enough to form a black hole.

There are some indications that observations of a few supernovae don't quite match the predictions for the creation of neutron stars, but that is a long way from proving the existence of these exotic objects. I [CN] would not be at all surprised if new types of astronomical objects are discovered in the coming years and decades, but before you ask I'm not the gambling type!

Can astronomers predict when there is likely to be a supernova visible to the naked eye?

James Clark (St Andrews, Scotland)

It is impossible to predict when any star will go supernova with any sort of accuracy. There are several massive stars in our Galaxy which are nearing the end of their lives, such as Betelgeuse in Orion, but they could last for another million years. The uncertainty lies in the fact that we don't know their mass exactly, and, even if we did, our theoretical models of stars are not precise enough to predict their date of death precisely.

But when Betelgeuse does go supernova, which will probably be some time in the next million years or so (don't hold your breath!), it will be spectacularly bright, outshining the Moon and being visible throughout the day.

When a star in our Milky Way explodes, would if affect us on Earth, and has this ever happened?

Ian Ross (Leeds, Yorkshire)

There are many examples of stars in the Milky Way that have already exploded and were visible with the naked eye. The most famous recent supernova was

Supernova 1987a, which occurred in February 1987. This was visible to the naked eye, but was not actually in our Galaxy. Rather, it was in the Large Magellanic Cloud, a small galaxy some 160,000 light years away.

The most recent recorded naked-eye supernova within our Galaxy was Kepler's supernova, which was seen in 1604 by the German astronomer Johannes Kepler. At its brightest it was as bright as the planet Jupiter, and was visible to the naked eye for around a year. The brightest recorded supernova occurred in 1006 and would certainly have been easily visible in twilight, and probably in daylight as well, remaining visible to the naked eye for around two years.

All the supernovae observed have been at least thousands of light years away, and so have had no physical impact on the Earth. The psychological and social impact would have been significant, as no way was known of creating or destroying stars, and the impression of the stars as being immovable objects would certainly have been challenged.

A supernova emits radiation at all wavelengths, from radio waves up to gamma rays. A particularly close supernova, nearer than say 30 light years, could produce enough high-energy radiation to kill us. Luckily, there are no stars in the vicinity of the Sun which are close to going supernova – the closest candidate is Betelgeuse in Orion, more than 400 light years away.

But supernovae have one very important effect – they are responsible for the creation of almost all the heavy elements we see around us. Hydrogen and helium were created in the Big Bang, and the elements up to iron are made in stars, but anything more massive needs huge amounts of energy to be created – such energy is provided by supernovae. These heavier elements are far less abundant that the lighter ones, but they are often particularly useful. Without supernovae, we would need to find other ways of producing electrical wiring (made of copper), plumbing (which used to be made of lead), and jewellery (gold, silver and platinum).

But aside from this, supernovae are crucial for distributing the material produced by stars through the Galaxy. It is almost certain that much of the matter that makes up the Earth, not to mention those of us who live on it, has been through a supernova at some point.

When Betelgeuse in Orion goes supernova, how bright will it be and for how long? Will it be dangerous to observe? Could it already have exploded, but the light has not reached us yet?

Al Kenny (Battersea, London), Thomas Collins (Liverpool) and Gary Walker (Banstead, Surrey)

When Betelgeuse explodes, it will be a spectacular sight to behold. It will be brighter than the Moon, and visible even during the day. It will peak in brightness after a few days or weeks and then gradually fade, probably remaining visible to the naked eye for several years. It would be the brightest object in the sky after the Sun, and the brightest stellar event ever seen.

With a mass around 20 times that of the Sun, Betelgeuse's life expectancy is only ten million years or so and its time is nearly up. But we can't predict its date of death accurately at all. For a start, the supernova occurs due to processes in the core, and all we can see is the surface of the star. Of course, it could go supernova next week, but it would take 427 years for the light to travel 427 light years to us. So there is a chance that it already has gone supernova and the light has yet to reach us.

How should the name Betelgeuse be pronounced?

Stephen Baskerville (Telford, Shropshire)

Like many star names, Betelgeuse originates from the Arabic language. The Arabic language uses a different script to the Latin alphabet, and so translations were tricky. In Arabic, the star was commonly called *yad-al-jauza'*, which means 'Hand of the Giant'. Mistranslations first turned this into *bedelgeuze*, through confusion over the Arabic equivalents of *y* and *b*.

In the nineteenth century, European astronomers readdressed the origin of the name, and were understandably confused. They decided that *bedelgeuze* must have originated from *bat al-jauza'*, on the misplaced assumption that it was (rather unfortunately) the 'armpit of the giant'.

As with many examples in language translations, the name has been anglicised in a number of ways. The main differences are in the pronunciation of 'Betel' (pronounced either Beetle or Bettel), and that of 'geuse' (pronounced juice, goose, gurz, or somewhere in between). There are also a number of variants on the spelling, such as Betelgeux.

Of course, this can all be avoided by using its Bayer designation of Alpha Orionis, but that's a lot less interesting.

Were you lucky enough to observe Supernova 1987a, and if so what were you feeling on seeing such a spectacle?

Brendan Alexander (Co. Donegal, Ireland)

One of us [PM] did in fact see the supernova (my co-author did not see the supernova so far as I know, though this may be because he was only four years old at the time. He must wait for the next one, which he may well see, but which I certainly won't). Having heard about it, and realising that staying in Britain was not going to be very successful, I jumped onto a plane and flew to South Africa. I must admit, I went there because it was almost certainly the only chance I had of seeing a naked-eye supernova and I did not intend to miss it. I did not mean to carry out any theoretical work, and was not equipped to do so. I merely disembarked from the plane, went to a dark area, looked up at the sky, and there was the supernova, which I estimated to be shining at the time at just below second magnitude (though others made it slightly fainter). It altered the entire look of that part of the sky.

The next day I returned to Britain well satisfied. Mission accomplished – I'd had my one view of a naked-eye supernova, even though the outburst had actually occurred so long before I was born and was a very long way away.

If two supernovae happened at the same time right next to each other, would they create a 'super-supernova'?

Thomas (Scunthorpe, Lincolnshire)

The chances of two supernovae happening next to each other are incredibly remote. To have any impact on each other, they would have to be two stars which were orbiting each other very closely. A supernova is caused in one of two ways: either by the core of a massive star collapsing when the nuclear fusion runs out of fuel, or when a white dwarf star exceeds a certain mass. A white dwarf increases in mass by pulling matter from a nearby companion which is in its latter stages of life. It is theoretically possible, though incredibly unlikely, that the white dwarf could be pushed over the critical mass at the same time as the companion star went supernova, but this would merely be a coincidence.

In the unlikely event that this did happen, I [CN] would speculate that the shockwaves from the two stars would collide between the stars and release an awful lot of energy. This would make for a spectacular supernova remnant!

How can several new stars be formed from the dust produced by just one supernova? Are the new stars very small, or was the star that went supernova very large?

Mark Jackson (Southampton, Hampshire)

For a star to go supernova, it has to be very massive, normally more than eight times the mass of the Sun. Such massive stars lose a reasonable fraction of their mass – as much as a third or more – during the later stages of their lives when they are puffing off their outer layers. In the supernova event itself, yet more of the mass is normally expelled in the explosion, with only a few solar masses being locked up in a neutron star or black hole. All in all, several solar masses of material are ejected into space from a single star that is massive enough to go supernova.

Stars come in all sizes, from tiny red dwarfs to huge stars hundreds of times the mass of the Sun. It is easier to form a smaller star than a larger one, so there are far more low-mass stars than there are high-mass ones. This means that the material from one supernova is enough to form a number of smaller stars.

But what it can't do is provide enough material for a new star as massive as the original, which would require material from number of supernovae. When a supernova occurs, it not only distributes material into space, it also sends shockwaves throughout the vicinity. These shockwaves sweep up matter that is already there and push it into denser clumps. It is in the densest clumps that the most massive stars form.

Galaxies

What would it be like at the centre of a galaxy?

Peter Bradford (Sydney, Australia)

In the centre of our Galaxy lies an enormous globe of stars thousands of light years wide. The night sky on a planet in that central bulge would be much brighter than ours due to the huge numbers of stars. The most massive stars that we know of in our Galaxy are found near the Galactic Centre, in the Arches Cluster. Such massive stars, up to around a hundred times the mass of our Sun, live for just millions of years – a mere moment when compared to the five-billion-year history of our Solar System. These stars live fast and die young, with too little time for life to form on any planets that might orbit them.

Right in the centre of the Galaxy lies an enormous black hole, with a mass equivalent to a million Suns. A searing hot disk of material orbiting the black hole emits radio waves, X-rays and gamma-rays, making its immediate neighbourhood rather inhospitable. While it would be fascinating to see such a place, I [CN] would certainly want it to be a return trip!

How did the spiral arms in our Galaxy form, and does the centre rotate faster than the outer rim?

Sean Gomez

First, what is a spiral arm? What it is *not* is a collection of stars moving round a galaxy together. Instead, it's more like a wave which causes the stars to bunch up and then spread apart again as it passes. Consider a wave on the ocean, where the wave moves along, but each little bit of water just moves in a small circle. From a distance, an ocean wave looks like a pile of water moving along as a unit, but in fact the molecules that make up each wave are constantly changing.

In a galaxy, it's not just stars that get bunched up, but also the gas and dust. When the clouds of gas and dust become denser, they form new stars. The most massive stars burn brightest, with a blue colour, but do not last very long. By the time the spiral arm density wave has passed, after tens or hundreds of millions of years, these hot blue stars have long since died, leaving just the less massive, dimmer, stars. So there are lots of stars between the spiral arms, they're just not very bright.

We should also consider the way in which a galaxy rotates. If the galaxy were like a solid disc, then the stars near the edge would have to be moving much faster than those further in to allow them to complete an orbit in the same time. For this to be the case, the outer stars would need to experience a much stronger gravitational pull towards the centre than the inner ones, and since they are further out from the centre this can't be the case. Alternatively, one might expect it to rotate like the planets in the Solar System, with those close in moving much faster than those further out. However, this would imply that all the mass was in the centre, while in a galaxy it is distributed throughout the disc – albeit with a fairly large bulge in the middle.

In fact, a galaxy behaves somewhere in the middle and, apart from in the very centre of the galaxy, all the stars move at about the same speed. However, since the stars further out have further to travel around their orbit, they take longer to make one complete revolution. This is just like runners running round a race track – those in the outer lanes have further to travel around the corners, which is why races have staggered starts.

So the stars nearer the centre of the galaxy move round more quickly than those further out, which causes density waves to wrap around the galaxy and creates the familiar spiral shape. Right in the centre, the spiral arms would be incredibly tightly wound, but in many galaxies, including ours, the spirals stop several thousand light years from the centre. Instead of spiral arms, the centre of our Galaxy is dominated by a bar-like structure, which, unlike the spiral arms, *does* rotate as a single unit. The formation process of the bar is not clear, but it is believed to be the cause of the spiral arms. In a *Sky at Night* programme, Professor Gerry Gilmore described it as being like a giant egg-beater, stirring up the Galaxy and causing density waves to spin off the end – the spiral arms in our Galaxy do indeed appear to be tied to the end of the bar. As a result, it is thought that the spirals are constantly changing over millions of years.

The true cause of spiral arms is not fully understood, and these are the favoured theories at the moment. These are constantly being adapted and improved, though since it takes so many millions of years for spiral arms to form, we can't actually observe the process taking place. We simply see snapshots in a wide range of galaxies, with no two looking exactly alike.

In some spiral galaxies, for example, the bar is much larger relative to the galaxy, giving it a very peculiar-looking shape. In others, there doesn't appear to be a bar at all, with the spirals continuing almost to the centre. The origin of these structures, called 'Grand Design Spirals', is thought to be different, caused by external influences. Such an influence might be another galaxy, passing by, stirring up the galaxy into a spiral shape like the Whirlpool galaxy.

If the Universe is expanding, why is the Andromeda galaxy going to collide with the Milky Way?

Andrew Brydges (Banstead, Surrey), Paul Smith (Bristol) and Peter Taylor (Epsom, Surrey)

Quite simply, this is due to gravity. The expansion of the Universe takes place on the largest scales, and the Andromeda galaxy is actually fairly close on cosmological scales. In fact, there is a group of a dozen or so galaxies in the 'Local Group' which are close enough to be gravitationally bound. Andromeda and our own Milky Way are the two largest members, and have been circling around each other for billions of years in a cosmic dance.

To measure the speed of a nearby galaxy such as Andromeda, we measure the speed at which its constituent stars are moving, and both the rotation of Andromeda and our speed relative to the centre of the Milky Way have to be taken into account as well. We know that Andromeda is moving towards us at around 100 km/s, but its motion 'sideways' relative to the Milky Way is much harder to measure. This sideways, or tangential, speed is unlikely to be zero, and could be as high as 100 km/s, although future measurements may refine this number somewhat.

If this tangential velocity is low relative to Andromeda's motion towards us, then it should collide with the Milky Way in around five billion years. If it is moving sideways a bit more, it will spiral round, delaying the collision until about ten billion years hence. What we know for sure, though, is that the two galaxies will collide eventually – they are simply not moving fast enough to escape that fate.

The collision won't be a single event, and the two galaxies will pass though each other a number of times before finally becoming a single merged galaxy.

What will happen when the Andromeda galaxy collides with the Milky Way? Will there be any effect felt on Earth?

Bob Hardy (Birmingham, West Midlands), Grant Mackintosh (Wigan, Greater Manchester) and Mark Bullard (London)

Galaxies are made of stars, and also clouds of gas and dust. When two galaxies such as the Andromeda galaxy and our own Milky Way collide, the effects of the various constituents will be different.

The stars are incredibly small compared to their separation – tens of millions of stars like our Sun could fit along the line between the Sun and the next closest star, so when two galaxies collide, the vast majority of the stars pass by each other like ships in the night. Actual collisions between stars are incredibly unlikely, and the stars will probably be moving too fast to form binary stars. A few may get close enough to get flung out into intergalactic space, and some will form the tidal tails which we see in merging galaxies such as the Antennae Galaxies and 'The Mice'.

The clouds of gas and dust, on the other hand, do collide. These colliding gas clouds provide ideal conditions for the formation of new stars. So while most of the original stars pass though, a new population of young, bright stars are formed near the collision site. The most massive of the new stars will live short lives, of around a million years, and end their lives in dramatic supernova explosions.

By the time the Milky Way and Andromeda collide, the Sun will probably have died, along with life on the Earth – at least in a form with which we're familiar. While the Earth itself may still be in orbit, it will be fried to a crisp by the red giant Sun, and then frozen solid as the Sun fades into a white dwarf. But ignoring such technicalities, we can consider the effect on a planet such as Earth.

As described above, it is unlikely that anything will happen to the Sun. The view from a planet, however, would be spectacular. As well as the stars in the Milky Way, there will be many of the stars in Andromeda visible as well. This rich vista will be complemented by the newly formed, young, bright stars – at least those not shrouded by the thick clouds of gas and dust.

These new stars would pose the greatest threat to life on a planet. The resulting supernovae would emit copious amounts of high energy radiation such as gamma rays. While an atmosphere and magnetic field make a good defence, they would not protect life such as us from supernovae within a few dozen light years.

In the centre of both galaxies lie two super-massive black holes, each millions of times the mass of a single star. When the merging is complete, these black holes will likely be in orbit around each other. The discs of gas and dust around each one will get close and may touch, setting off a new bout of star formation. Eventually, the two black holes may themselves merge, and what happens then is far from certain.

When this takes place, it is very unlikely any humans will be living on Earth, but for whoever is wandering though the Galaxy in a few billion years the view should be wonderful. Of course, they will have the issue of giving the resulting new galaxy a name!

Do galaxies such as the Milky Way ever shed stars from their outermost edges into intergalactic space? Are there any 'orphaned' stars floating alone in the space between galaxies?

Jim McKenna (Leicester)

Galaxies do not shed stars from their outer edges like mud off a cartwheel, but stars are sometime ejected. If two stars have a very close encounter, one of them (normally the less massive of the two) can be flung out. Most of the time, these stars are not thrown out of the galaxy entirely, but into a much wider orbit. These stars are often seen to move very quickly relative to their neighbours, and are called 'hypervelocity stars'.

Close encounters between galaxies can also result in stars being thrown out. This does affect the stars nearer the edge, which have a weaker gravitational link to their parent galaxy. The strong gravitational pull of the approaching galaxy can be comparable to that of their parent, and streams of stars are pulled into 'tidal tails', stretching for tens of thousands of light years. These celestial acrobatics can create stunning visual displays, and while most of the stars in the tails will return to their galaxy, a few will be flung into the intergalactic wilderness.

Considering the clarity with which light reaches us from such great distances, how much matter is there in deep space?

Charlie Stone (Poole, Dorset)

There is almost no greater understatement than saying 'space is big', or even 'really big'. While the Earth, Sun and planets seem pretty dense and massive to us, they are the exception rather than the rule. The Sun is large by human standards, at around 1.4 million km (800 million miles) across, but the furthest planet, Neptune, has an orbit with a diameter six thousand times that. The vast majority of the Solar System is almost completely empty space, filled with a light scattering of particles emanating from the Sun. The nearest star is four light years away, which is millions of times the Sun's diameter. The space between is not completely empty, but between the two there is only around one atom in every cubic centimetre of space (about the size of a sugar cube). By comparison, the air we breathe contains something like ten million million million atoms (ten to the power 19) in every cubic centimetre (give or take a factor of a few!). The material in empty space is largely comprised of hydrogen molecules.

We're all familiar with the effect that the Earth's atmosphere has on sunlight, with the particles scattering the light and turning the sky blue. Most of it still gets through without being affected, which is why the Sun is so bright. The majority of the Earth's atmosphere is below a height of around ten kilometres, which means that above every square centimetre of ground there are around ten million million million million molecules (10 to the power 25). That's certainly a lot, and it may seem astonishing that most of the sunlight passes by so many molecules without being affected. It is important to realise, however, that an atom or molecule is largely made of empty space, with the protons, neutrons and electrons making up a negligible fraction of the total volume.

Now, one could fit a lot of sugar cubes between us and the nearest star, but since each 'sugar cube' of space contains a single atom there are only around a few million million million atoms in all that distance – millions of times fewer than the number in the atmosphere. So when we point our telescopes at the stars, the scattering due to the material in interstellar space is tiny compared to the effect of our own atmosphere. Even the densest regions of space, such the centres of nebulae, are still much less dense than the air.

Of course, galaxies are much further away than stars, with the Andromeda galaxy being 2.5 million light years away. But intergalactic space is even emptier than the space within our Galaxy, and so there is still negligible scattering. The hydrogen gas does absorb a small about of the light, though, and over vast cosmological distances the molecules do add up. In fact, one of the methods of measuring the distances to the most distant objects known is by studying the absorption of optical light due to hydrogen between the stars and galaxies.

On larger scales still, the gas scatters microwave light that we see originating in the early Universe. The effect is small, since the scattering only works for ionised gas, in which the electrons have been stripped from the atoms, and this only happened when the first stars formed and started emitting light. The amount of such scattering we see is currently the best way of estimating when these first stars formed, currently estimated to be a hundred million years or so after the Big Bang.

If the planets and the Sun have weather and seasons, is it possible that galaxies and the Universe have weather and seasons?

David Reed (Corby, East Midlands)

First of all, we must define what we mean by weather and seasons. On the Earth, the weather is basically caused by air moving around (wind) and moisture condensing out of the clouds (rain, snow, hail, etc.). The movement of the air originates from the fact that the Earth is rotating, which causes high-altitude winds and variations in atmospheric pressure. These pressure variations, combined with changes in the heat coming from the Sun, cause the moisture to condense. Of course, this is a gross oversimplification of a very complex system, and I'm sure many meteorologists are currently cursing.

The seasons on the Earth are explained by the fact that the axis around which the planet spins is tilted with respect to the disc of the Solar System. As the Earth moves around its orbit, different regions receive varying amounts of solar illumination and therefore experience changes in their climate and weather.

All planets with atmospheres have weather, with many experiencing much more extreme conditions than those on the Earth. Most of the planets also have seasons to varying degrees, which depends on how tilted their axes are. For example, Uranus is tipped over by almost 90 degrees and therefore experiences huge seasonal variations. Conversely, Jupiter is almost completely upright and so has very mild seasonal changes.

The Sun's weather is slightly different, though can still be interpreted to take place in its atmosphere. Like all stars, the Sun emits a steady stream of particles, called the solar wind, which moves out through the Solar System. There are variations in the solar wind caused by flares and eruptions from the Sun's surface, which are in turn the result of small-scale changes in the Sun's magnetic field. The analogy to seasons is more tenuous, but the Sun's activity does wax and wane over a period of around 11 years.

On larger scales, it is probably fair to say that galaxies have weather. All galaxies rotate, with the stars, gas and dust moving round on timescales typically measured in millions of years. The intense radiation from stars in the galaxy, particularly hot, young stars or those that are in their final stages of their lives, acts to stir up the gas and dust. Supernovae, the explosions that occur when massive stars reach the end of their lives, create shockwaves that travel through space and compress the interstellar medium. Intense bouts of star formation can cause huge amounts of gas to be blown out of the galaxy, creating a fountain-like effect.

Seasons of galaxies are rather hard to conceptualise, and there really is nothing similar that we know of. The only tenuous analogy (and it is very tenuous!) is the activity associated with the black hole at the centre. We see some galaxies that have immense amounts of radiation emanating from their centres, thought to be due to the accretion of material around a black hole. These 'active galactic nuclei' are some of the brightest sources of radio waves in the sky, and it is thought that every galaxy could have experienced a period during which its black hole was accreting matter at a rapid rate and emitting vast quantities of radiation. The cause of the rapid accretion could be the merging of two galaxies, and so it might be possible for the cycle to repeat itself. Perhaps when our Milky Way Galaxy and the Andromeda galaxy collide in five to ten billion years the resulting galaxy will have a very active black hole while the influx of material is consumed.

What exactly is Hanny's Voorwerp?

Kevin Cooper (Fife, Scotland)

Hanny's Voorwerp is one of the most famous results of the Galaxy Zoo Project, which allows members of the public to classify galaxies and highlight any unusual objects. Found by a Dutch school teacher, Hanny van Arkel, this odd-looking green object was seen in images from the Sloan Digital Sky Survey. It lies close to a galaxy called IC 2497, though it was originally thought possible that the proximity could have been a coincidence. The name, by the way, derives from a Dutch word, which roughly translates as 'object' or 'thingamybob'.

After much study, including observations by the Hubble Space Telescope, the mystery of Hanny's Voorwerp is thought to be solved. Hundreds of millions of years ago, the black hole at the centre of IC 2497 experienced a surge in activity. It's not totally clear how long this would have been going on for, but we know that it has subsided now. The intense radiation from the active black hole caused the material in a nearby intergalactic cloud of gas to become energised, causing it to emit light at optical wavelengths. This cloud of gas is what Hanny van Arkel found.

All this actually happened more than 600 million years ago, with the light taking that length of time to travel across space to Earth. The reason that we can still see the Voorwerp is that the light that energised it had to take a slightly longer route to get to us. Rather than coming from the galaxy IC 2497 straight to us, the light travelled first to the Voorwerp, energised the material, and then travelled to us. Not a huge detour, but far enough to delay it by a couple of hundred thousand years.

The Voorwerp itself is nothing special in its own right, but what it allows us to do is identify a galaxy in which the active black hole has just been 'switched off'. Studies of IC 2497, and the black hole at its centre, may allow us to learn more about what causes such black holes to cease being so active, and in turn perhaps what causes their activity to begin in the first place.

I have read that some galaxy clusters are infused and surrounded by a halo of super-hot gas. Would such gas make life impossible within galaxy clusters?

Peter Mayhew (York)

The key thing to realise is that this gas might be very hot, but it is very tenuous indeed. Its high temperature causes it to emit a lot of X-rays, which might have an effect on life in the galaxies affected, but it probably wouldn't be fatal.

What causes galaxy filaments and the huge voids between them? Are they really the largest structures in the known Universe?

G Paul Hudak (Phoenix, Arizona) and Steve Hunt (Hedge End, Hampshire)

The origin of the galaxy filaments we observe is a combination of gravity and, perhaps surprisingly, sound waves. The very early Universe, at times less than a few hundred thousand years after the Big Bang, was incredibly hot and dense. The Universe was made of a mixture of ionised hydrogen and helium with the electrons stripped off by the intense radiation. In the first tiny fraction of a second after the Big Bang, quantum perturbations created small fluctuations in density throughout the Universe. These fluctuations created waves of varying density that spread out through the Universe – these were essentially sound waves. Their scientific name belies this fact, and they are properly known as 'baryonic acoustic oscillations'. These

Every dot in this image is a distant galaxy seen by the Sloan Digital Sky Survey, many of them billions of light years away. They are arranged in massive filaments and walls, separated by huge voids.

waves propagated at the speed of sound, which in the hot dense plasma was around half the speed of light. One property of plasma is that it interacts with light very effectively, and in the early Universe the resulting outward pressure was enough to offset the pull of gravity.

This was the situation until around 400,000 years after the Big Bang, when the temperature was low enough for the first atoms to form. The gas was still distributed fairly uniformly, but there were slight ripples in its density on the scale of a few hundred thousand light years. These ripples were incredibly tiny, but did have a characteristic scale. We can see this characteristic scale in the Cosmic Microwave Background, with the 'blobs' or warmer and colder regions of the Universe having a similar size across the map without forming a regular pattern of any sort.

It was at this point that the strong interaction between the matter and the light ceased and gravity started to take over. This allowed the gas to collapse under gravity and form the first stars, though this took a few hundred million years. In regions of the Universe that were slightly denser there were slightly more stars, and when they started forming galaxies there were slightly more of them as well. But the cosmic ripples were much, much bigger than a single galaxy, or even a large cluster of galaxies, and so to measure them we have to look at millions of galaxies distributed over enormous volumes of space. It is on these scales that we see the largest filaments of galaxies.

The first surveys to study galaxies on these scales were conducted in the 1970s and 1980s, but have been superseded by more recent projects. The largest of these is the Sloan Digital Sky Survey, which uses a 2.5-metre diameter telescope in New Mexico. It has mapped over a quarter of the sky and obtained measurements for almost 500 million stars, galaxies and quasars out to distances of almost two light years. In the Sloan map of galaxies, the cosmic ripples are not immediately obvious, but there is still a characteristic scale, now a few hundred million light years across, on which the distribution of galaxies and voids can be seen to have some sort of structure.

There is one more detail that is important to mention. The Universe does not only contain the normal matter that we're used to, but also large quantities of dark matter. This dark matter doesn't interact with light, which is why it can't be seen, but does feel the effects of gravity. In the early Universe, while the normal matter, also known as 'baryonic matter', was caught in the battle between the pressure of the intense light and the pull of gravity, the dark matter was simply collapsing under gravity. This affected the distribution of the first galaxies, and the study of these 'baryonic acoustic oscillations' is one of the best ways of measuring the properties and effects of dark matter in the early Universe.

Why does everything rotate – galaxies, planets, stars? What kick-starts this process?

Richard Swallow (Birmingham, West Midlands)

Rotation of a galaxy or solar system is very easy to start, but rather difficult to stop. Consider two stars moving past each other. Each exerts a gravitational pull on the other and so their paths change, and if the speeds are low enough they will swing round in a complete loop. These stars would then be in orbit around each other. In this way, rotation can easily start from two (or more) objects moving past each other. The same principle applies to stars, galaxies, planets and even the clouds of gas and dust that form stars and planets.

The rotation of an object, or a set of objects, has a property called 'angular momentum', which is essentially the amount of spin. Just as with normal momentum, angular momentum is always conserved. This means that it can be transferred from one object to another, but it can never be destroyed. It is dependent on the mass of the objects, their size or separation, and also on the speed at which they are spinning or orbiting. If a planet moves closer to a star for some reason, then it must start orbiting faster to keep the angular momentum the same. The principle can be easily observed by imagining an ice skater spinning on the tips of their skates. As they pull their arms in they get narrower relative to the axis around which they are spinning, and so they have to speed up to conserve angular momentum.

Consider a cloud of gas that is in the process of forming a star at its core. The cloud will be rotating, albeit slowly, due to the motion of all the particles of gas that make it up. As the cloud collapses it gets smaller, and so it most rotate faster to conserve the angular momentum. This is why the Sun spins, for example.

Angular momentum can be transferred between objects, particularly if they collide or pass very close to each other. This is the same principle that occurs on a snooker table; when the cue ball hits a coloured ball it transfers its normal momentum to it. If the cue ball was given some spin by the snooker player, then some of that rotation will also be transferred, which is what allows many of the trick shots.

Of course, a snooker ball does eventually stop rolling and spinning, largely because of friction between itself and the snooker table. Out in space there is rarely a frictional force in the same way – planets are not rolling around a table – but there is friction due to gravity. Specifically, the tides that objects create in each other, such as those caused on Earth by the Moon, can slow the rotation of a planet. The tides caused by the Earth on the Moon caused its rotation to slow down until its rotation relative to the Earth stopped. Since angular momentum must be conserved, to compensate for this reduction in rotation rate the separation of the Earth and Moon had to increase, and the Moon is now significantly further away than when it first formed.

So everything is rotating not because something started it spinning, but rather because nothing has stopped it.

Cosmology

The Expansion of the Universe

Wherever astronomers look in the Universe, galaxies are receding from us in every direction, making it appear that the Earth is at the centre of the Universe. We don't think of the Earth as being at the centre, but how do we know it is not?

Lynton McLain (London)

When we look out at other galaxies, we notice several things. Firstly, they are all around us, and there doesn't appear to be a preferred direction. It also doesn't seem that our particular region of the Universe is any different from any other. Galaxies are grouped into clusters and super-clusters, but there's nothing special about our galactic neighbourhood. But when we look at distant galaxies in detail, we notice that they seem to be moving away from us. As the Universe expands, the light from the galaxies is stretched to longer wavelengths, making them appear redder than they would if the Universe weren't expanding. Another way to interpret this is that all the galaxies are moving away from ours, which would seem to imply that we are somewhere special. This expansion does not apply on relatively small scales, such as when considering galaxies within the same

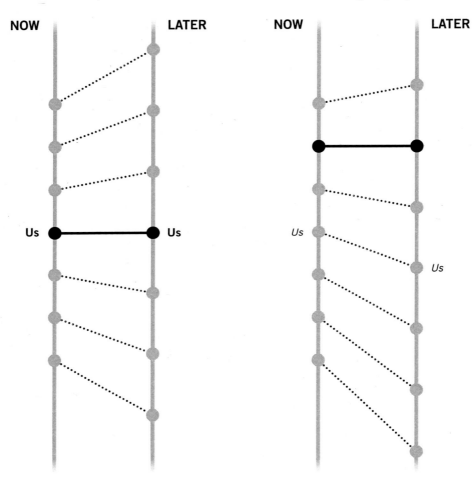

From our point of view

NOW   LATER

Us   Us

From a different galaxy's point of view

NOW   LATER

Us   Us

If galaxies were regularly spaced along a line with us in the centre, as shown on the left, then as the line (i.e. the Universe) expands the more distant galaxies end up further away. Since they seem to have moved further in the same length of time the more distant galaxies appear to have travelled faster than the closer ones. While this seems to imply we are at the centre, this is merely an illusion which occurs for every galaxy along the line, as shown for a different example on the right group, or cluster. On larger scales, however, it does *appear* as if every galaxy is moving away from us.

But appearances can be deceiving, and in fact the Milky Way is no more special than any other galaxy since, wherever you were in the Universe, you would see the same thing. We can create a simple example. Imagine a line of galaxies, each separated by rods a million light years long, and pick any galaxy on the line to be 'us'. The closest galaxy is one million light years away, the one beyond that two million, the next three million, and so on. Of course, in reality the galaxies are not so regular, but this can help to illustrate the concept.

If we stretch the rods so that adjacent galaxies are now 1.5 million light years apart, we see them all get further apart. Relative to the galaxy we've labelled as 'us', the nearest galaxy is now 1.5 million light years away, the one beyond that is 3 million light years away, and the next one 4.5 million light years away.

So, while the nearest galaxy has moved half a million light years further away, the next one has moved away by one light year, and the one after that by one and a half light years. The more distant galaxies have moved further, and since they have done so in the same amount of time, it seems that they are moving faster. We see the same thing in our real Universe, with more distant galaxies appearing to have moved away at a faster rate, which is what gives the impression that we are at the centre of the expansion.

But we can see from our simple line of galaxies that this illusion holds for *any* galaxy. Repeat the same experiment again and pick a different galaxy, and the same thing will happen, with more distant galaxies appearing to move away faster than the nearby ones. So, in an expanding Universe, *everyone* observes the illusion that they're at the centre of the expansion.

So if everyone sees an illusion of being at the centre, where is the real centre? Well, does there have to be one? It's entirely possible that the Universe is infinite in size, so that it goes on for ever in every direction – and an infinite

Universe can't have a centre. Even if the Universe is not infinite, it doesn't necessarily even have a centre. We could imagine it as being the surface of a balloon, expanding as the balloon is inflated, but there is no point on the surface of the balloon which is at its centre.

If there were a centre then that would be a special place, and one of the principles of modern cosmology is that there are no special places when considering the Universe on the largest scales. So it's not just that we are not at the centre of the Universe, but in fact that we don't even think there is a centre at all.

Do we know how far our Galaxy is from the origin of the Big Bang, and is there any debris remaining?

Frank Riley (Winsford, Cheshire)

The Big Bang didn't have an origin in terms of a location, since it took place everywhere. This may sound impossible but, as previously mentioned, we can imagine a simple analogy by representing the Universe as the surface of a balloon – not the air in the balloon, just the surface. We have to suspend reality for a short while, since this imaginary balloon is a perfect sphere and has no neck. As the balloon is inflated, the surface expands, but if we go back in time (more suspension of reality!) it contracts. When it gets so small that it is a single tiny point, we could ask a similar question to the one above: where on the surface of the balloon does the expansion start? The answer is the same as for the real Universe everywhere. The whole surface of the balloon is compressed into a tiny point, and so everything is at the start.

In terms of the debris from the Big Bang, you're looking at it! Everything you see, touch and taste has its origins in the Big Bang. The bulk of the work was done in the first three minutes, after which the Universe was made up of three-quarters hydrogen and one-quarter helium, with just tiny amounts of other elements. All the heavier elements were formed in stars, but the composition of the Universe hasn't really changed much over its 13.7-billion-year history. Although some has been converted into heavier elements, most of the hydrogen and helium created in the Big Bang is still around. While much of it is locked up in stars, planets and other objects, there are clouds of hydrogen gas in and around almost all galaxies.

Do we know how fast we are travelling through space relative to the rest of the Universe? Is anything in the Universe at a complete standstill, and not moving in any direction?

Dolores Myatt (Hemel Hempstead, Hertfordshire)

This question brings up the issue of a universal frame of reference, by which all motion can be measured. Since the Earth is going round the Sun, and the Sun is moving through the Milky Way, in this instance it would be more useful to consider the motion of our own Galaxy. The vast majority of the galaxies in the Universe appear to be moving away from us as the Universe expands. This motion is sometimes called the 'Hubble Flow', after astronomer Edwin Hubble who discovered that most galaxies appear to be receding. The recession is detected by measuring how much the wavelength of the light has been stretched by the expansion of the Universe. This moves the light towards the red end of the spectrum, hence why astronomers call it 'redshift'.

While most galaxies appear to be moving away, we find that some of the closer ones seem to be moving towards us. This is not unexpected, since the gravitational attraction of galaxies and clusters of galaxies counteracts the expansion of the Universe on such small scales. For example, our nearest large neighbouring galaxy, the Andromeda galaxy, is actually moving towards us, and both the Milky Way and the Andromeda galaxy are in a small group of galaxies which are being pulled towards a much larger group of galaxies called the Virgo Cluster.

Amazingly, we can actually measure the speed of our Galaxy relative to the 'Hubble Flow'. When we look as far as we can through the Universe, we see something called the Cosmic Microwave Background. The light has taken so long to travel from these distant reaches that we see the Universe as it was just a few hundred thousand years after the Big Bang – a mere blink of an eye compared to its current age of 13.7 billion years. We are seeing so far away that the Universe has expanded by a factor of a thousand since the light was emitted, redshifting what was once visible light into the microwave region of the spectrum.

This relic radiation was first detected in 1965, and appeared at first to be very uniform over the whole sky. A few years later, however, it was discovered that the redshift is not the same in every direction, with a slight increase in one direction and an equal and opposite decrease in exactly the opposite direction. This is observed because our Galaxy is moving relative to the frame of reference provided by the extremely distant Universe. And it's moving very quickly, at a speed of around 600 km/s (more than 1 million mph!). This is much faster than the speed of the Earth around the Sun, and even the speed of the Solar System around the Galaxy.

The cause of the motion, enigmatically known as the 'Great Attractor', was a mystery for several decades, partly because whatever is causing it is hidden behind the material in the disc of our Galaxy. The source of the motion is now thought to be a massive cluster of galaxies in the constellation of Norma, which is attracting not just our Galaxy and its immediate neighbours, but also the much larger Virgo Cluster. Every galaxy and cluster of galaxies in the Universe will be in a similar situation, being drawn towards another similar group. Given this, it is unlikely that there is a galaxy that is completely stationary relative to the expanding Universe as a whole.

Astronomers have observed that galaxies are moving away from each other, but how do we really know that this is due to the expansion of space itself, not simply the motion of the galaxies within a fixed space?

Andrew Smith (Clayton West, Yorkshire)

This is a very good question, and one that is not easy to answer fully here. First, let's start with the observations. The first evidence for the expansion of the Universe was found in the 1920s by Edwin Hubble, who was looking in detail at the light from relatively distant galaxies. In particular he was studying their spectrum, whereby the light is spread into its range of wavelengths, or colours, much like light passing through a prism. Rather than a smooth rainbow from red to blue, there are dark stripes in the spectrum of a galaxy caused by particular types of element absorbing specific wavelengths of light. Hubble compared these absorption lines to those measured in laboratories on Earth, and found that they were moved to longer wavelengths. In fact, all the lines in a particular galaxy were all moved towards the red end of the spectrum by the same factor. This effect was given the name 'redshift'.

There are in fact three possible ways of creating a redshift, all relating to the theories of relativity formulated by Albert Einstein. The first is a Doppler Shift, whereby an object's speed relative to the observer (i.e. us) causes the wavelength of the light to be increased or decreased. The same effect can be heard with sound. For example, when a police car zooms past with its siren blaring, the frequency of the sound when it is approaching is higher than when it is receding. In the case of the police car siren, the size of the effect is proportional to the car's speed compared with the speed of sound. In the case of light from distant galaxies, the effect is proportional to the velocity of the object compared with the speed of light. Light from an object that is receding is redshifted to longer wavelengths, while light from an object that is approaching is 'blueshifted' to shorter wavelengths. Since light travels at 300,000 km/h (186,000 mph), the effect of a velocity redshift is normally very small.

A second cause of a redshift is when the light is leaving or approaching an object with a very large mass. Light leaving a galaxy loses a tiny amount of energy when escaping the immense gravitational well. This 'gravitational redshift' effect is also normally very small.

The third method is normally called the 'cosmological redshift', and is caused by the expansion of the Universe. The equations that describe the expansion of the Universe assume that it is completely smooth, which is only true on the largest scales. When making a map of the Universe on a scale of billions of light years, it looks very smooth, with galaxies spread out in a foamy pattern. Consider taking a picture of the Pacific Ocean from space, from where it would look like a smooth blue surface. There are certainly waves on the ocean, but on such large scales they are inconsequential.

It is on these massive scales that the Universe can be considered to be expanding. The light that leaves a distant galaxy is shifted to a longer wavelength because the Universe has expanded between the time it was emitted and the time we measure it. The amount that it has expanded governs how much the wavelength of light is redshifted. The light from more distant galaxies has taken longer to travel, meaning that the Universe has expanded by a larger factor in the intervening period and so the light is redshifted more.

This interpretation of the cosmological redshift seems to suggest that space is expanding. Since space is defined as the absence of anything, it's not really clear what this means, and useful analogies for such a concept are hard to come by. You could interpret it to mean that space is being created in the voids between the galaxies, but that is somewhat problematic – what does it even mean to 'create space'?

When we consider the Universe at an earlier time, it was much smaller, so the clusters of galaxies were all closer together. How does that affect the measurement of distances? Was a light year a few billion years ago shorter than a light year today? Certainly not! But if clusters of galaxies have got further apart, how do we compare the Universe at different stages? Cosmologists tend to use a different measure of distance, where they correct for the expansion of the Universe by multiplying all distances by the appropriate factor. When using these units, which are called 'co-moving coordinates', clusters of galaxies tend to stay the same distance apart over time rather than moving apart. The catch is that a unit of distance actually gets larger with time – a 'co-moving light year' 7 billion years ago was around half the size of a co-moving light-year today. So the problem of how to interpret the situation is simply moved, from considering expanding space to requiring an expanding measuring stick.

If the equations describing the expansion of the Universe assume it is very smooth, does that apply in regions where it isn't so uniform? If you consider the scale of a cluster of galaxies, it certainly is not smooth. In our local group, for example, there are three large galaxies (the Milky Way, and the Andromeda and Triangulum galaxies), each with a mass equivalent to billions of Suns, along with around a dozen or so smaller galaxies. These dozen or so galaxies are spread over a space spanning a few million light years, with almost nothing in between.

That doesn't sound very smooth at all, which means that the Universe doesn't obey the very 'simple' equations that apply on the much larger scales. On these relatively small scales (since the Universe is billions of light years across, it seems fair enough to consider a few million light years to be small!), we really need only consider gravity. On these scales, gravity can cause galaxies to move within their clusters. This gives them a physical velocity, which adds an additional redshift or blueshift (depending on whether they're moving towards or away from us due to the normal Doppler shift). In the nearby Universe, these so-called 'peculiar velocities' can dominate over the cosmological redshift, and there are numerous galaxies that have a blueshift overall.

If the distances to the most distant galaxies are getting larger with time, can't we interpret that as a velocity? Well, yes and no. One can simply take the observed redshift and calculate the velocity that would create a sufficient Doppler shift to match the observations. For relatively nearby galaxies this seems fine, but at much larger distances a problem occurs. The speeds calculated in this way end up becoming greater than the speed of light, which we know to be impossible. The problem is one we've already encountered; measuring distances is very difficult and therefore we are not calculating a true velocity.

To properly calculate the speed, we would need to know the distance of the galaxy when the light was emitted, the distance to it when the light arrived, and the intervening time. But all we know is how much the light has been redshifted. There are a few ways of measuring the distances to some types of objects, but these are almost all very close on the scale of the Universe, and it's not easy to say which distance is being measured – the distance to the galaxy when the light was emitted or the distance when it arrived at Earth.

It would be much more satisfying to give a more clear-cut answer, but that simply isn't possible. The problem is that we're trying to make an analogy to something that we're familiar with, but no such thing exists that can describe the Universe as a whole – except the Universe itself!

In the expanding Universe, what is actually expanding – the space between galaxies, the space between stars, the space between planets, or what? Is the space between the Earth and the Moon also expanding?

Martin Fletcher (Croxley Green, Hertfordshire)

This question assumes that the interpretation of the expanding Universe is that space itself is expanding. As discussed in the previous question, that is one way of looking at it, but it has its own problems, notably that the concept of space expanding is nothing if not confusing. The Universe started out as a pretty boring, uniform place – although it was unimaginably hot and dense in its earliest moments. If you could see it, then it would be all but identical everywhere, and in every direction you could look.

This smooth, uniform place is the kind of universe that expands as one might expect, with everything getting further apart over time. But there's a problem, in that the Universe was *not* quite the same everywhere. Some bits were slightly denser than others, and it is these dense regions that ended up becoming the galaxies and clusters of galaxies that we see around us today. It is only when you consider the Universe on the largest scales that it looks smooth, with galaxies blurred out into a clumpy sea of tiny dots. This is how cosmologists see the Universe, with entire galaxies represented by a single tiny point, and it is on this huge scale that it is expanding.

But if you zoom in and look at a single cluster, the galaxies are most definitely not smooth, as they represent huge clumps of matter in the almost completely empty vacuum of intergalactic space. Such a clumpy environment doesn't obey the same rules as a smooth one, as forces such as gravity play a much larger role than those that are trying to push the Universe apart. Groups of galaxies are tied together into clumps by

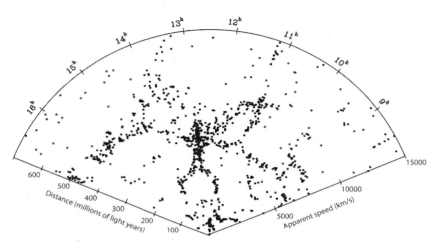

A slice through space showing the distribution of galaxies measured by a galaxy survey in the 1970s and 1980s. The distribution does not look random, with a 'Great Wall' seen at a distance of around 500 million light years, though the 'stick figure' in the centre is pure coincidence!

gravity, forming galaxy clusters. These clusters do not experience the expansion of space, but stay stuck together by gravity, which is much stronger on these relatively small scales.

What we've claimed is that gravity is too strong to stop galaxies and clusters of galaxies from expanding. But surely the massive clusters have their own gravitational attraction, and so can overcome the expansion just as easily? Well, adjacent clusters of galaxies *do* pull on each other, but so do all the other clusters in the Universe. And since on the largest scales the Universe is very smooth, there are roughly equal numbers of clusters pulling in each direction. The gravitational pull from all the clusters combined averages out to almost zero, meaning that the expansion of space is free to push them further apart.

If clusters of galaxies are too clumpy to experience the expansion of space, then so are individual galaxies and solar systems. So the space between stars, or the distance between the Earth and the Moon, is not expanding. The clusters of galaxies get further apart as the space between them expands, but they do not get any bigger themselves.

We return to our simple analogy of the Universe imagined as the surface of an expanding balloon. It must still be remembered that the surface of the balloon represents the Universe and that the interior should be ignored – that is simply providing a means by which to expand the surface. In this analogy, a common mistake is to draw the galaxies onto the balloon, so that as the surface (i.e. the Universe) expands they also grow bigger. As discussed above, this is not the case, and the galaxies are more accurately represented by pennies or buttons stuck onto the surface – they don't get bigger as the Universe expands, but they do get further apart.

In the balloon analogy, the Universe is split into two parts: the large-scale parts that can be considered smooth (and therefore expand over time), and the smaller bits where matter is more clumpily distributed. In reality, the Universe is not so simple, and there are grey areas in between. But rest assured that objects such as the Solar System, planets and people are not getting bigger. The gravitational force that keeps the Moon in orbit and the electromagnetic forces that bind the molecules in your body together are billions upon billions of times stronger than the expansive forces that push the galaxy clusters apart, at least on such small scales.

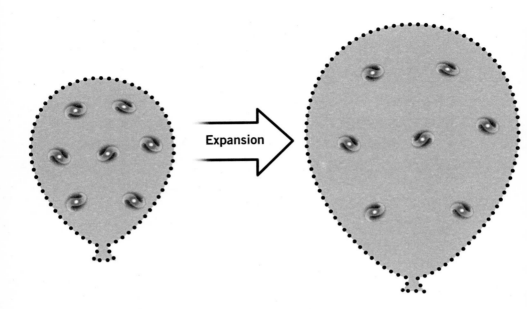

The Universe can be imagined as the surface of an expanding balloon, with galaxies stuck on. As the balloon expands the galaxies get further apart, but do not themselves expand.

I have read in Martin Rees's book that our Galaxy is moving towards the Virgo Cluster of galaxies at 600 km/s, and the Virgo Cluster is moving towards other clusters. Hundreds of galaxies, including ours, are being drawn towards a huge mass called the 'Great Attractor'. How can we know that we are not in a contracting universe with the 'Great Attractor' at its centre?

Peter Eggleston (Hexham, Northumberland)

Our Galaxy, the Milky Way, is a member of a group of nearly 20 galaxies, rather unimaginatively called the Local Group. This entire group of galaxies, which also contains the Andromeda and Triangulum galaxies, as well as a dozen or so smaller ones, is being pulled towards the Virgo Cluster, a much larger group containing hundreds of galaxies. There are also much larger groups, such as the Coma Cluster which contains thousands of galaxies and could be considered to be a cluster of clusters. The names of clusters simply refer to the constellations in which they are found.

Measurements of the distant Universe, some dating back to the 1960s, have shown that the Milky Way and the surrounding galaxies are indeed moving through space. Later measurements confirmed the speed as approximately 600 km/s, and that the motion is towards a point in the constellation of Centaurus. Since the discovery of this motion, the assumption has been that the cause is a huge supercluster of galaxies (a cluster of clusters!) with a mass equivalent to 10,000 Milky Ways. The difficulty with identifying the cluster, dubbed the Great Attractor, has been due to the fact that to see it we have to look through the disc of the Milky Way, where images are greatly confused by the many millions of stars. By comparing the speeds of other nearby galaxies, the distance was calculated at around 200 million light years – several times further away than the Virgo Cluster.

While our Galaxy blocks the view in optical light, such massive clusters show up very brightly in X-rays. Several careful studies in recent years have shown that the Great Attractor is somewhat smaller than expected, but that there is also a large concentration of galaxy clusters at a distance of around 500 million light years. This concentration became known as the Shapley Concentration, since it includes the Shapley Supercluster, a cluster of thousands of galaxies which was discovered by Harlow Shapley in the 1930s.

So many of the nearby galaxies are indeed being pulled towards this concentration of galaxies, but that's only part of the picture. We can see galaxies many times further away than the Shapley Supercluster, and most of these are not moving towards it. The gravitational attraction caused by this huge mass is a relatively local effect (if you can call several hundred million light years a local effect), slightly counteracting the expansion of the Universe in our own local neighbourhood.

Are the very distant galaxies being found by the Hubble Space Telescope still showing the same expansion as the nearer ones?

Ross E Platt (Vendee, Western France)

When we look at a distant galaxy we can examine how much the light from the galaxy has been stretched by the expansion of the Universe, something called its 'redshift'. This was discovered by Edwin Hubble in the 1920s, and led to 'Hubble's Law'. By examining relatively nearby galaxies, Hubble showed that their redshift is proportional to their distance from us – the light from a galaxy twice as distant has been stretched twice as much. In order to deduce this relationship, he needed to know their distance, something that is often hard to measure.

To get these galaxies' distances, Hubble studied a particular type of star, called a Cepheid variable star, which has a very predictable brightness. By comparing the predicted brightness of the star with how bright it actually looked, he could calculate its distance. These Cepheid variables are relatively close, so to calculate distances further out into the Universe we need more luminous objects with a predictable brightness. Luckily, nature has given us such an object in the form of a particular type of supernova, or exploding star, called a 'Type 1a supernova'. These supernovae can outshine an entire galaxy, and therefore are visible at huge distances.

The Hubble Space Telescope, named after Edwin Hubble, has been one of a number of telescopes searching the skies for these types of supernovae. For each one we then have a distance and redshift, so we can find out if Hubble's

Law still applies. And the answer is... sort of! The distant galaxies still appear to be receding, but the more distant ones seem to be receding at a faster rate. This tells us one of two things: either the distances are wrong, or the rate of expansion of the Universe has increased over the last few billion years.

It could be that the supernova behaved differently in the early Universe, either because they were made of a slightly more primordial combination of elements, or because they were in different environments. Either of these would throw off the predicted brightnesses, and therefore the calculated distances. But it's not clear that this would give a big enough discrepancy to explain the apparent change in expansion.

So if the Universe is expanding at a faster rate, why would that be? The current consensus is that it is a phenomenon known as dark energy, which causes the expansion of the Universe to accelerate. There is other evidence that something like dark energy exists (see later questions), but we don't yet have a handle on what it is.

The discovery of the apparent acceleration of the expansion of the Universe resulted in three of the leading scientists on the teams that initially discovered it, Saul Perlmutter, Brian Schmidt and Adam Reiss, being awarded the 2011 Nobel Prize for Physics.

If light can take so long to reach us here on Earth, is it possible that a lot of the objects we observe do not actually exist any more?

John Mahon (Melksham, Wiltshire)

It is indeed possible that some of the objects we see in the sky are no longer there. Light travels extremely quickly, at 300,000 km/s (186,000 miles per second), but astronomical distances are incredibly vast. Light from the Sun, 150 million km away, takes around eight minutes to reach us here on Earth, while light from Pluto takes seven hours to travel 7.5 billion km. This means that we see the Sun as it was eight minutes ago and Pluto as it was seven hours ago. But these distances are relatively small, and the light-travel time from stars is measured in years. The nearest star is four light years away, while the nearest large galaxy, the Andromeda galaxy, is 2.5 million light years distant. We are seeing the Andromeda galaxy as it was when most of our ancestors were still living in trees!

When we look at the most distant galaxies, we see them as they were billions of years ago, and certainly the more massive stars will have died since then as they don't live very long. Many of the galaxies will also have collided and merged with their close neighbours. So while the galaxies as a whole are likely still to be there, they will probably have changed considerably, and be made of new populations of stars.

If the Big Bang was a radial expansion of matter, why is almost everything in the Universe rotating?

Stephen Todd (North East England)

The reason is in the way everything forms. Stars and planets are formed from huge clouds of gas, while galaxies are formed from massive collections of stars. Let's consider the formation of a star, the precursor to which is little more than a large collection of molecules all moving in seemingly random directions. The particles slow down when they hit each other, and those in the densest regions collapse to form a central core. The rest of the cloud continues to move and the gravitational pull of the core causes the particles surrounding it to start orbiting it.

In physics, there's a quantity known as angular momentum, which is essentially the amount of spin something has. This can be the spin of a solid object, such as a planet or a spinning top, or the spin of a system such as a planet orbiting a star. We can't see angular momentum, but we can measure and calculate it – much like energy. One feature of angular momentum is that it is very hard to lose. It can be reduced by friction, which is why a spinning top eventually stops spinning. Colliding objects transfer angular momentum, which is why adding spin to the cue ball causes any ball it hits to also start spinning.

Not every particle will orbit in exactly the same direction, and they won't all be in circular orbits, but there will be a common direction of motion when the motion of all of them is averaged out. This common sense of rotation leads to a disc forming, which enforces the common sense of rotation. There will be occasional particles moving in different directions, but most move in the same way. Some of the angular momentum is lost in the collisions, but much of it remains in the cloud. As the cloud collapses, the angular momentum remains almost constant. Just like a spinning ice skater pulling in his or her arms, the cloud rotates faster. This means that even a very slow rotation of a large cloud of dust becomes a much faster rotation of the much smaller star.

The disc of gas left around the star is what the planets form from. Since most of the material is moving in the same direction, so do most of the planets. There are some smaller objects, mainly asteroids and comets, which orbit in a different sense, but most things in the Solar System are located in a disc and orbit the Sun in the same direction.

Galaxies are similar, but instead of forming from particles of gas they were formed from collections of stars. Stars don't generally collide, so it is even harder for them to lose angular momentum, which is why galaxies don't collapse into super-massive stars. Stars do exert a gravitational pull on each other, and this causes them to end up rotating in much the same way as planets. Just as in our Solar System, not everything in a galaxy orbits in the same way. For example, some stars in our own Galaxy are in orbits that are tilted with respect to the disc. And the smaller galaxies that orbit the Milky Way, such as the Large and

Small Magellanic Clouds, orbit in a different sense as well. So the sense of rotation of an object like a galaxy is a measure of the way *most* of the stars are moving, not necessarily all of them.

Is the Universe spinning?

John Robertson (Devon)

There is one conceptual leap to overcome when asking this question: relative to what? The question could be rephrased to ask whether the objects in the Universe are rotating in a common sense. The galaxies and clusters of galaxies are all moving, but could they all be rotating around a central point or axis? If you measured the direction of rotation of a large number of galaxies, which has actually been done, you would find that there is no preferred direction. Pretty much the same number of galaxies rotate clockwise (relative to our viewpoint from Earth) as anticlockwise. In terms of the direction of motion of galaxies, that is much harder to measure. We can measure the speed at which galaxies are moving towards or away from us, but not their motion across the sky – they simply take far too long to move any distance that is measureable from Earth.

We don't think that the Universe as a whole is spinning, and there is observational evidence to prove this from of the Cosmic Microwave Background. This is the afterglow of the Big Bang and the most distant thing we can see, making it an ideal way to look at the Universe on large scales. If the Universe as a whole were rotating, we would expect to see a subtle difference in the Cosmic Microwave Background. These effects have been searched for by many people, but not found.

The rotation of the Universe as a whole would also violate one of the principles of cosmology, namely that no place in the Universe is special. This is required by Einstein's theories of relativity, which we believe to be valid and correct throughout the Universe. If there were a point or axis around which the Universe rotated, there would be some locations that were more special than others, and a universal frame of reference against which all motion could be measured.

It has been known for some time that the Universe is expanding and that the further away an object is the faster it is moving. But since we see these distant objects as they were a long time ago, how do we know the Universe is still expanding today?

Tom Wood (Littlehampton)

We consider distant galaxies to be moving away from us because their light has been stretched to longer wavelengths. The stretching is calculated by measuring the wavelength of specific features in the spectrum of the light and comparing to the values measured in laboratories on Earth. This 'redshift' is not strictly speaking due to the physical velocity of the galaxies, but rather due to the expansion of the Universe over the time that the light has been travelling. We can compare these redshifts with the distance to the objects, though this can only be done for objects that we know the distance of. One particular type of supernova, a 'Type 1a', has a predictable brightness which allows its distance to be calculated and these exploding stars are so bright that we can measure them out to distances of billions of light years. When we look at more distant objects, the light from which has been travelling for a longer time, we see that more expansion has occurred than when we look at a closer object.

We can measure incredibly tiny changes in the wavelength, and therefore tiny expansions. The expansion of the Universe does change with time and matches our expectations. If we look at an object from which light has been travelling for a billion years, we see an expansion of less than ten per cent – so a billion years ago the Universe was ten per cent smaller than it is today. When we look at a galaxy that is so far away that the light has been travelling for eight billion years, we see that the Universe was about half its current size when the light was emitted. The light from the most distant objects we can see has been stretched by a factor of about nine. While we can't measure the distance to such objects, we can calculate that the light has been travelling for around 13 billion years – having been emitted less than a billion years after the Big Bang.

If at some point in the history of the Universe the expansion had stopped, we would see that the measured expansions would stop changing within a certain distance of Earth. There is no evidence that the expansion has stopped, and we even have evidence that it is now accelerating. Over most of the history of the Universe the expansion has gradually slowed down, but in the last several billion years it appears that the rate of expansion has increased. The currently favoured explanation for this is a mysterious force – 'dark energy'.

How come the expansion of the Universe is getting faster and not slower, as one would expect?

Sean Trow (Jersey) and Mervyn Pritchard (Marchamley, Shropshire)

This is one of the biggest questions in modern cosmology, and one to which there is no definite answer. As soon as it was established that the Universe was expanding, people set about trying to find out how fast. It was expected that the expansion would slow down, simply because of the gravitational pull of everything in the Universe. The fate of the Universe depends on how fast it was expanding, and how dense it is.

This is somewhat like throwing a ball straight up in the air. It travels upwards at first, but is continually slowing due to the Earth's gravity. Eventually, it slows to a stop and starts falling back down. Now imagine if you could throw the ball much, much harder, so that it travelled even further. It would still continue to slow down, but if you throw it at more than 11 km/s (24,000 mph) it would never actually stop. This critical speed, called the escape velocity, depends on the gravitational pull of the Earth, which in turn depends on its mass. In the case of the Universe, the critical quantity is its density; above a critical density and it will collapse on itself, below the critical density and it will expand for ever. But all this assumes that the Universe is only made up of matter and radiation.

In the 1990s, the picture became a lot more puzzling. Although measurements of the Universe on the largest scales seemed to indicate that its density is almost exactly equal to this critical value, astronomers simply couldn't find enough stuff. In fact, there were only enough galaxies to account for one-third of the critical density, even when including the mysterious dark matter. In addition to this conundrum, measurements of distant supernovae showed that the expansion of the Universe was in fact accelerating, and had been for several billion years.

The solution that is currently favoured by most cosmologists is called dark energy. It is a form of energy that pervades all space, but which exerts a pressure that acts to push everything apart. The cause of this mysterious energy is not known, and various theories have been proposed. The most commonly favoured (though that does not necessarily make it right!) is that the accelerated expansion is due to an inherent energy present in the vacuum of space. This energy density would be so very weak that in most cases it is not observable at all. This vacuum energy is a prediction of quantum physics, but there is no prediction of what its value might be. We have no way to measure or calculate it, but our best estimate places it at 30 orders of magnitude higher than what is needed to explain the accelerated expansion of the Universe. That's a discrepancy of a factor of a million million million million million! Somewhat embarrassing for cosmologists and quantum physicists alike, but since it's based on an estimate it is clear that there is much more work to be done.

So we don't know what causes dark energy, but all our measurements seem to indicate that there is something there that is causing the Universe to expand. It also fills the gap in the amount of 'stuff' in the Universe, bringing the total tally back up to the critical density measured by other experiments. It is of course possible that the theories are all wrong, and that there is no such thing as dark energy. But since it is now so crucial to our understanding of cosmology, there's a good chance that if the theories are wrong, they're *really* wrong!

Since the 'standard candle' used to probe the expanding Universe was proved to be inaccurate, how has it affected our understanding of the expanding Universe?

Scott Beresford (Birmingham, West Midlands)

The 'standard candles' used are better thought of as 'standardisable candles', as some work has to be done to calculate the distance carefully. The two main types used for extragalactic work are Cepheid variable stars and Type 1a supernovae. In both cases, the variation of the brightness can be used to deduce the intrinsic luminosity of the star. Once that is known, the distance can be calculated, since a more distant object would appear fainter than a closer one.

The Cepheid variable stars pulsate, in both size and luminosity, with a period that is linked to their average brightness. Since such stars are generally many thousands of times more luminous than the Sun they can be seen in other galaxies, and it was observations of a Cepheid variable star in what used to be known as the Great Andromeda Nebula that led Edwin Hubble to deduce that it was far beyond the realms of our own Galaxy.

But the relationship between the pulsation period and the luminosity of a Cepheid variable is not completely straightforward. For a start, there are two types of Cepheid variable – in fact, Hubble's initial calculation of the distance to the Andromeda galaxy was wrong because he assumed the wrong type of Cepheid. The pulsations also depend on the composition of the star, for example how many heavy elements such as oxygen, carbon and iron are present. While the composition can be determined by other means, there is still an intrinsic uncertainty in the distances calculated from Cepheid variables. While they were used by Edwin Hubble in the 1920s to show that the Universe was expanding, the rate of expansion was not well known.

Type 1a supernovae are much brighter than Cepheid variables, and are the result of a white dwarf star being destroyed when it reaches a critical mass. This mass is, in principle, the same for all white dwarfs and so it might be easy to expect that they all have the same brightness. But the details of the explosion depend on how fast the star is rotating, and what its exact composition is. What has been deduced from observations is that brightness is linked to the time that it takes the afterglow of the supernova to fade away. So to deduce the intrinsic luminosity, we have to first measure the brightness of the supernova over many days and weeks.

The most distant observed supernovae are so far away that the light left them when the Universe was less than half its current age. In the late 1990s, it was discovered that the most distant Type 1a supernovae appeared to be receding at a faster rate than they should be given their measured distances. The two possibilities are that the rate of expansion of the Universe is increasing, or that the distances to the supernovae are wrong.

The big question becomes: did these supernovae behave in the same way billions of years ago? If they have changed, then the assumptions used in calculating their intrinsic luminosities could be wrong, and therefore the distances would be off. For example, we know that the composition of stars has gradually changed over the history of the Universe, as successive generations became chemically enriched by the products of previous generations of stars. There is considerable debate over whether these differences could account for the effects seen, but the majority of astronomers now tend to agree that they are too small.

There are still those who disagree, and who believe the evidence for the accelerated expansion of the Universe is on thin ice. But there are now other experiments that have used different measurements, such as the large scale distribution of galaxies, to conclude the same thing. Everything points to the same model, and if the supernovae turn out to be misleading us, then the model could be left on shaky ground.

If the Cosmic Microwave Background is radiation from the Big Bang, then why can we still see it? Shouldn't it have travelled outwards at the speed of light, and therefore be well ahead of us?

Richard Jones (Cheshire)

The microwave light that we see as the Cosmic Microwave Background has indeed been travelling at the speed of light, but it has come from the distant reaches of the visible Universe. That means that it has taken 13.7 billion years to travel from its distant starting point to our telescopes today. The light that was in our location 13.7 billion years ago has also been travelling away at the speed of light, and is now long gone. In fact, there could be someone else billions of light years away answering the very same question.

When describing how far away galaxies are, the term light years is used. But what does this mean in an expanding Universe? If we say a galaxy is so many light years away, and light travels at a fixed rate, then next year the gap between us has increased. Are

distances revised to compensate for the expansion of the Universe or is the effect negligible?

Robert (Leicester)

Distances in cosmology pose a very difficult challenge for the very reasons posed in the question. The distance to a moving object depends on when you measure that distance. We're used to measurements being fairly instantaneous, but in cosmology that's not always the case. The distances are so great that the light takes a very long time to travel from where it was emitted to our telescopes on Earth. In the intervening time, sometimes measured in billions of years, the Universe has expanded – so do you quote the distance when the light was emitted (when the Universe was smaller) or the distance now?

The only handle we have for the distance to most objects across the Universe is their redshift – how much their light has been stretched by the expansion of the Universe. Using a standard model for the expansion of the Universe, we can calculate how long the light has been travelling. But turning this into a distance is a much more complex task, and it depends on how you want to imagine the Universe.

Let's consider the Universe as an enormous, flat rubber sheet, with galaxies scattered over its surface. As the Universe expands, the rubber stretches and the galaxies get further apart. Now how do you measure the distances? You could hold up a ruler to the rubber sheet, but that distance would then depend on how stretched it was when you made the measurement.

Let's consider a galaxy that, when we hold up a ruler to the rubber sheet, is three billion light years away. The light that is emitted from that galaxy, which one could imagine as a marble being rolled across the rubber sheet, travels at the speed of light and so one might expect it to take three billion years to reach us. As the light travels, however, the rubber sheet (i.e. the Universe) is being stretched, and the marble (i.e. the light) takes longer and longer to cross what used to be the same distance. It actually takes 13 billion years to reach us on Earth, by which time the Universe has expanded by a factor of around nine. If we now hold up a ruler again, the galaxy is much further away – in fact nine times further away, and the measured distance would be almost 30 billion light years. Both measurements are equally valid, but they give very different answers. The latter answer gives the impression that the galaxy has travelled 30 billion light years in 13 billion years, which would require it to travel faster than light.

There are other ways of measuring the distance. If the intrinsic luminosity of the object is known, as is the case with Cepheid variable stars and Type 1a supernovae, then its distance can be calculated in a different way. More distant objects look fainter, but when considering light from objects across the Universe the light is also dimmed by the expansion. This means that the calculated distance appears to be much, much greater than it really is, and in the case of the galaxy we considered earlier would come in at around the 270 billion light year mark!

All these different interpretations mean that cosmologists use two main measures when discussing distances in the Universe. The first is to use the redshift, which measures how much the Universe has expanded since the light was emitted. Since this is an observable fact there can be little argument, making the redshift the most common distance measure. If a distance is required, then the most common one of choice is to use the distance that would be found if a massive ruler could be held up and the distance instantaneously read right now – which for our example galaxy would be 30 billion light years. This is called the 'co-moving distance', since it removes the expansion, but as we saw above gives the impression that objects have travelled faster than light. In fact, what has happened is that the Universe itself has expanded faster than light.

How can it be that the Universe is larger than if it had been expanding at the speed of light since the Big Bang? Does this mean that the speed of light is not the fastest possible speed?

Mike Rosevear (Maidenhead, Berkshire), Molly Cutpurse (Grays, Essex) and Bryan Moiser (Beverley, East Yorkshire)

As discussed in the previous answer, this depends on what you mean by distance, since the measurement changes as the Universe expands. The confusion arises because the diameter of the visible Universe is often quoted as about 45 billion light years. When compared with the Universe's age of 13.7 billion light years, this can give the impression that objects have travelled faster than light, but you can rest assured that this is not the case. The distance quoted is the one that would be measured by an enormous cosmic ruler, held up and read off instantaneously.

But the light from the most distant depths of the visible Universe has been travelling towards us for over 13 billion years. This allows us to see the Universe as it was when it was a tiny fraction of its current age. However, we can't see all the way back to the Big Bang because for the first few hundred thousand years the Universe was opaque. The furthest we can see is something called the Cosmic Microwave Background, emitted when the Universe was less than 400,000 years old. When that light was emitted, the Universe was a much smaller place, and what we now see as a distant horizon was actually only 40 million light years away. The reason the light has taken so long to reach us is that the Universe has been expanding all that time, and since the light from the Cosmic Microwave Background started its journey it has stretched by a factor of more than 1,000.

So the speed of light is still the ultimate speed limit in the Universe, but while *no thing* can travel faster than light, *nothing* (i.e. empty space) can.

Is there any good reason to believe the entire Universe is entirely contained within our cosmic horizon? Could there be more galaxies beyond?

Geoff Robbins (Edinburgh) and Geoff Sargent (Portsmouth, Hampshire)

Our cosmic horizon is defined by the age of the Universe, as we can only see regions that are close enough for light to have travelled to us over the past 13.7 billion years. As time goes by, this horizon will grow, albeit very slowly in cosmological terms, and more galaxies will become visible. But will there come a point when this stops? The size of the whole Universe is not known – and in fact it could be infinite. Even if it is finite, however, that does not imply that the Universe has an edge.

Returning to our familiar analogy, consider the surface of a balloon, which has no edge but which is certainly not infinite in size. The Universe could well be similar, with our visible horizon representing some fraction of the entire surface. If you travel around the balloon, then eventually you return to where you started. Perhaps the same is true in our Universe. If we could see enough of the surface, then the galaxies we see in one direction would actually be the same ones we see in the opposite direction. Because of this, our example of a balloon should be treated with caution as it would be inaccurate to give the impression that the Universe is spherical.

Some scientists, however, are looking for hints that could give away the size of the Universe. By examining the largest scales we can see in the Universe, namely those in the Cosmic Microwave Background, the search is under way for subtle signatures of various effects, including a finite size to the Universe. It's a bold endeavour as it's not always clear exactly what is being looked for, but it suffices to say that nothing untoward has been found yet!

What is the mass of the entire Universe?

Paul (Dublin, Ireland)

We can't actually see the entire Universe, so determining its size and mass is impossible. What we can try to calculate is its density, or mass in a given volume. While we might not be able to measure the entire Universe we can see a lot of space, stretching for billions of light years in every direction, and in that space there are millions upon millions of galaxies. A galaxy like our own Milky Way contains the equivalent of a million million Suns, and since the Sun weighs two million million million million million kg, that makes galaxies pretty massive. These numbers get very large and unwieldy, so scientists would write the mass of the Sun as 2×10^{30} kg, which means a 2 followed by 30 zeros.

But the galaxies are pretty far apart, and are arranged in groups and clusters with immense voids in them. So what is the overall density? Well, it turns out to be pretty low. If the Universe were smoothed out, there would be the equivalent of just six protons in every cubic metre. Compare this with air, which we don't consider to be particularly dense. A cubic metre of air weighs about 1 kg which is equivalent to 600 million million million million protons. This means that to reduce the density of the air to the average density of the Universe we would have to expand every cubic metre until it reached beyond the Moon's orbit.

So the Universe is not very dense, but it is pretty big, and even a very low density could add up to a pretty large mass. The Universe as measured today is around 45 billion light years across. (See previous questions for why that *doesn't* mean that objects have travelled faster than light!) Assuming this volume, and the density given above, then the mass of the visible Universe is around 60 million million million million million million million kg (6 $\times 10^{43}$ kg, or a 6 followed by 43 zeros). That is the equivalent to a million

million galaxies like the Milky Way. Since the Milky Way contains around one hundred billion stars, there are an awful lot of solar systems out there!

If the Universe is expanding, will everything be out of sight one day?

Tony Roberts (Shoreham-by-Sea, West Sussex)

The Universe might be expanding, but as time goes on we can see further and further. This is simply because the light from even more distant objects has had time to reach us here on Earth. But as the expansion continues, the light from those most distant objects gets stretched more and more. As well as increasing the wavelength of the light, this also makes the objects appear dimmer. Eventually, the most distant objects will move so far away that their light can never reach us, and they will be invisible.

Closer objects, such as the Solar System and the Galaxy, are held together by gravity and these will not expand away. Eventually, however, after many billions of years, the last stars will fizzle out. If there are any people living in the Universe at that time, it will be an incredibly boring place!

How has the estimate of the age and size of the Universe changed over the history of *The Sky at Night*?

Hywel Clatworthy (Pontypool, South Wales)

The Sky at Night has covered the time of some of the most significant changes in our understanding of the Universe. The world of cosmology in the 1950s was dominated by one big question: was there a Big Bang? There was strong evidence by that point that the Universe was expanding, courtesy of Edwin Hubble and others, and the expansion fitted neatly into Albert Einstein's theories of general relativity.

A group of scientists, including Fred Hoyle from Cambridge, were proponents of the 'Steady State Universe'. Hoyle had triumphed in showing that most of the chemical elements were created in the centres of stars, and was not comfortable with the idea that the Universe had a beginning. In his theory, the Universe was expanding, but new matter was constantly created to fill the gaps. In this way, the Universe would constantly be changing, but when considered as a whole would be in the same state for eternity.

The opposing theory involved the concept that the Universe was smaller in the past. Taking the idea to its natural conclusion, there must have been a time when the Universe was much smaller. This was bolstered by observations of distant galaxies by radio astronomers, which indicated that the furthest reaches of the Universe are different from our local environment. The idea that the Universe had not been around for eternity seemed preposterous to some – the term 'Big Bang' was coined by the English astronomer Fred Hoyle in 1949, with some reports suggesting the name was meant to be disparaging (though Hoyle never admitted to this).

The nail in the coffin of the Steady State theory came in the 1960s. Two physicists working at Bell Labs, Arno Penzias and Robert Wilson, were trying to get to the bottom of static in radio communications. They found a constant signal coming from all over the sky, and could not find its source. It was deduced by Robert Dicke, an American theoretical physicist, that this could be radiation remaining from the afterglow of the Big Bang. This fitted in very well with the Big Bang model, as the early Universe must also have been so very hot and dense that it would have been dominated by intense radiation. Such a cosmic afterglow was independently predicted in the 1940s, and the discovery was surprisingly close to the predictions. We know this radiation now as the Cosmic Microwave Background, or CMB for short, and we see it as a constant glow over the whole sky, corresponding to a temperature of three degrees above absolute zero.

The CMB turned cosmology from a theoretical exercise into an observational science, and astronomers clamoured to find out as much as possible about the early Universe. The observations helped narrow down its age, initially putting it at somewhere around 10 billion years. This was slightly contradictory to some other evidence, which indicated that some stars were much older than that.

But the CMB also posed a number of problems for cosmologists. The early Universe seemed to have been almost exactly the same in all directions. The only way that different parts could have achieved the same temperature would be if light had been able to travel between them to equalise the energy. But the light from one side of the Universe is only just arriving at Earth, so it hadn't had enough time to get to the other side. And yet, somehow, the Universe has reached this incredibly uniform state.

A further problem was the calculated density of the Universe. It was known from Einstein's theories that there were three possible solutions. If the density was too high, then the gravitational pull of everything on everything else would slow down the expansion and eventually reverse it, culminating in a 'big crunch'. If the density was too low, then the Universe would continue to expand for ever, resulting in a 'big freeze'. Finally, there is a sweet spot in the middle, called the 'critical density', where the Universe would continue to expand but at an ever-decreasing rate.

The problem was that if the density were even a tiny bit different from the critical density, then we would not be here. Even one part in 10^{60} (1 followed by 60 zeros) would result in the Universe either being crushed to a pulp or ripped apart before life on Earth could evolve. Could this simply be a coincidence? As a rule, scientists are generally wary of a coincidence, especially one that is balanced on such a fine knife edge.

A common response to what was termed the 'flatness problem' was the anthropic principle. It stated that the Universe had to be this density because if it weren't then we wouldn't be here to ask the question. A seemingly valid answer, but not one that is very satisfying.

The solution to both these problems was proposed in the 1980s by an astronomer called Alan Guth. His theory, which he termed 'inflation', involved an incredibly rapid period of expansion in the very early Universe. This would expand the horizon very rapidly so that much larger parts of the Universe could reach the same temperature and density. If true, this would mean for certain that our own visible Universe was a tiny, tiny part of a much larger Universe, most of which is too far away for light to have travelled to us yet. Inflation would also solve the 'flatness problem', as the theory requires that the density approaches the critical value. This would be a much more satisfying answer than anthropic principle, though it still needs to be tested and verified.

By the 1990s, people had started making more detailed maps of the Cosmic Microwave Background, and had seen tiny variations. Parts of the early Universe were ever so slightly denser than others, and these over-densities became the sites of massive clusters of galaxies such as those we see around us today. NASA's Cosmic Background Explorer (COBE) and Wilkinson Microwave Anisotropy Probe (WMAP) satellites helped to make increasingly accurate maps, and started to help refine the estimates of what the Universe is made of. More recently the European Space Agency's Planck mission has been making more detailed maps of the entire sky.

The answer was startling, as it indicated that less than one-twentieth of the energy in the Universe could be attributed to normal atomic matter such as that which we and everything we see are made of. Around a fifth of the Universe is made of something called dark matter, of which there was evidence from other fields of cosmology and astrophysics. But, even combined, this only made up around a quarter of the energy density of the entire Universe. The rest is thought to be made of something which was called dark energy (cosmologists like to give things rather unhelpful and meaningless names). Dark energy and inflation both stem from theories of particle physics, the details of which are far beyond the scope of this book.

In the early twenty-first century, a consistent picture is finally taking form. The Universe is made of around 4 per cent matter that we're used to, around 23 per cent dark matter, and around 73 per cent dark energy. We also know that it is around 13.7 billion years old. Other aspects of the Universe are far more uncertain. For example, we have not yet discovered what dark matter is (a bold statement to write in a time when the Large Hadron Collider might be on the verge of discovering it!), and we don't really have a clue what dark energy is.

In other respects, nothing has changed since the 1950s. We might understand more about how the Universe has changed, and what occurred in its earliest moments, but we don't have a clue as to what caused the Big Bang in the first place. There are theories, but they are currently completely untestable. Perhaps, for the moment, this biggest of big questions is best left to the philosophers.

Is the Universe increasing in mass?

Steve Gayler (Poole, Dorset)

The short answer to this is no, at least not if you assume that mass and energy are equivalent. That's something that Einstein showed us, and is one of the reasons for the oft-quoted equation $E=mc^2$. Matter is being constantly turned into energy, for example when a star burns its nuclear fuel to create light. But the opposite can also happen, and a photon of light can decay into particles of matter. When we talk about the contents of the Universe, we normally talk about the energy density, accounting for the matter with its equivalent energy.

We can't see the entire Universe, just those parts that are close enough for light to have had sufficient time to travel to us. As time goes by, we can see further and further, bringing more and more galaxies into view. But if we take a particular volume of space at a certain time, for example the entire visible Universe that we can currently see, then on average nothing is entering or leaving it. For every photon of light that leaves the region we've selected, another one will enter.

But the Universe is expanding, causing that fixed region to grow in volume. While the energy content of the region may stay the same, the density will constantly be decreasing as the volume increases.

What shape is the Universe, and how do we know?

Peter Baker (Ascot, Berkshire) and Tom Stroud (Southampton, Hampshire)

Discussions about the shape of the Universe normally relate to how it should be treated on large scales. To do this, let's imagine that the Universe is actually two-dimensional. (Obviously, the Universe is not two-dimensional, but manipulations of three-dimensional space are notoriously difficult to visualise!) It's much easier or represent it with a two-dimensional surface, giving us a third dimension to move it around in.) Now imagine drawing a triangle on a piece of paper. Schoolchildren are taught that the angles within a triangle add up to 180 degrees, and on a flat piece of paper that would certainly be the case. A two-dimensional surface where angles in a triangle do add up to 180 degrees is said to have a 'flat' geometry.

Now imagine the surface of a sphere, say a globe of the Earth. From the Equator, draw a line heading due north to the North Pole, then turn through a right angle and head back to the Equator. Once there, turn another right angle to return to where the line started. What you have is a triangle drawn

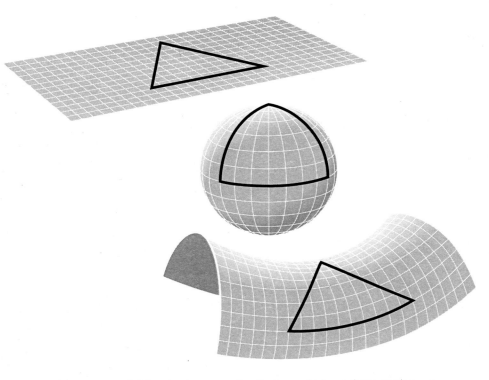

A large enough triangle drawn on the Earth would have three angles adding up to 270 degrees – more than if it was on a flat surface.

on a sphere, but all three angles in the triangle are right angles. That means the sum of the three angles is 270 degrees, not 180.

A shape such as this is said to have 'positive curvature', which means that the angles in triangles add up to more than 180 degrees. If you were to walk (or swim, or fly) along the lines you would think you were walking in a straight line at all times, unable to detect the curvature of the surface – it's only when looked at in three dimensions that the lines appear to be curved.

It is possible to imagine a surface where the angles of a triangle add up to less than 180 degrees. These are said to have 'negative curvature', and the simplest one to imagine is the shape of a horse's saddle, which goes down at the sides and up at the front and back. While the lines would look straight when viewed up close, from afar they would appear to bend outwards.

This all seems pretty abstract, and it may not be clear how drawing triangles on different shapes has anything to do with the Universe. Instead of drawing lines, we could imagine shining a beam of light. In a universe with positive curvature (e.g. a sphere) the beams of light bend towards each other, which makes things appear larger than they really are – the universe acts like a giant lens. In a universe with negative curvature, the lines curve away from each other and objects appear smaller.

So how do we go about measuring whether beams of light travel in straight lines? To do so would require knowing how large an object was in the first place, allowing us to compare that size with how large it appears. Luckily, we do have something of a known size, notably the features seen in the Cosmic Microwave Background, the afterglow of the Big Bang. When we look at the microwaves that are emanating from the early Universe, we see parts that were slightly hotter and denser than others. We actually understand the formation of these hot (and cold) spots very well – the early Universe may have been hotter and denser, but it was a pretty simple place to understand in terms of the physics.

We can then create a triangle with one corner here on Earth and the other two either side of a hot spot. The apparent size is exactly what it should be if all the angles add up to 180 degrees. That means that light has travelled in straight lines, and the shape of the Universe on these large scales is flat. We can do the same for objects that are a little closer to home than the most distant parts of the Universe we can see, using features such as the distribution of galaxies on massive scales. Basically anything that has a known size.

We know that the Universe seems to be almost completely flat. But we are not 100 per cent sure about the exact numbers – there's a little uncertainty, as there is with any physical measurement. The uncertainty means that there is a chance that we could one day measure signatures in the structure of the early Universe that imply that it is not flat on larger scales than we can see. It leaves room for other possibilities, such as the Universe being shaped like a football, with intersecting regions that are almost flat, but not quite. New measurements from the European Space Agency's Planck satellite will help refine the measurements further, and leave us more sure of what shape the Universe is.

How can we be sure whether the Universe is infinite or not?

Glenn Povey (Ipswich, Suffolk) and
Peter Wright (Weymouth, Dorset)

We actually *can't* be sure whether the Universe is infinite or not. The measurements to date tell us that the size of the entire Universe is probably much, much bigger than everything we see, but whether it's actually infinite or not is harder to measure.

What lies outside the Universe, and what is the Universe expanding into?

Thomas Work (Belfast, Northern Ireland), Kerry Young (London)
and Brian Murray (Liverpool)

The concept of something being outside the Universe is almost completely meaningless, as it involves the concept of there being space outside the Universe. Space as we understand it – the three dimensions of up-down, left-right and front-back – are only defined within the boundaries of the Universe. It is possible that the Universe we know is embedded in a higher-dimensional structure, but the higher dimensions will not be measured in the same way.

It is difficult to visualise the expanding Universe, but I compare it to an inflating balloon with the galaxies on the balloon's surface getter further apart with time. In this analogy, is there anything in the interior of the balloon?

Roger Clark (Brighton, East Sussex)

The analogy of an inflating balloon is a useful one because it gives the idea of an expanding space that doesn't have an edge. In this example, the Universe is the surface of the balloon, and all of space would be on its surface. The contents of the interior of the balloon are meaningless.

The problem arises because we are visualising the Universe as a two-dimensional surface in a three-dimensional world. Instead, try to imagine the surface of the balloon from the point of view of an ant crawling around on its surface. The ant (which for these purposes can't look up and so therefore has a two-dimensional existence) would only know the surface of the balloon. Providing the surface were big enough, it would seem to be flat to a tiny ant, just as the surface of the Earth appears to be flat from the point of view of us crawling around on its surface.

If the interior of the balloon is still causing problems, then you could try imagining the Universe as a large flat sheet which is expanding. The problem with that is that it's hard to get away from the idea of there being an edge, so the sheet has to be infinite in size. I'm afraid there really is no easy answer.

The Big Bang and the Early Universe

What existed before the Big Bang?

Gideon Kibblewhite (Bath, Somerset),
George (Blackburn, Lancashire), Ian Edge (Poynton, Cheshire),
Martin Newman (Bury St Edmunds, Suffolk) and
John Piper (Bexhill-on-Sea, East Sussex)

The concept of there even being a time before the Big Bang is generally considered to be inaccurate. In cosmology, space and time are treated as one entity referred to as space-time. It is generally considered that these came into existence at the Big Bang, and so before that time had no meaning. Asking what came before the Big Bang would be like asking what is north of the North Pole?

What is the recipe for a Universe, and how long does it take to prepare and cook till it's done?

Andi Ye (Whitby, North Yorkshire)

Before preparing a Universe, you need to make sure you have all the ingredients and utensils available. First of all, prepare a selection of fundamental particles, which are the main ingredients. You'll find these on the shelves marked 'quarks' and 'leptons', which include electron, muon and tau particles, as well as the tiny little neutrinos, which are a little hard to hold. Make sure that you get their antiparticle equivalents, but be careful to put in a tiny amount more matter than antimatter – this will be very important later. For the utensils, look in the cupboard marked 'Forces' and grab one of each of the strong nuclear force, the weak nuclear force, the electromagnetic force and the gravitational force. The forces come with 'exchange particles', and if you can find them it's worth throwing in a few Higgs bosons.

Now the easiest way to start off the baking is to try to get hold of a 'pre-inflated Universe'. These have already gone through all the trouble of an inflationary period, which saves a lot of hassle and a small amount of time. Not much time, around 10^{-35} seconds (a hundred million billion billion billionth of a second). The process involved in making this requires tremendous energies, and can be rather dangerous to reproduce. You'll recognise the inflated Universe because it will be about the size of an apple (we are making here just a visible Universe, as it is unclear what lies beyond and how far it goes), and will look exceedingly smooth all over.

To continue the process, you need to throw in all your ingredients and forces, not forgetting the all-important exchange particles that are required to make the forces work. To start the cooking, warm your oven to about 10^{28} degrees Celsius (or gas mark 1 billion billion billion).

Before you put the Universe in, make sure to stand back – in the first few trillionths of a second it will expand to fill the size of the Earth's orbit, around 300 million km across. In that small amount of time, it will also cool a great deal, by a factor of around a billion. The strong nuclear force will be acting on the quarks using 'gluons', and the Universe will be made of a quark-gluon plasma, the densest form of matter known, though there will also be a lot of intense radiation flying around. You should also make sure you have ear defenders on, as there will be fairly loud sound waves travelling through the Universe. These are simply due to tiny imperfections that were present in the pre-inflated Universe you started with. Don't worry, they're not dangerous, and sound like a very discordant rock concert.

After around a hundredth of a millisecond it will have cooled by another few million times, to a mere billion billion degrees, and expanded to around a light year across. The strong force, using gluons, will have tied the quarks up into particles called 'baryons'. Most of these are unstable and decay away in a tiny fraction of a second to produce a combination of electrons, neutrinos and photons. The only stable baryons are protons and neutrons, although even neutrons gradually decay into a mixture of protons and electrons. The most dominant constituent of the Universe will be photons, or particles of light. The electrons and their antiparticle equivalent, positrons, are continually colliding to create photons, though at these temperatures the photons can be spontaneously converted back into electrons and positrons.

This situation continues for the first three minutes, with photons turning into electrons and positrons, and back again, and neutrons slowly turning into protons. After three minutes, however, the temperature is as low as a billion degrees and the protons and neutrons can start to combine to form atomic nuclei. This process, called nuclear fusion, relies on the weak nuclear force, and will bind up all of the neutrons into nuclei such that they can't decay any more.

The final result of the battle between protons and neutrons is that the matter in the Universe will be made of around 70 per cent protons and 30 per cent neutrons. Around half of the protons will still be floating around on their own, but the other half will be locked into atomic nuclei such as helium. It is important that the temperature has decreased at the correct rate, as if it took longer then all of the neutrons would have turned into protons and there would be no elements in your early Universe other than hydrogen.

You must ensure that you keep the temperature decreasing, such that after around 15–20 minutes it drops below a few hundred million degrees. This stops the process of nuclear fusion and means that only the lighter elements are created – there simply isn't time for the heavier ones to form.

The temperature will also drop such that the photons can't decay into electrons and positrons. Providing you got the ratio of matter to antimatter just right when you put it all in, there should be no positrons left, and the electrons should have been decimated to around a billionth of their original population.

At this point, leave the Universe to cool down on its own. You may also want to find your nearest time portal and skip forward a few hundred thousand years, as this is when the next big change happens. The temperature will have cooled to a relatively chilly 3,000 degrees (though that's still about gas mark 200), which will allow the electrons to combine with the atomic nuclei and form the first atoms. This also makes the Universe transparent to light, and the photons will travel freely.

If you look closely at your visible Universe, which will by now be over ten million light years across, you'll notice that it looks slightly pockmarked. That's simply due to those tiny imperfections in the pre-inflated Universe. The sound waves that were propagating around have resulted in slight density variations, with some regions being slightly denser than others.

It is at this point that you can put away all but one of your utensils. The strong nuclear force is only needed if you're building or destroying protons, neutrons or other baryons, but all of those are tied up into atomic nuclei. The weak nuclear force is only necessary if you want to make or break the atomic nuclei, and they're quite happily sitting in the centres of atoms. And the electromagnetic force is busy keeping the electrons in the atoms and ensuring that the material in the Universe is electrically neutral. The only important utensil for the next hundred million years or so will be gravity, though you might want to keep the others nearby.

There is one crucial ingredient that we haven't mentioned yet, mainly because it was already included in the pre-inflated Universe. This is called dark matter, and is discussed at length elsewhere so won't be treated in any detail here. The key thing is that most of the forces have very little impact on the dark matter, with only gravity having any effect at all. In fact, you won't even be able to see the dark matter, but it is there. It is therefore at this time in your Universe's evolution, when gravity is the dominant force, that dark matter becomes important.

If you stare at the Universe, you'll see that the slightly denser bits are pulling the surrounding regions together, becoming denser and more massive. Watch it for long enough and the centres of the densest bits will become hot enough and dense enough to ignite nuclear fusion in their cores. The weak nuclear force will come into action again, creating heavier and heavier elements, and producing large quantities of light. This intense radiation invokes the electromagnetic force which ionises the surrounding medium, ripping the electrons from the atomic nuclei.

This period of reionisation is the last major change in the Universe, and the remainder of its evolution relates to relatively slight variations on the conditions present a few hundred million years after the Big Bang. The stars will collect into groups, called galaxies, and some will eventually have planets around them. After a long time, measured in billions of years, life forms may start to emerge. If you're feeling generous, you might even consider some of the species to be intelligent, though I wouldn't get your hopes up too far (I'm told that the ones to watch are the smaller aquatic mammals)! If you really want to test their intelligence, then I suggest you leave a message!

I have often heard the term 'pure energy' used in documentaries to describe the early Universe. Is it possible to have energy without matter?

P Lovering (Porthcawl, South Wales)

Einstein showed that energy and mass are equivalent, and that one can be turned into another. This is the basis behind the famous equation $E=mc^2$, where E is the energy, m is the mass of the particle, and c is the speed of light in a vacuum. This is a much-simplified version of Einstein's actual equation, and describes the situation for a stationary particle – the energy of a moving particle is even higher, and it is this principle on which experiments such as the Large Hadron Collider are based.

A feature of the standard model of particle physics is that particles can decay into a range of different particles – this is how nuclear fission operates. The particles in question are subatomic particles. Some may be familiar, such as protons, neutrons and electrons – the particles that make up atoms – but there is a whole zoo of other particles. Protons and neutrons are made up of particles called quarks, but there are also particles called pions, kaons and neutrinos. These particles can all be converted into other particles when they are bashed together, but only providing there is enough energy to create the required mass. But they can also decay into something that has energy but no mass, such as a photon of light. Those photons of light, which could be considered to be energy without mass, can decay back into particles that have a mass, with the mass created depending on the energy of the photon.

The experiments being conducted in the Large Hadron Collider at CERN in Switzerland rely on this conversion of matter. They take particles such as protons, or the nuclei of lead atoms, and speed them up to very close to the speed of light. This gives them an enormous amount of energy, and when they collide an enormous range of particles come out. The purpose of doing this in the Large Hadron Collider is to examine the particles that come out to see if there are any new ones we didn't know about.

The very early Universe was a much hotter, denser place than it is today, with the average energy of the particles being far higher than those which are used in the Large Hadron Collider. A sea of higher-energy particles was constantly changing from one form to another. Some of the energy will be in the form of photons of light, which have no mass. Energy is always locked up into particles of one type or another, but those particles do not necessarily have mass.

I have read that the rate of expansion during the 'inflationary' stage of the very early Universe was greater than the speed of light. How does this reconcile with the fact that nothing can travel faster than light?

Hugh Burt (Tamworth, Staffordshire)

There is no contradiction, as no objects are actually moving faster than the speed of light relative to each other. Rather, the expansion of space (or, to be precise, space-time) is occurring incredibly fast. In some senses, space-time is defined as the absence of anything, so while it's true that no *thing* can travel faster than light, *nothing* can expand at any speed.

The theory of inflation states that in the first 10^{-30} seconds (that's 0.000000000000000000000000000001 seconds, with 29 zeros between the decimal point and the 1) the Universe expanded by a factor of 10^{60} (that's a 1 followed by 60 zeros). Regions of the Universe that were originally very close are now so very far apart that there is insufficient time for light to travel between them – we say that they are beyond each other's horizon. This is very important because regions that are beyond each other's horizon shouldn't be able to exchange energy, and therefore there is no reason for them to look the same. But before the rapid inflation took place they were much closer together, within each other's horizon. This meant that for a very short time light could travel between them, and that contact enabled them to reach equilibrium, becoming almost the same density and temperature.

This feature of inflation solves a key problem that existed with the Big Bang theory for decades, namely that the Universe looks so similar in all directions. The most distant parts of the Universe that we see on opposite sides of the sky have only just entered our horizon, and so should not yet be within each other's. Since they are too far apart for light to travel between them they shouldn't have been able to equilibrate. When we study the distant Universe we see that it is remarkably similar in all directions, implying that it must have all been in contact at some point. While these regions of the Universe are too far apart now, before inflation they were much, much closer together. In the first tiny fraction of a second after the Big Bang these now distant regions were within each other's horizon, which explains why they are so similar today.

How do scientists know with such certainty the events that took place a fraction of a second after the Big Bang?

Bruce Jervis (Edinburgh, Scotland)

As we consider the Universe at earlier and earlier times, it actually gets considerably simpler to understand – largely because there was less complex structure present. In the first hundred million years or so after the Big Bang, the Universe was made almost entirely of hydrogen and helium gas. At earlier times, that gas was hotter and denser, and for the first 400,000 years of its history the Universe was actually opaque. The high temperatures stripped the atoms of their electrons and the resulting ionised gas, or plasma, constantly scattered the light. This is the furthest back we can see directly, often called the Surface of Last Scattering. The light that travelled through the Universe from that point is seen today as the Cosmic Microwave Background, an afterglow of the primordial fireball. We can measure the properties of the Universe at this age of 400,000 years, but to see further back we have to infer what took place from our observations and theories.

Closer to the time of the Big Bang, the conditions were so hot that even protons, which make up the nuclei of atoms, are broken down. This requires huge energies, but we can recreate the reactions in particle accelerators such as the Large Hadron Collider. Our observations in these laboratories and experiments are used to inform our theories of how the really early Universe behaved in its first few microseconds, but there comes a point beyond which we can no longer recreate the conditions in experiments on Earth. This is the point at which we have to rely solely on theories, and where the testable predictions end.

Cosmologists can think up as many whacky theories of the early Universe as they like, but to be proven the theory must make a prediction that can be tested. The theory of inflation is compatible with all the observations made, but it has yet to make a prediction that has been tested. To make matters worse, there are many theories of inflation that are all equally possible, given the data we currently have, but we have no way of telling which ones are correct – if any!

Since we can't see back to the inflationary era directly, we have to look at the impact it must have had on the later Universe. Theories of inflation predict that there should be a subtle signature visible in the Cosmic Microwave Background. This signature of inflation would be incredibly faint, but with the latest experiments such as Planck it may be possible to detect it. The likelihood is that if Planck sees the signature of inflation we will be in a position to say that we are more certain that inflation is correct, but the ability to deduce the details of exactly what occurred will rely on future missions that are still on the drawing board.

Was there a sound during the Big Bang?

Franklin Gordon (Sheffield, South Yorkshire)

First of all, let's consider what sound is. Sound is a pressure wave that travels through a material of some sort. We are familiar with it travelling through the air, but pressure waves can also travel through liquids and solids. For example, earthquakes produce pressure waves that travel through the interior of the Earth. As a pressure wave travels, parts of the material are bunched up closer together, becoming denser, while the adjacent regions are stretched apart, becoming less dense. The sound wave propagates though the material as these over- and under-densities travel along. The speed at which they travel depends on the density and composition of the material.

In the early Universe there were regions that were denser than others. The effect of these over-densities was not unlike the ripples on a pond, and the resulting waves of density propagated through the Universe. They propagated very easily, travelling at speeds of around half the speed of light. The result of these pressure waves was to create a pattern of over- and under-densities in the early Universe that we see today in the Cosmic Microwave Background. This marks the point, 400,000 years after the Big Bang, when the first atoms formed and when the density waves stopped travelling so easily though the Universe. The pattern that remained was frozen in to the matter in the Universe, and the denser regions eventually became massive clusters of galaxies that we see today.

The intensity, or loudness, of sound waves is measured by how dense the over-densities are relative to the under-densities. We traditionally measure the volume in decibels, which are a slightly unusual unit. This scale is useful because the range of volumes that can be heard by the human ear is so wide. Every increase of ten decibels means that the over-densities are ten times denser relative to the under-densities. So 20 decibels is ten times louder than 10 decibels, 30 decibels ten times louder than 20, and so on.

The variations in density throughout the early Universe were incredibly weak, at just one part in 100,000, but that still corresponds to somewhere around 110 decibels. If you could go back and listen to it, this would not be loud enough to do any significant damage – about the same volume as a loud rock concert! The sound would also be much too low for the human ear to hear – about 50 octaves too low in fact.

Dark Matter and Dark Energy

What are dark matter and dark energy, and do they really exist?

*Paul Foster (Clapham, London), Ann Ibrahim (London) and
Ken Mackintosh (Horsham, West Sussex)*

To discuss this, it is useful to examine the evidence behind the existence of
dark matter and dark energy. The evidence for dark matter has been around
since the 1930s, when astronomer Fritz Zwicky realised that galaxies in
the Coma Cluster (a massive cluster of galaxies found in the constellation
of Coma Berenices) are more tightly grouped than they should be. The
clustering of galaxies is determined by their gravitational attraction, and
therefore by their mass.

The standard method of weighing galaxies in those days was to use their
brightness – essentially measuring the amount of starlight, dividing by the
amount of starlight from a star like the Sun, and then multiplying by the
Sun's mass. What Zwicky realised was that the mass required to explain
their clustering was hundreds of times the mass that could be accounted
for with their starlight. He termed the remainder of the matter, which he
deduced must not be shining, 'dark matter'.

Over the next few decades, much of the discrepancy in the two estimates
of the mass of galaxies was attributed to matter that shone at other
wavelengths. For example, radio astronomy revealed the discovery that the
mass of hydrogen and helium gas between the stars is almost ten times that
of the stars themselves. But that still left a considerable amount of matter
that was unaccounted for.

In the 1970s, an American astronomer called Vera Rubin was studying the rotation of galaxies themselves, and discovered that they were behaving in an unexpected way. Most of the mass of a galaxy is concentrated in the centre, and one would expect that the stars further out to be orbiting more slowly – just as the outer planets in our Solar System orbit more slowly than the inner ones. But what Rubin and her team found was that the stars on the outer edges of the galaxy were orbiting too quickly. There were two possible solutions: either the galaxy was more massive than was previously thought, or the equations of gravity were wrong. If the galaxy was more massive, then the additional mass must be distributed much more smoothly than the stars themselves, and astronomers spent a long time looking for what it might be. All that was known was that it gave off little or no light, but still had a mass and therefore a gravitational pull on other matter.

Slowly, the various candidates were ruled out after searches failed to find them. Careful searches for small black holes scattered through the galaxy returned nothing. Astronomers turned to small, faint objects in the spherical halos of galaxies – they called them Massive Compact Halo Objects, or MACHOs! Although there are plenty of stars and other objects that are very faint, there are simply not enough to account for the missing mass. The remaining candidate was a new type of matter, but one that didn't interact with light at all. This matter was not so much dark as completely transparent, or invisible, but Fritz Zwicky's term 'dark matter' has stuck. The particles are theorised to exist by particle physicists though to date none have been found. The collective name given to these particles by astronomers was 'Weakly Interacting Massive Particles', or WIMPs (a very suitable alternative to MACHOs!).

A further big piece of evidence in the search for the missing mass was the study of the distant Universe. The distribution of matter in the form of galaxies could only be explained if there was more there than could be seen by any telescope. The search for the dark matter particles is still under way, but it is making progress. The Large Hadron Collider at CERN is producing reactions with enormous energies that could produce tiny amounts of dark matter. Since we can't see dark matter, it won't be directly detectable, but the particles are expected to decay into particles of 'normal' matter that *can* be detected.

While there's not yet any definitive proof of what dark matter is, most astronomers expect that it will turn out to be these previously unseen particles. A small number are still searching for possible modifications to Einstein's theory of gravity that could explain the observations, but there has been little progress on that front.

The discussion about what dark energy is will be much shorter, simply because we know far less. Even taking into account the dark matter, around 70 per cent of the energy (i.e. 'stuff') in the Universe is still unaccounted for. Added to this, something appears to be causing the expansion of the Universe to accelerate. Several possible theories have been put forward, the most popular one being the energy of the vacuum of space itself. While the Universe expands, the density of matter and radiation decreases but the density of this vacuum energy would remain constant. If this is correct, it would have started to drive the expansion outward at ever-increasing rates several billion years ago.

We have no way of predicting from theories what the vacuum energy is, and even the best guesses are way out from what is required to explain the accelerating expansion Universe. Quite simply, we just don't know!

What is the latest information about dark matter and dark energy?

Chris Geraghty (Cannock, Staffordshire) and Rik Whittaker (Manchester)

The latest information on dark energy and dark matter are the results of surveys of hundreds of thousands of galaxies. Although dark matter does not shine and therefore cannot be seen, it does have a mass and therefore exerts a gravitational force. One of the side effects of large masses such as galaxies is that they distort light passing close to them. This bending of light by strong gravitational fields is called gravitational lensing, and was predicted by Einstein in his theory of gravity. A massive cluster of galaxies will distort the light from background galaxies, and change their shapes. Most of the time the galaxies simply look a little stretched and distorted, but sometimes the images are spread into large arcs. If the effect is strong enough there can even be multiple images of the same galaxy visible!

Gravitational lensing allows astronomers to map out where the matter is in galaxy clusters. This allows us to see where the greatest concentrations of dark matter lie without being able to see it directly. The techniques to study this are getting more and more sophisticated all the time, and can now map the distortions of galaxies over large swathes of sky.

The background galaxies, the light from which is distorted by the gravitational lensing effect, are often at huge distances. The vast distances mean that these measurements probe the expansion of the Universe. Any study of the expansion of the Universe sheds light on dark energy, and these studies have helped pin down its strength.

But there's one more measurement that is crucial for understanding dark matter and dark energy. The furthest back we can see in the Universe is the Cosmic Microwave Background, radiation from the early Universe dating back to just 400,000 years after the Big Bang. Structures are visible in the

Cosmic Microwave Background, caused by very slight over-densities in the early Universe, and we can simulate the early Universe to investigate what is required to generate the measurements that we see.

These careful techniques mean that we are truly in the age of precision cosmology. To match the various measurements, we now know that 72 per cent of the Universe is made of dark energy, around 23 per cent is made of dark matter, and less than 5 per cent is made of the atoms and molecules that constitute everything we see around us. If that doesn't make you feel small, I'm not sure what will!

If all things have an equal and exact opposite, such as matter and antimatter, is there any evidence for anti-dark matter?

Terry Leese (Camberley, Surrey)

The work of physicists in the early twentieth century showed that for every fundamental particle known there is an exact opposite particle, called its antiparticle. So there are anti-protons, anti-electrons and anti-neutrons, and so on for all the particles that constitute the matter we are made of.

It is thought that dark matter is made of different types of particles that do not interact with light and therefore cannot be seen. Despite their peculiar nature, these particles are similar in some respects to the 'normal' particles that we're used to and so they should also have antiparticles. The most likely discovery method for dark matter is in a particle accelerator such as the Large Hadron Collider, and it is very likely that the discovery will be of both a dark matter particle and its antiparticle counterpart.

Gas clouds collapse under gravity to form stars. Would we expect dark matter to collapse under gravity, and what would result from this?

Steve Jones (Bedford)

Gravity is the force that dominates how dark matter is distributed in the Universe. When we study the distribution of dark matter, we find clumps of it centred on the locations of galaxies and galaxy clusters. In fact it's the other way around – the dark matter formed the clumps due to gravity and the galaxies formed in the centre of the clumps.

When normal matter, such as that in gas clouds, collapses under gravity, other effects start to play a part. Collisions between the particles mean that the gas clouds cool down and collapse further. The gas can also radiate away energy, and it is the radiation combined with the collisions that allows it to become denser in the cores of the clouds, eventually leading to the formation of stars. On the scale of galaxies, similar processes lead to the formation of discs such as that which makes up the bulk of the structure of our Milky Way.

Dark matter, on the other hand, does not interact with anything – even itself – and therefore can't radiate away energy or cool due to collisions. Without these interactions, the dark matter can't collapse further than large, roughly spherical balls.

The dark matter and normal matter are tied together by their mutual gravitational attraction. The early Universe was filled with an almost completely uniform sea of matter (both normal and dark), with only slight over-densities. The regions that were slightly denser had a greater gravitational pull and therefore collapsed under gravity, becoming denser still. Since around 80 per cent of the matter in the Universe is dark matter, this dominated the gravitational collapse. The normal matter followed the dark matter, and eventually became dense enough to form stars.

Ironically, since dark matter only really feels gravity, and is not affected by collisions or radiation, we can simulate how it behaves much more easily than normal matter. Huge computer simulations of large regions of the Universe can recreate its initial conditions and predict the distribution of dark matter at various stages throughout the Universe's history. The complicated bit is accurately predicting what the normal matter does, as this involves many other aspects of physics. After all, the formation of stars and galaxies is incredibly complex, and something we still do not understand fully.

The results of these simulations seem to match the observations of the distributions of dark matter relatively well, and to a large extent the normal matter. For example, the distribution of galaxies on the largest observable scales in the Universe – billions of light years – agrees with the simulations. On much smaller scales, such as the scale of a single galaxy like the Milky Way, the details of the physics of normal matter are much more important. For several years, the simulations predicted that there should be many smaller galaxies scattered around our own – more than were actually observed. Part of the problem was that these tiny galaxies are incredibly faint and hard to find, and a relatively large number have now been found. But the observations are leading to changes in our understanding of how dark matter and normal matter behave. This greater understanding of the behaviour has led to a better idea of what the dark matter particles might be, allowing particle physicists to start looking for them in particle accelerators. We are probably many years off definitively identifying dark matter, but we are getting closer all the time.

If we can't detect it or observe it, how can we be sure that dark matter exists and isn't simply something we've invented to make the observed data fit the predictions.

Simon Foster (Steeton, West Yorkshire) and Craig Sohail (London)

To prove the validity of a scientific theory or hypothesis, such as the existence of dark matter, the theory needs to meet all the observations that have been made. But more importantly it needs to make a prediction that can be tested and used to distinguish it from other theories. The initial evidence for dark matter relied upon the gravitational force that stars and galaxies feel. This was found to be much larger than could be accounted for by the matter we could see. A possible solution was that there was a significant amount of matter that does not shine at any wavelength, but there were competing theories. For example, the possibility that gravity is weaker on large scales than suggested from Einstein's equations of gravity.

In recent decades, there have been additional pieces of information that have led most scientists to lean in favour of dark matter over modified theories of gravity. One of the first was the structure of the early Universe, seen in the Cosmic Microwave Background. In the very early Universe the dark matter and normal matter behaved differently, with the dark matter simply collapsing under gravity while the normal matter also felt the effects of the intense radiation whizzing around. The structures seen in today's Universe can only be explained if the amount of dark matter was around four times the amount of normal matter – a number which is in surprisingly good agreement with that found from the study of stars and galaxies.

We can now map out the distribution of dark matter, which we can't see directly, through its gravitational effects on the normal matter, which we can see. The incredible masses warp the light from galaxies that lie beyond, creating distorted images that allow astronomers to map where most of the mass lies in galaxy clusters. This effect, which is predicted by Einstein's theories of gravity, is called gravitational lensing, and is now being used to map the distribution of dark matter on massive scales across the Universe.

The results are also in good agreement with the predictions, with every galaxy and cluster of galaxies surrounded by an enormous halo of dark matter. A key piece of information came from studying two clusters that are in the process of colliding. The clusters, called the Bullet Clusters have recently (in astronomical terms!) passed through each other, but the various components of the clusters behave very differently. When two clusters pass through each other, the stars and galaxies do not, in general, actually collide, rather they pass through, affected only by their mutual gravitational attractions. This is similar to the behaviour of the halos of dark matter which surround each cluster. In contrast, the gas which is spread throughout the cluster can be considered as a fluid, and the two gas clouds do collide and create massive shockwaves that travel through space.

The results of studying this pair of clusters were incredibly illuminating. They revealed that, as expected, the gas in the clusters had formed large shockwaves. In contrast the galaxies had passed by each other like ships in the night, and are still in the form of two roughly spherical clusters. The prediction was that dark matter should behave in a similar way to the stars and galaxies, and so should lie in the same place. If there is no dark matter, then the main mass of the clusters should lie with the gas, and if there is it should be near the galaxies. When observations of the gravitational lensing effect were made, the majority of the mass of the clusters was found to be located in the same place as all the galaxies – matching the predictions based on the existence of dark matter.

Today the existence of dark matter is accepted as very likely by most astronomers, but considerable scepticism will remain until the particles that make up dark matter are conclusively found and identified.

Do you think the case for dark matter and dark energy is proved? Do they even make sense? Is it not more likely that we have got our sums wrong or incomplete?

Karen Cappleman (Kent) and Robert Ince (Preston, Lancashire)

The cases for dark matter and dark energy are very different, partly because of how sophisticated the two theories are. For dark matter, the current theory states what the particles might be that make it up, and therefore we can search for those particles in particle accelerators. The evidence for dark matter being made of particles which experience gravity but do not emit, absorb or scatter light is strong, but many people will not be convinced that it is real until it has been seen in the laboratory.

Dark energy is altogether different. The evidence points to there being *something* that is causing the rate of expansion of the Universe to accelerate, but we don't know what that something is. Even what is generally considered to be the most likely candidate for the origin of dark energy, an energy density that is present in the vacuum of space itself, cannot predict the strength of the effect. In fact, the best estimate for the vacuum energy based on theoretical predictions is a factor of a million million million million million higher than the effect we see due to dark energy!

What is important to remember is that dark energy is simply a name for something we don't understand, and is only a decade or so old as a concept. Compare this to Newton's theory of gravity from 1687. It is less than a century since Einstein showed that Newton's theory of gravity was not quite correct, so for 300 years the scientific community had to deal with the fact that something wasn't quite right with their understanding of the Universe. For example, Newton's gravity could not accurately predict the orbit of Mercury (though it was pretty close), whereas Einstein's could.

But even Einstein didn't get everything right! His equations predicted that the Universe should be either expanding or contracting, something which he found to be inconceivable at the time. He added a further term to account for the fact that the Universe was completely static (which he believed it was), and then rued that decision when a decade later Edwin Hubble showed that the Universe is in fact expanding.

Even with this little hiccup, the simultaneous development of Einstein's theory of gravity and the field of quantum mechanics created a fundamental change in physics. It opened up whole new areas of research which are fundamental to the world we live in today. Without quantum mechanics and relativity, we would have no computers, no lasers and no satellite navigation systems, to name but a few. So it is possible that the discovery of what dark energy really is could be the start of a new era in physics.

Even if we discover conclusively that either dark matter or dark energy are not real at all we will know that our understanding of the Universe is wrong on some level, and that in turn will invigorate a period of intense research to find out why.

Will discoveries made by the Large Hadron Collider have any impact on astronomical science?

Ken Askew (Leicestershire)

Astronomy and particle physics are closely related, particularly when considering the very early Universe. The experiments in the Large Hadron Collider (LHC) collide together atomic nuclei and create tremendous energies, comparable to those present in the first fractions of a second after the Big Bang. At such high energies, it is possible to split protons and neutrons into their constituent quarks, making what is known as a 'quark-gluon plasma'. These quarks combine together to make all sorts of other particles, which allows particle physicists to study scales that are otherwise completely unobservable, even by studying the centres of stars.

Experiments such as these have allowed cosmologists to understand the origin of the matter in the Universe. Such experiments are also investigating the reason why there is more matter than antimatter in the Universe. There should have been equal amounts created in the Big Bang, but most of it was annihilated. There is a subtle difference between matter and antimatter that means that matter has won out, at least in our region of the Universe.

Over the past few decades, particle physicists have shown that there is a whole zoo of fundamental particles, which go by names such as electrons, muons, quarks and neutrinos. There are theories, however, that there is a whole new level of particles, which mirror those we know in some ways but are much more massive. These 'super-symmetric' particles are one of the best candidates for dark matter. One of the properties of these particles is that they do not interact with normal matter, and so we can only see them if they decay into particles that we can actually measure.

The really interesting reactions are very unlikely to take place, and the only way they are observable is by creating hundreds of millions of reactions every second. Most of the reactions have relatively mundane results, but every now and again there is an interesting set of products. With immense computing power, these interesting reactions are picked out and studied in greater detail. It will take time but if these super-symmetric particles exist, the LHC should be able to find them.

Given that we can observe the Cosmic Microwave Background as predicted by Big Bang theory, why haven't neutrino detectors found evidence of a Cosmic Neutrino Background?

Rob Schottland (Sedona, Arizona, USA)

Neutrinos are a type of subatomic particle that we know exists but which we know very little about. This is largely due to the fact that they are so hard to measure, since neutrinos do not interact with matter very well at all. In fact, we don't detect the neutrinos at all, but rather the effect they have on material they pass through. As neutrinos travel through matter, there is a tiny, tiny chance that they will interact with an electron in one of the atoms. This electron will begin moving incredibly quickly – faster than the speed of light through water – and emit a characteristic pattern of light. This pattern of radiation, which is the equivalent of a sonic boom, is named after Pavel Cherenkov, the Russian physicist who characterised it and was awarded the 1958 Nobel Prize for Physics.

Since the chance of neutrinos causing Cherenkov radiation is so small, most detectors use large quantities of material to increase the chances of a neutrino interaction. For example, the Super-Kamiokande experiment in Japan uses a tank, 40 metres wide and filled with 50,000 tons of water. If a neutrino passes through the water and interacts with an electron, some of the 11,000 detectors around the edge of the sphere pick up the flash of Cherenkov radiation.

The number of neutrinos in the Universe is staggeringly high – in a single second somewhere around 300,000,000,000,000 neutrinos pass through your body! Luckily, they have no effect at all – to be sure of stopping a neutrino you would need a slab of lead a light year thick.

Neutrinos come from a number of sources in the Universe, with many of those detected on Earth originating from the Sun and nuclear reactors.

Huge numbers are also emitted by supernovae, which are massive stars exploding at the ends of their lives, and in fact is how the vast majority of the energy of a supernova is released. The flash of light can outshine a galaxy, but the energy released in neutrinos is hundreds of times greater. In 1987, a supernova was observed in the Large Magellanic Cloud, a small galaxy around 160,000 light years away. Just as the flash of light was seen, a brief burst of neutrinos was detected. It was one of the best pieces evidence for what causes a supernova. Although only around 20 neutrinos were detected between all the experiments around at the time, this event led to the start of neutrino astronomy. Since they are so hard to detect, it is difficult to pinpoint the direction they originate from, though experiments are continually getting better.

Neutrinos were also created in the early Universe. They were released around a second after the Big Bang and, in a similar way to the Cosmic Microwave Background, those neutrinos are travelling through space and being detected here on Earth. The standard model of the early Universe predicts that at any given moment there should be a few primordial neutrinos in every cubic centimetre of space, though since they are so hard to detect their existence has not been confirmed. While the Cosmic Microwave Background is a direct probe of the Universe at an age of around 400,000 years, measuring the Cosmic Neutrino Background would allow us to directly study the Universe at an age of less than a second – much closer to the Big Bang itself.

Do neutrinos have mass, and if so could they be dark matter?

Spencer Taylor (Rochdale)

In the standard model of particle physics, it was originally assumed that neutrinos had absolutely no mass, much like photons of light. However, results of experiments conducted with neutrinos generated in nuclear power plants, and with neutrinos originating in the Sun, indicate that they probably *do* have a mass, but that it is very small. This relies on the fact that there are three types of neutrino (called flavours) and that a neutrino can switch between the different flavours. If the theory is correct then they must have a mass, but all the experiments demonstrated was that the masses were very small and that the three flavours had slightly different masses.

The best information on the mass of the neutrino actually comes from cosmology, as measurements on the rate of expansion of the Universe can help constrain the best estimates of the neutrino mass. In 2012, the upper limit was around one-millionth of the mass of an electron, and since an electron is around one two-thousandth the mass of a proton, that's pretty light! The mass is so small that it can't yet be measured accurately, and all we can do is put a maximum limit on it, and even this number is an upper limit on the sum of the masses of all three flavours, so the mass of each one will be lower still.

So we do know that neutrinos have a mass, and therefore will be affected by gravity. Since we can't see them very easily at all (see the previous question), they would seem to fit the bill for being a good candidate for dark matter. The problem is, they're not quite massive enough, even if their mass is right on the upper limit discussed here. So they may well be responsible for *some* of the effects attributed to dark matter, but they can't account for all of it. The search continues – stay tuned!

Could the 'missing mass' in the Universe have been captured by black holes?

KJ Thomas (Manchester)

As soon as it was realised that there was some 'missing mass' in the Universe, people started theorising as to where this mass might be. Black holes were an obvious candidate, as they are relatively massive and don't give out any light. They fell into a category of objects called 'Massive Compact Halo Objects' (MACHOs), which also included neutron stars, brown dwarfs and old, faint white dwarfs.

The first thing to say about black holes is that we've never actually seen one, though we have remarkably good evidence that they exist. Einstein's theory of relativity predicts that when matter reaches a certain density it should collapse to such a dense state that no light can escape. There are two general types of black hole. The first is a supermassive black hole, one of which is thought to lie at the centre of every large galaxy – including our own. These are millions of times the mass of our Sun and their formation is linked to the formation of the galaxies themselves, though it's not totally clear which came first, the galaxy or the black hole – the astronomical equivalent of the chicken and the egg problem. These black holes shouldn't be hard to find as they're surrounded by massive galaxies, and there certainly aren't any lying in the outskirts of our own Galaxy.

The second type is dubbed a stellar-mass black hole. These are thought to be formed when a star several dozen times the mass of the Sun dies at the end of its life. When the nuclear fusion stops in its core, the star can no longer support its huge mass against its own massive gravitational pull. A certain fraction of the material collapses and forms a black hole in the centre, the mass of which will depend on the mass of the original star. It's possible that there are some that are a fraction of the Sun's mass, though most are probably several times that. If there were many massive stars around, then there should be a great deal of these black holes.

The question becomes: how do you see something that is black against the black backdrop of outer space? Einstein comes to the rescue again, thanks to his prediction of the effect that a large mass has on light. The gravitational field created by a massive object causes light to be bent, magnifying and distorting the light coming from behind. We see this relatively often, but it is normally caused by galaxies or entire galaxy clusters. It does also occur with much smaller objects, though the effect is much smaller. If there are black holes in the outer regions of our Galaxy, then they would appear to move against the background of more distant stars and galaxies. If one were to pass between us and a background star then the black hole's gravity would magnify the light of the star and cause a short increase in brightness. The effect is called 'microlensing' and the same phenomenon would be seen if any massive object passed directly in front, perhaps a brown dwarf or even a planet, making this method suitable for searching for all types of MACHOs. The variation in brightness is quite predictable, but the chances of it happening are very rare.

To increase the chances of finding them, teams of astronomers pointed their telescopes continuously at the Large and Small Magellanic Clouds. These two small galaxies lie more than 160,000 light years away, but are close enough that millions of individual stars can be seen. Between us and them is the Galactic Halo, a roughly spherical volume that surrounds our Galaxy and is where the majority of these MACHOs should reside – if they are real. A very small number of these microlensing events were seen, but many fewer than would be expected if black holes and other MACHOs were responsible for the majority of the missing mass attributed to dark matter.

Origin of the Elements

How were the first hydrogen atoms formed during the Big Bang?

John Youngs (London)

A hydrogen atom is the simplest atom possible, consisting simply of an electron orbiting a proton. Heavier elements, such as helium, oxygen and iron, have a nucleus that contains a greater number of protons along with a similar number of neutrons, and also have more electrons around them. Protons and neutrons like to stick together, but can be kept apart if the temperature is above about one billion degrees. Likewise, electrons like to go into orbit around the nuclei of atoms, but can be prevented from doing so at temperatures above a few thousand degrees.

For the first few hundred thousand years after the Big Bang, the temperature was high enough to prevent electrons from becoming attached to nuclei, and the Universe was ionised. So before that point, we only need consider the atomic nuclei – the protons and neutrons. Until about three minutes after the Big Bang, the Universe was too hot to allow protons and neutrons to stick together. Since a proton is the nucleus of a hydrogen atom, it is valid to consider the matter in the very early Universe to have been composed of hydrogen nuclei and lots of free neutrons. Any neutrons that were flying around would have gradually decayed, to form protons (more hydrogen nuclei) and electrons.

As the Universe expanded it also cooled, and around three minutes after the Big Bang the temperature cooled enough to allow protons and neutrons to start sticking together. This process is called nuclear fusion, and is the same process that takes place in the core of the Sun. It only occurs when the temperature is at tens of millions of degrees or higher. The neutrons that hadn't decayed into protons previously became locked into the nuclei of heavier elements. These include helium (two protons and two neutrons), but also variations on hydrogen called deuterium (one proton and one neutron) and tritium (one proton and two neutrons). Deuterium and tritium are very similar to hydrogen in most senses, because they behave the same chemically – the extra neutrons don't have much effect.

This process only continued for around 20 minutes, because after that the temperature became too cool for nuclear fusion to take place. At that point, the matter in the Universe was made of around 75 per cent hydrogen and 25 per cent helium, with very small amounts of deuterium, tritium and lithium (which has three protons and either three or four neutrons). There was not time to make any of the heavier elements such as oxygen, carbon and iron before the temperature dropped below this limit.

After that, the expansion and cooling of the Universe continued. Around 400,000 years after the Big Bang, it cooled enough to allow the electrons to go into orbit around the nuclei and the first proper atoms were formed. The Universe remained in this state, full of neutral hydrogen and helium gas, for hundreds of millions of years. It was around that time that the first stars formed, which ionised the gas around them and started nuclear fusion in their cores. This fusion continued converting hydrogen into helium and heavier elements, but has barely made a dent in the proportion of hydrogen in the Universe – it still lies at around 75 per cent.

I know that elements are created in stars, and that in supernova explosions the heavier elements are rapidly produced. But how can the huge range of elements become spread so widely through the Universe to give the mix we see on Earth?

Rufus Segar (Worcestershire)

The elements in the Universe are not as widely spread out as it might at first appear. We certainly have a healthy range here on Earth, but we are in a very special location. On the whole, the composition of the Universe is not vastly different from shortly after the Big Bang, after which the matter in the Universe (here we refer just to normal matter, and ignore dark matter) was made of 75 per cent hydrogen, 25 per cent helium and a tiny smattering of lithium. As soon as stars formed, the nuclear fusion in their cores started converting hydrogen into helium and then into other heavier elements. This is where most of the carbon, nitrogen and oxygen come from in the Universe, along with a selection of other elements such as silicon, magnesium, calcium and iron. The even heavier elements, such as lead, gold and uranium, are created when really massive stars die in supernova explosions.

But the important thing to realise is that stars account for less than ten per cent of the matter in the Universe, with the rest being composed of the neutral hydrogen and helium gas that was present after the Big Bang. The main reason for this is that star formation is a relatively inefficient process. About 90 per cent of the material in a dense gas cloud doesn't end up in stars, but is pushed back out into space. The reason for this is the pressure exerted by starlight itself, which pushes most of the very light atoms away.

Stars don't just have an effect on the gas clouds during their formation, and, as they live out the main part of their lives, they exert a stellar wind which blows through space. Hotter, brighter stars have a more intense wind, and it can be strong enough to blow enormous bubbles in space. An example of such a bubble is Barnard's Loop, located in the constellation of Orion, which is around 600 light years across. But these stellar winds are just the start. Towards the end of their lives, stars become bloated to hundreds of times their original size and tend to shed their outer layer. These layers are still primarily composed of hydrogen and helium, but contain trace amounts of heavier elements. These outer layers are puffed off, forming what is called a planetary nebula, which is really just the ejected outer layers of a dying star. In their final moments, massive stars explode in violent supernovae. The explosion is huge and creates massive shockwaves that travel through space, spreading the chemically enriched material into the surrounding regions. When shockwaves meet, they can cause pockets of gas to increase in density and start a new generation of star formation.

This process has repeated itself many, many times. While the Sun is five billion years old, over a third the age of the Universe, more massive stars live much shorter lives. Stars that are 20 times the mass of the Sun, such as Betelgeuse, only live for about ten million years, and more massive ones have shorter lifespans still. In the past 13 billion years of the Universe's existence, there has been plenty of time for hundreds of generations of these stars to have formed and died, chemically enriching the environment and spreading the products around.

By the time our Sun formed around five billion years ago, the gas clouds in the Milky Way had been chemically enriched to give them small amounts of carbon, oxygen, silicon, calcium, iron and so on. The composition of the Sun is 75 per cent hydrogen, 24 per cent helium and 1 per cent oxygen, with tiny amounts of other elements. These heavier elements might be very rare in stars and the Universe as a whole, but they are more common on planets. For a start, in the cold vacuum of space they tend to react together to form molecules such as water (hydrogen and oxygen) and carbon monoxide (carbon and oxygen). Also present are tiny grains of interstellar dust, composed primarily of carbon, oxygen, silicon and iron.

The grains of dust and the heavier elements are too heavy to be pushed away by the light from a star like the Sun, and end up forming a dusty disc around it. Compared with the interstellar gas clouds, these discs have a far higher abundance of heavier elements, and it is from these discs that planets form. The end result of the whole process is that a planet like the Earth is very chemically diverse. Very roughly, it is made of around 30 per cent iron, 30 per cent oxygen, 15 per cent magnesium, 15 per cent silicon, 2 per cent aluminium and 2 per cent calcium. The remainder is made of a wide range of elements, and less than 0.3 per cent of the Earth's mass is hydrogen.

Remember, however, that stars make up around ten per cent of the matter in the Universe, and planets an even tinier fraction; despite all this local chemical composition, the Universe is still broadly the way it started.

The End of It All

Will the Universe ever end, and what is the best theory for the end of the Universe?

Bruce Goodman (Colchester, Essex), James Partington (Spain) and David Bate (Cheltenham, Gloucestershire)

If the question 'Where did we come from?' is the biggest question, then the question 'Where will it all end?' is arguably the second biggest. The two are inextricably linked, as the past evolution of the Universe gives an indication of its fate. All we can do, however, is extrapolate our theories and make guesses based on the physics we understand.

In around five billion years, the Sun will have died, ending its life as a dim white dwarf star. The Earth will probably still be here, but will be first burned to a crisp when the Sun becomes a red giant, and then frozen solid as the light goes out. More stars will continue to be born, however, and this will probably continue for tens of trillions of years. After that, the Milky Way will have consumed its supply of gas and dust and be composed of white dwarfs, neutron stars and brown dwarfs. None of these give off much light and so the Galaxy will be a much dimmer place.

In the meantime, the Milky Way will have collided with the Andromeda galaxy, forming one much larger galaxy, but even that galaxy will not stay the same for ever. Over aeons of time, the stars will either be flung out into intergalactic space or their orbits will decay and they will fall towards the centre. Many of the stars that fall to the centre will fall into the black hole, swelling its mass to thousands of times what it is currently. The same processes will happen with the galaxies in galaxy clusters; most will be likely flung into intergalactic space, while others will fall towards the centre and form super-massive galaxies.

On larger scales, the fate of the Universe is more uncertain still. Our current model involves the Universe expanding at an ever-increasing rate. As well as pushing the galaxy clusters apart, this expansion will also lower the temperature in the Universe. The relic radiation from the Big Bang, which we currently see as an almost completely uniform temperature of around three degrees above absolute zero, will continue to cool. We see distant galaxies at longer wavelengths as the light from them is stretched by the expansion of the Universe, and this process will continue. In the end, the Universe will almost be completely dark.

That is not the end of the story, however, and if a dim, dark Universe filled with black holes and the remnants of stars sounds bleak it will probably get worse. Stephen Hawking showed that black holes radiate energy, slowly losing mass, and so even these will decay. Even the simplest forms of matter will not be safe, as it is thought that even protons can decay into lighter types of particles. This means that the brown dwarfs, white dwarfs and neutron stars will gradually dissolve, though on timescales of a billion billion billion billion years or more. Since protons decay so very, very slowly, the process is incredibly hard to measure, and the timescale could be wrong by huge factors, so these numbers are incredibly uncertain.

This bleak future is only one possibility, based on the best guess using the observations of the fraction of the entire Universe that we can see. It could be that our part of the Universe is different to others, in which case the end result might be different. Other parts of the Universe could be much denser, in which case the whole thing could collapse in on itself in a 'Big Crunch' (the opposite of a Big Bang). We simply don't know, and there may never be a way of knowing, but that doesn't stop some cosmologists from trying to work it out. You never know, it might just work and we might eventually find out with more certainty what the fate of the Universe is. In the meantime we'll just have to wait and see – though possibly for a very, very long time!

The Multiverse and Extra Dimensions

Is there a possibility that other Big Bangs have occurred in different locations?

Roy Abrams (Liverpool)

It is possible that Big Bangs have occurred elsewhere, and some scientists would say that it is very likely. Some very speculative theories about the nature of the Big Bang indicate that it should have happened many times – possibly even an infinite number of times. The concept of many universes is called the 'multiverse', and these other expanding universes could be very different from our own, with different physical laws. Perhaps ours is the only one where conditions allow the formation of atoms, let alone stars, planets and life.

Imagine the Universe as being represented by a two-dimensional plane, not unlike a sheet of paper. If there was another parallel two-dimensional universe some distance above or below the first, then there would be no way of anyone in the first sheet of paper being aware of the second sheet. In the real Universe, which we see as three-dimensional, an additional universe would not be 'above' in the traditional sense, but could be some distance away in a fourth spatial dimension. Even if our Universe expanded for ever in three dimensions, it need not ever meet the other universe, just as the two pieces of paper could be stretched as much as possible without ever meeting.

If there are other universes out there, how would the predictions of the end of our Universe change as a result of one or more other universes 'colliding' with our own?

Gil (Peterlee, County Durham)

It depends on the nature of the collision. If the other universe was expanding in the same three dimensions that ours resides in, then they could collide in the 'traditional sense'. It's possible that the effect of a universe in such close proximity would be seen through its effects on the most distant objects we can see, though no such signs have been seen. This would imply that the properties of the Universe as a whole could be different from the properties of the region we can see, which might affect the final fate of the Universe.

The additional universes would be separated from our own in a fourth spatial dimension, which is rather hard to imagine. It is the equivalent of two pieces of paper lying parallel, but separated by a small distance. In his theories of higher-dimensional spaces, Stephen Hawking refers to the three-dimensional universes as 'branes' (I believe derived from the word membrane). One theory is that it was collisions between these branes that caused the Big Bang, though there is no way of proving or disproving the theory as yet.

In the multiverse interpretation of quantum cosmology, in how many universes is Miley Cyrus President of the USA?

Maude Agombar (Salisbury, Wiltshire)

One possible interpretation of the Universe is that we live in one among many. In fact, it is possible that there is an infinite number of universes. In an infinite number of universes, every possible combination would occur somewhere, at some time. In some, for example, the entire works of Shakespeare would have been written by monkeys typing random letters on typewriters. In others, Miley Cyrus would indeed have been President of the USA. How likely it is would affect how many times it would occur, but it would still occur an infinite number of times – even a small fraction of infinity is infinity! Now isn't that a scary thought?

Do you think there will ever be another scientific explanation for the origin of the Universe other than the Big Bang?

Andrew Hindmarch (Surrey)

My [CN] feeling is that the Big Bang theory is based on solid scientific evidence and that it won't be disproved. However, other aspects of our cosmological model are on much less firm ground. Dark matter, for example, has yet to actually be identified (though that's a bold thing to write in a book which will be printed and published during a period when active searches seem to be getting closer). Without an observation to prove its existence, it is hard to consider the theory to be proven, though certainly there is far more evidence for dark matter than other competing theories. Dark energy is particularly susceptible to becoming a victim of scientific progress. I base this assessment largely on the fact that all we can say is that we think there is something which is having an effect, but we don't know what that thing is.

It is important that the scientific community doesn't back itself into a corner and close its eyes to alternatives. Some of the greatest delays to scientific progress in the last few hundred years have been due to the refusal of people to accept new ideas. Just as in the world of commerce, there are many benefits to be gained from competition. Scientists who interpret results in different ways and therefore support opposing theories will often support new experiments. The crucial thing that must happen is that personal feelings should be removed. Believing that something is true simply because you'd prefer it that way, or because that would make things easier, is not an appropriate way to conduct scientific research.

Other Worlds

Other Planets

Will we ever be able to build a telescope large enough to directly observe extra-solar planets?

David Cockayne (Birmingham)

This one is easy to answer – we already have! In 2008, teams using the Gemini and Keck telescopes on Hawaii announced that they had directly observed three planets orbiting a star 128 light years away in the constellation of Pegasus. These telescopes are amongst the largest optical telescopes on Earth, with the primary mirrors of the Keck telescope being 10 metres across. Nevertheless, to see such detail the effects of the atmosphere have to be taken into account, and it was only with the latest techniques that these observations were possible.

Not long after these images were released, astronomers digging through data from the Hubble Space Telescope discovered a planet orbiting the star Fomalhaut in Pisces. This planet is not dissimilar to Jupiter but orbits much further from its parent star, embedded in a dusty disc.

While we have now directly imaged these planets, we have not been able to see any detail on them. That will require much larger telescopes, which have a much greater resolution. Telescopes are being designed with aperture diameters in the range 20–40 metres. These extremely large telescopes will still need to combat the effects of the atmosphere, but in principle will be able to see much more detail. It will be some time before we can see oceans and landmasses on other planets!

How do scientists find out the gravity of a planet?

Marilena (Cyprus)

The gravity on the surface of a planet depends on its mass, and also its size. Larger planets tend to be more massive, and therefore tend to have a larger gravitational pull on their surface. Jupiter, for example, has a mass around three hundred times that of the Earth but, because it is so much larger (about ten times the diameter), its surface gravity is only two and a half times that on Earth. In the Solar System we know the masses of the planets very well, simply by studying the way they interact with other astronomical bodies such as their moons.

In other solar systems, the masses of planets are harder to determine. Many of these extra-solar planets are discovered by examining the effect they have on the star. Technically a planet doesn't orbit a star, but rather both star and planet orbit the centre of mass of the system, called a 'barycentre'. Since a star is so much more massive than a planet, it is affected much less, but it does tend to wobble a small amount. Very careful observations can detect this slight wobble, which tells astronomers the mass of both the star and the planet. The situation is complicated slightly because these other solar systems are normally tilted at an unknown angle with respect to Earth, and that tilt affects the apparent size of the wobble.

The gravity on the surface of a planet also depends on its size, which the above method can't tell us. That can normally only be worked out if the planet happens to pass directly between us and the star, which is only possible if the planet's orbit lines up almost perfectly with our view from Earth. At these great distances we only see the dip in light as the planet blocks a small amount of the star's light, but the amount of starlight blocked tells us just how big the planet is. If we know that *and* we've detected how much it makes the star wobble, then we can work out the surface gravity of a planet. For example, a planet called CoRoT-3b, which orbits a star 2,000 light years away in the constellation of Aquila, would have surface gravity more than 20 times that on Jupiter. It's unlikely we'll ever want to go to that particular planet, though, as it orbits its star at a tiny fraction of the Earth's distance from the Sun, whipping around its orbit in a little over four days.

Kepler is surveying only a tiny slice of the sky, and to date has recorded well over 1,000 potential planets. What area of the sky is *Kepler* currently surveying?

Richard Coville (Canada)

The *Kepler* mission, launched in 2009, is surveying a small region of the sky in the constellation of Cygnus the Swan. This region was chosen because it is very rich in stars, but will not be blocked by the Sun at any point. *Kepler*'s field of view is around ten degrees across – about the size of a fist at arm's length – but that is only one four hundredth the total area of the sky. Nevertheless, there are still a huge number of stars visible, and *Kepler* monitors around 150,000 of them. Most of the stars chosen are similar to the Sun, but not all are known to have planets around them.

Kepler detects the tiny dip in brightness as a planet passes in front of its parent star. A dip that looks convincing is labelled as a candidate planet, and the number of these candidates is currently in the thousands and rising rapidly. To detect whether the planet is really there, three equally spaced dips must be observed. For a planet like the Earth this could take three years of searching, so the confirmation that the planets are real can take some time.

As the results from the *Kepler* probe become more and more exciting, how far away are we from finding a second Earth-like planet?

Martin Hickes (Leeds)

The planets found so far by a range of telescopes and experiments cover a wide range of masses, sizes and orbits. This is largely due to the methods used to find them, which tend to be better at picking up planets that are larger, more massive, and orbit closer to their star. The goal of *Kepler* is to find a planet like the Earth, i.e. one that has a similar size, a similar mass, and orbits at a similar location relative to its parent star. To do this, *Kepler*'s detectors are incredibly sensitive, so that they can see the smallest dip in brightness as a planet passes in front of its star.

We are continually getting closer to an Earth-like planet, and the results come in incredibly rapidly. At the time of writing, planets have been found in their stars' habitable zones, i.e where liquid water could exist on the surfaces of rocky planets, but none of these are known to be rocky. *Kepler* has also found planets that are roughly the same size as the Earth but these orbit much closer to their parent star.

How likely is it that the exoplanets currently being detected have moons, and do you think that a large moon orbiting a planet such as the Earth is necessary for life to evolve?

Bryan Upfield (London)

In our Solar System almost all the planets have moons, and the giant planets have dozens of them, so it is very unlikely that planets in other solar systems do not also have moons. But the Earth, with its relatively large Moon, is unique, and most moons are much smaller relative to their parent planet.

It is thought that our Moon was formed when a giant body roughly the size of Mars crashed into the Earth around 4 billion years ago, causing a large amount of material to be thrown off and over time to form the Moon. What is very hard to work out is how likely such a collision is to happen. Since we have yet to see a moon outside our own Solar System we have only the one example and so a statistical analysis is difficult. Simulations of the conditions that were thought to exist in the early Solar System indicate that such collisions are not horrendously unlikely, but they are not necessarily common. A recent estimate was that somewhere between one in four and one in 45 planets the size of the Earth could have a moon like ours, but there are many assumptions made in these studies.

The effect of the Moon on the evolution of life is very hard to evaluate. We know that it has an effect on the Earth, but not whether that has affected life in any significant way. For example, the presence of a large moon stabilises a planet's axis; the Earth's axis is tilted at around 23 degrees relative to its orbit around the Sun, but this axial tilt does not vary much. In contrast the planet Mars, which has two tiny moons that are just 12 and 20 kilometres in diameter, has experienced huge tilts in its axis over the history of the Solar System.

If the early Earth had experienced such large shifts, would life have been affected? It's hard to say, though the weather on Earth would have experienced large changes. Primitive life tends to be fairly tolerant of temperature changes, and more advanced life might have been able to adapt to the conditions providing they were varying slowly enough.

The other major effect of the Moon is the tides it causes on Earth. The Moon formed slightly closer to the Earth than it is currently, and so the tides would have been higher. I have heard it said that the tides may have helped life make the move from the oceans, where it first formed, onto land. The tides would have meant that the marine creatures could spend increasingly longer times out of the water by moving up the shoreline, giving them a gentle introduction to the drier environment. This is conceivable, but the fossil record is not complete enough at these distant times. Whether a lack of tides would have delayed, or prevented, life's movement onto land is not clear.

Life Elsewhere

Has anyone yet produced an accepted formula that gives a probability of life elsewhere in our Solar System, or elsewhere in the Universe?

Mark Bullard (London)

The most widely cited equation, or formula, designed for this purpose was proposed by astronomer Frank Drake in the 1960s. The equation, as Drake has commented, is meant to be used to explore the factors involved in determining the possibility of life elsewhere, rather than to give a definitive answer. In its original form, Drake's equation was used to give an estimate of the number of civilisations that we could communicate with, symbolised by the letter N, and is often written as:

$$N = R \times F_P \times N_E \times F_L \times F_I \times F_C \times L$$

The number is calculated by multiplying together a range of numbers and probabilities. The first, R, is the rate of formation of stars that are suitable for life to exist around. In our Galaxy, the Milky Way, there is roughly one star being born per year, and we believe that most stars are probably capable of harbouring life in principle. So we could guess that R is equal to 1.

The second symbol, F_P, is the fraction of those stars that have planets around them, and we can also estimate this. We think that most stars form in a similar way, from a large cloud of gas and dust. Once the star has formed, the leftover material forms a disc around it, and that disc forms planets. We have seen numerous examples of stars with these dusty discs, and lots of stars with planets around them, including binary stars. Let's be optimistic and say that every star can have planets around it. So F_p is also equal to 1.

The symbol N_E is for the number of Earth-like planets in each of these solar systems, which could be interpreted to mean the number of planets in the habitable zone – the zone around the star in which the temperature allows liquid water to exist. This we don't know yet, but it is something that the *Kepler* mission is trying to find out. We certainly know of lots of systems that have massive gas giant planets very close in to their stars. These planets probably formed further out and then moved inwards, which could prevent Earth-like planets from forming. Unfortunately, these massive, close-in planets are much easier to detect than Earth-like ones, and so dominate our current lists of planets. We do, however, know that there are rocky planets out there, and that some are at reasonable distances from their stars – in fact some are very close to being in a habitable zone. This has to be a guess, but let's go with half of all planetary systems containing planets in the habitable zone. So N_E is equal to 0.5, but that is only a guess – we should have a better idea of that number in a few years when *Kepler* has returned its results.

The fourth symbol is F_L, and is the fraction of planets in the habitable zone on which life forms. This is where the guesses start to become really controversial. Since life on Earth seems to exist in a very wide range of environments, it is tempting to suspect that it can arise anywhere. But the one thing life is very good at is adapting, and it could be that the earliest life forms arose in the perfectly idyllic conditions of early Earth (warm and wet), and simply adapted to exist in these harsh conditions over hundreds of millions of years. If that's the case, then the chance of life arising might be a billion to one or less! It could also be that we are the result of a complete fluke, and that the chances of life occurring are absolutely minuscule, though that's a little depressing. There are many different ideas about this and there has been no firm evidence either way. This number is only meant to represent the formation of life in its most basic form, so for the moment I'll be an optimist and assume that life will form anywhere it can, so F_L is equal to 1.

If we stopped here and multiplied together all the numbers that we've calculated so far, then we would have the rate at which new life springs into being in our Galaxy. We would have:

$$N = R \times F_P \times N_E \times F_L$$

Using the numbers we've estimated, there would be life springing up on a new planet every two years. The Milky Way has been around for quite a long time – at least around 10 billion years – and so that would mean that life would have evolved billions of times. But remember that we guessed at a few of the numbers involved. It might turn out that Earth-like planets are not as common as we guessed here, or that life does not form as readily as we've assumed, both of which could reduce that number hugely. For example, if only one in ten stars had an Earth-like planet, and the chance of life arising on it was one in ten billion, then the number would drop from billions to around 1. If that's the case, then the Earth could be the only planet harbouring life in the entire Milky Way.

The remaining terms in Drake's Equation refer to how life evolves. F_I is the fraction those life-harbouring planets on which life evolves to become intelligent. It's obviously happened once here, but could that just have been luck? If we weren't around would chimpanzees or dolphins have evolved to become the dominant species on the planet? Who knows?

The term F_C is the fraction of those civilisations that develop technology capable of transmitting into outer space. Again, who is to say whether the development of electricity and radio communications was inevitable?

The last term is the length of time that the civilisation continues to transmit signals. The transmissions could stop for a number of reasons. It could be that the civilisation is destroyed by a natural disaster, or that it destroys itself in a nuclear war. Or perhaps they just *decide* to stop transmitting. For example, the signals escaping from Earth are weakening as our technology becomes more efficient and less energy is radiated out into space.

We can make educated guesses at most of these numbers, but that is it. In the 1960s only the first one – the rate of star formation – was known, while now we have a slightly better idea about the formation of planets. But even so, the estimates of the number of life forms that could exist in our Galaxy range from one (just us) to billions, simply by changing the assumptions made.

Why is life important to the Universe?

Kevin Sommerville (New York)

There are two ways of addressing this question. One could ask, 'Does the Universe care whether there is life in it?' Of course, as far as we're aware the Universe can't think for itself, and so the answer becomes philosophical at best. Certainly we as life forms have no physical effect on anything beyond our own planet, aside from a few tiny space probes travelling through space, and even the most distant ones haven't got much further than the edge of the Solar System.

On the other hand, we could ask 'Is it important to us whether life exists?' and this is almost a sociological question. From a personal and scientific point of view, many of us are greatly interested in whether there is life elsewhere, and it would certainly help to put us in our place. Does the existence of life elsewhere make us less special as a species, and what if that civilisation is as intelligent as us? This might have implications for those with religious or spiritual beliefs, but I [CN] am far from qualified to discuss that here.

In science fiction, the discovery of life elsewhere is often depicted as ushering in a new era of worldwide peace, ending all wars, though that is probably a somewhat utopian view. In some other works, worldwide unity is frequently due to the threat of domination or extermination from a hostile alien race.

Discussions of the discovery of extraterrestrial life often end up turning into discussion of the implications, and so my conclusion would probably be that the existence of life *is* important to us, but not necessarily the Universe itself.

Is it possible that life such as that on Earth formed millions or billions of years ago elsewhere in the Universe?

Gary Partington (Spain)

This is certainly possible, though it's hard to say how likely it is. The Earth formed around four and a half billion years ago, shortly after the Sun. In its infancy, the planet was a molten ball of rock, constantly being pelted by the debris that was still present in the early Solar System. Volcanism blighted the surface, spewing noxious gases into the atmosphere. It was around half a billion years before conditions were suitable for life, which took hold several billion years ago. Since those early days, life has evolved considerably, with entire classes of species all but dying out (dinosaurs) and others springing up to fill the void (primates). It is often claimed that life sprang up as soon as the conditions allowed, and through evolution and natural selection evolved rapidly into much more advanced species. However, who is to say that there weren't many 'false starts' in the first few billion years of the Earth's history that were swiftly obliterated by an asteroid impact? If these were primitive enough they would have left no fossil record.

At around five billion years old, the Sun is far from the oldest star in the Universe, and there are billions of stars like the Sun which have formed over the 13-billion year history of the cosmos. The very early Universe was a much more primordial place, with far lower concentrations of heavy elements such as carbon, oxygen, silicon, iron and so on. Planets are primarily made from these heavy elements, and life as we know it would not be able to exist without some of them. Life (at least in forms we are familiar with) probably wouldn't have been possible for the first period of the Universe's existence simply due to the relatively limited chemistry possible with the ingredients present. The chemical evolution of the Universe was much more rapid in its early days, and so it is likely that within a few billion years the chemical composition would have been suitable for life. This means that there would be stars that formed billions of years before the Sun that are orbited by Earth-like planets. Any life that formed here would in principle have had a head start of billions of years over that on the Earth.

Whether that life is still around now is a different issue. The Sun will very gradually increase in brightness over the next few billion years and, while the associated temperature increase on the Earth will be tiny over human lifetimes, after a billion years or so the oceans will probably boil off. While microbial life may be able to survive, this will probably make most of the animal kingdom extinct. A few billion years after that and the Earth will be burnt to a cinder as the Sun becomes a red giant, and may even be destroyed in the outer layers of the massive star. A few hundred million years after that and the Sun will wither into a faint white dwarf star, making the entire Solar System uninhabitable by any forms of life that rely on sunlight. The same is probably true in other solar systems and, without some form of interstellar travel, any other life will probably die out. Of course, in a billion years technology can advance significantly, and so we might discover that these ancient civilisations are already living out amongst the stars.

I read once that the odds of inorganic chemistry creating life were more than twice the number of all the stars in the Universe. If that's correct, the odds have been beaten once – could they really be beaten twice?

Karen Cappleman (Kent)

All life relies on complex molecules that make up our proteins and DNA, which are very sensitive to the arrangement of the atoms that make them up. A strand of human DNA is primarily made of hydrogen, oxygen, carbon, nitrogen and phosphorus, but there many billions of molecules. Changing the order of the molecules changes the DNA, and most combinations would not be suitable for life to exist. The chances of such a specific arrangement of atoms and molecules occurring naturally are absolutely tiny, and even taking into account the vast amount of time that life has had to evolve the chances are still very small. So small, that the chances of life arising even once in the entire visible Universe are vanishingly small. We know it has arisen once (us!), but these assumptions would imply that the odds of it having arisen twice are tiny.

Perhaps there is some sort of driving force that makes the life-supporting combinations more stable, or more likely. An intriguing prospect, but one that would involve aspects of chemistry that we are not yet aware of. Or maybe there was an initial form of life that is much simpler but which we have not yet discovered.

But we also know that the assumptions above are not entirely accurate. We are continually finding more and more complex chemicals out in the depths of space. We have even seen amino acids – the building blocks of proteins – in meteorites that have fallen to Earth. This means that life didn't have to start from scratch but had some basic building blocks, though the odds are still small. Biologists are trying to understand the way in which life is formed, though efforts to create life in the laboratory have so far been fruitless.

What are the chances of life on the newly discovered exoplanet Gliese 581g?

Karl (Stoke on Trent)

The planet Gliese 581g is a very controversial planet. Its parent star, Gliese 581, is known to have four planets around it, called Gliese 581b, c, d and e (in the standard notation, Gliese 581a is the star itself). The discovery of two further planets (Gliese 581f and g) was announced in 2010 by a group using the Keck telescope, but the team using the HARPS instrument on the European Southern Observatory's 3.6m telescope could not find it in their data. The disagreement is because the evidence for these two additional planets is rather weak, and could be due to contamination in the data caused by the other planets, particularly Gliese 581d.

The confirmation, or otherwise, of the planet will require more observations, and it is likely that the debate will soon be over one way or the other. In the meantime, however, we are free to speculate. If it is really there, then Gliese 581g is a planet a few times the mass of the Earth with an orbital period of around 36 days. This places it rather close to its parent star, but since the star is a dim red dwarf, the planet would still be in the 'Goldilocks zone', a region around the star that is the right temperature for liquid water to exist.

Whether there is life on the planet is much harder to say. With such a cool, red sun it would almost certainly be very different to anything we are familiar with. Knowing this will require much more detailed observations of the planet to establish the chemical composition of its atmosphere – if it has one.

Out of the number of massive gas giants found outside our own Solar System, are we looking at their moons for signs of potential life?

Paul Foster (London)

With our current technology the discovery of moons of planets in other solar systems is beyond us, as they are far too small to be detected by the methods we normally use to find the planets. However, evidence from our own Solar System suggests that moons of giant planets are very common, so we are pretty sure they must exist elsewhere.

A large moon such as ours can have a small affect on its planet which might be measurable. As the moon orbits it pulls on the planet slightly, causing it to wobble. The wobble of the planet will change the precise timing of its motion around its star, and this might be detectable by experiments such as *Kepler*.

Calling All Life Forms...

We've sent signals from Earth now for over 50 years. Would other civilisations be able to detect these signals if they were on the receiving end?

Derrick A Edwards (Leicester)

We have been leaking radio signals into space for around 60 years, and those first radio waves have travelled 60 light years. However, as the signals travel further, they become more spread out and harder to detect. Most of the signals are also restricted to a very narrow range of radio frequencies, which distinguishes them from most natural astronomical signals.

When we look for signals from alien civilisations, we look for similar types of transmissions, simply because that's what *we* are emitting – but who is to say that alien civilisations use the same technology as us? Perhaps they communicate using X-rays, and have been constantly beaming X-rays out into space. If they have the same idea as us, they might be looking for X-ray transmissions from planets, which we have not been transmitting in large amounts at all.

Do we know if any of the star systems in range of radio signals emanating from Earth have any signs of a planet in the 'Goldilocks zone'?

Barry Holland (St Helens)

Let's assume that the Earth has been radiating radio waves for 60 years. That includes not only the odd deliberate signal, but also the 'leakage' from terrestrial television and radio transmissions. The earliest radio waves, travelling at the speed of light, have reached 60 light years. Within that distance, we know of around a hundred planets. The vast majority of these are gas giants and most orbit incredibly close to their parent star, though a few orbit further out.

The 'Goldilocks zone' is normally defined as the region around the star where liquid water can exist. For smaller, dimmer stars this is closer in than for the larger, brighter ones. Whether liquid water is present also depends on the planet's atmosphere, which generally increases the surface temperature slightly.

One system that is notable is located around the star 55 Cancri. There are five planets that we know of. The star itself is slightly smaller than the Sun, and so the nominal habitable zone would lie a little further in. Of the five known planets, three orbit much too close to their star, while a fourth orbits too far out. This is a great shame from the point of view of the habitable zone, as one of the inner planets is what is called a 'super Earth', being just over eight times the mass of Earth and around twice the diameter. Sadly this planet, called 55 Cancri e, orbits at a distance of just 2 million km, whipping round in less than 18 hours, and so would be baked to a cinder. There is, however, a larger planet orbiting at roughly the same distance as Venus is from the Sun. With a slightly cooler star, the planet could lie close to the Goldilocks zone, but the planet is a gas giant somewhere between Neptune and Saturn in terms of mass. If it has any large moons with thick enough atmospheres, then perhaps those are habitable. Unfortunately, we are some way from detecting the presence of moons of extra-solar planets, and so further speculation will have to wait.

A second intriguing example is the planet orbiting the star HD 85512, which is around 35 light years away. The star is somewhat cooler than the Sun, but the planet orbits closer in, just inside where Mercury's orbit would be. The planet is a few times the mass of the Earth, and so could potentially be rocky. The temperature on the planet's surface would depend on the amount of cloud cover, but a rough guess can be made. Using a set of assumptions, such as that the atmosphere will not be too dissimilar from our own in terms of composition, it can be calculated that the surface temperature could be suitable for the existence of liquid water. These are only rough calculations, however, and we can only be sure if we actually study the light from the atmosphere of this planet directly.

The field is moving incredibly quickly, and it is entirely possible that by the time you read this an Earth-like planet will have been found in the Goldilocks zone of a nearby star. In the October 2011 edition of *The Sky at Night* we asked Dr Giovanna Tinetti to have a guess at how long this would take, and she put her money on finding an Earth-like planet within a year!

Is there any scientific effort to address the question 'Should we answer the call if ET rings?'

Martin O'Flaherty (Liverpool)

Discussions about this issue often centre on the reason for the communication in the first place. Perhaps ET would like to share knowledge and expand everyone's understanding of the Universe, in which case a frank and honest conversation would be beneficial to both parties. But there is the possibility that an alien race might be looking for targets for conquest, whether they want to mine the Earth for its resources or simply pack humans up into their lunchboxes. In this case, of course, we probably shouldn't answer, though by the time we realise that it might be too late. If the communication looks to be specifically targeted at Earth, then it's likely that they've detected our presence – they might even be on their way already!

Many people have voiced the opinion that we shouldn't communicate with aliens because of the risk of them coming to destroy us. However, one would like to think that if they've managed to achieve interstellar communication and travel then they would have moved beyond destruction and war. But what if they are far more technologically advanced than us? We might look to them as sheep and cows do to us, in which case would they start clothing themselves in human skin and eating us with herbs and spices?

If we do receive communication from elsewhere, then there is a much more immediate problem to be overcome – who should speak on our behalf? Would we want the USA to lead the conversation, as happens in many science fiction stories? There are discussions at the international level, such as at the United Nations, of what to do in this situation – both in terms of whether to respond and what we should say. Such decisions can seem laughable at times, based in the realm of science fiction, but if that communication from ET does arrive it will probably be too late. In the meantime, the consensus tends to be that while we can't keep our presence a secret, we probably shouldn't advertise it too widely until we've made up our mind what to do if someone answers.

Would it be sensible and worthwhile to use the Low Frequency Array (LOFAR) for SETI research?

Alan Tough (Elgin, Moray)

LOFAR, or the Low Frequency Array, is an enormous radio telescope being built that stretches across Europe, including a station in Chilbolton, Hampshire. The array is not, however, comprised of radio telescopes that we are familiar with, but rather a network of radio antennae. These work in a similar way to television and radio aerials, picking up signals from a large area of the sky simultaneously. The power of LOFAR is the ability to combine the signals from huge numbers of antennae simultaneously, allowing astronomers to look at any particular location in great detail. Since the combination of signals is performed during the computer analysis, it is in principle possible for LOFAR to look in multiple directions simultaneously.

This would seem to make it ideal for SETI (the Search for Extra-Terrestrial Intelligence), but there are many demands on the telescope for other purposes. There is, of course, nothing to stop people taking the data from LOFAR and sifting through them for artificial signals.

Closer to Home

Is it likely that any form of life will be discovered elsewhere in the Solar System?

Wendy Lewis (Maidstone)

If we discover life elsewhere in the Solar System, it is likely to be very simple. But there are hotspots where we think it might be possible for microbes to exist. The first place people looked was Mars, though it seems unlikely that any life exists there now unless it lies deep beneath the surface. Based on this, most experiments have looked on Mars for evidence of past life rather than current life. We know that Mars was a much warmer, wetter world hundreds of millions of years ago, thanks in part to the thick atmosphere that it has since lost. We have found clays deposited on Mars that must have been formed in what would best be described as a tropical environment – though it doesn't look like there were any rainforests on early Mars.

In the 1970s and 1980s the *Voyager* spacecraft flew past the giant planets Jupiter and Saturn. These planets are huge gas giants, made almost entirely of thick gaseous atmospheres that we don't believe are suitable for life. But what interested the astrobiologists was not the planets themselves but some of their moons. Jupiter's moon Europa is an ice-covered world, but a dense network of ridges and crevasses indicates that the icy surface is floating on a lake of liquid water. The water is kept warm by heating due to the intense tidal forces of Jupiter. If the sub-surface ocean is in contact with a rocky interior, then it's possible that life exists in the dark depths. The life would not be something we are familiar with, as it would need to get its energy from somewhere other than the Sun. We know of microbes on Earth that rely on geothermal energy from the rocks, or on the heat generated by 'black smokers' on the ocean floor, though all these life forms probably evolved from microbes on the surface. Missions have been proposed to melt or drill through the European ice, which is probably around a hundred kilometres thick over most of the surface, though realistically they are probably decades away.

A similar phenomenon was seen in the 2000s by the *Cassini* satellite orbiting Saturn. One of Saturn's tiny moons, Enceladus, has geysers of salty water erupting from fissures near its south pole. The observations indicate that Enceladus has a sub-surface ocean similar to Europa's, although we know that it is a salty ocean and therefore in contact with a rocky ocean floor. Whether this ocean and the 'fountains of Enceladus' are permanent features is unknown, as they could be present for relatively short periods of time.

One of the most promising places we could look for life is Saturn's largest moon Titan. After Mars, this is arguably the most Earth-like place in the Solar System, though it has some crucial differences. It is large enough to hold on to a thick hazy atmosphere, which the *Huygens* probe descended through in 2004–2005. We see clouds, lakes and rivers on the surface, and we've even seen the effects of seasonal rains filling up lakes and then emptying along rivers. But Titan, at a billion miles from the Sun, is far too cold for liquid water to exist, let alone clouds made of water vapour. Instead, the liquid that shows a cycle of evaporation and precipitation is methane and ethane. These are hydrocarbons – combinations of hydrogen and carbon – though it is possible that life could exist in these conditions.

Where should we concentrate our future efforts in terms of finding life in the Solar System?

Paul Foster (Clapham, London)

In terms of searching for life, I would say the most interesting of the moons is Europa. If there is life in the sub-surface ocean then we would know that it must have evolved in very different conditions to those on Earth, which would make life in other solar systems much more likely. Of course, Mars is considerably closer and therefore easier (and cheaper) to travel to. The tests for life are very delicate, and it may well be that we won't know for sure whether there is life on Mars until a manned mission has visited and dug down through the soil.

Although spacecraft are built under very clean laboratory conditions, how sure are we that we are not contaminating the atmospheres and surfaces of other bodies with Earth matter, especially when we leave detritus behind?

Shirley Morgan (Maidenhead)

There are incredibly tight regulations about the contamination of alien worlds with Earth-based material. The severity of the rules depends on the nature of the particular body in question, largely whether it may have life on it. For example, the Moon and Mercury are completely devoid of life, and therefore the regulations are less strict than those for missions to Mars or the outer planets, where simple life forms may be present. Spacecraft are always built in incredibly clean laboratories, largely because the presence of dust or other contaminants can cause problems for the spacecraft itself, let alone any potential alien microbes.

There is one further preventative course of action that is taken, and that is to destroy the spacecraft before it can contaminate another world.

While spacecraft would not be intentionally put on a collision course with a potentially life-bearing planet or moon, if left to their own devices they could eventually get caught by a moon's gravitational pull and crash. At the end of its mission, in 2017, the *Cassini* probe will be deliberately flown into Saturn's atmosphere. As well as providing our only in-situ test of the cloud layers, this will also ensure that the spacecraft can't possibly crash down onto the surface of Titan, Enceladus, or any of the planet's many other moons.

Should we not look close-up at comets for signs of an alien signature?

Sandy (Scotland)

There is a theory that life originally evolved on comets, and was delivered to Earth in an impact. It is generally believed that a reasonable fraction of the Earth's water – possibly all of it – was delivered to Earth by comets. We have also detected the presence of amino acids – complex molecules that are the building blocks of proteins and DNA – in meteorites that have fallen to Earth, but there has not been any sign of life itself.

Of course, that's not to say for sure that it couldn't exist. Comets warm up considerably if they approach the Sun, though they fall into a deep freeze as they move further out away from the Sun. There is also no liquid water on the surface of comets, only solid ice. As sunlight warms the surface the ice sublimates, turning straight into a vapour, and is ejected from the comet. If life has evolved there it would have to be able to exist deep in the icy interior, hibernating during the comet's long passage through the outer Solar System.

The possibility of life on comets is largely not believed, and I [PM] find it rather unlikely. That is not to say that we should not look for it, however. The best way of doing this would be to visit a comet and make measurements on its surface, or to bring back samples to Earth. We have samples from a comet's tail thanks to the *Stardust* probe, but not from the surface of one. I remain sceptical, but am always willing to be proved wrong!

Some of the recently discovered extra-solar planets have startlingly short orbital periods. How can we be sure that we are not observing partially constructed or segmented Dyson spheres?

Steven Ford (Haydon Bridge)

This is a very intriguing question. A Dyson sphere is a theoretical concept that originated with the American scientist Freeman Dyson. He theorised that a sufficiently advanced civilisation could construct a sphere that completely surrounded their star. The material would have to be mined from planets, moons and asteroids, requiring technology way beyond our wildest dreams at present. The advantage of such a sphere would be that the interior surface, all of which would in principle be habitable, would be enormous, and that it would be possible to utilise almost all the energy from the star itself. A variation on the theme is a 'ring world', where a ring is constructed rather than a full sphere.

Of course, such structures are currently firmly in the realm of science fiction, with absolutely no observational proof. There are several reasons why the observed planets could not be fragments of a sphere. Firstly, most of the measurements are made by detecting the wobble of the star due to the gravitational pull of the planet. If the planet were replaced by a sphere of material, then the gravitational pull of opposing segments would cancel out, resulting in a much smaller wobble. Secondly, we are now able to study the atmospheres of some of these planets, and detect the presence of a range of molecules.

Of course the final reason for not believing them to be spheres should be what is known as Occam's Razor. Is it more likely that a planet exists close to a star, or that an advanced civilisation has built an enormous sphere in just the right way to make it look like a planet passing in front of the star? I'm afraid that, while it can be very appealing to think of such weird and wonderful concepts, I can't see it being possible that we are observing them.

Manned Space Exploration

The Story So Far

In April 2011, we celebrated 50 years of manned space exploration. What do you see as its greatest achievement during that time and what would you hope that the next 50 years will bring?

David Nixon (Huddersfield), Carol Owen (Chorley, Lancashire)

What is the greatest achievement of the first 50 years of space travel? I [PM] think I have got to say proving that 'it can be done'. Before Yuri Gagarin's flight in 1961, there were so many famous astronomers, including Astronomers Royal, who ridiculed the entire idea. They were shown to be entirely wrong, and to show that people can live and work in space is the best achievement of the first half-century.

What can we look forward to in the next 50 years? If we work together, there is so much we can do. It depends in my view upon two things – politics and finance. For space travel must be international, and this depends on the quality of world leaders. (Looking round the present collection of world leaders inspires me with no confidence at all, but I hope that I'm wrong.)

If all goes well, we'll have more manned missions to space and I would hope a base on the Moon's surface. So far as our travels are concerned, I can't see us getting any further than that, because travelling to Mars involves spending weeks in space in full exposure to the Sun's radiation. Until we overcome the radiation problem, Mars is out of reach. I'm sure we will do it, but whether we do it in the next fifty years remains doubtful – we must hope for the best.

Which astronaut has flown the furthest in space over his career?

Kevin Taylor (Gloucester)

As far as we can tell, the current record is held by the Russian Cosmonaut Sergei Krikalev, who has so far notched up 803 days, 9 hours and 39 minutes in space. He took his first spaceflight in 1988 to the Russian space station *Mir*. His second flight, in 1991, was of note as it lasted more than ten months. The long duration was simply due to a problem with getting a replacement flight engineer up to orbit, requiring Sergei to do a double shift in space, but in the meantime the USSR collapsed. He is therefore sometimes referred to as the last citizen of the USSR.

But *Mir* wasn't Krikalev's only home from home. In the 1990s and 2000s he flew on the Space Shuttle and served on the International Space Station. But Sergei Krikalev will almost certainly not hold the record for much longer. Following his lead is another cosmonaut, Kaleri Yurievich, who has so far spent just over 770 days in space. With a typical stint on the Space Station lasting around six months, it is likely that Yurievich will take the record during his next spaceflight.

Spending 800 days in space corresponds to over 10,000 orbits of the Earth, clocking up a staggering 140 billion km on the odometer! This is far higher even than the *Apollo* missions, where the return journey to the Moon and back is around 800,000 km. But of course the *Apollo* astronauts have travelled the furthest from Earth, reaching a distance of around 400,000 km compared with a few hundred kilometres to low-Earth orbit. The most distant humans ever were the crew of *Apollo 13* who, in their disaster-struck spacecraft, executed an engine burn to send them around the far side of the Moon and safely back to Earth (the film is remarkably faithful to the actual events). It is unlikely that the record held by Jim Lovell, Fred Haise and John Swigert, set in 1970, will be broken at any point in the near future.

Of all the astronauts and cosmonauts you have met, which did you find the most interesting and why?

Andrew R Green BSc (Hons) FBIS, FRAS (Cambridge)

This is a difficult question to answer. I [PM] met most of the astronauts up to the year 2000, and came to know some of them very well. I will say one thing: they are all very different people. Take for example the first two men on the Moon, Neil Armstrong and Buzz Aldrin – Neil does not like publicity, and is very retiring, whereas Buzz Aldrin is a publicist, in the best sense of the word. I have found that the American and Russian astronauts, although different, all share one or two characteristics. All of them have more than the usual share of courage, ability and common sense.

I find it very hard to select any, but the very first man to go into space was Yuri Gagarin. I met him on several occasions before his sad and untimely death in an ordinary aircraft crash. I like Gagarin because he was going into the complete unknown. It was suggested that any space traveller would be hopelessly space sick or hopelessly giddy, but this was not so and Gagarin proved it. When he came down, most of the familiar 'bogies' had been disproved. All those who followed Gagarin had at least some idea what to expect – he hadn't.

The View from Above

Why, when we see footage of astronauts on the lunar surface or images of Earth from a great distance, do we not see any stars, just an inky blackness?

Stephen Millership (Stockport)

It is simply an issue of contrast. The Sun appears to be more than a billion times brighter than the nearest star, purely because it is so much closer. The Earth and Moon reflect a reasonable fraction of the light that hits them, and so their surfaces are still much, much brighter than the rest of the stars. If you take a camera and try to take a picture of the stars in the night sky, you will find that a reasonable exposure length is needed – probably a fair few seconds to get a decent image. Do something similar with the Moon, and you will find that even with a short exposure the Moon is incredibly bright. Any image you see that shows the features on the Moon's surface along with background stars, unless it is taken during a lunar eclipse, is almost certainly a composite image made of several different exposure lengths stitched together.

Have any of the astronauts actually seen the Great Wall of China from space?

Camelia Galvin (Liverpool)

There is an old story that the Great Wall of China can be seen from the Moon. Of course it can't! The Great Wall is by no means complete and it would be very hard to recognise from a great altitude. Parts of it can be picked out on some photographs from the International Space Station, but it is certainly not conspicuous – it is much too narrow.

Why do space missions always show us the Earth, but never the stars? Is it possible to recognise constellations such as Orion from the Space Station?

John Hennessey (Sheffield) and J Hooper (Bishopstoke, Hampshire)

One of the main reasons for this is that they're looking the wrong way most of the time. The International Space Station has an observation room, called the 'cupola', which is on the Earthward side, but there is nothing similar on the far side.

When the Space Station is on the daylight side of the Earth, the brightness of the planet and the station itself would completely overwhelm the background stars, for the reasons discussed in an earlier answer. If the astronauts looked out of the far side of the Space Station during the night time, when both the station itself and the Earth were dark, they would be faced with a couple of problems. Firstly, the sky would be moving relatively quickly due to the station's rapid orbit around the Earth. This would mean that long-exposure photos would be tricky to achieve without some accurate tracking of the sky. Secondly, there would be so many stars visible. As anyone who has been to a site with a really dark sky will know, observing the sky in such conditions can actually be rather confusing. The brighter stars that make up the constellations can be hard to pick out from the fainter ones that we don't normally see, and identifying the familiar shapes such as Orion and Cassiopeia can be rather difficult.

We are all familiar with images of the Earth and Moon taken by astronauts, but what does the Sun look like from orbit?

Christopher Harper (Nailsea, Bristol)

Neither of us has ever been into space, and there are indeed very few pictures of it, so we need to rely on the account of an astronaut who has seen it. The British-born astronaut Piers Sellers, who has appeared on *The Sky at Night*, explained that the Sun is an incredibly bright white ball, set against a dark black background. It also appears to move incredibly quickly, since the International Space Station orbits the Earth every hour and a half or so. Sunrises and sunsets take a few seconds, and the entire horizon glows bronze and gold for a brief moment before the Sun suddenly appears in all its brilliant glory. Because it reflects the sunlight the station goes through similar colour changes and one can only imagine what a wonderful sight it must be to see with one's own eyes.

How big does the Earth look from space?

Felix Pelling, age 8 (Newport, Wales)

Most astronauts don't actually go that far from Earth. The International Space Station, for example, is only around 300 km above the surface of the Earth, and the Hubble Space Telescope is around twice that. To put this in context, if the Earth were shrunk to the size of a football then the Space Station and Hubble would be less than a centimetre above the surface.

So from orbit the surface looks pretty big, filling half the sky, which is why most images of the Earth from space only show a small portion of the planet. The situation is different, however, if you go to the Moon. The astronauts on the *Apollo 8* mission were the first to see the Earth from that distance, and the sight must have been stunning. In fact, it is often claimed

A photograph of the Earth from space, taken by the *Apollo 17* astronauts in 1972.

that the most reproduced image in the world is the image of the Earth from space taken by the *Apollo 17* astronauts on their way to the Moon. It's hard to say whether this claim is really true, particularly in the digital age, but it certainly sounds plausible.

Of course, there are spacecraft that have travelled even further, and various missions, notably the *Cassini* and *Voyager 1* spacecraft, have captured images of the Earth as a tiny blue dot in an image, which is certainly enough to make one feel very small indeed!

What does space look like?

Matthew Manship, age 8 (Newport, Wales)

Well, one can't see space itself, since space is defined as the absence of anything, but the view *from* space is one that must be very impressive indeed! One of the biggest differences must be that the sky is very dark even when the Sun is up, since there is no atmosphere to scatter the light around. Piers Sellers described the colours as incredibly vivid, with the Earth's oceans appearing the brightest blue you've ever seen.

The other place that people have been to is the Moon, and it is often imagined that it is a very grey place. But the astronauts who have been there say that it is not, and that there are flecks of colour all over the lunar surface.

Do astronauts have a nice time in space?

Ama Boateng, age 7 (Newport, Wales)

As with some of the previous questions, for this we need to turn to someone with more experience in such matters. Piers Sellers told *The Sky at Night* that he had a wonderful time in space, and would recommend spaceflight to everybody. Seeing the world whizz by must be wonderful, and the whole experience one of the most exciting experiences possible. I'm sure it's hard to describe just how much fun it is, and so Piers offered to take everybody with him – though sadly that is not in his power. If you do ever get to go into space yourself, then do let us know just how beautiful it is!

Is it possible for anyone at all to become an astronaut, and if so how would I prepare to become one and who would I apply to?

Sam (North England)

Astronaut training takes a very long time, and normally follows from a good strong education. You typically have to be a scientist, an engineer, a medical doctor, or a pilot, although a small number of schoolteachers have travelled into space. This is primarily because of the roles that astronauts fulfil while in space. While there are of course the pilots who fly the spacecraft, there are scientists and engineers who perform the scientific experiments and more technical parts of the missions.

There are also many stringent physical tests that need to be passed, as the journey into space puts a great deal of strain on the body. We wish you all success, but for full details we would have to direct you to the European Space Agency or NASA.

I am 9 years old (nearly 10). Do you think it would be possible for me to become the first girl on Mars when I become an astrophysicist? Will travel to Mars be possible by then?

Sushila (Devon)

There is no reason why not. Of course you will have to go through all the training and all the qualifications. The main trouble about reaching Mars is the radiation, and this is something we have not yet solved. By the time you are grown up we may well have done so.

If you get to Mars and we are still around don't forget to send us an e-mail or text message!

The International Space Station

How big is the International Space Station, and what does it look like inside?

Erin, age 8 (Newport, Wales)

The International Space Station is pretty big, and the habitable volume is around the size of the cabins of two jumbo jets. In fact, it doesn't look too dissimilar, since the main spaces are lined up in a long tube, though there are a number of bits sticking off the sides. The various segments are made by different nations, such as America, Russia and Europe. Each one has its own feel. On *The Sky at Night*, Piers Sellers described the Russian areas as being like a Jules Verne old-world habitat, while the American ones are more futuristic-looking.

As well as the habitable areas, there is a lot of other structure to the Space Station as well. A main truss carries the solar panels and radiators, and a number of robotic arms and docking ports adorn it at various locations.

The European Space Agency's Automated Transfer Vehicle is a stunning piece of hardware. Are there any plans to allow crew members to get to the International Space Station within the ATV? Is burning it up after its mission not a waste of such a valuable and fully functioning vehicle?

Richard Walder (Eastbourne, East Sussex)

The Automated Transfer Vehicle (ATV for short) could be converted into a manned crew vehicle, but there is a significant amount of infrastructure

The International Space Station, photographed against the backdrop of the Earth.

required as well. For a start, the *Ariane 5* rocket that launches it is simply not designed for manned capsules and the vibrations on launch would kill anyone on board. Secondly, manned missions require additional support on the ground or at sea for when the capsule returns to Earth. While the USA deployed its navy to collect the *Apollo* capsules there is no equivalent for Europe, so it would require the commitment of a number of nations' naval resources to fulfil the same purpose.

The ATV currently has three main roles. Firstly, it takes tonnes of crucial supplies up to the station, including food and water. Secondly, it provides an equally crucial boost to lift the Space Station into a slightly higher orbit – reserving the fuel on board the station for the manoeuvres required for collision avoidance and so forth. And thirdly, it acts as a rubbish dump.

Although packaging is kept to a minimum, there is still a fair amount of waste generated on the Space Station. It would be careless to simply jettison such waste out of an airlock – to do so would only add to the space debris problem – and so the ATV is used for stowage of old equipment and other waste.

The ATV can't remain docked to the Space Station permanently, as the docking port is needed for future missions, so once it has fulfilled these roles there are three possible courses of action. The first would be to move it away, which would leave it susceptible to collision with space debris, and its orbit would eventually decay until it burnt up in the atmosphere, though some parts would probably reach the ground. A second option would be to move it to a higher orbit, where it is away from the majority of junk in orbit, and where it would not experience such severe orbital decay. However, since it would be full of rubbish, it is not clear there would be a future use for it. The third option is to allow it to re-enter the Earth's atmosphere and burn up in a predictable way. When done in a controlled manner, anything that reaches the surface can be made to hit the ocean rather than populated areas.

Of course, if it is ever converted into a manned capsule, the occupants will not be in favour of any of these options, and a controlled re-entry is the only possible option.

I once saw what looked to be a very bright star directly overhead which suddenly blinked out. Could it have been the reflection from the Space Station disappearing as the solar panels moved? Is it possible to track the Space Station's position?

Rochard Tolbart (Lanvallec, France)

This is quite possible. The International Space Station can be very brilliant, even brighter than Venus when the solar panels are in a favourable position.

When visible, the Space Station can be seen to move relatively quickly through the sky, normally from west to east, typically taking a few minutes to complete its journey. It is only a few hundred kilometres up, but this means that it can remain in sunlight for a couple of hours after sunset down on the ground. Although it does change its orientation slightly over time, this would not be sudden, and it probably disappeared because it went into the Earth's shadow. You can track the location of the brightest satellites online, including at the excellent website www.heavens-above.com.

Dangers of Space Travel

How much radiation hits the surface of the Moon compared to the Earth, and how did the spacesuits manage to protect against it? Can they be used to clean up radiation here on Earth?

John Restick (Irvine, Ayrshire)

The radiation received in low-Earth orbit is not too dangerous, equivalent to 2 or 3 chest X-rays per day. This sounds high, but is actually fairly small when compared with the radiation normally received throughout a lifetime. On the Moon the situation is different, and the radiation is more dangerous. In fact, any astronauts on the surface of the Moon during a solar flare would probably be killed.

The spacesuits are designed to protect against some of the radiation, but not all of it. The knowledge transfer is actually the reverse of what is suggested in the question, with the technologies used in the nuclear industry being used to protect astronauts, so in fact spacesuits are being used to help clear up radiation on Earth. At the moment, we have much more experience with nuclear reactors than spaceflight, but perhaps in the future that may change and spaceflight will be used to advise the applications here on Earth.

The Foreseeable Future

Now the Space Shuttle has been retired, what are the prospects for future manned space travel?

Steven (Edinburgh)

At the present moment, we depend upon the Russians and their *Soyuz* capsule, though China, Japan and India will probably have manned vehicles in the foreseeable future. The *Dragon* capsule made by SpaceX, a commercial company in the USA, is a possibility, along with a number of competitors. It is likely that these private companies will be used, along with the Russian vehicles, to take astronauts to the Space Station. We should also remember the possible development of European manned space capsules, based on the Automated Transfer Vehicle that currently acts as a cargo transport, though that is some way off.

NASA are in the process of developing a multi-purpose crew vehicle that could be used to take astronauts to a range of destinations, be that Earth orbit, a nearby asteroid, a satellite in need of repair, or even Mars. The crew vehicle will be launched on a new rocket, but the first routine flights of that are not likely until the end of the decade.

Will so-called 'space tourism' ever become available to the general public, rather than just the very rich?

Gary Holmes (Swadlincote, Derbyshire)

I [CN] would say that there is no reason why not. After all, space tourism is to us what normal airtravel would have been to the Victorians. Although the cost is currently very high, the first aeroplane journeys were similarly expensive. The key development will be the use of low-altitude spaceflight for travelling from one place to another, at which point it will become economical and affordable – at least until the fuel runs out.

When the USA decided to beat the USSR to the Moon, they scrapped the elegant X-15 spaceplane programme for the more expedient Saturn V delivery system. Why haven't current space programmes pursued this approach to manned spaceflight?

Gwyn Roberts (Cramlington, Northumberland)

A number of programmes along these lines are being planned, including one here in the UK called Skylon, though they are at a relatively early stage. With Skylon, for example, the current effort is focused on simply proving that the *concept* is correct. The immediately obvious advantage of a spaceplane is that it can be reused, though that was never fully achieved with the Space Shuttle. The next major step is to develop an engine that can act like a jet engine in the air, but a rocket engine in space. Both use a combination of hydrogen and oxygen as fuel, but in the lower atmosphere the oxygen can be extracted from the air itself. The major challenge is developing an engine that works at both low and high speeds, and that can keep everything cool enough.

Spaceplanes such as Skylon are likely to be at least a decade away (unless the military unveils a miraculous new design that they've been working on in secret!), so for the moment we're stuck with good old-fashioned rockets.

I remember all the excitement surrounding manned space missions and the first Moon landings when I was a kid in the 1960s. There were predictions of men on Mars by the end of the century and even manned missions to Jupiter. Are you disappointed in the lack of manned exploration beyond Earth orbit for the foreseeable future? I most certainly am!

George Jones (Liverpool)

I [PM] am disappointed, but I suppose I ought to have expected it. For heads of nations to get together and work in harmony is something we have never achieved yet, and until we do we are not going to make progress – and neither do we deserve to. As I've said over and over again, the main problem is radiation. Somehow, we've got to learn how to deal with that before we can set out for Mars.

Are there any plans for manned missions to the outer Solar System?

Kathy Fowler (Stockport, Cheshire)

It is too early to start thinking about the outer Solar System. We must first be quite sure that we can travel safely not only to the Moon but also to Mars. There are also a number of logistical challenges in making such long journeys, not the least of which is being able to take enough food!

Given the enormous success of robotic missions to the planets, and the advances in computing power since the *Apollo* missions, have we seen the last of manned spaceflight beyond biology experiments in low-Earth orbit?

Brendan Alexander (Co Donegal, Ireland), Dan Donnelly (Southampton, Hampshire) and Paul Scott (Plymouth, Devon)

I would say not. Say what you may, but there are things that humans can do that robots simply can't. Some things are only possible with an intelligent and adaptive response to events, and at the moment robots cannot think for themselves with anywhere near the capacity of the human brain. I find it hard to imagine that the human race is not destined to explore the Solar System and become comfortable working in the cold, hard vacuum of space. Eventually, I would hope that manned space exploration will be as routine as reaching low-Earth orbit is today, or conducting experiments over the winter in Antarctica.

Do you think Britain should be more actively involved in manned space exploration?

Ben Slater (Claverdon, Warwickshire)

Britain has a relatively minor involvement in manned space exploration, but we focus most of our research on unmanned, robotic missions. Manned space missions can serve a purpose, normally where the flexibility and adaptability of a human are key to the mission's success. For example, most of the research being conducted on the International Space Station is in the form of experiments which are run by people.

But manned missions also have a huge potential to inspire people into science. A great many people were inspired by seeing people walk on the

Moon, and the impact of that on the fields of physics and astronomy is probably immeasurable. As a child of the Space Shuttle era, I [CN] was brought up with manned space flight being a regular, if not routine, occurrence, though the majority of scientific discoveries over the past 50 years have been from unmanned missions.

These unmanned satellites do not get the publicity of the space telescopes, with many being involved in telecommunication and Earth observation. An example is Envisat, an Earth-observation satellite which has been monitoring our planet's surface and providing key information following natural disasters around the globe. A number of UK-based companies are world leaders in satellite manufacturing, and in the fields of astronomy and space science Britain is incredibly strong on the world stage. For example, the UK led the design, build and operation of the SPIRE instrument onboard the Herschel Space Observatory, and is leading the MIRI instrument on the James Webb Space Telescope, the successor to the Hubble Space Telescope. A field in which the UK is developing a lot of expertise is that of micro-satellites, tiny but functional satellites which are relatively cheap to build and launch. These can be far more efficient when large satellites are not needed, and are probably the way much of the industry will go.

In Britain we haven't had a rocket programme since the Black Arrow project was cancelled in the 1970s, and so these satellites have to be launched on foreign launch systems. This is often the European Space Agency's *Ariane* rocket, but in the future it is possible, some would say probable, that the rockets being designed and built by private industry will become the dominant method of launching satellites and instruments into space.

In my view, manned missions need to justify the additional cost and effort involved with providing support for people onboard. There is a lot of expertise around the world, primarily from the USA and Russia, but lately also from countries such as China. The cost involved in building up our own expertise in this area would be huge, and I would say that we are right to stick to what we're really good at, which is unmanned missions.

There is nothing to stop us being involved in future manned missions, though. For example, there has been a lot of excitement about future manned missions to Mars. In my view (though of course ESA and NASA don't ask me personally!), such a mission needs to justify the presence of people on board. There is no reason the UK can't use its expertise in planetary science to play a key role in this mission, even if it is not in the glamorous role of walking on the red planet.

A Moon Base

What would it take to get the USA, Europe and Russia together to have a manned scientific base on the Moon in the next 30 years, like that in Antarctica?

P Raiswell (Norwich)

It would take all the nations involved to elect sensible leaders, who can serve mankind and not only themselves. This, unfortunately, may be some way ahead of us yet, and at the time of writing there is no sign of it. Until we learn to work together we are not going to get very far – the remedy is in our own hands. (Personally, I [PM] would take all the current world leaders, put them in a spacecraft, and send them on a one-way journey to Alpha Centauri!)

There are of course many other nations with an interest in space research: China, India and Japan to name only three. If there is another space race, I expect it will be between the West and China. I hope there isn't another space race, however, because it puts true cooperation back by many years.

We know that the Moon is a varied and fascinating place. If the next mission to land on the Moon was suddenly back on, where would you want it to land and why?

Julia Wilkinson (Rochdale, Lancashire)

I [PM] am sure it was right to call off the Moon landings after number 17. If we'd gone on, we'd have learnt more about different areas of the Moon, but probably nothing fundamental, and sooner or later something would have gone wrong, with tragic results. If I had to choose a site now for the next mission, I would unquestionably go to Aristarchus, the brightest crater on the entire Moon with an unusual surface, and where a number of transient lunar phenomena (TLP) have been reported. So Aristarchus is my choice. Others may have many different ideas.

I [CN] would go for the south pole of the Moon, as it is the one location where there are peaks in almost permanent sunshine. The crater nearest the south pole is called Shackleton Crater, after the famous explorer to Earth's south polar region. This would provide an excellent place to put solar panels for power, and would have relatively easy access to parts of the Moon not visible from Earth. There have even been proposals for a roving base. While that would allow the ability to move to different locations and examine the Moon in more detail, the primary goal of a mission to the Moon would seem to be to prove that we can set up a base on another astronomical body. For that, I would say a static base is more suitable.

When we have a base on the Moon, what will be the first kinds of experiments to be carried out?

James West (Kenilworth)

I [PM] would say medical research, a physics laboratory and an observatory. A lunar hospital may sound far-fetched now, but it will soon be a reality. There is so much medical research that can be carried out on the Moon that can't be carried out down here on Earth.

There would probably be further investigations into the possibility of growing plants in lunar soil. While it also sounds far-fetched, it may be possible to develop some species that can thrive. Of course, there won't be substantial crops for many years, and lunar residents may have to resort to eating lichens, mosses and dandelions.

Should there be international collaboration to make further Moon landings, or should we set our sights directly on Mars?

Andrew Dean (Oakham, Rutland)

I [PM] would say we've got to conquer the Moon first. I believe the first trip to Mars won't be to Mars at all, but in fact to its tiny satellite Deimos, with the development of an international base there.

The American administration has proposed a journey to visit a near-Earth asteroid. This would provide different challenges to landing on the Moon or Mars, and would allow us to prove that people are able to live and work in deep space, well away from the gravitational pull of planets or satellites. Such experience will be vital if we are to be able to service spacecraft in locations far from Earth.

Could it be possible to one day have automated industry on the Moon to build technology, generate power, and mine the regolith?

Paul Metcalf (Suffolk)

I [PM] see no reason why not, and there is no reason why we shouldn't. There are arguments about destroying the pristine surface of the Moon, but the Moon has never had any life on it to complain. Automated technology is already very well developed here on Earth, and the Moon is an ideal place to deploy it. The manned missions into space should be reserved for activities that require an intelligent, adaptive operator, and the routine tasks left to robots.

Living On Mars

Will people land on Mars in our lifetime?

Dee Parker (Essex), Nick Howes (Cherhill, Wiltshire), William Arinze (Kingston, London) and Trevor Erry (Bromwell, Kent)

If we solve the radiation problem, then yes, but without that, then no. We have the technology to take craft to Mars and are well on the way to developing the ability to return them, but we are at a loss as to how to deal with the solar radiation that would be fatal to any Martian explorers.

What are the logistics involved in a manned mission to Mars, and what would the minimum return journey duration be, including the stay on the planet?

N.J. Anderson (Southsea, Hampshire)

I [PM] would foresee a base on the satellite Deimos before heading down to Mars. It's much easier to land on Deimos – in fact more of a docking operation than a landing. From there, trips down to Mars would be significantly simpler. In terms of a round-trip duration, it would probably be a couple of years. The journey time to Mars is about six months, and a similar duration to return, and the opportunities come up roughly once every two years. So six months out, a year on the planet's surface, and then six months back from Mars.

Of course, leaving Mars is significantly more difficult than leaving the Moon due to the higher gravity, and so more fuel would be required. The easiest way of obtaining the fuel would be to extract the key components from Mars itself, probably from sub-surface water ice. Of course, any explorers would also need to eat, and so the ability to produce food and drink while on Mars would be a key requirement. Water is already recycled on the International Space Station, but growing food is much more complicated. The Martian soil is not without nutrients, but making plants hardy enough to survive will be challenging.

Is a mission to Mars really feasible given the amount of time it would take and the radiation the astronauts would be exposed to?

Jeff Brown (Whitstable, Kent)

We do not currently have all the technology required to visit Mars, but we are on the way to developing much of it. For example, we know we can land probes on Mars and are developing the capability of returning them, and so a return trip is a matter of technological engineering rather than fundamental science. There are other technologies, such as the production of fuel on Mars, for which we know the processes required but which we have yet to demonstrate on a large enough scale. The development of these technologies will take time, and very likely a number of unmanned probes to the Martian surface and back, before we ever try them with people on board.

Would you support volunteers being sent on one-way missions to Mars?

Paul Connelly (Manchester)

It is very rare for people to sacrifice their lives in the service of science, at least knowingly. It's not clear that we would gain a whole lot from such a venture, and I imagine the public outcry would be rather loud. Besides, there would probably be a distinct shortage of volunteers, and you can certainly count both of us out!

The setting up of a permanent colony on Mars is a long, long way off, but I [PM] believe such a thing will exist at some point in the future. When such a facility is there, then sending people to live their lives on Mars would definitely be possible, and I'm sure there would be more volunteers.

If offered by NASA, would you swap your 700 shows in return for a one-way trip to Mars?

Graham Hall (Barry, Wales)

Quite simply, no, thank you very much!

Having been born after the space race and Moon landings, I feel part of a generation that has given up on manned space exploration. Will the new focus towards Mars reignite a new space race in my lifetime?

Nigel Somerville (Coleraine, Northern Ireland)

I [PM] hope it won't be a space race, but a spirited collaboration. Given the right leadership, it could happen so easily. It is merely a case of choosing the right leaders and having their policies continue for longer than an election period – so far we have been singularly unsuccessful at that!

I have heard that Mars has no magnetic field, and so can't protect its atmosphere from the solar wind. If this is so, how will we be able to terraform the planet if it can't hold its atmosphere?

Peter Ainsworth (Manchester)

If we did decide to terraform Mars, we'd have to replenish the atmosphere, which with technology of the (very far) future could probably be done. A thicker atmosphere will create more of a shield from higher energy particles, which may be enough to protect any explorers or colonists. There are also pockets of magnetic field over the surface of Mars, thought to be due to particular rock formations, and while these are incredibly weak compared to the Earth's magnetic field they may provide some small protection from solar radiation.

Worlds Apart

Do you think it will be possible to live on another planet, and how long do you think it will be before we do so?

Robert Gaughan (Ealing, London) and
Mike Haywood (Sittingbourne, Kent)

I'm sure that it will one day be possible for people to live on another planet indefinitely, and even reproduce there. In our Solar System, Mars seems to be the only possible destination, and the first manned missions there are decades off. In terms of full-scale colonies, I would say that we are at least century away, though there can be little doubt that it will eventually happen. It is simply a matter of overcoming the technological challenges.

Is there an easy way to terraform a planet, and how far away from planetary engineering are we?

Terence Gibbons (Durham)

Terraforming is an immense feat of engineering, and we are nowhere near at the moment. The scale of the industry involved is absolutely huge. Planetary atmospheres are also incredibly complicated, and depend on a careful balance of many factors. These can range from the balance between oxygen and carbon dioxide, which on Earth is controlled by plant life, to the absorption of carbon into the oceans. One of the biggest problems with trying to recreate the Earth's atmosphere on another planet is that we don't even know exactly how it works, and we'd be sure to miss something crucial. Some of the largest mass extinctions on Earth are suspected to have been due to sudden climate change, possibly caused by volcanic activity or the sudden release of methane from the oceans. After all, we would look particularly stupid if we allowed an extinction event to take place on a planet we had just terraformed and populated.

For the time being, terraforming lies in the realm of science fiction. Mind you, television itself would have been science fiction a couple of hundred years ago!

The Distant Future

If you could travel to anywhere in the Solar System, where would you like to visit and why?

Colin Ashley (Wokingham, Berkshire), Andrew Halford (London) and Steve Attwood (Birmingham)

Another question I [PM] find very hard to answer. There are so many places I would like to go, provided of course there was a guarantee of a return ticket. All in all, I think I'll go back to Mars. After all, it's less unlike the Earth than any other planet, and although there are no Martians, or little green men, there's still the chance of finding very primitive life forms.

I think I [CN] would like to visit Titan, Saturn's largest moon. It's the only other place in the Solar System we know of that has lakes and rivers, albeit made of hydrocarbons such as ethane and methane rather than water. It would be a truly alien world, with stunning vistas. Of course, the skies wouldn't be very clear due to its thick atmosphere, but on the way there I'd hope to have a wonderful close-up view of the planet Saturn and its magnificent rings!

If you could travel to any part of the Universe instantly and come back alive, where would you like to visit?

Paul Coomber (Gloucester)

I [PM] would find this question easier to answer if I knew more about the Universe, for we have to remember that once we go beyond our tiny Solar

System our knowledge is very restricted. Certainly I would like to go to a planet where life might not be intolerable, but as yet I can't name one. I think, Chris, this is more your line...

I [CN] would take advantage of the opportunity of seeing some of nature's most stunning sights. I think a point way out beyond the Galaxy would be an ideal place to get a view of our local part of the Universe, seeing both the Milky Way and the Andromeda galaxy from afar. This would provide an unprecedented view of the far side of the Galaxy and give a sense of scale that simply isn't possible from here on Earth. I'd also take a decent telescope, though, as I'd want to try to get a picture of home – or at least the Sun – from such a great distance.

Do you think it will ever be possible for us to travel to another star system?

Ben Slater (Claverdon, Warwickshire), Brian Rothwell (Manchester),
Neil Rathod (Essex), Paul Foster (Clapham, London),
Tim Graham (Kingston-upon-Thames, Surrey) and Philip G (Canterbury)

I [PM] am not going to say it's impossible, because nothing is really impossible. What I will say is that we will never do it by any propulsion method we can visualise at the moment. There must be some fundamental breakthrough and I've no idea what form it would take. Time travel, teleportation, warp travel... all these are science fiction at the moment. We must remember that television was science fiction around a century ago. Of course, other races far in advance of ourselves may have managed this, and have mastered the secrets of interstellar travel. This means that if they so wished they could visit us, and flying saucers and UFOs are not absolutely out of the question. All I can say is, I would like to see one land. If it did, and a little green man came out, what would I say? I would say, 'Good evening, tea or coffee?'

Just as TV films are disassembled, transmitted and reassembled for viewing instantaneously, might it be possible to perform a similar process in the future to transport human bodies to distant planets once a receiving facility has been established?

Arthur Moore (Leeds)

This would be teleportation, which for the moment is firmly in the realm of science fiction. In television, the particles that make up the image are completely different from those of the original, and are not transmitted instantaneously. The signals are transmitted using radio waves, and so travel at the speed of light. While on Earth the time delay is inconsequential, transferring images from Earth even to the nearest star in this way would take more than four years.

It might seem in principle that it could be possible to record the state (i.e. position and velocity) of every atom in the human body, transmit that information, and put another set of atoms into the same state. There are logistical challenges, such as the fact that there are billions of billions of billions of particles in a human body, and one of the most fundamental problems with such a procedure is something called the Heisenberg Uncertainty Principle. This states that it is impossible to know the location and speed of anything with complete accuracy, which means that even recording the exact state of all the atoms in a human body is impossible, and so recreating it accurately enough at the other end would also be impossible.

Space Missions

Space Navigation

How many spacecraft do we still retain contact with, and how much do we know about their locations and journeys?

Carl Kirby (London)

After more than 60 years of the space age, there are a great many satellites and spacecraft, launched for a very large range of purposes. There have been thousands of launches, but the vast majority of spacecraft do not go beyond Earth orbit. The majority are either Earth observation satellites, normally either for military purposes or environmental monitoring, or communications satellites. One reason for there being so many is that there are more than fifty countries building satellites. Around half of the satellites ever launched have since burned up in the Earth's atmosphere as their orbits have decayed, though there are some which are in orbits too high for this to happen.

A small number of Earth-orbiting satellites are for research, the two most famous probably being the International Space Station and the Hubble Space Telescope, and a fraction of them are dedicated to astronomical research. There are also around 40 operational orbiting observatories, working at different wavelengths. By comparison, there are nearly 50 observatories that are still in orbit but no longer operational, and they are all tracked using ground-based radar and telescopes.

Heading much further out, there are over 20 operational probes scattered through the Solar System, most either orbiting or on the surface of other planets or the Moon, and others travelling through the Solar System. There are nearly three times as many artificial spacecraft that are still somewhere out in space but no longer working. Most of these are not actively tracked, but their locations are fairly accurately known by predicting their orbits and trajectories.

The most distant operational satellite is *Voyager 1*, which is an impressive 17 billion km (nearly 11 billion miles) away from Earth. So how do we track such distant objects?

Well, that's thanks to a network of radio dishes around the world called the Deep Space Network. Roughly equally spaced around the world (in California, Spain and Australia) the three facilities provide full-time communications with spacecraft throughout the Solar System. The network comprises some of the biggest radio telescopes in the world, with the largest being 70 metres in diameter, and they allow the positions and velocities of spacecraft to be measured very accurately. This does, however, rely on knowing the positions fairly precisely, as such large radio telescopes can only observe a tiny part of the sky at any time and a manual search can take a long time. It also relies on the spacecraft working correctly, since they must be emitting radio waves in the direction of the Earth – otherwise it is easy to 'lose' spacecraft, as happened with the *Mars Observer* in 1993!

Once the radio dish has locked onto the spacecraft's position, its velocity is measured by 'Doppler shift' of the transmission, whereby the spacecraft's speed towards or away from Earth changes the exact frequency of the radio waves ever so slightly. At the start of the space age, such as during the

Apollo era, this was a painstaking process which had to be done manually by telescope operators, though now automated computer processors make it much faster and more efficient.

When the telescope has tuned in to the transmissions, the communications can begin. With most missions, it is often a case of getting data back down to Earth, and the spacecraft beams its signals back towards us. The antennas on spacecraft are much more modest than those on Earth, and the rate of transmission is incredibly small. For example, at the normal rate the information is transmitted back to Earth by the *Voyager* spacecraft, it would take around ten seconds to transmit a single text message. The communication is not always one-way, though, and sometimes the mission operators need to send new instructions during the same session. It is quite rare for operators to talk to their missions in 'real time', so such instructions are normally queued up in advance.

Could you please explain the basic principles of space navigation which enables spacecraft to make amazing rendezvous with planets, comets etc.?

Rob Beeton (nr. Henley-on-Thames, Oxfordshire)

Moving a spacecraft is very different to moving a vehicle on the ground or in the air, for two main reasons. Firstly, there is no air resistance, so when you give something a push with its rockets or thrusters it won't slow down unless you give it another push in the opposite direction. This is why some probes whizz past planets or asteroids without stopping – the only way of slowing down enough to enter orbit would be to carry large quantities of fuel.

Secondly, *everything* is moving, so all speeds have to be measured relative to something else. We're used to talking about the speed of cars or aeroplanes in miles per hour, and this is always relative to the ground. That's entirely fair enough when on the Earth – after all, the ground isn't going anywhere! But in space it's very different because even the Earth is moving, as it travels round the Sun at around 30 km per second – a whopping 67,000 miles per hour!

If we want to send a probe to Mars then that speed is certainly useful, because we need to go much faster to overcome the Sun's gravitational attraction just enough to get us out to Mars' orbital distance, which is around 75 million kilometres further out from the Sun than the Earth. A bit of maths and a good knowledge of the laws of gravity will tell you how much fuel you need, and then you just have to go away and build a big enough rocket. In fact, the equations needed are simply the ones worked out in 1687 by Sir Isaac Newton.

But that's only part of the problem, because at the time your probe gets out to Mars' orbit, you also need Mars to be in the same place, otherwise there's very little point in making the journey. This is actually just a question of timing, and is why missions to Mars only launch roughly every two years – this is how often the Earth and Mars are in the best places in their orbits relative to each other.

But even when it gets there, which will take several months, your trusty space probe will be going so fast relative to Mars that if left to its own devices it would fly right past the planet. It would need to slow down quite considerably to go into orbit, which requires a bit more fuel – though some probes get a helping hand by flying through the outermost layers of Mars' thin atmosphere and using friction to slow them down. For encounters with much smaller bodies, such as asteroids or comets, it is more normal for spacecraft to fly straight past. An exception is the Japanese *Hayabusa* probe, which touched down on asteroid Itokawa and returned samples to Earth (though the journey back was very eventful, after a string of bad luck befell the probe).

So what if you want to go further? Well, there's only so far you can get with a normal rocket, and we can't build them big enough to send spacecraft right out of the Solar System. Instead, almost all probes use a technique called a gravitational slingshot to give a speed boost. By flying past a planet or moon in the correct way, a spacecraft can either increase or decrease its speed. This was used extensively by the *Voyager* spacecraft in the 1970s and 1980s, enabling *Voyager* 2 to fly past Jupiter, Saturn, Uranus and Neptune over the course of a 12-year interplanetary mission.

The equations involved might have been drawn up more than 400 years ago, but it all gets very complicated when dealing with planets that are moving and a spacecraft whose mass is changing as it burns fuel. Advances in computing have helped enormously, allowing scientists to run detailed simulations to cover all eventualities. Sometimes things sadly go wrong, either due to human error or equipment malfunction. In 1999, the *Mars Climate Orbiter* was sent on an incorrect trajectory after an embarrassing mix-up between metric and imperial units. As a result it dived too deep into the Martian atmosphere and was destroyed. And more recently, the Japanese *Akatsuki* probe to Venus failed to enter orbit because of a problem with the rockets. With *Akatsuki*, however, all is not lost, as there will be another chance to enter orbit when it passes the planet again in 2016.

We have trouble running public transport to time on our planet, but how on earth do scientists manage to send spacecraft out into the Solar System to arrive on time and to land with such accuracy on another world?

Ian Drain (Portsmouth, Hampshire)

Almost all aspects of a spacecraft's mission are programmed in great detail in advance. The launches are carefully timed to ensure the journey will be as straightforward as possible, and the thruster firings are all pre-programmed. The position and speed of the spacecraft are carefully checked after every manoeuvre, with follow-on manoeuvres executed if necessary.

It doesn't always go to plan, however. The main culprit is normally equipment failure, often involving either thrusters or moving parts. This is why spacecraft are designed to be as simple as possible, generally using reliable components such as explosive bolts rather than electric motors. These are less susceptible to damage which might occur during launch, when the probe will experience huge vibrations.

But spaceflight is still a complicated business, and a reasonable proportion of missions don't actually succeed. In the early days, this was often due to a failure of a rocket, either exploding on launch or failing to reach orbit. Nowadays, this happens less often, though there is still the odd accident. In 1996 the first *Ariane 5* rocket self-destructed less than a minute after launch, because of a software bug. Two consecutive *Taurus* rockets failed in 2009 and 2011, when the fairing which protects the payload failed to separate, leaving the rockets much too heavy. And of course the most tragic launch failure, which occurred on 28 January 1986, was when the Space Shuttle *Challenger* tragically broke apart less than two minutes into its flight, resulting in the loss of all seven crew members.

Missions to other planets are often less successful than one might imagine, too. Of the 38 missions to Mars since the 1960s, only half have been successful. The majority of the failures were in the 1960s and 1970s, and mostly from the USSR, though NASA had its own string of spectacular bad luck in the 1990s when it lost three of its six Mars missions.

The loss of missions is tragic, but we must remember that there are many, many successful missions which have performed far above their design parameters. The *Voyager* spacecraft are still going strong after more than 40 years in space. And the Mars rovers *Spirit* and *Opportunity* have both long outlived their original mission lifetime of 90 days. *Spirit* lasted six years before becoming stuck in a sand trap, and *Opportunity* has travelled more than 30 km over the surface of the red planet. *Cassini* is continuing to discover what weird and wonderful surprises are harboured by Saturn and its many moons, from the methane lakes of Titan to the fountains of Enceladus. This exploration of the ringed planet's system requires a large number of manoeuvres, though wherever possible the mission operators use gravity slingshots from the moons to adjust *Cassini*'s course, saving the precious fuel for when it is required.

After more than 50 years of the space age, mankind's ability to send probes around the Solar System is only increasing, with more and more missions doing us proud.

How is it that spacecraft are able to avoid collisions with unobservable space rocks and other debris that might be randomly traversing their intended path?

Ian Zanardelli (London)

Space is not entirely empty, and there are billions of tiny particles of dust in the Solar System, as well as much larger rocks, asteroids and planets. But space is also really big, and the chances of collisions are very small. The problem is that when they do happen, the collisions can do considerable damage because of the high speeds involved. There is very little that can be done about the collisions, as most of the particles are far, far too small to be seen, let alone tracked. Of the spacecraft that have been lost en route to their destinations, it is possible that some were caused by impacts from space debris, though there is no way of knowing for sure.

To protect against such impacts, most spacecraft have shielding on their leading surfaces, which become pock-marked by impacts of tiny micrometeorites. The biggest problem, though, is not from particles of dust or rock, but from cosmic rays. These are very high-energy particles, normally protons and electrons, which travel close to the speed of light and can wreak havoc with electrical circuits. They have so much energy that if they hit a piece of computer memory they can actually change what is stored. The computers are often designed to mitigate against such circumstances, though this sometimes involves the spacecraft entering 'safe mode'.

Sometimes they do cause serious problems, however, and suspected cosmic rays caused a malfunction in one of the instruments onboard the Herschel Space Observatory in late 2009. The malfunction caused a critical piece of the instrument to be damaged beyond repair, and it was only saved by the presence of a backup system. After the event, software updates ensured that a similar problem could not occur again. Thankfully, such problems are few and far between.

I understand that asteroids on a collision course with Earth are dangerous, and I am glad they are now being investigated; but what about space junk? I imagine it consists of small bits that do no damage when they fall but do they clump together? Are they dangerous to spacecraft or the Earth, and is there any way to collect the debris?

Jessica Allen (Ipswich, Suffolk) and Janet Jubb (Glossop, Derbyshire)

Space junk is a serious concern for spacecraft in orbit, and there are millions of pieces. Most of them are very small, sometimes just frozen particles of unused fuel or flecks of paint. These tiny pieces do not normally penetrate spacecraft, although they can do some damage. Most spacecraft have some form of shielding to protect their vital components, particularly those that might be inhabited by people. Any surfaces which are returned to Earth from orbit, such as the Space Shuttles, are inspected to gather information on these tiny particles. There have been occasions when tiny impact scars have been seen on the Shuttle windows, but none have posed a threat to the integrity of the spacecraft or the safety of its crew.

In 2006, the Space Shuttle *Atlantis* was found to have a small hole, less than 3 mm in diameter but over a centimetre deep, in one of its payload bay doors. If the object that caused that hole had hit an astronaut on a spacewalk, it would have done serious damage. Estimates are that over a six-hour spacewalk an astronaut has a 1-in-31,000 chance of being hit by a small piece of space debris.

Although these pieces are very small they pack a big punch when they hit something. This is because objects in Earth orbit are typically moving at around 27,000 km per hour (17,000 miles per hour). The collisions are not normally head-on, but the average collision speed is still about 36,000 km per hour (22,000 miles per hour).

Anything larger than a marble is big enough to be seen from the ground, using either radar or optical tracking telescopes. Although they can't always be tracked, these can still pose a significant threat to spacecraft, and are too large to shield against. For example, an aluminium sphere 1 cm in diameter, about the size of a standard marble, would have the same impact energy as a cricket ball travelling 2,600 km per hour, or a small car travelling at 60 miles per hour.

Objects larger than a cricket ball are actively monitored and tracked, and satellites (at least those with thrusters) are normally moved out of the way if there is a chance of a collision. And there are much larger pieces, ranging from leftover rocket stages to defunct satellites. In 1996, a French communication satellite was hit by a piece of a rocket that had exploded years beforehand. The piece of debris was around the size of a briefcase and tore off part of a long boom. A decade later, the Chinese caused controversy by deliberately destroying a satellite, creating thousands more pieces of debris. And in 2009 the inevitable happened, when a non-functional Russian satellite collided with a US Iridium satellite, adding further debris to the total.

Most of the pieces of debris have decaying orbits and eventually burn up in the atmosphere after anywhere from a few days to a few years. In fact, some objects are intentionally burned up in the Earth's atmosphere, though where possible they are targeted at the ocean to avoid falling over inhabited areas. It is rare for pieces to make it to the ground, though some can do. The first American space station, *Skylab*, re-entered the Earth's atmosphere in 1979, with some chunks striking Western Australia. The largest man-made object to be re-entered to date is the 135-tonne Russian space station, *Mir*, which was intentionally brought down over the Pacific Ocean in 2001, after an impressive 15 years of service.

With space becoming more and more crowded, efforts are under way to reduce the amount of space junk. While there is little that can be done about the pieces that are up there, mission controllers are working to reduce the debris created by future missions. There are a number of proposals for doing so, but none of them are really feasible with today's technology.

At its closest point, Mars will receive an electronic signal some three minutes after transmission from Earth. So a signal sent to command a Mars rover will arrive after three minutes, and the results viewed three minutes later. In the meantime, the rover could have come to grief and no one would know. How do scientists cope with this real-time problem?

Brian Crane (Norwich, Norfolk)

Mars orbits slightly further out from the Sun than the Earth, at a distance of around 225 million km (140 million miles), compared with Earth's 150 million km (93 million miles). These might be small distances on astronomical scales, but they're still appreciable, even to radio transmissions which travel at the speed of light – a zippy 300,000 km per second (186,000 miles per second). When Mars is opposite the Sun in the sky (what astronomers call 'opposition'), it is at its closest point to Earth, around 75 million km away, but even then light takes around three minutes to travel to us. At its furthest point from Earth, when it is around the other side of the Sun, it takes more like 15 minutes.

So Brian is absolutely correct: a signal from Earth will take at least three minutes to get to Mars, and at least another three to get back. How do the rovers *Spirit* and *Opportunity* avoid crashing into anything? Well, first of all, like most space missions, the rovers are not driven in 'real time' – that is, there isn't anyone with a joystick driving them (as fun as that would be). All the driving is planned well in advance. And secondly, they travel very slowly, so they don't go very far in six minutes. Of course when they're near the edge of a cliff, such as when the *Opportunity* rover drove to the edge of Victoria Crater, 'not very far' could be far enough to send them over the edge, so the drivers are very careful.

But *Spirit* and *Opportunity* have another trick up their sleeves. As well as sending instructions (such as 'drive forward two metres', 'probe that rock', etc.), the mission operators can also send software updates. Both rovers have some automatic software that allows them to monitor their surroundings using 'HazCams' while driving, and to stop if they see a potential problem. Sadly, this didn't stop *Spirit* from getting stuck in a hidden sand trap, ultimately leading to its demise, but *Opportunity* is still going strong. Driving further and faster than before, *Opportunity* has made the impressive 12 km journey to the rim of Endeavour Crater.

Of course, there are probes much further out than Mars. The most distant probe we're still in contact with is *Voyager 1*. Launched in 1977, it is now more than 17 billion km (10 billion miles) away from Earth. Light takes over 16 hours to travel this distance, making a round trip nearly a day and a half long. It's a good job it doesn't like meaningful conversation!

Rockets and Propulsion Systems

It required enormous rocket engines to launch the *Apollo* crew from the Earth, but how did the much smaller rockets on the lunar lander lift the craft from the Moon? The Moon is smaller and has less gravity, but that does not seem enough to explain the discrepancy.

Nick Stone (Bournemouth, Dorset)

Nick is correct that the Moon is smaller, and therefore the gravitational pull at its surface is lower – about one-sixth that on the Earth's surface. But gravity is not the only difference. Let's compare the two cases briefly: the Saturn V rocket that launched from Earth, and the Lunar Module (LM) that returned from the Moon. The Saturn V rocket which launched the *Apollo* astronauts from Earth was composed of three stages, and between them they provided around 500 times as much thrust as the much smaller rocket that lifted the Lunar Module from the Moon. But they were lifting *very* different objects. The Saturn V, which was over 111 metres (363 feet) tall weighed in at around three thousand tonnes at launch. But the vast majority of that was fuel and rocket stages, which were dropped off as their fuel was used.

In fact, the Saturn V was only designed to take about 45 tonnes to the Moon, and around two-thirds of that was the Command and Service Modules, both of which stayed in lunar orbit, while the 15-tonne Lunar Module descended to the Moon. And on lift-off from the Moon, the descent stage remained there, leaving just the ascent stage to return to lunar orbit – and that only weighed about five tonnes.

Lunar module (descent stage)
10 tonnes

Lunar module (ascent stage)
5 tonnes

Command module
5 tonnes

Service module
25 tonnes

The entire Lunar Module, which travelled to the Moon tucked behind the Command and Service Modules, weighed just 15 tonnes, and only the 5-tonne ascent stage needed to lift off from the Moon. Only the 5-tonne Command Module returned to Earth.

So the mass difference is the major factor in why the rockets are such different sizes: one is lifting three thousand tonnes off the Earth's surface, while the other is lifting just five tonnes from the Moon. In principle, there's no limit to the mass of object we can get to the Moon, it's just a case of accelerating it to a high enough speed that it can escape Earth orbit. But the larger the mass, the larger the thrust you need. This is why the Saturn V rockets were built in stages, with the spent stages falling away when their fuel was exhausted. This decreased the mass of the rocket, and meant that the later stages needed less powerful engines.

The vast majority of spacecraft and satellites launched today go into low-Earth orbit, which is a few hundred kilometres above the surface. A relatively small number go into Geostationary Orbit (about 36,000 km away) or beyond, requiring an additional rocket stage to be used. For that reason, the Saturn V is still the most powerful launch vehicle ever built. In 1973, a Saturn V launched the American space station *Skylab* into orbit, along with an *Apollo*-style Command and Service Module, which all weighed around 90 tonnes. The mighty Saturn V even managed this without the use of the third rocket stage, yet none of the today's rockets could even begin to match it.

How long is a light year, and how long at current spacecraft speeds would it take to travel one light year?

David (Oswestry, Shropshire)

Light travels pretty quickly, at around 300,000 km (186,000 miles) every second, which equates to around one foot per nanosecond. At the start of the twentieth century, Albert Einstein realised that this speed is the ultimate speed limit in the Universe, and as far as we know nothing can travel faster. Furthermore, because the speed of light (in a vacuum) is constant we can measure huge astronomical distances by the time it takes light to traverse them.

So while 300,000 km is a long way, it's not very far in astronomical terms. In fact, it's only three-quarters of the way to the Moon. So radio transmissions to the *Apollo* astronauts took over a second to get to them, and the reply took just as long to get back. The Sun, at a distance of 150 million km (93 million miles), is eight minutes away in terms of the light-travel time, so from Earth we are actually seeing the Sun as it was eight minutes ago. We can call this distance eight light-minutes.

Area of detail shown on page 356

Launch escape system

Apollo Payload (to the Moon)
45 tonnes

Third stage
120 tonnes

Second stage
480 tonnes

Height: 111 metres

First stage
2,300 tonnes

The mighty Saturn V, the most powerful
rocket ever built, weighed in at 3,000 tonnes
and stood 111 metres tall, and was designed
to send a mere 45 tonnes to the Moon.

Pluto, for example, is around six light-hours away. So if you're ever looking at Pluto through a telescope in the middle of the night, remember that you're seeing it as it was at around teatime! But even this is only a tiny fraction of a light year. Travelling 300,000 km every second, over the course of a year light can cover nearly ten million million km (six million million miles). That's more than 60,000 times the distance from the Earth to the Sun, and over 2,000 times the distance from the Sun to the most distance planet, Neptune.

But even this vast distance is still only on our doorstep. Proxima Centauri, the nearest star to us, is a little over four light years away. The fastest man-made object to leave the Solar System is the *Voyager 1* spacecraft, which gained speed using gravitational slingshots around Jupiter and Saturn. It is now 16 light-hours away, but that is less than a five-hundredth of a light year. Although the Sun's gravity is constantly slowing *Voyager 1* down, the spacecraft is too fast to be stopped. At its current speed of 17 km per second it would take *Voyager 1* 17,000 years to travel one light year. With today's technology, interstellar travel requires a lot of patience.

For man to reach beyond our Solar System would require propulsion not in use today. Can you conceive of an energy form that would propel future manned space exploration? Einstein said that the speed of light could not be surpassed, but could he have been wrong?

Jamie Smith (Pudsey, West Yorkshire)

The rockets in use today to launch spacecraft are all based on chemical reactions, normally the reaction between hydrogen and oxygen. This is how the Saturn V rocket sent *Apollo* astronauts to the Moon in the 1960s and 1970s. The principle of rocket flight is fairly simple, and is based on the conservation of momentum. The momentum of an object is its mass multiplied by its velocity, and without *external* forces the total momentum of something must stay constant. A tiny bit of fuel ignites, and sends material speeding out the back of the rocket. To compensate, and to keep the total momentum constant, the rocket accelerates forwards (which in the case of rockets is usually upwards relative to Earth), but since it is so much more massive than the fuel streaming out the back it only gains a little bit of speed. It therefore takes a lot of little bits of fuel to send the rocket upwards, which is why the Saturn V was 111 metres tall and weighed 3,000 tonnes, all to get the 45 tonnes of *Apollo* spacecraft to the Moon. As discussed previously, the majority of the weight of the Saturn V is the rocket, including the fuel required to get the immense craft off the ground.

The same principle can be used, with a different mechanism for sending the fuel out the back at high speeds. From the early days of rocket development, back in the 1940s and 1950s, US scientists were looking at using nuclear explosions instead of the chemical reaction. While a launch from the ground would cause a lot of nuclear fallout (unfeasible on both environmental and political grounds!), it was considered to be a viable option in space. While there would not be significantly more thrust provided by a nuclear rocket than by the chemical rockets in use today it would be much more fuel efficient, with a relatively small amount of fuel required to get the same thrust.

This 'Project Orion', as it was called, was always controversial, but was finally ended by a nuclear test ban which prohibits nuclear detonations in space. Even without the political problems, there are a number of serious technical challenges. For example, the rocket has to be able to withstand the detonation of a nuclear bomb behind it, and at a rate of roughly one detonation per second. The technique was suggested for interplanetary or even interstellar travel, with theoretically achievable speeds of around one-tenth the speed of light. This would cut the journey time to Alpha Centauri to decades rather than millennia, but would require far larger structures than we can currently build in space. It was even suggested that the nuclear explosions be replaced with antimatter explosions, though the creation and storage of sufficient quantities of antimatter, which annihilates normal matter when they come into contact, is far beyond our current capabilities.

A technology that is in use on current spacecraft is the ion engine. This works on the same principle, sending tiny quantities of fuel out the back at high speeds, but the fuel in this case is charged particles, or ions. The ions are accelerated to high speed using electric fields, so there are no explosions involved. And while the resulting thrust is very low, making such technology unsuitable for rocket launches, the engine is incredibly efficient. This kind of propulsion is ideal for long voyages, and was used on the *Hayabusa* mission to the asteroid Itokawa, as well as the *Dawn* mission to the asteroid Vesta and the dwarf planet Ceres. While the ion engine provides *Dawn* with a constant but gentle push, it is not powerful enough to launch a rocket, which still requires the chemical reactions we are used to.

But there are methods which do not rely on carrying fuel on board. A solar sail, for example, uses the very slight pressure generated from sunlight hitting a surface to propel craft. The force is incredibly small, and the sail is made of microscopically thin sheets of material spread over large areas. The Japanese *Ikaros* mission uses a sail less than a hundredth of a millimetre thick and around 20 metres across. The sail is also fitted with solar panels to provide power for the communications equipment and scientific instruments, and the reflectivity of the sail can be changed to provide the ability to steer. *Ikaros* travelled to Venus and was a successful technology demonstration, as was NASA's smaller *Nanosail-D*, which performed tests in Earth orbit. The next step planned by JAXA, the Japanese space agency, is to launch a much larger solar sail which could be combined with an ion engine to travel to the planet Jupiter.

These technologies are based on our current technical abilities, but the world of science fiction goes far beyond what we can achieve at present. Propulsion methods such as 'hyperdrives' and 'warp drives' are generally based on the concept of warping space, or travelling in an additional dimension. Others use the idea of using or creating a wormhole, a tear in the fabric of space which links up with another part of space many light years away. While wormholes are mathematically possible in some circumstances, they are not thought to be stable and we certainly have no evidence that they even exist. To make it worse, the experience of entering a wormhole would likely be similar to that of entering a black hole, and we don't know any way of surviving that.

So forgetting fanciful ideas of hyperspace, it's possible that we'll develop or discover a propulsion technology which is more efficient than the ion drive, or more powerful than our chemical rockets. If Robert Bussard was right in the 1960s, we might be able to use electric fields to gather hydrogen from interstellar space and power nuclear fusion engines. It would be a weak thrust, but over the course of a century or so a craft could achieve reasonable fractions of the speed of light, though would never be able to break that speed limit. The interstellar travel time would be reduced to centuries, though on reaching their destination the ship's inhabitants would be the descendants of the original crew.

We know of no way of accelerating anything to faster than the speed of light. That this limit exists is one of the requirements of Einstein's theory of relativity, and there is not yet any evidence to suggest that the theory is wrong.

So it looks like the speed of light is going to remain the ultimate speed limit for a while. But I [CN] wouldn't want to prejudge what our descendants could achieve. If you're reading this in the year 1,000,000, a part of me is really hoping that you're doing so while lying on the beach on an idyllic planet, bathing under the glow of two suns and speaking in alien tongues to the native inhabitants. But that will have to stay as my dream for a while yet, I suspect.

Solar System Exploration

Is it possible to send a person to Venus, land on the surface for 20–30 minutes despite the enormous pressure and heat, collect a rock sample and then leave?

Paul Metcalf (Suffolk)

The first probe to land on another planet was the Soviet *Venera 7* lander in 1970, which returned data from Venus's surface for 23 minutes. In fact, the USSR had a great deal of success with Venus missions. In total, nine Soviet probes landed on the surface and successfully sent back data. The survival record is held by *Venera 13*, which transmitted for just over two hours.

The problem, as Paul correctly states, is the temperature and pressure. On the surface, the temperature soars to 450 Celsius (840 Fahrenheit), and the pressure is nearly 100 times that on Earth. There would be immense challenges involved in keeping someone alive in those conditions. If all the astronaut is doing is collecting a rock sample, then I would say don't bother sending them – just send a robotic lander. It's much cheaper, it's been done before, and the consequences of failure are somewhat smaller!

One feature that hasn't been achieved before is the return to Earth. To make the return rocket a feasible size, it would be sensible to return just a tiny capsule containing the rock. But the rocket and its fuel would also need to be protected from the temperature and pressure. While rockets involve hot, explosive reactions, the hydrogen and oxygen fuel is normally stored in liquid form, relying on very cold temperatures. This doesn't bode very well for a planet with surface temperatures above the melting point of lead.

Venus surface: An image from the surface of Venus, taken by the USSR's *Venera 13* spacecraft. The spacecraft survived the immense temperature and pressure for just over 2 hours.

Do you think that Europa should be the prime candidate for robotic exploration in the Solar System considering its potential for hosting extraterrestrial life?

Ben Slater (Claverdon, Warwickshire)

I [CN] think Europa, Jupiter's icy moon, is an incredibly important place to explore, though I don't expect it to be easy. A liquid ocean is thought to exist below the thick layer of ice, and if there is life there it is expected to be below the surface. The thickness is unknown, but is thought to be hundreds of kilometres thick in places, making it very difficult to penetrate.

To make matters worse, the surface of Europa is covered with fissures, so it is possible the surface will change over time. The problems with finding a landing site are compounded by the fact that there is no atmosphere to make parachutes useful, so the spacecraft will need a sophisticated landing system. Additionally, spacecraft in the Jupiter system are plagued by incredibly high levels of radiation from the giant planet's strong magnetic field, which severely limits their lifetime. So while I sincerely hope we explore Europa some day, it won't be easy and it is likely to be several decades before any significant progress is made.

How likely do you think it is that a *Cassini*-like mission might be sent to Uranus, and what might we expect it to find or explain?

Gareth Wilkes (Oxford)

Missions to the outer planets are very challenging and expensive, and take many years, in fact decades, to develop and come to fruition. Take, for example, the *Cassini* mission to Saturn. The project was originally proposed in the 1980s, based on the success of the *Voyager* missions, which flew past Saturn in the early 1980s, but was not launched until 1997. Missions like *Cassini* have a defined set of questions they would like to answer, and in the case of Saturn there are many questions. Specific questions the team wanted to answer included the relationship between the atmospheric cloud layers and its interior, and the variations seen in the planet's magnificent rings.

Saturn is also graced with a large family of moons, and there was specific interest in Titan, one of the largest moons in the Solar System which is surrounded by a hazy methane-rich atmosphere. To investigate this planet-sized moon, *Cassini* carried on board the *Huygens* lander, which descended through Titan's thick atmosphere and produced amazing images of the surface.

But some of the most amazing results from *Cassini* were not direct answers to those questions. Take, for example, the tiny, icy moon Enceladus, which was suspected to harbour a liquid ocean beneath its surface. What was not expected, however, was the jets of salty water being vented from fissures near the south pole of Enceladus, which not only confirmed the presence of the sub-surface ocean but also revealed details of its composition.

By comparison, Uranus is a very different system. It has a ring system, but nowhere near as extensive as Saturn's, and its family of moons does not contain such interesting cases as Titan or Enceladus. The planet itself is considerably smaller, being an 'ice giant' rather than a gas giant, with a thick atmosphere covering a relatively large solid core, and investigation of this atmosphere is sure to yield interesting results.

What is possibly most interesting about Uranus is its past. The planet has been knocked on its side, possibly due to an ancient collision. When *Voyager 2* visited Uranus in 1986, the north pole was pointed directly towards the Sun. Two decades later, a quarter of the way round its long orbit, Uranus has just passed its equinox, and in another twenty years the south pole will be continually sunlit with the northern hemisphere in perpetual darkness. The resulting seasonal variation must be very extreme equivalents of those seen at the Earth's poles. The system may harbour clues as to the cause of Uranus's peculiar orientation.

It is also thought that Uranus has moved around considerably throughout the Solar System's history, perhaps even switching places with the outermost planet Neptune. Such planetary motions are predicted by computer simulations of the formation of the Solar System, and are thought to be a common occurrence in other planetary systems that we see. Investigations of Uranus could provide vital clues as to the Solar System's history. In addition, it now appears that planets with masses similar to Uranus and Neptune are among the most common in the Galaxy, so finding out more about them will be important for understanding these alien solar systems.

As with *Cassini*'s investigation of Saturn, it is likely that the most interesting discoveries would be the accidental ones, which were not predicted or looked for. But unfortunately, there is simply not currently the scientific interest in Uranus that there was in Saturn. While there was a proposal to launch a mission there, it was unfortunately not deemed worthy of further development by the European Space Agency. A mission to Uranus would be fascinating, though I [CN] think it is therefore rather unlikely that one will be launched in the foreseeable future. The next large-scale interplanetary missions are likely to be to Jupiter or Saturn, which I'm sure still have a whole host of surprises left in store for us.

With all the effort and time that has gone into the *New Horizons* probe to Pluto, why does it have such a short operational window when it arrives? Is there any possibility of it approaching other Kuiper Belt objects, such as Eris, Sedna or Makemake?

Kevin Cooper (Fife, Scotland)

New Horizons had the fastest launch of any spacecraft, at almost 60,000 km per hour (37,000 miles per hour), which meant that it already had sufficient speed to be able to leave the Solar System despite the gravitational pull of the Sun. Previous probes, such as *Voyager 1* and *Voyager 2*, achieved this escape velocity by flying past the massive planets Jupiter and Saturn, using their gravity to pick up speed. *New Horizons* also passed Jupiter and picked up enough extra speed to shave nearly three years off its journey.

By the time it reaches Pluto in 2015 *New Horizons* will have slowed a little due to the Sun's gravitational pull, but will still be travelling at 50,000 km per hour (31,000 miles per hour). That is far too fast to go into orbit, for which it would need to be travelling at a fraction of the speed, and it doesn't have enough fuel to slow down enough.

New Horizons will be asleep for most of its eight-year journey from Jupiter to Pluto, and will only wake up less than a year before the flyby. It will pass within around 10,000 km (6,000 miles) of Pluto and 27,000 km (17,000 miles) of its large satellite Charon. The detailed measurements will take place for several weeks either side of the closest approach, but the radio signals will be so weak that it will take another nine months for the spacecraft to transmit all the information back to Earth.

Pluto is located in the Kuiper Belt, a region of the Solar System around five billion kilometres from the Sun, an analogue to the much closer asteroid belt and populated by icy bodies ranging from dwarf planets like Pluto down to little more than rubble. At over 2,000 km across, Pluto is one of the largest Kuiper Belt Objects known, but the region is thought to contain thousands of objects over 100 km in diameter. There's a lot of space at such a large distance from the Sun and these objects are very widely spread out, but mission planners hope that they can direct *New Horizons* towards one or more of these other objects. The other large bodies that we know about, such as Eris, Sedna and Makemake, are unfortunately on the other side of the Solar System. These bodies orbit the Sun very slowly, taking hundreds or thousands of years to complete an orbit, so *New Horizons* can't simply wait for them.

There are currently efforts under way to find any other objects that exist close to *New Horizons'* flight path. Astronomers do this by staring at patches of sky and looking for any moving objects. The job is harder than usual because Pluto, and therefore also *New Horizons'* flight path, is in the direction of the centre of our Galaxy, meaning that the picture is confused by thousands of background stars.

Even without these additional encounters, *New Horizons* will be entering unexplored territory. While the two *Voyager* craft will always be further away, they are both heading in directions away from the main disc of the Solar System. *New Horizons*, by comparison, is travelling in the plane of the planetary disc, and so will be the first spacecraft to explore the Kuiper Belt. This region is very hard to observe from Earth, so having a probe in situ should reveal a great deal about this region of the Solar System, possibly providing clues as to its formation.

Why was the impactor of *Deep Impact* spacecraft made out of copper?

Philip Corneille (Belgium)

The *Deep Impact* mission visited the comet Temple 1, and released an impactor which produced an artificial crater in the nucleus of the comet. The impactor was around the size of a washing machine and weighed around 300 kg. Colliding with the surface at over 20,000 miles per hour, it made a crater around the size of a football field, and sent a large amount of material up into space. The flyby craft observed this ejecta in great detail, in particular the chemical composition.

The impactor was made primarily out of copper in order to minimise the chemical reactions between it and the comet itself, ensuring that the material the flyby craft examined was as pure as possible.

What is the furthest distance man has ever travelled in space?

Khalid Bourne (London)

There are several ways of measuring this. In terms of manned space flight, the furthest man has travelled from Earth is to just beyond the Moon, around 400,000 km (250,000 miles) away. This is peanuts compared to the scale of space, and the vast majority of our exploration has been by robotic missions. In these stakes, the *Voyager* spacecraft hold the record, and will never be caught by any mission launched to date. The *Voyager 1* spacecraft, launched in 1977, is now 17.5 billion km (10.9 billion miles) from the Earth, which is more than 110 times the Earth-Sun distance. Such spacecraft don't travel in straight lines, and *Voyager 1* swept past Jupiter and Saturn on its way out of the Solar System, travelling a total of 23 billion km (14 billion miles).

What for you, Sir Patrick, was the biggest surprise discovery for a space mission?

Alex Tym (Cheshire)

One of the biggest surprises has been the revelation that Saturn's tiny satellite Enceladus is shooting out fountains of water, which means there must be an underground ocean there. But Enceladus is so small it simply ought not to have anything of the kind, and we have to admit that we are completely puzzled. We may not find out more until we send a manned expedition there, and that's not likely to be for a long time yet.

The *Cassini* probe has actually flown through the plumes and studied what they're made of. The fountains appear to come from markings on the surface which have been named 'Tiger Stripes', now known to be deepish valleys only around a hundred metres across at their deepest. The existence of an ocean of liquid water deep inside Enceladus is a complete enigma!

Which space-exploration mission has had the most 'real world' benefit for mankind?

Earl Robinson (Ledbury, Herefordshire)

Space-exploration missions have two major benefits. The first is the most obvious: the advance in our scientific knowledge of our Solar System and the Universe at large. The second is the development of technology and the economic impact that this provides. Many of the technological developments are apparent in our everyday lives, from cordless power tools to smoke detectors, and from medical thermometers to the aerodynamics of golf balls.

It is not necessarily true to say that these technological developments wouldn't have come to fruition without the space programme – after all, NASA were not the first to think of attaching a battery to a power drill!

But the key impact was that NASA *needed* these technologies and so had to develop them, providing some stimulus into the relevant industries.

One could argue that the most beneficial mission was *Sputnik 1*, the first satellite launched in 1957 by the USSR. That proved that space travel was possible, and encouraged rapid development over the following decades. Today, satellites are crucial to many aspects of our lives, from navigation systems to monitoring of large regions following large scale natural disasters.

In terms of space-exploration missions, I [CN] would highlight the fleet of solar observatories, which probe the impact of the Sun on our planet. The Sun has a significant effect on our climate over very long time periods, and in fact the motion and orientation of the Earth and Sun are the dominant influences on our planet's climate over tens of thousands of years. The effect of the Sun on the climate on shorter timescales is much smaller, though is currently undergoing intense study. The knowledge gained will inform us as to whether the Sun is likely to make matters better or worse over time, on top of the changes caused by our impact on the planet.

In addition to the climate, solar flares and ejections of material can threaten many systems that we rely on in our everyday lives. These are accompanied by high-energy particles, which can damage satellites in orbit, as well as electrical and communication systems down on Earth. Such flares and ejections pose a serious threat to astronauts travelling in space, and is arguably the biggest problem presented As we gradually extend our technological fingers further out into space we make ourselves more susceptible to what is often termed 'space weather', and studying it is crucial for the future.

The Bizarre
and Unexplained

If what we knew about the Universe was placed into percentages, how much would be theory and how much would be fact?

David Duly (Co Antrim, Northern Ireland)

There are very many ways of thinking about this, but perhaps the best is to consider what fraction of the contents of the Universe we understand. The current cosmological model includes dark energy and dark matter, which are discussed in more detail elsewhere. Dark matter is material that we can only detect through its gravitational effects. The best indications are that there is around five times as much dark matter as 'normal' matter – i.e. that which everything we see, hear and touch is made of. While we know how much there is, we don't really know what it is made of, and it is fully justifiable to call dark matter a theory at the moment.

Dark energy is even more theoretical, in that we only know that *something* seems to be causing the expansion of the Universe to accelerate. What that something is we know not, and so dark energy is certainly theoretical – even Saul Perlmutter, one of the co-discoverers of the apparent effect of dark energy, has said that it is a place holder term for something as yet unknown. The truly astonishing thing is that dark energy seems to account for around 73 per cent – almost three-quarters – of the energy density of the entire Universe.

That leaves 27 per cent for the normal and dark matter, which is split into around 22 per cent for dark matter and 5 per cent for normal matter. So only around a twentieth of all the 'stuff' in the Universe is normal matter, which we believe we understand reasonably well. And if it wasn't bad enough, only around a tenth of that is stars – the rest is gas and dust between the stars.

This sounds like we know almost nothing, but it must be remembered that almost all the discoveries in astronomy have been led by observations, rather than by theories. Edwin Hubble measured the expansion of the Universe in the 1920s, Fritz Zwicky deduced the presence of 'dark matter' in the 1930s, and teams of astronomers studying supernovae in the 1990s discovered that the expansion of the Universe seems to be accelerating. And our knowledge is continuously expanding. The theory of dark energy is only a little over ten years old, so before that we only knew of a quarter of the Universe. Around 60 years before that we had no knowledge of the possible existence of dark matter, meaning that we only knew of a twentieth. Before the advent of radio astronomy we didn't have a true feel for quite how much gas was in the Universe, so we only really knew of the stars – limiting ourselves to less than one per cent of the contents of the Universe. It was only in the 1920s that we had proof of galaxies outside our own, and since we believe there are somewhere in the region of 100 billion galaxies in the visible Universe, we were only surveying a tiny, tiny fraction of it.

Even many of the known facts are contested, some more justifiably than others. The Big Bang and the expansion of the Universe are widely accepted, though there are a small number of scientists who are trying to find plausible alternative theories to match the observations (so far without success). The presence of dark matter is not completely accepted, with some astronomers (admittedly a minority) investigating the possibility that Einstein's theory of gravity needs to be modified when applied on the largest scales. Dark energy is the most controversial of these, partly because it is a very young idea (15 years is nothing on the normal timescales of fundamental scientific discoveries!) and partly because there is no understanding of what it might actually be, something that makes all scientists rather uneasy. It is simply a name assigned to an observational effect.

Relativity and the Speed of Light

How do we measure the speed of light, and how do we know it is constant?

Rob Hawthorne (Sky at Night cameraman) and Mike Poole (Manningtree, Essex)

The speed of light was first measured using the motion of Jupiter's moons, observing them pass into Jupiter's shadow or cast a shadow on the planet's cloud-tops. It was Ole Rømer who, in 1676, found that the transits of the moons were earlier than predicted when Jupiter was closer to us, and later when it was further away. The reason was that the transits were happening exactly when predicted, but the light took slightly longer to get here when Jupiter was further away, meaning that we observed the transit slightly later. Rømer thus calculated that light travelled at such a speed that it would take 22 minutes to cross the Earth's orbit.

In the 1720s, James Bradley observed that the precise positions of the stars change if you are moving relative to them. This is similar to the reason why the front windscreen of a moving car gets so much wetter than the rear windscreen, though obviously involving much higher speeds! Over the course of a year the Earth does just that, and by observing the star Gamma Draconis, which passed almost directly overhead from Bradley's location, he calculated that light travelled 10,210 times faster than the Earth travelled around its orbit, making the Earth's orbit around 14 light-minutes across.

One of the most precise calculations of the speed of light is to accurately calculate the frequency and the wavelength of a light beam, as the two multiplied together give the speed of light. We now define the speed of light as being 299,792,458 metres per second. In fact, it is exactly that value, as in 1983 the General Conference of Weights and Measures decreed that 'The metre is the length of the path travelled by light in vacuum during a time interval of 1/299 792 458 of a second.'

Thus any further changes to the speed of light are in fact changes to the definition of the length of a metre. This definition is in keeping with that used by Albert Einstein, who treated space and time in a similar way, and used the speed of light to convert from a unit of space to a unit of time.

If the speed of light is variable over significant periods of time then we would need a good deal of rethinking. It appears in some of the most fundamental laws of physics, and so would change the way atoms behaved. Our measurements of the early Universe indicate that atoms have not changed their behaviour, which means that either the speed of light has remained constant, or some other fundamental 'constants' have changed their value to compensate.

Why can nothing travel faster than the speed of light, and what would be the benefits if we could?

Arthur Holden (Woodstock) and Steven Halley (Bridgwater, Somerset)

First of all, it would contravene all of Einstein's theories. Secondly, if you could travel at the speed of light your mass would become infinite and time would stand still, one of which could be considered a disadvantage and the other an advantage. We accelerate particles to within 99.999 per cent of the speed of light in particle accelerators, but we can't actually get any closer due to the immense energies required.

There have been reports from the OPERA experiment, based at CERN in Geneva, that sub-atomic particles called neutrinos have been observed to travel a fraction faster than the speed of light. The experiment relies on precisely timing how long the neutrinos take to travel from a source to a detector 700 kilometres away. It was observed that the neutrinos appeared to arrive around 60 billionths of a second earlier than they should of had they travelled at the speed of light, thus breaking the fundamental speed limit by a tiny amount. Of course, the measurement is incredibly difficult, and relies not only on precise timings, but also on very accurate measurement of the distance they have travelled.

There is much investigation taking place as to the cause of this potentially paradigm-shifting result, though most physicists (including the team who made the measurement) are of the opinion that there are probably additional anomalous effects that have not been taken into account, possibly with the measurements of distances or time. At the same time, different experiments around the world are attempting to reproduce the measurement, though so far none has been successful. Of course, by the time you read this the situation may well have changed (such is the danger with discussing such recent results!), though I [CN] find it very unlikely that Einstein will be proved to be incorrect.

If a spaceship travelling at the speed of light produced a 'headlight' beam, would that beam be travelling at twice the speed of light?

Adrian Alemson (Douglas, Isle of Man)

Well, a spaceship can't travel at the speed of light, so let's imagine one travelling at three-quarters the speed of light. One of the things that Einstein taught us was that the speed of light is a constant and identical for all observers, no matter where they are or how fast they are travelling. So the spaceship would measure the light leaving at the speed of light, and any oncoming vehicles would see it approaching them at the speed of light. This sounds very contradictory, but is just one of many weird effects of travelling at very high speeds.

To a stationary observer, the craft would be approaching very quickly, and so the light would be tremendously 'blueshifted', being shifted up in frequency by a significant factor. At three-quarters the speed of light, that factor is around 50 per cent, so the wavelength of the headlight would appear to be 50 per cent shorter than it would be if the spacecraft were standing still. If the spacecraft had red headlights, then they would appear blue to anyone they were approaching. Similarly, if the spacecraft approached a red traffic light, it would see it as blue – just think of the mayhem on the intergalactic highways!

If the speed of light cannot be exceeded, then what is the relative speed of separation of two objects travelling at more than half the speed of light in opposite directions?

Phil Clarke (Hastings, East Sussex)

One of the odd features of Einstein's theory of relativity is that, when travelling at high speeds, distances and time durations seem to be changed relative to those of someone who is not moving. If two spacecraft left the Earth in opposite directions at half the speed of light, then they would see each other receding at around four-fifths the speed of light. If they increased their speed to four-fifths the speed of light, then to each other they would appear to be travelling away from each other at 97 per cent of the speed of light. No matter how fast a speed they travelled at, they would never observe each other travelling at more than the speed of light.

If a photon travels at the speed of light, it presumably experiences no time passing, so are photons immortal?

Maude Agombar (Salisbury, Wiltshire) and Peter Belcher (Chichester, West Sussex)

The faster an object moves, the shorter the length of time it experiences relative to something that is not moving. Since a photon travels at the speed of light, it experiences no time passing. So while we see a photon take eight minutes to travel from the Sun to the Earth, from its point of view that journey would take no time at all.

So a photon is not really immortal; it simply doesn't experience time at all.

If light travels at 300,000 kilometres (186,000 miles) per second, how fast does 'force' travel? If the Sun were to suddenly 'disappear', how long would it take for the Earth's orbit to be affected?

Andrew Timms (Sussex) and Colin Andrew Price (Northwich, Cheshire)

The force of gravity travels at the speed of light, and so the Sun's loss would be felt just over eight minutes after the Sun disappeared. Of course, anyone still on the Earth would see the Sun disappear at exactly the same time as its gravitational effect stopped, so from our point of view the two things would occur simultaneously.

Does a photon of light have a mass?

Paul (Weymouth, Dorset) and Ken Stephenson (Cockermouth, Cumbria)

A photon has no mass at all. It does have momentum, though, but that is related to the energy of the photon and not to its mass – a photon's momentum is its energy divided by the speed of light. This is the origin of a phenomenon called 'radiation pressure', whereby the momentum of a photon of light can be transferred to an object that absorbs or reflects it, which is how solar sails work.

If you know where the Earth is in relation to other celestial bodies, can you predict where it will be in the future and send a radio signal?

Malcolm Dewey (Bognor Regis, West Sussex)

We can work out fairly accurately where the Earth will be in relation to other celestial bodies, at least over human timescales. Over longer timescales, say millions of years, small effects from tiny objects in the Solar System can add up to generate a large uncertainty in where the Earth can be. The same is true of most of the other large objects in the Solar System, such as the planets. The smaller objects, such as asteroids and comets, are particularly susceptible to tiny effects, sometimes being observed in a slightly different position from where they were expected to be and their positions can sometimes be hard to predict over as short a time as years or decades.

Radio waves travel at the speed of light, which is not an infinite speed but it is pretty quick. It equates to around one foot (30 centimetres) every billionth of a second. This means that every signal we send is in effect communicating with the future, and every signal we receive originated in the past. We often use the speed of light to measure the vast distances in astronomy, with one light year – the distance light travels in one year – being around 10 million million kilometres (6 million million miles). There are examples which can be used to measure shorter distances. For example, the Moon is around one light-second away, so the *Apollo* astronauts were relaying information with a one-second delay, with ground control hearing about it around a second after it actually happened. (During that intervening second the Moon moves about one kilometre around its orbit, though this is too small a distance to require any compensation in terms of communication equipment.) The Sun is just over eight light-minutes away, so radio waves from the Sun tell us what was happening eight minutes ago. The most distant planet, Neptune, is around four light-hours away.

The speed of light is so fast, however, that actually sending useful messages into the future is not possible. Let's consider the Earth moving around the Sun. In another six months, the Earth will be on the other side of the Sun. If we were to send a radio signal in that direction now, however, it would take only around 16 minutes for the signal to get to that point, whizzing straight past and continuing out through the Solar System. In six months' time, the signal we emitted would have travelled a reasonable fraction of the distance to the next nearest star.

Of course, if you were on a spaceship half a light year away, your radio signals would take six months to reach the Earth and so, by the time they got to the Solar System, the Earth would have moved to the other side of the Sun. The situation is slightly more complicated because the signals you would be picking up from the Earth would have left six months previously, so the position you were measuring would be out by six months as well. This is not a problem yet, however, as all the space probes we have ever launched are at distances measured in light-hours. Even the furthest probe from Earth, *Voyager 1*, is only 17 light-hours away, which pales in significance to most astronomical distances.

Why do we say light travels as a wave, rather than in a straight line?

David Gay (Hull)

The proper term for what is usually called 'light' is an 'electromagnetic wave'. It is a combination of electric and magnetic fields oscillating up and down in a wave-like motion. The distance the light moves between consecutive oscillations is called a 'wavelength', and tells us the colour of the light.

The wave does, however, travel in a straight line. Imagine a string, held tightly between two people, which is plucked to start a little wave. The string wiggles up and down, making a wave, but that wave travels along the string in a straight line.

Of course, the path of light can be bent, if it is reflected off a mirror, refracted through a lens (or any other material with a different refractive index), or diffracted around a sharp edge. The same is true of many other waves as well. Waves in the ocean travel in straight lines, but at each point the individual bits of water simply move in small wiggles. This is why a boat out at sea does not get pushed along by the waves, but instead bobs up and down. Water waves are also 'refracted' in a sense, as the shallow water near a beach bends their path to cause them to travel directly towards the shore.

As the furthest galaxies are observed to be accelerating, are their clocks running much slower? Is the age of the Universe 13.7 billion years to an observer in the most distant galaxy?

Alan Jones (Finchley, London)

The apparent acceleration of the distant galaxies is due to the expansion of the Universe, and not because they are really moving away from us with a physical velocity in the normal sense. Therefore the normal rules of time dilation do not apply. Of course, we see the most distant galaxies when the Universe was a lot younger, as the light takes such long periods of time to travel through the cosmos. If we could pick up signals from a cosmic alarm clock in the most distant galaxies observed, it would not yet have passed one billion years.

However, anyone living in that galaxy would be in the same situation, seeing the Milky Way as it was billions of years ago, though they would still measure the Universe as being the same age as we do, at 13.7 billion years.

How much slower does time pass near the Sun than it does on Earth due to the gravitational effect?

Paul Foster (Clapham, London)

The gravitational time dilation on the surface of the Sun is a few million times higher than that on the Earth's surface, and yet clocks would appear to tick a tiny amount slower. The difference would mean that clocks on the surface of the Sun would gain a second every ten days or so.

A somewhat smaller effect is the difference between the time experienced in Earth orbit compared with that on the surface, with the difference being measured as a few parts in ten million million. While this sounds negligible, it means that the clocks on global positioning system (GPS) satellites lose around 45 microseconds per day compared with those on the ground, with around 7 microseconds per day gained by the fact that the GPS satellites are moving very quickly. Since the entirety of GPS is based on timing, these offsets are significant, and would create errors amounting to tens of kilometres per day if not compensated for!

Gravity

**If photons of light are massless, how does gravity bend their path
or prevent them from leaving a black hole?**

Peter Burgess (Gloucester)

The action of gravity can be interpreted as the warping of space (and time).
This means that anything travelling through that region of space – even
photons – will travel along a curved path. In fact, the mass of the objects
that is travelling through space doesn't even matter.

A frequently discussed physics thought experiment is to drop a bullet at
the same time as firing one from a gun sideways. Both bullets actually hit the
ground at the same time, since they both experience the same acceleration
due to gravity – it's just that the one fired from the gun has travelled a
significant distance horizontally as well.

A photon of light experiences the same acceleration due to gravity, and
so a laser beam fired sideways would in principle hit the floor at the same
time as both bullets. The problem is that the photons are moving so fast that
they quickly run out of ground, but if there were enough ground then this
is what would happen. The fact there is not enough ground is what limits
this to being a 'thought experiment', which is merely imagined rather than
actually carried out.

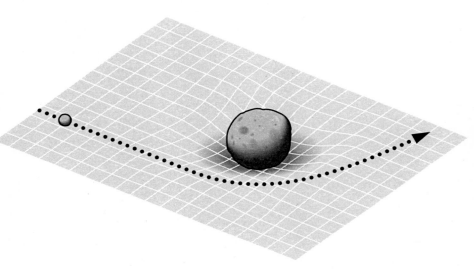

The distortion of space-time by gravity is similar to the distortion of a rubber sheet by a weight. All particles will travel on curved paths, just like a marble rolled across the sheet.

Is gravity really a force, or is it just our perception of the way space is warped by the presence of matter?

Roy Waghome (Leigh-on-Sea, Essex)

To all intents and purposes, in day-to-day life gravity can be thought of as a force, and is well described by Newton's equations, which he wrote down way back in the seventeenth century. For a full treatment of the effect, however, one must consider Einstein's theories of gravity, where it is better imagined as a distortion of space-time. The way this distortion manifests itself is to give the appearance of an attractive force between two objects.

For the vast majority of purposes, Newtonian gravity is accurate enough, and most space probes do not have to take Einstein's theories into account.

The full Einsteinian treatment is only normally required when dealing with incredibly high gravitational fields, such as those near a black hole.

How do we know that gravity has the same strength throughout the whole Universe?

Peter Burr (Brighton)

We don't *know* that it has the same strength, but all the evidence indicates that it has. However far away galaxies are, they appear to experience the same force of gravity as we do, indicating that the action of gravity is the same at the far reaches of the Universe as it is closer to home. For example, the size of a star depends in part on the strength of gravity, and stars in distant galaxies appear to have the same range of sizes as those in the Milky Way.

There are some theories that incorporate changes to the strength of gravity over large distances, though these relate to the force between two in particular circumstances, rather than an intrinsic variation in the strength of gravity throughout the Universe. These theories would mean that the strength of gravity does not decrease with the square of the distance (the well-known 'inverse-square law'), but in some other way. These theories of modified Newtonian gravity are a possible alternative to explaining the observations attributed to dark matter, but they have failed to explain all the observations and are currently ruled out by the majority of cosmologists.

Does gravity have a speed? If so, how is it measured?

Daniel Howard (Beeston, Nottingham)

As far as we can tell, it has the same speed as light. It's hard to be sure, because all observations only travel at the speed of light, so measuring anything faster than that is very hard.

If the technology was available to us, would it be possible to travel to a point in space where we would not be under the influence of gravity?

Steven (Ashton-in-Makerfield, Greater Manchester)

It is very hard to imagine that there is any place where the overall force due to gravity is exactly zero. Gravity reaches an infinite distance, but gets weaker and weaker. It is possible to imagine a location in the Universe where the gravitational pull of all the galaxies in every direction happen to cancel each other out, but the actual existence of such a location is impossible.

Are gravity waves just a convenient theory to fit our observed facts?

Richard Saddington (Huddersfield, West Yorkshire)

Gravitational waves are a prediction of the theory of gravity, though these were an exercise in theoretical physics rather than an attempt to explain particular facts. While we have never detected gravitational waves, there is considerable effort under way to do so. These measurements rely on detecting tiny variations in the stretching of space due to the passing of a gravitational wave. Just as a sound wave causes the expansion and compression of air (or any other medium), a gravitational wave would cause the expansion and contraction of space-time itself. But the effect is very weak, and even when measuring over lengths of kilometres the stretching predicted is a tiny fraction of the size of a single atom. Such detections also have to be isolated from local effects such as earthquakes, lorries passing by, or even clouds passing overhead!

Although we have not yet detected any gravitational waves, we have good reason to trust in Einstein's theories. A key observation was made in the 1970s, when a very special pulsar was discovered. A pulsar is the remains of a star that was several times more massive than the Sun and which went supernova and left behind a neutron star. This neutron star is emitting beams of radio waves from its magnetic poles, and one of these beams sweeps across the Earth as the neutron star rotates on its axis. Every rotation results in a pulse of radio waves which are detected on Earth, and such objects are called pulsars. The pulsar in question rotates incredibly quickly, spinning on its axis 17 times every second. The rotations of pulsars are one of the most stable and predictable effects we know of, but the timing of this pulsar was seen to not be completely regular. The slight changes in the timing of the pulses led astronomers to deduce that the pulsar was in a binary system with another neutron star and, as it orbited, the radio pulses were taking different times to travel to Earth, sometimes arriving a little earlier than expected and sometimes a little later. This second neutron star is also likely to be emitting similar radio waves from its magnetic poles, but its orientation is suitable to cause the beam to point towards Earth. The two neutron stars, each of which is less than 20 kilometres across, orbit each other in less than eight hours.

The startling discovery, and the one that applies to gravitational radiation, was that the orbits of the pulsars were shrinking. The shrinking is very slow, with the orbital period decreasing by less than a thousandth of a second every year. This decrease in the orbit means that the system is losing energy, and the only way we know that it can do that is through gravitational waves. The loss of energy is in agreement with Einstein's theories, bolstering support for general relativity. The discovery of this binary pulsar, called 'PSR 1913+16', earned Joseph Taylor and Russell Hulse the 1993 Nobel Prize for Physics.

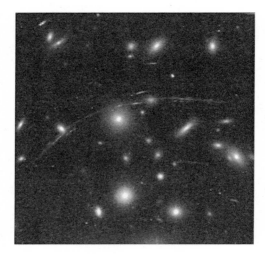

The immense mass of the galaxy cluster Abell 1689 distorts the light from background galaxies, stretching their images into long arcs.

If light is bent by gravity, then surely the light from distant stars and galaxies has no relation to their actual positions in the sky. Does this affect our understanding of the Big Bang and the Universe as a whole?

Sean Tully (Twickenham, London)

The effect of gravity on light over huge scales is there, but it is very small, and we can measure it so well only thanks to the exquisite images from telescopes today. The distortion of the light, called gravitational lensing, is very dependent on the mass of whatever is doing the lensing. Normally this is due to a galaxy or cluster of galaxies, but smaller objects can have the same effect. In 1919, two simultaneous expeditions were mounted to make careful observations of a solar eclipse in an effort to detect the deflection of light from background stars caused by the Sun. The expeditions were largely successful, and Einstein's theories had one of their first pieces of experimental proof.

Today, the studies of gravitational lensing are one of the best methods we have of measuring the distribution of dark matter. In this way, these distortions have a very profound effect on our understanding of the Universe.

Black Holes

What is on the other side of a black hole?

Maude Agombar (Salisbury, Wiltshire), Chirag Bajaria (London)

Frankly, we simply do not know what is on the other side of a black hole – though perhaps one day we will find out. There are theories as to what happens, but none have been proven. For example, it is predicted that the nature of time and space become reversed, which is something we find extremely hard to imagine!

What happens to all the matter being sucked into black holes?

Gordon Parr (Norden, Rochdale)

We do not know what exactly happens when material falls into a black hole, as we simply don't have the physical knowledge to explain it. One thing that is important to note, however, is that black holes do not simply suck everything in like a vacuum cleaner in space. Rather, material can quite happily orbit a black hole as the Earth orbits the Sun. It is only if the material gets too close that it ends up falling in, never to return.

What size would the mass condense to at the centre of a massive black hole, such as the one at the centre of our Galaxy?

John Thorne (Cardiff)

The only size that is important with respect to a black hole is the event horizon, which is the point beyond which not even light can escape. The size of the event horizon depends on the mass of the black hole, and we can look at a few examples. For example, a black hole with the same mass as the Earth would have an event horizon around a centimetre across. A black hole with the same mass as the Sun, which is nearly a million times more massive than the Earth, would have an event horizon a few kilometres across.

Supermassive black holes, such as the one thought to lie in the centre of our Galaxy, have a mass equivalent to a million Suns, and therefore an event horizon millions of kilometres across – several times the size of the Sun.

Would the escape velocity be different in different black holes, and would it be possible for one to expand so much that the Earth would be affected?

Louise Duggan (Co Longford, Ireland)

When discussing the 'edge' of a black hole, we are usually referring to the event horizon. This is the point at which the escape velocity reaches the speed of light, and so nothing can escape – not even light. There are only three properties of black holes that seem to be able to vary significantly: their mass, how fast they are rotating, and their electrical charge.

The mass of a black hole determines the distance at which the escape velocity reaches the speed of light, which to all intents and purposes can be considered to be their size. Remember that it is perfectly possible for objects to be in orbit around a black hole. If the Sun suddenly turned into a black hole it would shrink to a few kilometres across but would still have the same mass. The Earth would continue to orbit as it does today, though it would get rather dark!

As discussed in the previous question, a black hole as massive as the one in the centre of our Galaxy, which has a mass equivalent to a million

Suns, would have an event horizon several million kilometres across. This is a few times the size of our Sun, and so still much smaller than the Earth's orbit. There are odd effects close to the event horizon of a black hole, however. Objects can be in stable orbits around a black hole as close in as a few times the size of its event horizon, though the exact distance that material can safely orbit is dictated by how fast the black hole is rotating. Any closer, and their orbits decay and the material falls in.

Much further out than this and the adverse effects are vanishingly small, with the black hole having the same gravitational effect as a star of the same mass. While black holes have serious effects in their immediate vicinity, there are none nearby that could ever have any adverse effect on the Earth.

What happens to the gravitational field at the event horizon of a black hole?

Colin Spragg (Carmarthen, South Wales)

Nothing particularly special happens at the event horizon of a black hole. The gravitational attraction simply gets strong enough that the escape velocity reaches the speed of light. Since nothing particularly special happens, it would in principle be possible to cross the event horizon without even realising it.

This may sound surprising, but a strong gravitational pull is not necessarily a problem. The real difficulties arise when the gravitational pull at one end of an object is much stronger than the gravitational pull at the other, an effect similar to that which causes tides on the Earth. The important effect is not how strong the gravitational pull is, but rather how rapidly it changes with distance from the centre. This is a cosmic equivalent of the statement that it is not falling that hurts, it's hitting the ground!

In the case of most black holes, such as those that are remnants of dead stars, these tidal forces become very strong well before an object crosses the event horizon. But for a supermassive black hole the event horizon is much larger, and can be so far from the black hole that the tides at that distance are not very strong at all. This would mean that someone flying past a black hole could fly through the event horizon without being ripped apart, or possibly even noticing. Of course, once within the event horizon they would never be able to escape and so eventually the tides would become strong enough to be rip them apart – at which point they would certainly notice!

What would it look like to fall into a black hole?

Ray Finnegan (Shrewsbury, Shropshire)

The best description of what one would experience is 'spaghettification', which is simply to say that objects are stretched out until their atoms are pulled apart. If you were falling in feet-first, then the gravitational force near your head would be much less than that at your feet, which would therefore be pulled at a faster rate, stretching you out like a piece of spaghetti. Of course, once you become spaghettified, it is likely that you wouldn't know much about it for very long at all!

Since matter falling into a black hole experiences time dilation which reaches infinity as it enters the black hole, surely from our point of view no matter should yet have entered the black hole. Where is the error in my physics?

Geoff Puplett (Shropshire)

On the face of it, this would seem to be accurate, though you are right that it seems paradoxical. As a person nears a black hole they would seem to move more and more slowly from the point of view of a distant observer, so should they not appear to stop completely as they passed the event horizon? There is one way of thinking about it that may help. Imagine that the way of monitoring time is to pick up the ticking of someone's watch. As person 'A' falls into a black hole, person 'B', who sits at a safe distance, would hear the ticks get further and further apart as the effect of time dilation increases. But after a certain number of ticks, 'A' would cross the event horizon, and no more ticks would be able to leave the black hole. So person 'B' would eventually hear the last tick from 'A'. Now replace the ticks with photons of light, and you'll see that person 'B' can only pick up a certain number of photons of light from person 'A' before they cross the event horizon.

Time dilation is only one of the effects of a black hole. The huge mass means that light experiences a gravitational redshift as it climbs out of the gravitational well of the black hole. So not only do the ticks get further and further apart, but the signals get weaker and weaker, and are stretched to longer and longer wavelengths. This is why the surface of a black hole does not glow brightly, as all the photons that are leaving it are so incredibly weak that they carry very little energy indeed.

Is 'black hole' a cosmological misnomer? Should it be 'black sphere or globe', and is there any requirement that all black spheres be spherical or globular?

John Richmond (Surrey)

The name black hole originates from the American physicist John Wheeler and, like many names in astronomy, is particularly misleading. Firstly, they are not holes; a black hole is spherical since it is defined by its gravitational field. And secondly, they are certainly not black. After all, an object that cannot be seen cannot have a colour. If you were to look at a black hole, all you would see is the distorted light from whatever lay behind it. Though it must be admitted that 'black hole' sounds rather more catchy than 'invisible sphere'!

Do black holes eventually swallow up the galaxies that surround them, including the dark matter? If they do, could black holes eventually combine and merge with each other to crush the Universe back down to a singularity?

Simon Hewitt (London)

To discuss this we must look so far into the future that all we can do is speculate. While black holes will eventually swallow up much of the material around them, as each particle's orbit slowly decays, the process will be very slow. So slow, in fact, that a significant fraction of the stars in galaxies will be flung out into intergalactic space before they can be consumed. What happens to them is much more uncertain, and of course they may end up being captured by a different black hole.

In terms of black holes merging, if the latest theories involving dark energy are to be believed, then in trillions upon trillions of years the Universe will have expanded so much that the remaining black holes will be so far apart that they will have very little effect on each other at all.

Does every galaxy have a black hole at its centre?

Jon Gould (Somerset)

So far as we can tell, every large galaxy does harbour a massive black hole at its centre. This is thought to be so even in some of the larger globular clusters, which are much less massive than a typical galaxy but which are still very dense at their centres. An example of this is Omega Centauri.

The best evidence for the black hole at the centre of our Galaxy is the motion of the stars in its immediate vicinity. They orbit so quickly that this can only be explained by an object millions of times more massive than the Sun. Since we can't see anything there, the only thing it can possibly be is a black hole.

We've even seen evidence of two black holes in the cores of merging galaxies. It is expected that these will eventually merge, probably on a relatively short timescale in astronomical terms, so one has to get lucky to see a galactic collision at just the right time.

If all the matter and energy in the Universe were located in one single place, creating a 'mega-massive' black hole, what would be the diameter of the event horizon of such an object?

Tim Sheridan (London)

The answer to this question is somewhat surprising, and also a little non-intuitive. We must first clarify what we mean by an event horizon, which is technically called the Schwarzschild radius after the German physicist Karl Schwarzschild who first derived the relevant equations. For a given mass of object, the Schwarzschild radius is the radius at which the escape velocity reaches the speed of light. If an object is smaller than the Schwarzschild radius, then it is a black hole; if it is larger, it is not. For example, the Schwarzschild radius for something the mass of the Sun is around three kilometres, and since the Sun is much, much larger that this it is not a black hole – which is rather fortunate for us.

The entire visible Universe is incredible massive, and is probably only a small fraction of the entire thing – most of which we can't see because light has not had sufficient time to travel far enough. We can estimate that the visible Universe contains roughly one trillion galaxies (a trillion is one million million), each of which has a mass equivalent to a trillion Suns. Using these numbers, the Schwarzschild radius would be hundreds of billions of light years, much larger than what we can see today. The interpretation of this is that we are inside the Universe's event horizon, which simply means that we can never leave it!

Such calculations are interesting, but make far more assumptions than are appropriate for such a complex beast as the entire visible Universe. The calculations for the Schwarzschild radius are suitable for a single source that exists in isolation, and which is also relatively small compared to the size scales being studied. When we consider scales comparable to the Schwarzschild radius or smaller, as in the case of the Universe, we should really take into account the complex effects of general relativity – something that there is not space to do here. So while they are interesting and fun to consider, these calculations do not really apply to the Universe as a whole.

Could two black holes collide, and if so what would happen when they did?

Peter Underwood (Harrietsham, Kent), Robert Smith (Durham) and Maude Agombar (Salisbury, Wiltshire)

Yes, they can, just as two planets or stars can collide, though the occurrence is very rare. It only really happens when two black holes are in orbit around each other, most likely the remnant of a binary star system, both components of which have died and become black holes. Such binary black holes will gradually spiral in towards each other, eventually merging to create a more massive black hole. In doing so, they would emit gravitational waves, and the collision of two black holes is one of the signatures that the current gravitational wave detectors are searching for – though none have been found yet.

Every large galaxy we have studied appears to have an extremely massive black hole in its centre, and when two galaxies merge the two black holes would eventually merge together. The black holes themselves aren't visible, but the incredibly hot material surrounding them emits X-rays. In 2011, observations with the Chandra X-ray satellite showed that the galaxy NGC 3393 appears to have two massive black holes in its centre, most likely the result of the merger of two smaller galaxies around a billion years ago.

Unexplained Phenomena

What was the phenomenon that the Three Wise Men followed to Bethlehem?

Brian Mills (Hildenborough, Kent)

When considering the star of Bethlehem we have to admit that we do not have a great deal to guide us, and we are also decidedly unsure about our dates. The one thing about which we can be absolutely certain is that Christ was not born on 25 December AD 1. He cannot have been born in the year 0, because there was no year 0. In our calendar, therefore, the year 1 BC was followed immediately by AD 1, and this has caused confusion in our own time, when it was widely believed that the new millennium would begin on 1 January 2000. Predictably, governments fell into this trap, and declared a public holiday on the last day of 1999. The new millennium actually began on 1 January 2001. In any case, the entire issue is meaningless, and is only relevant to the Christian creed.

So when was Christ actually born? Again, there is no general agreement. The British astronomer and historian David Hughes, who has probably given as much attention to the problem as anyone else, prefers 7 BC. If we take this as being the earliest possible date, and 4 BC as the latest, we have a time span of three years, and this helps us pin down any celestial phenomena. Anything before 7 BC or after 4 BC can probably be ruled out, and this narrows our search a great deal.

But the real problem is the lack of information. The star of Bethlehem is mentioned in the Bible only once, in the Gospel according to Matthew, and nowhere else. So let us begin by quoting Matthew, Chapter 2 verses 1–2 and 7–10:

> [1] In the time of King Herod, after Jesus was born in Bethlehem of Judea, wise men from the East came to Jerusalem, [2] asking, 'Where is the child who has been born king of the Jews? For we observed his star at its rising, and have come to pay him homage …'
>
> [7] Then Herod secretly called for the wise men and learned from them the exact time when the star had appeared. [8] Then he sent them to Bethlehem, saying, 'Go and search diligently for the child; and when you have found him, bring me word so that I may also go and pay him homage.'
>
> [9] When they had heard the king, they set out; and there, ahead of them, went the star that they had seen at its rising, until it stopped over the place where the child was. [10] When they saw that the star had stopped, they were overwhelmed with joy.

That is absolutely all. The other Gospels are silent, and the star is not mentioned anywhere else, so our information is very limited from the outset. There are also translation issues, particularly in that seeing a star 'at its rising' could equally mean 'in the East'. I wonder how many theories have been put forward to explain the star? I [PM] believe that there are several possibilities:

1: The whole story is a myth, in which case we can have no idea of its origin.
2: The star was supernatural.
3: The story was invented by Matthew to add colour to his account of the nativity, or was added later by another author.

4: The star was a genuine astronomical phenomenon.

5: The star was a UFO – or, if you like, a flying saucer – dispatched to Earth by some alien civilisation far away in space.

What, then, about the Wise Men? They may have been Zoroastrians, a cult founded in 1000 BC. Zoroaster was a monotheist, a person who believed in only one god, and who believed there was a time when a king would change the realm into one of security and peace. Something which, alas, has not yet happened.

The magi were well respected, and were very influential. Of course they were astrologers as well as stargazers, and this is a very important point, because for them the appearance of the star, assuming it appeared, was primarily of astrological importance. So let us examine the various possibilities. Possibility 1 (the whole story is a myth) can tell us nothing at all. And possibility 2 (the star was supernatural) is frankly beyond the realm of this book. Possibility 3 (that Matthew may have invented the story) is conceivable, but somehow it doesn't seem likely. Leaving 4 for the moment, we come to possibility 5 (the star was a spaceship). We will not say that this is absolutely impossible, for there must be many people in the Universe who are far more advanced than we are, but this doesn't seem very probable. So we come back to number 4: was the star a genuine astronomical phenomenon?

First of all, we can rule out Venus, Jupiter and any other bright star or planet. Remember, the wise men were stargazers primarily, and were very familiar with the sky. If they were fooled by Venus, they would hardly have been very wise.

So we must list a few requirements: (1) the star must have been unusual; (2) it must have been conspicuous; (3) it may have been seen only by the wise men; (4) it must have appeared during the period from 7 to 4 BC; (5)

either it cannot have lasted for long, or it must have appeared, vanished, and reappeared at a suitable moment; (6) it must have moved in a way quite unlike any normal star or planet.

Candidly, the only object of the night sky which could fulfil all these requirements is a flying saucer – and this we have discounted. So we must try to find something that satisfies most of the requirements.

It must have been unusual, for otherwise the wise men would have expected it. It must also have been conspicuous, but the likelihood that it was seen only by the wise men is another limitation. Had it appeared over a much larger range, others would have seen it. Moving in a way quite unlike that of another star or planet, really does not fit many of the options, so let us see what we find if we delve deeper. Can the star have been a comet? Halley's Comet came back at least ten years before the dates in question, and anyway it does not fit the other requirements. The possibility of a brilliant supernova has been suggested often enough, but a supernova does not suddenly appear and then vanish. If it had been a supernova, it would have lasted for a long time, and Herod would have seen it. Neither would it have moved in the way the star of Bethlehem was said to have.

A theory favoured by a great many people, though not by me, is that the star was due to a planetary conjunction, i.e. two planets appearing very close to each other. Just occasionally this can happen, and there was a conjunction of Jupiter and Saturn in 7 BC. However, I feel that this can be ruled out straight away, because it would not have been really spectacular, it would have lasted for some time, and anyone could have seen it. Moreover, the planets were never close enough to merge into one object as seen with the naked eye. The two brightest planets are Venus and Jupiter, and when close together they make a brave showing, as they did, for example, on the 23 February 1999 when they were only 8 minutes of arc apart. Way back in

1818 (3 January), Venus actually occulted (i.e. obscured) Jupiter, but there is no record of this, partly because the planets were close to the Sun at the time, and partly because it would only have been visible from a poorly populated area in the Far East. The next occultation of Jupiter and Venus will be seen at an elongation of 10 degrees from the Sun, on 14 September 2123.

We seem to be disposing of most of our possibilities, but the vital point is that the star of Bethlehem, if it were anything at all, was seen only briefly and by a few people in a restricted area. At this point, I would put forward the only theory I believe can account for what St Matthew says. It is possible that the star of Bethlehem was in fact two brilliant meteors. Meteors may appear from any direction at any moment, and they can be really brilliant. Occasionally, a meteor may outshine the Moon, or even the Sun. Suppose, therefore, that the Wise Men saw a brilliant meteor (a fireball) reaching across the sky and lasting for some seconds before finally vanishing in the direction of Bethlehem. After a few minutes or possibly an hour or two, another meteor appeared, following exactly the same path. This would have been very unusual indeed, but it does fit the facts except for the suggestion that the star stopped over the birthplace of Christ. No meteor can do that.

I feel myself coming back to a statement attributed to Sherlock Holmes: 'If something mysterious is found, eliminate all the impossibilities. When you have done this, the least improbable of the remainder, however far-fetched, must be the truth.' So the suggestion made here is that although two meteors do not by any means answer all the problems raised by the star of Bethlehem, they do so more successfully than any other theory. The chances of us finding any further evidence now, after so long a time, is negligible. This means, that the mystery must remain. Make up your own mind!

Is there any truth in the idea that Planet X, or Nibiru, exists, or that it poses a danger to Earth?

Many, many people, including Rebecca Kitteringham (Halifax, West Yorkshire), David Butler (Larkfield, Kent) and Brendan Malone (Rugby)

This relates to the idea that there is a planet, or smaller object, in the outer Solar System that will eventually collide with the Earth. In short, there is absolutely no proof that a planet of this kind exists, and who suggested the name Nibiru I know not. If a planet like this did exist we would certainly know by now because of its gravitational pull on bodies we can see, but there is absolutely no trace of anything of the kind. There have also been surveys of the regions that have come up empty, apart from finding objects that are roughly the same size as Pluto. All these objects stay well in the outer depths of the Solar System. Certainly there are no planets lurking that could possibly be any danger to Earth.

The greatest danger to Earth from anything in the Solar System comes from objects that orbit near Earth, of which there are a reasonable number. These are all asteroids, and none has been found yet that poses a threat. There's no guarantee we won't find a dangerous near-Earth asteroid, but numerous groups are constantly on the look-out for them, diligently scanning the skies.

A large monolith has been seen on Phobos. Can you explain what it is?

Mike Keating (Tooting, London)

It is a perfectly ordinary piece of rock and there is nothing unusual about it. Phobos is littered with rocks, and some of them look fairly square, especially when combined with shadows. It is so easy to see an

What looks like a regular monolith on the surface of Phobos is actually just a trick of the light.

ordinary rock, and then try and turn it into something unusual. There are some people who will make up remarkable stories about very ordinary features. The classic case here is the 'face on Mars' photographed from the *Viking* spacecraft, which does from one aspect look very like a face. The appearance was due to a combination of the relatively low resolution of the images and the lighting conditions, and seen from another angle it bears no resemblance at all. Another more recent example was a rock which, from the point of view of *Spirit*, did look an awful lot like a human form sitting on the Martian surface.

We have to admit that some people will let their imaginations run riot!

Patrick Moore
and The Sky at Night

What was the event that inspired you to take up astronomy with such a passion?

Adrian Barnard (Didcot, Oxfordshire)

Quite simply, reading a book when I was just seven years old. It was called *The Story of the Solar System*, by GF Chambers, and I read it through and was hooked. It had belonged to my mother, who was mildly interested. In fact it was an adult book, but my reading was all right and I had no problem with it. As I sit here in my study and look at my mantelpiece I can see that little book together with its companion, *The Story of the Stars*. Both were published in 1898!

What was the first thing you saw through a telescope?

Julia Wilkinson (Rochdale, Lancashire)

The Moon! A family friend, Major AE Levin, had his observatory at Selsey, where I now live (I didn't back then), and with his 6-inch telescope showed me lunar craters. I was seven years old, and since that moment the Moon has been my main astronomical interest.

A few of the many books in Patrick's study, including the ones that inspired him to start astronomy.

After years of observing, what aspect of astronomy gives you the most personal satisfaction now?

Lulu Hancock (Dudley, West Midlands)

There are really two answers to this. First and foremost, the joy of using my telescopes to introduce people to the sky – particularly youngsters. Your beginner of today is your researcher of tomorrow, and I know plenty of teenagers and pre-teens who have started off in my observatory, and have since left me far behind. Secondly, the thrill of observing never fades. There is always something new to use and something new to discover.

What has been your most exciting observation seen through your own telescopes? If you could see any sight again, what would it be?

Adrian Bright (Littlebury, Essex), Ray Sharman (Hunston, Chichester) and Adam Bootle (Romford, Essex)

My most exciting observation? I think I've got to say the transit of Venus, in 2004. These transits occur very occasionally. There are two, separated by eight years, and then no more for over a century. The 2004 transit passed right over my Selsey observatory, and we had quite a gathering there – telescopes of all kinds and varieties, and many astronomers. Venus came into view round the tree at the end of my garden, and a minute or two later drew on to the Sun's disc as a black circle. We watched it for the next 2-3 hours as it crossed the disc and moved off the other side.

So the transit of Venus was a great day. I would love to see the last transit of the century, in June 2012, but it's not so well seen from my home in Selsey. Most people are going east, but if I were fit enough I would go to North Norway, where there is a midnight sun. Sadly, I doubt if I'll be fit enough to go, but I'll make it if I can.

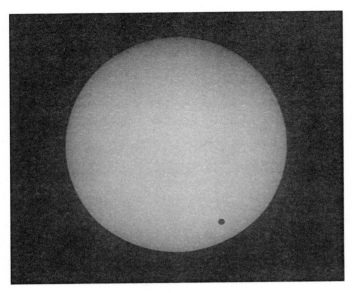

Venus passing across the disc of the Sun in 2004 during a transit. It was photographed by Adrian Janetta from Northumberland using a 10" telescope and a solar filter.

After looking up to the skies over the years you must have seen some amazing sights that many of us have yet to see, and viewed celestial objects and their changing states with awe and wonder. With that in mind, what would be the one object in the sky that, if it were gone, you would miss observing the most?

James Fewings (Portsmouth, Hampshire)

The most spectacular thing I've ever seen is a total eclipse of the Sun – there is nothing quite like it. But the object I would miss most? My main subject has always been the Moon, and without the Moon our night sky would seem very barren. I'd also hate to lose Saturn with its rings!

Of all the wonderful observatories and telescopes in the world (professional or amateur) that you have visited, which one has been your personal favourite?

John Pilbeam (Hailsham, East Sussex)

My favourite telescope, not counting my own, is the Lowell Telescope at Flagstaff, Arizona. It is a 24-inch refractor, and Lowell used it to make his observations, which included the 'canals' of Mars. When I had my first view of Mars through Lowell's telescope, I wondered whether I would see canals. I'm delighted to say that I didn't!

I've done a lot of work with the Lowell Telescope, particularly before the first landings on the Moon, and it's definitely my favourite.

My dad thinks the galaxy M81 is better than M82, but I strongly object. M82 has lots of cool dust, but what does M81 have? Which is your favourite of these two, and why?

Sophie, age 11 (Cheltenham)

A very difficult question to answer. M81 is a much more perfect galaxy, and M82 is irregular and ragged. But M82 does contain some unusual and fascinating objects, so that must get my vote. Although both are always worth looking at!

How many episodes of *The Sky at Night* still exist in the BBC archive?

Gary Holmes (Derbyshire) and Robin Flegg (Middlesex)

I think there have been a total of 715 episodes of *The Sky at Night*, though obviously that number is going up by one a month! We've had one episode per month ever since 1957, and there have been several 'specials', so keeping count can be tricky. Not every episode ever broadcast still exists, unfortunately, though the record is complete for the recent past.

The first episodes of *The Sky at Night* were broadcast live and were not recorded. The later ones were recorded, but videotape was expensive, and many tapes were wiped and reused. A few more have been lost in the depths of the BBC archives, sadly, though now and again they crop up. In 2011 a copy of an episode from 1963 was found, which featured an interview with my old friend Arthur C Clarke. I think of all the episodes that could have been found, this would have been one of my favourites.

Has Patrick presented every single episode of the programme since 1957? If so, has he never had a holiday?

Terry Fairhall (Chessington, Surrey)

I have never taken a holiday at the time of *The Sky at Night*, and I have missed just one episode. I ate a goose egg that turned out to be the wrong kind of goose egg. I was rushed into hospital, dangerously ill. That was the only episode I was unable to get to. If I could find that wretched goose, I would wring its neck. Otherwise, I haven't missed any at all.

I had one trip that wasn't actually a holiday, but a round-the-world trip for the 55th *Sky at Night* episode. One of our stops was Hawaii, where there is a range of world-class telescopes. Our producer made a complete hash of the aeroplane bookings, and we had to spend three extra days in Hawaii. Oddly enough, it happened twice!

Patrick using the 24" telescope at Lowell Observatory, near Flagstaff, Arizona.

Of all _the Sky at Night_ programmes, do you have a favourite, or a most memorable?

Steve Elliott (Farnborough, Hampshire), Mark Icke (Birchington, Kent), Gordon Rogers (Oxford) and Gary Partington (Spain)

My most memorable _Sky at Night_ may seem to you rather an odd choice. I'd been very busy mapping the 'libration areas' of the Moon, right on the edge of the Earth-turned hemisphere, which is very difficult to observe. Under extreme conditions, a little of the far side is turned in our direction and we can see it. We were filming a _Sky at Night_ on one of these occasions, and I was actually making a drawing of a crater on the far side of the Moon – that's one programme I'll never forget.

In all of the historic events that you have covered in the show's history, which one single _Sky at Night_ episode do you think was the most significant and why?

Robert Bell (Darlington)

I must give my own personal answer to this, I suppose. The very first _Sky at Night_ was broadcast in April 1957, and we were ushered in by a comet, Arend-Roland. That was my first view of that comet through my telescope, and was broadcast live. Sadly, we'll never see that comet again, on its way out of the Solar System it was affected by the gravitational pull of Jupiter and thrown into a hyperbolic orbit so that it will never come back. I wonder where it is now? I wish it well!

Could you pick out that one moment in all the televised episodes that you recall with the greatest excitement, and wish you could relive?

Mark Hill (Neilston, East Renfrewshire)

My greatest excitement was during the Moon landings, when I heard Neil Armstrong's voice: 'The Eagle has landed.' We all knew the tremendous risks the astronauts were taking, and there was so much that could have gone wrong. We all felt tremendous relief!

Are there any episodes that contain mistaken predictions or theories that might be best forgotten?

Jamie Richardson (Carlisle)

Like most other people (not counting politicians of course), I've made a great many mistakes in my time. One of these concerned my own favourite subject, the Moon. There was a longstanding argument as to how the Moon's craters got there – were they due to meteoric impact or volcanic action? I was a strong supporter of the volcanic theory. I remember one programme when I put forward a few justifications, which I'm sure were convincing, but I was later proven completely wrong. The craters are all due to impacts.

I remember an episode in the 1980s about Venus. I made a few serious statements about Venus, which were backed up by the best scientific evidence, and every one of which proved to be wrong. We live and learn…

Patrick in his study with one of the globes that are used on the set of *The Sky at Night.*

Over the history of the programme, you must have interviewed some 'greats'. Is there anyone you remember especially well?

Dave Jones (Bognor Regis, West Sussex)

On *The Sky at Night*, I've interviewed many great astronomers. If I had to pick the greatest of them all, I'd pick Sir Bernard Lovell, the great radio astronomer responsible for the Lovell Telescope at Jodrell Bank. I'm pleased to say that he is still with us at the age of 98.

Which event that you have covered gave you most trouble?

Jeff Brown (Whitstable, Kent)

The event that gave me most trouble was a total solar eclipse. It was in 1999, and the zone of totality ran right through Cornwall, where I was. Needless to say, the preceding and following days were brilliantly clear, and the actual eclipse day was cloudy. We made our broadcast as the rain pattered down, and said things like 'dear me', 'tutt tutt' and 'what a pity'.

What are the globes that are behind Patrick in his study on *The Sky at Night*?

Gerald Hutt (Okehampton, Devon)

They are globes of the Moon and planets. The Moon globes were sent to me by the Russians at the time when they were sending their probes round the Moon, and had used some of my lunar maps. Some of the early Moon globes sent by the Russians show blank areas on the far side of the Moon, which hadn't then been mapped. The details were filled in later by orbiting spacecraft, both Russian and American.

Other globes I've acquired in various ways. One, which I can see on my mantelpiece now, I acquired in a very odd way indeed. In 1954, when I was still in an air-force uniform, Oxford University asked me to go down and look at some of the things in their observatory library. I complied and made the trip. As I started to leave, I noticed a little globe in the waste paper basket. I marched back into the observatory and said, 'This is a 1910 Niesten globe of Mars.' 'Yes,' they said, 'we know. We didn't want it.' Thanks very much, I have it now – a proud possession!

One of Patrick's mother's drawings of alien life.

What are the cartoon-like pictures that can sometimes be seen in Patrick's study? They seem to be of very strange creatures. Has the work been published?

Ellen Harteijer (Amsterdam) and Michael Winfield (Derbyshire)

Strange is the right word! They were drawn by my mother, who was a very talented artist, and allowed her imagination to run riot. She must have done over 20 pictures, all of which are hanging round my house. She published one book, *Mrs Moore in Space*, in which all these are reproduced. They are certainly unlike anything else.

My mother had skills at music and at art. I inherited the music, but not the art!

How many cats does Patrick have? Are they named after famous astronomers or celestial bodies?

Lara and Jonathon (Hertfordshire)

I've got a very beloved cat, Ptolemy, who is jet black. I've had him since he was a tiny kitten, and I wouldn't be without him for anything. A friend of ours had a cat and that cat had kittens. I met the kitten, which put his head against my hand and I heard every word that kitten said.

Why Ptolemy? Well, Ptolemy was the greatest of the old Greek astronomers, but that wasn't the reason for the name. My uncle was a barrister, but at one stage he threw out the Law and went on stage as a leading actor in the opera *Amasis*. They were doing one of these operas in London, with a Greek backdrop. They'd just had a black kitten and called it Ptolemy. So when my kitten came along, he also became Ptolemy. I've often told him that story, and I'm sure he understands it – very intelligent cat!

Is Patrick really the only living person to have met the first man to fly, the first man in space, and the first man to land on the Moon? A truly remarkable and astonishing fact if true.

John Roach (Aberdeen)

I can't be sure I'm the only one, but certainly I met Orville Wright, Yuri Gagarin and of course Neil Armstrong. Whether anyone else has met all three, I know not. On the whole, I rather doubt it. Orville died in 1947, so his life did overlap those of Yuri and Neil.

Did you choose the objects in your Caldwell catalogue for any special reason, or were these favourites of yours from your own personal observing in both hemispheres?

Mark Chamberlain (Hereford)

I've got to admit that the Caldwell catalogue began very light-heartedly. I'd been in my observatory observing Jupiter and, when it finally set, I amused myself by looking at various star clusters and nebulae. I thought that since Messier only catalogued just over a hundred of these, there must be many he left out. Either because there was no chance of mistaking them for comets, in which he was mainly interested, or because they were too far south to be seen from France, where he lived. Just for fun, I set about making a catalogue of the same number of objects that can be seen easily with a small telescope. Unlike Messier, I began in the far north and went to the far south. But what to call it? I couldn't call it the Moore catalogue as, like Messier, that begins with 'M'. My name is actually double-barrelled, Caldwell-Moore, so I called it the Caldwell Catalogue.

Frankly, I thought no more about it. I sent a copy to *Sky and Telescope* magazine, and assumed they'd throw it in the waste paper bin. They didn't; they published it, and it caught on. Surprisingly, the catalogue is now rather widely used.

I made one mistake: I called it after my own name. One rather uncharitable gentleman from BAA accused me of trying to publicise my own name, which is not what I intended at all. But it's too late now. People seem to find the catalogue useful, and I'm glad they do.

What has been your greatest achievement over your career?

Michael Murphy (Lisnaskea, Co. Fermanagh)

The only thing I've done, with my books and my programmes, is to try to interest other people and bring them into astronomy. Whether I've succeeded is for others to judge, but at least I've tried. If I've done anything in the scientific world, that's it.

What has been the most surprising or significant discovery in astronomy or cosmology over your lifetime?

Vicki Wallace (Co. Donegal, Ireland), Philip Corneille (Belgium) and Stephen Case (Pembroke Dock, Pembrokeshire)

I would say the discovery of 'microwave background radiation', but I will leave it to my co-author to elaborate, as he is an astrophysicist and I am not. Over to Chris!

The Cosmic Microwave Background (called the 'CMB' for short) was discovered in 1965 by Arno Penzias and Robert Wilson, pretty much by accident. They were trying to detect radio waves from our own Galaxy, the Milky Way, using a large radio telescope at Bell Labs in New Jersey. What they found was that there was radio emission coming from all over the sky, on top of the galactic emissions. They ruled out every possible cause they could think of (including, famously, clearing out bird droppings from inside the radio antenna!), until the only source left was the Universe itself.

Such radiation was predicted to exist by physicists in the 1940s, but the actual detection of it was the first conclusive evidence of the Big Bang theory and, to mark the importance of their discovery, Penzias and Wilson were awarded the 1978 Nobel Prize for Physics.

Research into the Cosmic Microwave Background has been a rich field for decades, and in the 1990s, three decades after the CMB's discovery, the two lead scientists of the COBE satellite, George Smoot and John Mather, were awarded the 2006 prize for their research.

CMB research continues, and the Planck satellite is currently making the most detailed ever map of the CMB over the whole sky, giving cosmologists an excellent view of the early Universe. Combined with measurements from many other experiments, the CMB helps us understand the age and density of the Universe with remarkable accuracy, how it has evolved over billions of years, and even how fast the Earth is moving through space.

What single technological advancement over the last 53 years has facilitated the greatest increase in our knowledge and understanding of the cosmos?

Tony Davies (Shoreham-by-Sea, West Sussex)

I think we've got to say here the development of electronics in astronomy. Old-fashioned photography has gone out, and electronic devices have taken over. They have led to amazing advances, in all branches of science, not just astronomy. Coupled with the advances in electronic computing, they have allowed discoveries astronomers could only dream of even as recently as a decade ago. So I must say the advent of the Electronic Age.

Which future astronomical discovery would you most like realised today?

Andrew Kelly (Manchester)

The discovery I'd like above all others is the reception of an intelligent message from outer space. This would confirm that we are not alone in the Universe, and that life is undoubtedly widespread.

I'm sure it is possible, and I'm sure we are very far from being alone, but saying that is one thing and proving it is quite another. I hope that proof will come in my lifetime, but I admit that I am very far from being confident.

What do you think will be the subject of the 1000th *Sky at Night* programme, or after another 700 episodes?

Geraint Day (Swindon, Wiltshire) and Glyn Harper (Isle of Man)

I would hope that the 1000th *Sky at Night* would come from the surface of Mars or some other world. I would like to be there, but I'm afraid that's hardly likely. I always have the feeling that we might be able to broadcast the programme from another world, but not in the foreseeable future. We've got to conquer the radiation problem first, and so far we've no idea how to do that.

I was a pupil from a school Patrick previously taught at, with an interest in astronomy. I appeared in a BBC trailer with Patrick for *The Sky at Night* on its 10th anniversary, and have kept a keen interest in astronomy since. I now have a son a bit younger than I was then; what would you recommend I do to stimulate his and similar children's interest in astronomy?

Mark Bennett (London)

Dear Mark, I'm not sure how old your son is, but I would do three things. I would buy him a pair of binoculars, I'd make sure he has some books to read, and I would take him to a planetarium. Those are the three things I'd recommend.

If you are anywhere near my hideout in Selsey, bring him in! It would be good to see you again – I'm sure you've changed since our last meeting. Best wishes, Patrick

The Sky at Night encouraged me to go to university and study Space Science. What is required, 30 years on, to encourage the next generation to have an interest in this field, both as a hobby and as an academic subject?

Chris Sidwell-Smith (Leicester)

I would say that the way to interest future generations is the same as it's been for your generation and mine. Make reading matter available, go to the nearest planetarium, join an astronomical society, and equip yourself with some optical equipment – a pair of binoculars is the ideal way to start.

For those interested in astronomy in the form of academic research, then a firm grounding in physics and maths is crucial. But research also requires a keen interest in the subject, so keep gazing at the stars.

Glossary

This glossary makes no attempt at being at all complete. It merely gives one or two of the less familiar terms we use in this book. Readers will be familiar with most of them but possibly not quite all!

Alt-Az mount A telescope mounting which is aligned with the horizon, on which the telescope may be swung freely in any direction.

Altitude In astronomy, the angular height of an object above (or sometimes below) the horizon. The zenith has an altitude of 90 degrees.

Angular momentum The amount of rotation, or spin, that an object has around a given point or axis. It is calculated by multiplying together the mass of the object, the square of its distance from the axis, and the rotational velocity around the point or axis.

Aphelion Furthest distance of a planet or other body from the Sun in its orbit.

Asteroid A small Solar System body. Most of the best-known asteroids move around the Sun between the orbits of Mars and Jupiter.

Aurorae Also known as 'polar lights', specifically Aurora Borealis (Northern Lights) and Aurora Australis (Southern Lights). They occur in the Earth's upper atmosphere, and are caused by charged particles emitted by the Sun.

Automated Transfer Vehicle An unmanned cargo ship built and launched by the European Space Agency to resupply the International Space Station.

Azimuth The bearing of an object in the sky, measured from north (0°) through east (90°), south (180°) and west (270°).

Barycentre The centre of gravity of a group of objects, such as the Earth and Moon, or the Sun and planets. In the case of the Earth-Moon system, because the Earth is 81 times as massive as the Moon, the barycentre lies well inside the Earth's globe.

Binary star A stellar system made up of two stars, genuinely associated, and moving around their common centre of gravity. The revolution periods range from millions of years for very widely separated visual pairs down to less than half an hour for pairs in which the components are almost in contact with each other. With very close pairs, the components cannot be seen separately, but may be detected by spectroscopic methods.

Black hole An object with such a high mass in such a small space that nothing can escape, not even light.

Brown dwarf A small star with a mass less than around a twelfth that of the Sun, but more than 13 times the mass of Jupiter. A brown dwarf cannot sustain the fusion of hydrogen in its core, but can burn deuterium.

Celestial Sphere A sphere onto which the locations of stars, planets and galaxies are projected. Positions are normally given in right ascension and declination. The equator and poles of the celestial sphere are aligned with the Earth's, but it does not rotate.

Cepheid variable A type of short-period variable star, very regular in behaviour, the name of which comes from the prototype star, Delta Cephei. Cepheids are astronomically important because there is a relationship between variation periods with their real luminosities, so that their distances may be obtained by sheer observation.

Cluster, globular A group of many thousands of stars that formed together and which are bound together by gravity.

Cluster, open A group of stars that formed together but which will eventually disperse.

Comet A small icy body in orbit around the Sun, left over from the creation of the planets. When comets come close to the Sun they can lose material, creating the characteristic tail.

Constellation A pattern of stars in the sky. The stars in any constellation are not really related to each other, because they are at very different distances from the Earth.

Corona The outermost part of the Sun's atmosphere, made up of very tenuous gas. It is visible with the naked eye only during a total solar eclipse.

Cosmic Microwave Background (CMB) Microwave radiation from around 400,000 years after the Big Bang, released when the Universe cooled enough to become transparent. Tiny fluctuations in the CMB show us the temperature and density of the early Universe.

Cosmic rays High-velocity particles reaching the Earth from outer space. The heavier cosmic-ray particles are broken up when they enter the upper atmosphere.

Cosmology The study of the Universe considered as a whole.

Dark energy The name given to a form of energy that makes up more than two-thirds of the energy density of the Universe, and which seems to cause it to expand at an ever-increasing rate.

Dark matter Matter that does not emit, absorb or scatter light, and which can only be observed through its gravitational effect on other objects.

Day, solar The mean interval between successive meridian passages of the Sun, i.e. the points at which the Sun is due south. The length of a solar day varies through the year, but on average it is 24 hours long.

Day, sidereal The interval between successive meridian passages, or culminations, of the same star: 23 hours 56 minutes and 4.091 seconds. This is the true rotation rate of the Earth.

Declination The angular distance of an object above the celestial equator, analogous to latitude measured on Earth.

Deuterium An isotope, or variation, of the hydrogen element, but with one proton and one neutron in the nucleus.

Doppler effect The apparent change in wavelength of the light from a luminous body which is in motion relative to the observer.

Dwarf planet A member of the Solar System moving round the Sun in the same manner as a planet, but much smaller. The best-known dwarf planet is Pluto.

Eclipse, lunar The passage of the Moon through the shadow cast by the Earth. Lunar eclipses may be either total or partial. At some eclipses, totality may last for approximately 1.75 hours, though most are shorter.

Eclipse, solar The blotting-out of the Sun when the Moon is directly between the Earth and the Sun. Total eclipses can last for over 7 minutes under exceptionally favourable circumstances. In a partial eclipse, the Sun is incompletely covered. In an annular eclipse, exact alignment occurs when the Moon is in the far part of its orbit, and so appears smaller than the Sun; a ring of sunlight is left showing round the dark body of the Moon. Strictly speaking, a solar 'eclipse' is the occultation of the Sun by the Moon.

Ecliptic The apparent yearly path of the Sun among the stars. It is more accurately defined as the projection of the Earth's orbit onto the celestial sphere. The planets move through the sky close to the ecliptic plane.

Electron Part of an atom; a fundamental particle carrying a negative electric charge.

Element An atom containing a specific number of protons, neutrons and electrons.

Equator, celestial The projection of the Earth's Equator onto the celestial sphere.

Equatorial A mounting in which the telescope is set up on an axis which is parallel with the axis of the Earth. This means that one movement only (east to west) will suffice to keep an object in the field of view.

Equinox The equinoxes are the two points at which the ecliptic cuts the celestial equator. At an equinox, day and night are of the same length.

Escape velocity The minimum velocity which an object must have in order to escape from the surface of a planet, or other celestial body, without being given any extra impetus.

European Space Agency (ESA) A treaty organisation that provides for cooperation among European states in space research and technology.

Event horizon The 'boundary' of a black hole. No light can escape from inside the event horizon.

Exoplanet, extra-solar planet A planet orbiting a star other than the Sun.

Filter In astronomy, a device that only lets through specific wavelengths of light. Filters can be 'broadband', e.g. letting through red light, or 'narrowband', letting through only a narrow range of wavelengths, usually a range emitted by a particular element.

Finder A small, wide-field telescope attached to a larger one, used for sighting purposes.

Fraunhofer lines The dark absorption lines in the spectrum of the Sun, or any other star. The lines are caused by the absorption of light by particular elements and can be used to deduce a star's composition.

Galaxy A system made up of stars, nebula and interstellar matter. Many, though by no means all, are spiral in form.

Galaxy cluster A group of galaxies that are bound together by gravity.

Gamma rays Radiation of extremely short wavelength and of very high energy.

Gravitational wave A type of radiation distinct from electromagnetic radiation, and which is caused by the movement of masses. Gravitational waves are manifested as distortions in space.

Halo, galactic The spherical-shaped cloud of stars round the main part of a galaxy, made primarily of dark matter but also containing relatively small numbers of stars.

Infrared radiation Radiation with a wavelength longer than that of visible light, ranging from approximately 7,500 Angstroms to 300 microns.

International Space Station A space station in orbit around Earth, built by an international collaboration including the USA, Russia, Europe, Japan and Canada. Construction began in 1998 and was completed in 2011.

Interstellar medium The material between the stars in a galaxy, made of gas and dust.

Ion An atom which has lost or gained one or more electrons, and so has respectively a positive or negative charge.

Ionisation The addition or removal of an electron from an atom, often caused by the emission or absorption of radiation.

Kuiper Belt A belt of small bodies moving round the Sun near the orbit of Neptune.

Libration Relating to the Moon, the wobble of the Moon as it spins, allowing us to see narrow regions that would normally be considered to be on the far side.

Light year The distance travelled by light in one year.

Local group A collection of galaxies, of which our Galaxy is a member.

Luminosity The intrinsic brightness that an object has, irrespective of its distance.

Magnitude, absolute The apparent magnitude that the star would have if it could be observed from a standard distance of 32.6 light years.

Magnitude, apparent The brightness of an object in the sky. Lower numbers correspond to brighter objects. The brightest star in the sky, Sirius, is of magnitude -1, while the faintest stars visible to the naked eye from a dark sight are of magnitude 6. The Sun has an apparent magnitude of -27.

Meteor A piece of cometary debris. When it dashes into the Earth's atmosphere, it burns away to produce a shooting star.

Meteorite A solid body from space landing on the Earth. Most meteorites come from the asteroid belt.

Nebula A cloud of gas and dust in space, inside which new stars are being formed.

Neutrino A fundamental particle similar to the electron but with no electric charge and a very small mass. Neutrinos are hard to measure as they do not interact strongly with matter.

Neutron A fundamental particle with no electric charge, found in the nucleus of an atom.

Neutron star The remnant of a massive star that has exploded in a supernova. A neutron star has a mass similar to the Sun but is only 10–20 km across.

Oort cloud An assumed spherical shell of comets surrounding the Sun, at a range of about one light year.

Parsec The distance at which a star would have a parallax of one second of arc: 3.26 light years, 206,265 astronomical units, or 30.857 million million kilometres.

Perihelion The position in the orbit of a planet or other body which is closest to the sun.

Period, orbital The period that a planet or other object takes to orbit the Sun, or that a satellite takes to orbit its primary planet.

Period, sidereal The period of revolution of a planet on its axis.

Photon A particle of light, which carries energy but has no mass.

Photosphere The visible surface of the Sun or another star.

Planet An object orbiting the Sun or another star that has a sufficiently high mass to have become spherical and to have cleared its own orbit of other material.

Plasma Ionised gas, normally at very high temperatures. The surface of the Sun is made of plasma, as was the very early Universe.

Precession The movement of the axis of rotation of a spinning body such as a planet.

Proton A fundamental particle with a positive electric charge, found in the nucleus of an atom. The nucleus of the hydrogen atom is made up of a single proton.

Pulsar A neutron star with a strong magnetic field and jets of radio waves that sweep across the Earth as it spins on its axis.

Quasar The core of a very powerful, remote active galaxy. The term QSO (quasi-stellar object) is also used.

Red giant A star nearing the final stages of its life, which has swelled up to tens or hundreds of times its original size.

Redshift The stretching of the wavelength of light, either due to the source moving away from the observer, due to it having left a gravitational field, or due to the expansion of the Universe.

Relativity A theory formulated by Albert Einstein, which describes the behaviour of an object travelling at high speed or with a high mass.

Right Ascension A coordinate used to give positions on the celestial sphere, similar to longitude used on the Earth.

Satellite A natural or artificial object that is orbiting another astronomical body such as a planet.

Solar wind A flow of atomic particles streaming out constantly from the Sun in all directions.

Solstices The times when the Sun is at its maximum declination of approximately 23.5 degrees; around 22 June (summer solstice, with the Sun in the northern hemisphere of the sky), and 22 December (winter solstice, Sun in the southern hemisphere).

Spectroscopy The study of the spectrum of light, usually allowing the composition of an object to be studied.

Spectrum The range of wavelengths, or colours, of light that an object emits. The spectrum of an object can be used to deduce its composition.

Sunspot A dark area on the surface of the Sun that is slightly cooler than its surroundings.

Supernova A colossal stellar outburst, involving either (1) the total destruction of the white dwarf member of a binary system, or (2) the collapse of a very massive star.

Terraforming The process of making another planet or astronomical body inhabitable by adjusting its climate.

Transit The passage of one object in front of a larger one, blocking some or all of the light.

Variable stars Stars which change in brilliancy over short periods. They are of various types.

White dwarf A very small, very dense star which has used up its nuclear fuel, and is in a very late stage of its evolution.

Zenith The observer's overhead point (altitude 90°).

Zodiac A belt stretching round the sky, to either side of the ecliptic, in which the Sun, Moon and principal planets are to be found at any time. (As such, they will always be observed against one of 13 constellations.)

Zodiacal light A cone of light rising from the horizon and stretching along the ecliptic; visible only when the Sun is a little way below the horizon and thus will often be obscured. It is due to thinly spread interplanetary material near the main plane of the Solar System reflecting sunlight.

References

Academic papers are often cited in the following style, with the journal in italics and the volume in bold: <Author> (<Year>) <Journal> **<Volume>** (<Issue>), <page>: "<Title>"

Observing

p30 (Gavin Hall): Large Binocular Telescope Observatory website: www.lbto.org

p40 (John Royle & Aiden Stone): British Astronomical Society webpage: http://www.britastro.org/dark-skies/bestukastrolocationmap1.html

p48 (Ian Downing & Mick Scutt): Antikythera Mechanism Research Project website: http://www.antikytheramechanism.gr/

Further reading

British Astronomical Association website: http://britastro.org

Ian Ridpath (ed.), *Norton's Star Atlas and Reference Handbook* (20th edn., Addison Wesley, 2003)

Stellarium, freely downloadable planetarium software available from www.stellarium.org

The Moon

p76 (Peter Barton): Hartung (1976) *Meteoritics* **11** (3), 187: 'Was the formation of a 20-km diameter impact crater on the Moon observed on June 18, 1178?'

p78 (Andy Cook): Jutzi and Asphaug (2011) *Nature* **476**, 69: 'Forming the lunar farside highlands by accretion of a companion moon'

Further reading

Lunar Reconnaissance Orbiter website: http://www.nasa.gov/lro

Patrick Moore, *Patrick Moore on the Moon* (Cassell Illustrated, 2006)

The Solar System

p89 (John A Tomkins): McDonaugh (2001) *International Geophysics* **76**, 3: 'Chapter 1. The composition of the Earth'

p89 (John A Tomkins): Professor Alan Fitzsimmons, BBC *Sky at Night*, episode 700

p90 (David Gay): Professor Alan Fitzsimmons, BBC *Sky at Night*, episode 700

p94 (Paul Smith): Professor Alan Fitzsimmons, BBC *Sky at Night*, episode 700

p97 (Bart van der Putten): Dr Lucie Green, BBC *Sky at Night*, episode 700

p98 (John Moore): Dr Lucie Green, BBC *Sky at Night*, episode 700

p99 (Alison Barrett): Dr Lucie Green, BBC *Sky at Night*, episode 700

p103 (Alex Mackie): Edberg et al. (2010) *Geophysical Research Letters* **37**, L03107: 'Pumping out the atmosphere of Mars through solar wind pressure pulses'

p111 (Alex Andrews): Professor Alan Fitzsimmons, BBC *Sky at Night*, episode 700 *p116 (Jon Culshaw)*: Professor Alan Fitzsimmons, BBC *Sky at Night*, episode 700

p116 (Derryck Morton): NASA Planetary Data System Standards Reference, Chapter 2: Cartographic Standards: http://pds.nasa.gov/tools/standardsreference.shtml

p118 (Rob Johnson): Sheppard and Jewitt (2003) *Highlights of Astronomy* 13, 898: 'The Abundant Irregular Satellites of the Giant Planets'

p120 (Carl Harris): Kerr (2008) *Science* 319, 21: 'Saturn's Rings Look Ancient Again'

p120 (Carl Harris): Poulet et al. (2003) *Astronomy and Astrophysics* 412, 305: 'Compositions of Saturn's rings A, B, and C from high resolution near-infrared spectroscopic observations'

p122 (Anne Edwards): Porco et al. (2005) *Science* 307, 1226: 'Cassini Imaging Science: Initial Results on Saturn's Rings and Small Satellites'

p123 (Nigel Asher): Planetary Society blog post: http://planetary.org/blog/article/00002471/

p123 (Ben Slater): Soderbolm et al. (2010) *Icarus* 208, 905: 'Geology of the Selkcrater region on Titan from Cassini VIMS observations'

p123 (Ben Slater): Cornet et al. (2011) *LPI Science Conference Abstracts* 42, 2581: 'Geology of Ontario Lacus on Titan: Comparison with a Terrestrial Analog, the Etosha Pans (Namibia)'

p124 (Edward Ignasiak): Professor Alan Fitzsimmons, BBC *Sky at Night*, episode 700

p127 (Gerard Gilligan): Professor Alan Fitzsimmons, BBC *Sky at Night*, episode 700

p128 (Chris Stinson): Morbidelli (2005) 'Origin and Dynamical Evolution of Comets and their Reservoirs' http://arxiv.org/abs/astro-ph/0512256

p129 (Roy Jackson): USNO website: http://aa.usno.navy.mil/faq/docs/minorplanets.php

p129 (Roy Jackson): IAU Resolution B5 (2006) 'Definition of a planet in our Solar System'

p129 (Roy Jackson): IAU Resolution B6 (2006) 'Pluto'

p131 (Rebecca Taylor): Sedna: http://www.gps.caltech.edu/~mbrown/sedna/

p131 (Rebecca Taylor): Sagan and Khare (1979) *Nature* 207, 102: 'Tholins: organic chemistry of interstellar grains and gas'

p131 (Rebecca Taylor): Barucci et al. (2005) *Astronomy and Astrophysics* 439, L1: 'Is Sedna another Triton?'

p133 (Alan Davis): Universe Today article: http://www.universetoday.com/14486/2012-no-planet-x/

p135 (Mark Bullard): Q61 Genda and Ikoma (2008) *Icarus* 194, 42: 'Origin of the ocean on the Earth: Early evolution of water D/H in a hydrogen-rich atmosphere'

p135 (Mark Bullard): Callahan et al. (2011) *PNAS* 108 (34), 13995: 'Carbonaceous meteorites contain a wide range of extraterrestrial nucleobases'

p135 (Mark Bullard): http://www.nasa.gov/topics/solarsystem/features/dna-meteorites.html

p135 (Mark Bullard): Hartogh et al. (2011) *Nature* 478, 218-220: 'Ocean-like water in the Jupiter-family comet 103P/Hartley 2'

p136 (Dave Annear): Drouart et al. (1999) *Icarus* 140, 129: 'Structure and Transport in the Solar Nebula from Constraints on Deuterium Enrichment and Giant Planets Formation'

p137 (Gerald Hutt): Sekanina (1968) *Bulletin of the Astronomical Institutes of Czechoslovakia* 19, 343: 'A dynamic investigation of Comet Arend-Roland 1957 III'

p137 (Gerald Hutt): Marsden (1970) *Astronomical Journal* 75 (1), 75: 'Comets and nongravitational forces III' *p138 (Gillian Ann Jackson)*: Mainzer et al. (2011) *Astrophysical Journal* **743** (2), 156: 'NEOWISE Observations of Near-Earth Objects: Preliminary Results'

p142 (Ingrid van Dam): USGS website: http://pubs.usgs.gov/gip/geotime/age.html

p142 (Duncan Borrington-Chance): JPL small-body database browser: http://ssd.jpl.nasa.gov/sbdb.cgi

p143 (Les Stringer): NASA Science website: http://science.nasa.gov/science-news/science-at-nasa/2003/29dec_magneticfield/

p145 (Ron Sexton): W. McDonough 'The composition of the Earth', Chapter 1 in Earthquake Thermodynamics and Phase Transformation in the Earth's Interior, Volume 76 (2000), available online: quake.mit.edu/hilstgroup/CoreMantle/EarthCompo.pdf

p146 (Rosemary Davis): Thommes, Duncan and Levison (2003) *Icarus* **161**, 431: 'Oligarchic growth of giant planets'

p146 (Rosemary Davis): Thommes, Duncan and Levison (1999) *Nature* **402**, 635: 'The formation of Uranus and Neptune in the Jupiter±Saturn region of the Solar System'

p146 (Rosemary Davis): Scientific American Blog: http://blogs.scientificamerican.com/basicspace/2011/07/26/jupiter-sneaked-up-on-asteroid-belt-then-ranaway/

p149 (Ronald Mallier): Schroeder and Smith (2008) *MNRAS* **386**, 155: 'Distant future of the Sun and Earth revisited'

p149 (Ronal Mallier): Villaver and Livio (2007) *Astrophysical Journal* **661**, 1192: 'Can planets survive stellar evolution?'

p150 (Baz Pearce): Professor Alan Fitzsimmons, BBC *Sky at Night*, episode 700

Further reading

Cassini Solstice Mission website: http://saturn.jpl.nasa.gov

Patrick Moore, *Mission to the Planets: The Illustrated Story of Man's Exploration of the Solar System* (Cassell Illustrated, 1995)

Solar Dynamics Observatory website: http://sdo.gsfc.nasa.gov

Voyager website: http://voyager.jpl.nasa.gov

Stars and Galaxies

p158 (Alec Bordacs): Galaxy Map: http://galaxymap.org

p172 (Russell Aspinwell): Herschel Space Observatory: http://herscheltelescope.org.uk and http://www.esa.int/herschel

p189 (Andrew Brydges etc.): Lord Martin Rees, BBC *Sky at Night*, episode 700

p197 (Kevin Cooper): Lintott et al. (2009) *MNRAS* **399**, 129: 'Galaxy Zoo: "Hanny's Voorwerp", a quasar light echo?'

Further reading

John Bally and Bo Reipurth, *The Birth of Stars and Planets* (Cambridge University Press, 2006)

ESA's Hubble website: http://spacetelescope.org

Galaxy Zoo: http://www.galaxyzoo.org

Patrick Moore and Robin Rees, *Patrick Moore's Data Book of Astronomy* (2nd edn., Cambridge University Press, 2011)

Cosmology

p203 (Lynton McLain): Lord Martin Rees, BBC *Sky at Night*, episode 700

p207 (Dolores Myatt): Kogut et al. (1993) *Astrophysical Journal* **419**,

1: 'Dipole Anisotropy in the COBE Differential Microwave Radiometers First-Year Sky Maps'

p213 (Martin Fletcher): John A. Peacock, *Cosmological Physics* (Cambridge University Press, 1998)

p213 (Martin Fletcher): John A. Peacock (2008) 'A diatribe on expanding space' http://arxiv.org/abs/0809.4573

p213 (Martin Fletcher): Francis et al. (2007) PASA **24** (2), 95: 'Expanding Space: the Root of all Evil?'

p216 (Peter Eggleston): Cooperstock, Faraoni and Vollick (1998) *Astrophysical Journal* **503**, 61: 'The Influence of the Cosmological Expansion on Local Systems'

p218 (Ross E Platt): Reiss et al. (1998) *Astronomical Journal* **116**, 100: 'Observational Evidence from Supernovae for an Accelerating Universe and a Cosmological Constant'

p218 (Ross E Platt): Perlmutter et al. (1999) *Astrophysical Journal* **517**, 565: 'Measurements of Omega and Lambda from 42 High-Redshift Supernovae'

p229 (Robert): Ned Wright's Cosmology Calculator: http://www.astro.ucla.edu/~wright/CosmoCalc.html

p233 (Paul): National Solar Observatory webpage: http://www.cs.umass.edu/~immerman/stanford/universe.html

p234 (Hywel Clatworthy): Penzias and Wilson (1965) *Astrophysical Journal* **142**, 419: 'A Measurement of Excess Antenna Temperature at 4080 Mc/s'

p242 (Thomas Work etc.): Lord Martin Rees, BBC *Sky at Night*, episode 700

p244 (Andi Ye): Steven Weinberg, *The First Three Minutes: A Modern View of the Origin of the Universe* (Basic Books, 1993)

p255 (Paul Foster etc.): Lord Martin Rees, BBC *Sky at Night*, episode 700 *p258 (Chris Geraghty and Rik Whittaker)*: Rubin, Ford and Thonnard (1980) *Astrophysical Journal* **238**, 471: 'Rotational properties of 21 SC galaxies with a large range of luminosities and radii, from NGC 4605 (R = 4kpc) to UGC 2885 (R = 122 kpc)'

p258 (Chris Geraghty and Rik Whittaker): Zwicky (1937) *Astrophysical Journal* **86**, 217: 'On the Masses of Nebulae and of Clusters of Nebulae'

p262 (Simon Foster and Craig Shail): Clowe et al. (2006) *Astrophysical Journal* **648**, 109: 'A Direct Empirical Proof of the Existence of Dark Matter'

p262 (Simon Foster and Craig Shail): Markevitch et al. (2004) *Astrophysical Journal* **606**, 819: 'Direct Constraints on the Dark Matter Self-Interaction Cross Section from the Merging Galaxy Cluster 1E 0657-56'

p265 (Ken Askew): LHC: CERN Brochure 'LHC: The Guide' http://cdsweb.cern.ch/record/1092437/files/

p265 (Ken Askew): Professor Brian Cox, BBC *Sky at Night*, episode 700

p268 (Spencer Taylor): Square Kilometre Array website: http://www.skatelescope.org

p277 (Bruce Goodman etc.): Adams and Laughlin (1997) *Reviews of Modern Physics* **69** (2), 337: 'A dying universe: the long-term fate and evolution of astrophysical objects'

Further reading

Professor Peter Coles's blog 'In the Dark': http://telescoper.wordpress.org

John Gribbin, In search of Schrodinger's Cat: Quantum Physics and Reality (revised edn., Black Swan, 2012)

Steven Weinberg, *The First Three Minutes: A Modern View of the Origin of the Universe* (Basic Books, 1993)

WMAP website: http://wmap.gsfc.nasa.gov

Other Worlds

p284 (David Cockayne): Direct Imaging: Marois et al. (2008) *Science* **322**, 1348: 'Direct Imaging of Multiple Planets Orbiting the Star HR 8799'

p288 (Martin Hickes): Dr Lewis Dartnell, BBC *Sky at Night*, episode 700

p288 (Martin Hickes): Borucki et al. (2011): 'Kepler-22b: A 2.4 Earth-radius Planet in the Habitable Zone of a Sun-like Star': http://arxiv.org/abs/1112.1640

p288 (Martin Hickes): Fressin et a. (2011) 'Two Earth-sized planets orbiting Kepler-20': http://arxiv.org/abs/1112.4550

p294 (Kevin Somerville): Dr Lewis Dartnell, BBC *Sky at Night*, episode 700

p298 (Karl): Vogt et al. (2010) *Astrophysical Journal* **723**, 954: 'The Lick-Carnegie Exoplanet Survey: A 3.1 M_Earth Planet in the Habitable Zone of the Nearby M3V Star Gliese 581'

p298 (Karl): Anglada-Escudé and Dawson (2010) arXiv pre-print: 'Aliases of the first eccentric harmonic : Is GJ 581g a genuine planet candidate?': http://arxiv.org/abs/1011.0186

p300 (Barry Holland): Habitable Planet: Kaltenegger, Udry and Pepe (2011) 'A Habitable Planet around HD 85512': http://adsabs.harvard.edu/abs/2011arXiv1108.3561K

Further reading

The Extrasolar Planets Encyclopaedia: http://exoplanet.eu

NASA Kepler website: http://kepler.nasa.gov

Fabienne Casoli and Thérèse Encrenaz, *The New Worlds: Extrasolar Planets* (Springer, 2007)

Manned Spaceflight

p312 (Kevin Taylor): Astronaut biographies http://www11.jsc.nasa.gov/Bios/

p316 (Christopher Harper): Piers Sellers, BBC *Sky at Night*, episode 700

p318 (Ama Boateng): Piers Sellers, BBC *Sky at Night*, episode 700

p318 (Sam): NASA Astronaut Selection and Training http://spaceflight.
nasa.gov/shuttle/reference/factsheets/asseltrn.html

p320 (Erin): Piers Sellers, BBC *Sky at Night*, episode 700

p320 (Richard Walder): ESA's ATV website: http://www.esa.int/atv

p324 (John Restick): Piers Sellers, BBC *Sky at Night*, episode 700

p337 (Peter Ainsworth): Professor David Southwood, BBC *Sky at Night*,
episode 700

Further reading

NASA International Space Station website: http://www.nasa.gov/station

NASA Orbital Debris website: http://orbitaldebris.jsc.nasa.gov

Space Missions

p343 (Carl Kirby): National Goegraphic 'Fifty Years of Exploration':
http://books.nationalgeographic.com/map/map-day/2009/10/29

p247 (Iain Drain): Professor David Southwood, BBC *Sky at Night*, episode
700

p359 (Jamie Smith): JAXA Ikaros website: http://www.jspec.jaxa.jp/e/
activity/ikaros.html

p359 (Jamie Smith): NASA Dawn website: http://dawn.jpl.nasa.gov

p364 (Paul Metcalf): Venera 13 webpage: http://nssdc.gsfc.nasa.gov/nmc/
masterCatalog.do?sc=1981-106D

p368 (Kevin Cooper): New Horizons website: http://www.nasa.gov/
newhorizons/

p370 (Philip Corneille): Deep Impact webpage: http://www.nasa.gov/deepimpact

p371 (Earl Robinson): Benefits of the Space Program: http://techtran.msfc.nasa.gov/at_home.html

Further reading

Patrick Moore, *Mission to the Planets: The Illustrated Story of Man's Exploration of the Solar System* (Cassell Illustrated, 1995)

NASA's Voyager website: http://voyager.jpl.nasa.gov

Bizarre and Unexplained

p373 (David Duly): NASA WMAP website: http://wmap.gsfc.nasa.gov

p376 (Rob Hawthorne and Mike Poole): Romer and Cohen (1940) *Isis* **31**, 328: 'Roemer and the First Determination of the Velocity of Light (1676)'

p376 (Rob Hawthorne and Mike Poole): Bradley (1729) *Philosophical Transactions of the Royal Society of London* **35**, 637: 'Account of a new discovered Motion of the Fix'd Stars'

p376 (Rob Hawthorne and Mike Poole): Resolution 1 of the 17th meeting of the CGPM http://www.bipm.org/en/CGPM/db/17/1/

p385 (Peter Burgess): Professor Brian Cox and Lord Martin Rees, BBC *Sky at Night*, episode 700

p388 (Richard Saddington): Hulse and Taylor (1975) *Astrophysical Journal* **195**, L51: 'Discovery of a pulsar in a binary system'

p388 (Richard Saddington): Taylor, Fowler and McCullock (1979) *Nature* **277**, 437: 'Measurements of general relativistic effects in the binary pulsar PSR1913+16'

p388 (Richard Saddington): Nobel Prize website: http://www.nobelprize.org/nobel_prizes/physics/laureates/1993/press.html

p397 (Simon Hewitt): Lord Martin Rees, BBC *Sky at Night*, episode 700

p397 (Jon Gould): Fabbiano et al. (2011) *Nature* **477**, 431: 'A close nuclear black-hole pair in the spiral galaxy NGC3393'

p401 (Brian Mills): The Bible, New Revised Standard Version (1989)

p401 (Brian Mills): Patrick Moore, *The Star of Bethlehem* (Canopus Publishing Limited, 2001)

Further reading

Jim Al-Khalili, Black Holes, *Wormholes and Time Machines* (2nd edn., Taylor & Francis, 2012)

Russell Stannard, *The Time and Space of Uncle Albert* (Faber and Faber, 2005)

Patrick Moore and *The Sky at Night*

p420 (Ellen Harteijer & Michael Winfield): Gertrude L. Moore, *Mrs Moore in Space* (Creative Monochrome, 2002)

p423 (Vicki Wallace etc.): Nobel Prize website: http://www.nobelprize.org

Further reading

Patrick Moore, *80 Not out: The Autobiography* (Contender Books, 2003)

Index

Acknowledgements

Any book of this kind is surprisingly challenging, for careless mistakes can easily creep in. In this book, so far as we can tell, they haven't, and this is due to the care taken by the editorial and design team that put it together. The book originates from the 700th episode of *The Sky at Night*, which was a great success thanks to the efforts of the whole team. Special thanks to Jane Segar (nee Fletcher) for her hard work on the programme, as well as the book itself. Without her, we rather doubt whether this book would ever have seen the light of day.

For the programme itself Sir Patrick is regularly joined on screen by Dr Chris Lintott, Paul Abel, Pete Lawrence and Dr Chris North. But the key to the programme is the guests that come to tell us about their work, both their professional research and amateur astronomy activities. For the 700th programme we were lucky to be joined by Dr Lewis Dartnell, Prof. Alan Fitzsimmons, Dr Lucie Green, Dr Brian May, Astronomer Royal Lord Rees and Prof. David Whitehouse, not forgetting our question master Jon Culshaw.

The Sky at Night has a very small team and even smaller budget, which 'beams' in the people it needs to make it happen. Behind the scenes, it relies on the hard work of Executive Producer Bill Lyons and the production team from BBC Birmingham: Linda Flavell, Tracey Bagley, Leena Marwaha, Gemma Wooton, Stella Stylianos, Natalie Breeden, Keaton Stone and Tom Prentice. Not forgetting, of course, the camera, lighting and sound crew – Rob Hawthorn, Rob Lacey, Martin Huntley and Andy Davis – who every month transform Patrick's study into a studio. Then there are the incredibly skilled editors, in particular Matthew Jinks, Stephen Killick, Martin Dowell, and Simon Prentice, all of whom have pieced together the programmes over recent months and edited out our fluffs and mistakes!

For this book we are grateful to the readers who so kindly agreed to help check its factual accuracy, particularly Paul Abel, Alan Fitzsimmons, Edward Gomez, Will Grainger, Pete Lawrence, Chris Lintott, Stuart Lowe, Derry North and Gabi North.

Special thanks to all those who have provided splendid photographs and illustrations, which they have so kindly allowed us to use. Without them, it is certain that neither *The Sky at Night* nor this book would be the success that we hope they are.

Picture Credits

BBC Books would like to thank the following individuals and organizations for providing photographs and for permission to reproduce copyright material. While every effort has been made to trace and acknowledge copyright holders, we would like to apologize should there be any errors or omissions.

Pg 13 – Patrick with his 15" reflector/Patrick Moore; Pg 16 – The Plough/Richard Palmer Graphics; Pg 22 – International Space Station/Ralf Vandenbergh; Pg 27 – Reflecting and refracting telescopes/Richard Palmer Graphics; Pg 32 – Large Binocular Telescope/Photo courtesy of Aaron Ceranski and the Large Binocular Telescope Observatory (The LBT is an international collaboration among institutions in the United States, Italy and Germany); Pg 33 – Sketch of Saturn/Patrick Moore; Pg 34 – Patrick with his 12 1/2" reflecting telescope/Patrick Moore; Pg 39 – Photograph of star trails/Stewart Watt; Pg 46 – Jupiter/Anthony Wesley; Pg 58 – Full Moon/Jamie Cooper; Pg 61 – Gravitational pull of the Moon/Richard Palmer Graphics; Pg 65 – Phases of the Moon/Richard Palmer Graphics; Pg 71 – Total solar eclipse/Alan Clitherow; Pg 79 – Mare Ibrium/Julian Cooper;

Pg 86 – Solar System/Richard Palmer Graphics; Pg 93 – Cloud tops of Venus/ NASA/NSSDC Photo Gallery; Pg 100 – Solar prominence/NASA; Pg 120 – Rings of Saturn/NASA/JPL/Space Science Institute; Pg 125 – Hyperion/ NASA/JPL/Space Science Institute; Pg 129 – Voyager 2's image of Triton/ NASA/JPL; Pg 153 – Motion of nearby stars/Richard Palmer Graphics; Pg 160 – Map of our own Galaxy in the infrared/NASA/JPL-Caltech; Pg 199 – Galaxy redshift sample/M. Blanton and the Sloan Digital Sky Survey (SDSS) Collaboration, www.sdss.org; Pg 204 – Spacing of galaxies/ Richard Palmer Graphics; Pg 214 – Distribution of galaxies/Smithsonian Astrophysical Observatory/Gellar & Huchra (1989); Pg 216 – The Universe as an expanding balloon/Richard Palmer Graphics; Pg 240 – Curvature of Earth/Richard Palmer Graphics; Pg 317 – Photograph of the Earth from Space/NASA (Image ID number AS17-148-22727); Pg 321 – International Space Station against Earth/STS-119 Shuttle Crew/NASA; Pg 356 – The Lunar Module/Richard Palmer Graphics; Pg 358 – Saturn V/Richard Palmer Graphics; Pg 365 – Surface of Venus/NASA (Image ID number: YG06847); Pg 386 – The distortion of space-time by gravity/Richard Palmer Graphics; Pg 403 – Galaxy cluster Abell 1689/NASA, N. Benitez (JHU), T. Broadhurst (The Hebrew University), H. Ford (JHU), M. Clampin (STScI), G. Hartig (STScI), G. Illingworth (UCO/Lick Observatory), the ACS Science Team and ESA; Pg 407 – Monolith on the surface of Phobos/NASA/Mars Global Surveyor; Pg 410 – A few of the many books in Patrick's study/BBC Books; Pg 412 – Venus passing across the disc of the Sun in 2004/Adrian Janetta; Pg 415 – Patrick using the 24" telescope at Lowell Observatory/Patrick Moore; Pg 418 – Patrick in his study/Patrick Moore; Pg 420 – One of Patrick's mother's drawings of alien life/Patrick Moore.